Total Loss

D1403137

Reviews of the first edition

'Besides being gripping reading, there is a wealth of information to be learned about the actions of others in emergencies: what worked and what didn't work. . . an invaluable book for the sailor.'
Yachting

'Sure, you can learn from your own mistakes, but wouldn't you rather learn from theirs?'
Sailing

'From a wide variety of sources, here are 40 stories of tragedy at sea. . . the tales provide gripping if sometimes unsettling reading and many valuable lessons.'
Cruising World

'The stories will make the reader a better, or a retired, sailor.'
WoodenBoat

'This is a good book to read beside a warm fire. It's an absorbing, non-fiction account of recreational boating disasters. The 40 stories are all of pleasure boat mishaps and run from the ridiculous to the sublime. But they are instructive. . . Steps could have been taken to avoid the tragedy.'
Maine Boating

'Much of this book's charm derives from the individual personalities of the contributors. To lose a boat must be a great embarrassment, at the very least, but many of these contributors have managed to retain a sense of proportion and even humor, and are to be admired for having the courage to share their experiences with other sailors. These accounts are, without exception, interesting, often instructive, and sometimes hilarious.'
Mid-Gulf Sailing

'The book should be required reading for anyone going offshore. It will heighten your appreciation of the many things which can go wrong. . . Skippers who keep their mistakes to a minimum will find they have less need of good luck to stay afloat.'
Classic Boat

Total Loss

A COLLECTION OF 45 FIRST-HAND
ACCOUNTS OF YACHT LOSSES AT SEA

Second edition

Edited by Jack Coote
Revised by Paul Gelder

S

SHERIDAN HOUSE

*Dedicated to all sailors who have suffered the heartbreaking loss of
their yacht after a life and death struggle. And let us not forget the
courage and resourcefulness of their rescuers. This book is a requiem
for all their brave spirits.*

This edition published by Sheridan House Inc.
145 Palisade Street
Dobbs Ferry, NY 10522
www.sheridanhouse.com

First edition 1985
Second edition 2002

Library-of-Congress Cataloging in Publication Data

Total loss: a collection of 45 first-hand accounts of yacht losses at sea / edited by Jack
Coote: revised by Paul Gelder— 2nd ed.
    p. cm.
  Includes index
  ISBN 1-57409-146-8
  1. Yachting–History. 2. Shipwrecks–History. 3. Yachting–Safety measures. I. Coote,
Jack. II. Gelder, Paul.

GV812.T67 2002
797.1'246–dc21

                                             2001049720

Printed in Great Britain

ISBN 0-57409-146-8

Contents

Preface   xi
Acknowledgements   xiii

Part one: STRESS OF WEATHER

1 The cat without nine lives   3
The loss of Pete Goss's jinxed catamaran *Team Philips* in an
Atlantic storm

2 No escape at Fécamp   10
Nigel Porter describes the loss of his Sadler Barracuda *Riot*
in the 2000 Cross-Channel Great Escape Race

3 Mayday for *Maybee*   15
Rolled by a freak wave and dismasted, Gordon Stanley's
Rustler 31 was abandoned north-west of Cape Finisterre

4 The sinking of *Galway Blazer*   21
Taking part in his fourth solo transatlantic race in 1996,
Peter Crowther's famous yacht sank in two minutes taking
on 'a torrent of green water'

5 A short race across the Atlantic   25
Jason Baggeley was 12 days out from Plymouth on the
2000 Europe 1 New Man Star Singlehanded Transatlantic
Race when his 30ft yacht was knocked down twice

6 Fastnet rescue   32
The loss of *Griffin* in the famous Fastnet 1979 race is
written by her navigator, Stuart Quarrie and the skipper
who rescued *Griffin*'s crew, Alain Catherineau

7 Capsize! How I lost *Gulf Streamer*   38
Phil Weld and his crew were trapped for five days in his
trimaran when she capsized on her way to England

8 Capsize of *Rushcutter*   **51**
Anthony Lealand and crew took to the liferaft when the
30ft sloop he was delivering from New Zealand to Australia
was rolled through 360°

9 So near and yet . . .   **60**
Caught in a storm in the Bass Strait with bilge pumps out
of action, Keith Douglas Young describes a fatal run for
shelter on a hazardous shoreline

10 Sea dark, sky crying   **68**
In one of the most dramatic rescues in the history of ocean
racing, Isabelle Autissier was airlifted off her stricken yacht
920 miles from Adelaide

11 Oopsie Daisy!   **78**
Lionel Miller's Catalac catamaran *Lazy Daisy* was capsized
by a 'survival' wave off the East Coast of Scotland

12 Surviving Hurricane Assault   **84**
Bob Payne describes the loss of a 48ft ketch caught in a
Caribbean hurricane and abandoned after four knock-
downs

13 'I am not going to die!'   **93**
During a round Britain and Ireland trip John Passmore
encountered the worst June conditions since records began,
leading to the capsize of his Heavenly Twins catamaran

Part two: FAULTY NAVIGATION

14 The fatal reef   **101**
Peter Middleton's blue water cruiser ran hard aground on a
coral reef in the Bahamas

15 The loss of *Keelson II*   **108**
Hugh Cownie's Vancouver 32 was wrecked on a reef at
night on the Caribbean island of Nevis

16 Song – the final episode   **115**
Singlehanded sailor George Harrod-Eagles suffered the

double indignity of losing his 26ft sloop off the east coast
of Puerto Rico and then having the wreck looted

17 Last time over
122

Ann Griffin describes how tiredness, a wrongly identified
lighthouse and a coastal current conspired to wreck their
yacht

18 A gaffer's grave
126

Michael Millar's mistaken estimate of tidal currents en
route to Northern Brittany cost him his gaff-cutter

19 *Chartreuse* on the rocks
134

Paul Newell recalls how his 31ft sloop *Chartreuse* sank after
taking the inside Needles passage during a singlehanded
race round the Isle of Wight

Part three: FAILURE OF GEAR OR RIGGING

20 Four pumps – and still she sank
141

In hurricane force winds Bruce Paulsen's schooner sank for
lack of working bilge pumps

21 The wicked old *Martinet*
148

Bob Roberts graphically describes the loss of Thames
sailing barge *Martinet* through blocked bilge pumps

22 The end of an OSTAR
154

When the port float on Peter Phillips's 35ft trimaran *Livery
Dole* snapped off it was time to launch the liferaft

23 The death of *Banba*
160

Malcolm Robson retained his sense of humour in adversity
when 1200 miles east of New York everything seemed
against him

24 What went wrong?
164

Merrill Robson describes how a broken rudder caused the
loss of *Maid of Malham* halfway between Panama and
Tahiti

25 The tri that broke up 167

Luck runs out for the backyard-built multihull *Triventure*. Crewman Malcolm Beilby describes the drama

Part four: FAILURE OF GROUND TACKLE OR MOORING LINES

26 A gallant Dutchman 175

Margaret Wells describes the loss of *Maaslust*, one of the Dunkirk Little Ships, off Selsey Bill

27 *Girl Stella*'s going 182

A premonition ignored; a broken stern line and Frank Mulville's *Girl Stella* is destroyed in a 'safe' cove

28 Bad luck in Boulogne 194

Even in harbour a yacht can be at great risk if conditions change. Clementina Gordon's yacht sank in Boulogne

29 *Thelma* parts her cable 197

An anchor chain sawn clean through by coral 'as if with a file' caused the loss of A W (Bob) Roberts' gaff-cutter in the Pacific Cocos Island

Part five: COLLISION

30 Run down or rescued? 203

Niels Blixendrone-Moller describes his disastrous rendezvous with a tanker in the Atlantic

31 Fatal flotsam 207

Josh Hall's collision with a container during the 1994–95 BOC Around Alone Race

32 Anatomy of a sinking 214

Joe Bass's life-and-death struggle alone aboard *Sea Crest*, his Brewer 44, after striking a submerged object two days out from the US Virgin Islands

33 That sinking feeling   222
Noel Dilley and crew hit a UFO (unidentified floating
object) off Casablanca

34 The loss of a 'friend'   227
An afternoon sail from Plymouth saw Peter Jackson's yacht
sink after striking a submerged log five miles from the
breakwater

35 Hard chance in a nutshell   232
Peter Tangvald's 32ft *Dorothea* sank 40 miles south of
Barbados at night. He owed his life to a 'brave little
dinghy'

36 Whalestrike   240
Jerome Poncet's says *au revoir* to his 44ft ocean racer after a
pod of killers strike. George Marshall tells the story

37 There she blows   248
During the Cape to Rio race a 32ft sloop was struck by a
blue whale. Anthony Hocking describes the drama

Part six: FIRE OR EXPLOSION

38 LPG – a disaster waiting to happen   259
The 55ft Nicholson yacht *Lord Trenchard*, owned by the
armed forces, was destroyed in a gas explosion off Poole
Town Quay. First Mate Gavin McLaren survived to tell the
story

39 A blazing yacht in the Ionian   264
A sailing holiday in the Mediterranean turns to disaster
with an engine fire as fellow flotilla sailors Derek and Carol
Asquith come to the rescue

40 *Strumpet* was gone!   267
A Camping Gaz lamp on a hook was the chief suspect
when Henry Irving's 28ft yacht caught fire, melted away
and sank off Skegness

41 Chance in a lifetime   271

A 34ft motor-sailer becomes a floating cauldron, with the
inflatable dinghy stuck in a cockpit locker, as skipper
C Binning and crew have a lucky escape

42 One touch of the button   275

When a spark from a new starter motor set fire to James
Houston's boat, the flares and lifejackets were in the
saloon and the inflatable dinghy was melting

Part seven: BEING TOWED

43 Typhoon Brenda and the tow   283

Towed from the path of a typhoon in the South China Sea,
Major Philip Banbury tells of the loss of *East Wind of the
Orient*, a Contessa 38

44 The loss of *Jester*   289

Michael Richey describes how he abandoned *Jester* after a
knockdown – and her subsequent loss under tow by a bulk
carrier

45 *Mischief*'s last voyage   299

The great 20th century explorer and adventurer H W (Bill)
Tilman's eloquent epitaph for his Bristol Channel pilot
cutter lost off Greenland

Preface

As Jack Coote wrote in the preface to the first edition of this book 16 years ago, this is not a pessimistic book. Its intention is not to discourage anyone from setting out in a well-found yacht having made sound preparations for a voyage. Neither should the book be considered a morbid or voyeuristic exercise.

The sailor who loses a yacht, for whatever reason, has lost a partner in great adventures. As Frank Mulville wrote in the chapter *Girl Stella's* Going: 'A boat has a soul, a personality, eccentricities of behaviour that are endearing. It becomes part of a person, colouring his whole life with a romance that is unknown to those who do not understand a way of life connected with boats. The older a boat becomes, the stronger the power . . . people look at boats with wonder and say "She's been to the South Seas", or "She's just back from the North Cape", and the boat takes on a reputation in excess of that of its owner.

'A boat is always there – you never stop worrying about her whether you are aboard or ashore. She may be laid up in some safe berth for the winter or hauled out of the water in a yard . . . wherever you may be, a part of your consciousness is always reserved. Men lie awake worrying about their bank balances, their waistlines, their wives, their mistresses actual or potential; but sailors worry about boats.'

For Mulville the loss of *Girl Stella* was 'a dead weight of responsibility that settled heavily on his shoulders . . . a score that could never be wiped clean'.

For Mike Richey there could also be 'no going back' after the loss of *Jester*. As he watched her recede into the distance, 'looking as trim and pretty as ever' he realised how much he had loved her. 'Men personalise their boats as no other artefact. I felt I had failed her, that I should have stayed with the boat . . . It was one of the unhappiest moments of my life,' he recalled.

Bill Tilman wrote that the loss of *Mischief* meant the loss of more than a yacht. 'I felt like one who had betrayed and then deserted a stricken friend . . . I shall never forget her.' Bob Roberts confronted a sight that almost broke his heart when he saw *Thelma*, the gallant 27ft vessel that brought him safely through fair weather and foul for 7000 miles, pounding on the rocks on a lonely Pacific shoreline. Coral had cut through the anchor chain like a file.

The chances of having to 'abandon ship' are as small as being involved in an air or rail crash. A reasonably competent yachtsman can expect to sail for a lifetime without ever having to face the kind of dramas described in the following pages. Nevertheless, it can happen, and perhaps that's why the awful finality of the term 'total loss' holds such a fascination for most sailors.

There are many reasons why yachts are lost at sea. Some are obvious and others strange or even unexplained, like some of the accounts in this book. But it is fortunate, indeed, that most of those who have suffered and survived such loss are willing, sometimes even eager, to recount their disasters through a genuine desire to pass on the lessons that can be learned from what they endured. The lessons deserve to be remembered, as do the boats.

PAUL GELDER

Acknowledgements

This book could not have been compiled without the co-operation of many people. As the late Jack Coote acknowledged in the first edition, the idea for the book came from Julian van Hasselt of Kelvin Hughes. He did some preliminary work on it before handing the project to Jack. The late Peter Tangvald had once intended to put together a similar book and generously shared some of his research.

The editors of sailing magazines on both sides of the Atlantic have given permission to use extracts from their publications, including Sarah Norbury, editor of *Yachting Monthly*, and Andrew Bray, editor of *Yachting World*.

Among those who wrote accounts especially for the book are Jason Baggeley, whose *Ana* was lost in the 40th anniversary Singlehanded Transatlantic Race in 2000, and Gavin McLaren who survived the gas explosion aboard *Lord Trenchard*. Stuart Quarrie, navigator of *Griffin* in the notorious 1979 Fastnet Race, also wrote his account specially for the book, as did Henry Irving (*Strumpet*), Ann Griffin (*Northern Light*) and Merrill Robson (*Maid of Malham*).

Yacht club journals often contain exciting, well-written accounts of incidents experienced by members and the following editors and contributors are to be thanked: the editor of the *Royal Cruising Club Journal* and Alain Catherineau for his part of 'Fastnet Rescue' and Brigadier D H Davies (acting on behalf of the late WH Tilman) for '*Mischief*'s Last Voyage'; the editor of the *Journal of the Royal Naval Sailing Association* and George Marshall for 'Whalestrike' as well as Peter Phillips for 'The End of an OSTAR'; the editor of the *Cruising Association Bulletin* and Margaret Wells for 'A Gallant Dutchman'; the editor of the *Old Gaffers Association Newsletter* and Michael Millar for 'A Gaffer's Grave'; the editor of *The Silhouette Owner* and Clementina Gordon for 'Bad Luck in Boulogne'; the editor of the *Clyde Cruising Club Journal* and Lionel Miller for 'Oopsie Daisy'; the editor of the *Lowestoft Cruising Club Journal* and George Harrod-Eagles for '*Song* – the Final Episode'.

For permission to use excerpts from books, I have to thank Martin Eve of Merlin Press and the late Frank Mulville for '*Girl Stella*'s Going' as well as Edward Arnold Ltd and Miss Anne Roberts for 'The Wicked Old *Martinet*', and the family of Phil Weld for the extract from '*Moxie - the American Challenge*', a book which is a collector's item for any sailor's library.

Peter Crowther (*Galway Blazer*), Hugh Cownie (*Keelson II*), Niels Blixendrone-Moller (*Nuts*), Joe Bass (*Sea Crest*), and Noel Dilley ('That sinking feeling') were also generous in sharing their experiences so candidly.

Part one:

Stress of weather

Pete Goss's Team Philips *rescued by a 67,000 ton container ship.*

1 The cat without nine lives

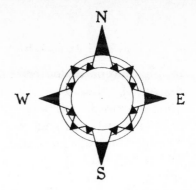

Yacht *Team Philips* (120ft catamaran)
Skipper Pete Goss (39)
Crew Andy Hindley (32), Alex Bennett (24), Graham Geoff (40), Paul Larsen (30), Richard Tudor (34) and Phil Aikenhead (55).
Bound from Totnes, Devon, on sea trials and, eventually, Barcelona for The Race
Date of loss 10 December 2000
Position 900 miles west-north-west of Land's End

She was the most revolutionary yacht built in Britain to date and captured the imagination of the British public like few other projects. She was the nautical equivalent of the Starship Enterprise *– an exotic, revolutionary craft that challenged the philosophy of ocean racing. With a budget of £4 million, Pete Goss used Third Millennium Star Wars technology to build a giant state-of-the-art 120ft rocket ship – 'the wildest piece of kit that anyone has seen on water!' he claimed.*

L aunched on the River Dart, in the quintessential English town of Totnes, Devon, in January 2000, it was bigger than the centre court of Wimbledon, but weighed no more than 44,000 lbs. The 70ft-wide catamaran was set to contest the fastest non-stop ocean dash around the globe, The Race – a no-rules, no-limits global drag race for the most hi-tech yachts on the planet. The prize was a million dollars and Pete Goss was Britain's brightest hope. Computer predictions suggested he could do it 65 days. The Jules Verne record stood at 71 days 14 hours and 18 minutes.

Tragically, *Team Philips* never even got to the start line.

The catamaran's designer, Adrian Thompson, had gone 'back to nature' for the concept. He looked at birds of prey, fish and evolution – 'the best designer in the world'. But since evolution takes millions of years, Thompson used a computer – 'to speed things up a bit!'

'If you watch a dolphin, it cuts through the water with minimum drag,' he said. 'Think of a grasshopper and an elephant. One is frail, but nimble. The challenge for us was to develop something slender, lightweight, but strong.'

But it wasn't strong enough.

'Have you ever seen with a fish with a flat top? Have you ever seen a sea-gull's wing with supports?' enthused Goss. 'I don't think of it as a boat . . . this project is more like something from aerospace or Formula One racing cars. I want the trailblazers of tomorrow to learn from what we are doing today,' exclaimed Goss, Britain's new all-action hero, an ex Royal Marine, who adopted an 'open house' policy as half a million people visited the shed to see the craft take shape.

Team Philips, named after her Dutch title sponsor, was built of exotic materials like Kevlar (used for bullet-proof vests) and titanium metal. The structural engineering was by Martyn Smith, who designed the sharp end of Concorde. The 135ft unstayed wing masts were like a section of massive aircraft wing. *Team Philips* was designed to sail at over 40 knots (47mph) and the pod in which the crew slept and ate had to be mounted on rubber shock absorbers. On a yacht of this size, you'd expect a crew of 10–15. *Team Philips* was designed for a crew of six, including Goss, to keep down weight, with reduced stores. The entire boat was controlled by just four winches.

Wave-piercing technology, developed for high speed boats used by the Special Forces, meant the vessel would fly a hull out of the water in just 12 knots of wind. At top speed (over 40 knots) the yacht would be clocking almost 50mph – faster than most ski boats, most seabirds and most fish. If you laid all the carbon fibre filaments in *Team Philips'* structure end-to-end they would stretch to the moon and back 200 times.

In March 2000 – days after her maiden voyage and the naming ceremony in London by Her Majesty Queen Elizabeth – *Team Philips* left Dartmouth and headed into the Atlantic for sea trials to the cheers of 100,000 well-wishers. Twenty-four hours later she was being towed into the Isles of Scilly supported by air bags after a catastrophic structural failure. In winds reported to be no more than 24 knots and with seas of 5–6ft a 45ft section of the port hull had snapped off. The starboard hull was also cracked. It was an agonising moment in the history of British yachting. And for those who had followed one of the most professionally managed campaigns it was a terrible blow. The craft was unceremoniously towed back to the building shed in Totnes where the problem was identified as a failure of the unidirectional carbon strakes (strips) that run the length of each hull.

The bonding of the carbon laminates to the honeycomb Nomex core had not worked.

But never one to give up, Goss, acknowledging that his project was at the cutting edge of technological advances, repaired her. *Team Philips* was relaunched on 25 September, only to suffer another devastating setback two weeks later with a broken bearing at the base of her port mast which saw her limping back home for a second time.

The final twist to the saga came on the morning of 10 December, 2000, after Goss and his six-man crew set off from Dartmouth on Saturday 2 December to sail around the British isles. All had seemed to be going well on this 'third time lucky' outing as the team gingerly took the giant catamaran on its Atlantic shakedown cruise.

'We wanted a stern test of the boat before setting off for the much more settled conditions of the Mediterranean, so we really have dived in with both feet by heading 60° north. It's wickedly windy and very rough but we have grins from ear to ear,' said Andy Hindley, First Mate.

They rounded the north of Scotland in a force 8 and Goss said *Team Philips* felt strong and safe, despite the uncomfortable seas. He decided they would continue west into the Atlantic. With navigator Hindley regularly in contact with shoreside weather expert and router Lee Bruce, they planned to stay in favourable following winds to the north of the relentless depressions.

The crew were not pushing the boat. Generally they were broad-reaching with one reef more than they needed while they got used to handling the huge cat. The acceleration of the boat proved remarkable. Coming out of tacks boat speed would leap from single figures to more than 20 knots in around three seconds. The speed topped 35 knots.

Ultimately *Team Philips* was heading for the Mediterranean and the start of The Race. The plan was to hook round the west side of a depression that would take them into the more regular westerlies to the south and provide them with a favourable wind angle to lay Gibraltar.

But a large depression with 70-knot winds was hovering over Newfoundland 350 miles away and was forecast to remain there for 24 hours. On board *Team Philips* the crew were expecting to see 35–40 knots and were waiting for the wind to veer to the south-west and then west as they crossed the front preceding the depression. They saw the barometer drop as expected as they touched the eastern extremity of the depression.

The sea was becoming increasingly lumpy and confused and as *Team Philips* headed south the crew wondered why the wind hadn't veered.

Instead of staying static, the east side of the Newfoundland depression defied the forecast and became elliptical, creating three separate intense mini-depressions, often known as 'bombs'. At lunchtime on Saturday 9 December, *Team Philips* was in the northern part of one of these. Over the course of three hours the barometer, already dangerously low, dropped by a further 18mB in three hours. 'We didn't really know why it was happening,' said Goss, 'but we knew we were in something pretty big.'

The intense low was kicking up waves from a third direction, the east, adding further confusion to the sea. 'We were in this cauldron of very big waves with lots of energy, completely unpredictable,' said Goss. 'There was no way of working out where it was coming from or where it was going. Occasionally in the cockpit you could see these very, very high rogue waves which would shoot off at twice the speed of all the other waves.'

The crew, thinking the depressions would head north-east, set a course to the south-west to get into a more regular wave pattern. But the boat took a hammering. The central pod, slung high above the waterline between the catamaran's two crossbeams, was being slammed by waves.

At the height of the storm the impact of three waves in quick succession ruptured the pod at the bottom of the winching cockpit, just forward of the aft beam. Despite the pod's carbon fibre construction, the split began to grow larger and whenever a wave struck, the gap would open by as much as three inches.

The structure of the pod was disintegrating and the crew were concerned that if the catamaran endured these conditions for much longer the pod might collapse into the water, taking the accommodation and all their navigation and communications equipment with it. It might also rip off the aft steering cockpit along with the vital hydraulics for the steering system.

With someone on the helm they could survive the conditions, but if they lost their steering they would be utterly at the mercy of the sea. The catamaran had emergency tiller bars which fitted to the top of each rudder stock but the crew did not feel they would be able to control the boat with these in the prevailing conditions.

As they came more under the influence of the depression, the waves became larger but more regular and the wind more ferocious. The anemometer four metres above the deck showed 56 knots but the sea state indicated it to be closer to 70 knots. This lasted for eight hours and Goss described it as one of the worst storms he'd ever been in.

They turned the boat around and ran before it. At the outset of bad weather they had dropped the mainsails and streamed warps, including their 300yd long 1in anchor line and their sea anchor. Even dragging all this and with the wing masts feathered fore and aft, the boat speed recorded was 32.5 knots.

'We had huge breaking seas. At times we had the transoms 20ft under water with the waves lapping over the steering cockpit. At times we had the bottom of the rudder tips, which have a 6ft draught, about 10ft out of the water,' said Goss.

With the centre pod becoming increasingly unsafe, the crew were huddled in the starboard hull in their survival suits with their grab bags. The most valued items on board at that moment, reported Mark Orr, Managing Director of Goss Challenges, were their Musto Gore-Tex socks and a hot cup of tea. The hull is normally used for stowage and is a rabbit's warren of bare carbon bulkheads and structural floors. It was not designed as living accommodation, particularly in a storm.

Meanwhile, Goss remained resolutely on the helm, keeping the boat on track down the waves, with Hindley at the chart table in the centre pod liaising with Lee Bruce and feeding Goss regularly with mugs of sweet tea. By this time the Maritime Rescue Co-ordination Centre at HM Coastguard in Falmouth had been alerted and were monitoring the situation. It was not looking good.

The crack in the pod was getting worse. Although the wind was beginning to ease, the waves remained large and another depression was forecast to strike within 10–12 hours. It seemed unlikely that the pod would survive another battering. If they lost the steering there was every chance the boat would capsize during the next depression. If the crew ended up in the freezing North Atlantic in mid-December it was likely that someone – possibly all of them – would die. Some of them, Goss included, had young families. They were heading north-east, away from the shipping lanes and the longer they left it, the longer it would take to rescue them.

At 2355 GMT Goss agreed with the MRCC that they should issue a Mayday, with a view to abandoning ship. At the time *Team Philips* was lying at 52°44'N 28° 12'W, 900 miles west-north-west of Land's End. The *Hoechst Express*, a 294m 67,680 tonne container ship belonging to the German company Hapag-Lloyd, responded to the call.

On board *Team Philips* the Inmarsat Mini-M satellite radio had been ripped off the deck after it had become entangled by a flailing sheet. The Inmarsat A satcom terminal on board the *Hoechst Express* was not functioning so communications between the vessels and the MRCC were carried out by Inmarsat-C telex. To help with communications, the MRCC asked the RAF to scramble a Nimrod from their base in Kinloss, Scotland.

At 0400 Captain Edzard Ufer on board the *Hoechst Express* had *Team Philips* on radar and soon after was in VHF communication with Goss, working out how they would go about the rescue. With the large sea still running it was hard to locate *Team Philips*. The RAF Nimrod dropped a green flare to indicate her position. Expertly Captain Ufer slowed his massive ship, passed *Team Philips* and spun the *Hoechst Express* around and brought her to a standstill, leaving the catamaran in her lee.

With no sails up and still streaming lines *Team Philips* had been sailing at nine knots but in the lee of the ship's 24m freeboard she slowed down and, with the help of the starboard engine, Goss was instructed to manoeuvre her along the starboard side of the ship.

The wind may have dropped but a 30ft sea was still running. Warps were dropped down to the boat and an attempt was made to secure her alongside but rise and fall between the two vessels was some 30–40ft. 'There was one particularly big wave when we were perhaps 50ft away and this breaking crest came between us and we lost sight of her. That gives you some idea of the sea state,' explained Goss.

With the mooring lines slack, *Team Philips* was moving fore and aft considerably, occasionally crashing into the ship as her 135ft-tall port unstayed mast slapped against the ship's hull like a giant fly swat. The brunt of the impacts was taken by the bulbous cockpit around the foot of the port mast but one bang bent the tip of her port bow.

Rope ladders were dropped down from the ship's main deck along with a net. The ship's crew would not open the lower pilot door for fear that *Team Philips* would damage it. By 0550 the first crewman had clambered to safety. This involved waiting for the catamaran to be on the peak of a wave and then hurriedly climbing the ladder before the next wave came along, or before they were swatted by the mast. As sailmaker Graham Goff climbed the ladder, the mast slammed into the hull just four feet away from him. Twenty-five minutes later all the crew, including Goss, who was the last to leave, were safely on board the *Hoechst Express*. *Team Philips* was cast off and left to fend for herself in the North Atlantic.

The crew had left one wind generator working and the Inmarsat C terminal was switched on. This enabled their shore team to poll the position of the boat. Positions from the stricken catamaran were being received for some time after she was abandoned.

On 13 January, 2001, a beacon signal was picked up by satellite and confirmed at regular intervals. Goss Challenges, working with Falmouth Coastguard, began a second extensive air search in a corporate jet aircraft chartered for £10,000. Despite good visibility, Goss and his logistics manager Nick Booth had no sightings of *Team Philips*.

As a report in *Yachting World* magazine indicated, even if *Team Philips* was recovered, the integrity of her structure was 'highly suspect'. So ended the short career of this popular ill-fated craft of the 21st Century.

'I think she'll turn up somewhere, eventually . . .' said Mark Orr. 'She could go north or south. She could turn up in the Arctic pack ice, or drift to the west coast of Ireland.'

Footnote

Just as Mark Orr predicted, wreckage from *Team Philips* was washed ashore six months later as far apart as Iceland and Ireland.

A large piece of wreckage, a section of bow, was located in May 2001 off the Irish coast, 50–60 miles west of Donegal Bay. It was first spotted by a Norwegian seismic survey vessel, MV *Geo-Pacific*. The section of wreckage measured some six to seven metres and had the logo 'Let's make things better'.

A day later, a massive section of the port hull was seen some 800 miles away off the coast of the Vestmannaoyer Islands, in south-west Iceland. A boat went out to tow the slender blue hull back to port. Along one side was the www.teamphilips.com website address. On the inner side of the hull, poignantly, were the names of the hundreds of people who had made donations to the project. Later, one of the two wingmasts was found on Iceland's south coast and one of the beams was also reportedly discovered.

This account is extracted from articles in *Yachting World* and *Yachting Monthly* magazines and information from the *Team Philips* website

Lessons learned

With such a leading-edge project, and such an untried, revolutionary craft, perhaps the biggest lesson is that you need to allow plenty of time for sea trials. The sea will always exploit any weakness. Goss was out to test his boat to the limits. The circumstances were exceptional in every way. But sailors should never be pressurised by deadlines which might put them in the wrong place at the wrong time.

Goss realised that he and his crew were drifting away from the shipping lanes and the longer he delayed making a decision, the longer rescue would take. As Mark Orr, Managing Director of Goss Challenges, said of the abandonment: 'It was a difficult decision but we have always underpinned this project with safety and seamanship. It was not a panic decision, but a decision taken in the interests of safety.'

2 No escape at Fécamp

Yacht *Riot*, a Sadler 45 Barracuda
Skipper Nigel Porter
Bound from Brighton, Sussex, to Fécamp, France
Date of loss May, 2000
Position off the entrance to Fécamp Harbour

Nigel Porter describes the loss of his Sadler Barracuda yacht, Riot, *in a severe storm during the cross-Channel Great Escape Race to Fécamp in May 2000.*

There were 102 yachts taking part in the annual Royal Escape Race from Brighton to Fécamp. The event, organised by Sussex Yacht Club, commemorates the escape to France of King Charles II from Cromwell's Republican army in 1651, following the execution of his father. The king's escape vessel was a little coal brig, *The Surprise*. My yacht was a Sadler 45 Barracuda called *Riot*.

Aboard I had what I regarded as a strong cruising crew, rather than a racing crew. But we had a great variety of experience between six of us. John had sailed from childhood, with three Atlantic crossings to his credit and was a Cape Horner, too. Helen, local chairperson of the Sail Training Association, was also a Cape Horner, having circumnavigated against the elements on one of Chay Blyth's steel yachts, *Nuclear Electric*. She had also sailed for many years in a variety of yachts. Bob, a yachtsman for 18 years, was a keen navigator. Chris was a dingy sailor who had moved up to bigger boats and Jennie had taken to the water about eight years ago and gained much experience. Lastly, there was me. A sailor from my student days, 55 years previously, the last 20 of them as owner/skipper. My crew had sailed many miles together in all sorts of weather.

We split up into three watches of two, with an hour on the helm each. The forecast was discouraging: southerly, backing SE force 2–3 at first then building to force 4–5 and eventually veering SW force 2–3. It was going to be a slowish trip. We had plenty to eat and drink and in view of the forecast didn't expect much excitement.

As a 'cruiser' embarking on my first race in a fleet of over 100 boats, I was pleased we got off to a trouble-free start, crossed the line two minutes after the gun and made up a little distance on some competitors before we reached the first mark.

At this point the fleet split, some going south-east, against an ebbing neap tide. We chose to use the tide and go south-west in the hope that when the tide flooded east it would give a bit of a lift towards Fécamp. The wind was fluky and *Riot* was not surging along in her usual fashion. Even so, we were easing ahead of the nearer boats. The cross-track error on the GPS was building, however. A round of bacon sandwiches helped raise morale. The helmsman changed hourly and the chart plot slowly crawled southward, but not on the course we wanted.

By noon we were not even level with the Meridian light vessel. Then the wind freshened and backed a little so that we could head east more and, with the help of the flood tide, reduce the cross-track error.

By 1500 hours we were just south of the east-bound shipping lane and the plotter showed us bang on course for Fécamp.

'Not so bad. We'll be in by 2200 hours,' I announced confidently.

This was the last time we had any cause for self-congratulation. From then on the wind and the weather played increasingly vile tricks on us.

Back home, severe conditions were forecast and during the day a storm warning had been broadcast. The first boats arrived in Fécamp by 1830. But the bad weather would not appear until after 2000.

The wind shifted further and increased and we had to start tacking to stay anywhere near our course. It was also plain that we would lose the favourable tide and need to get further east.

As the light faded, so the wind shifted and strengthened. Time to put two reefs in the main and roll in a bit of the genoa. We all checked our lifelines were securely hooked on. Matters were not going according to plan or forecast! The boat took all this and was going at her usual rapid pace with Helen at the wheel enjoying some very good sailing. Suddenly the wind whipped round through 180° and we had a crash gybe and were sailing back towards Brighton at 10 knots. With the wisdom of hindsight, I wished we'd kept going.

No damage was done. As we began to sort ourselves out, Chris exclaimed 'My God, Nigel look behind you!'

Down to the west there was a black wall of threatening cloud which seemed to be roaring towards us. The main was reefed right down and the genoa reduced to a rag, just in time. Then the front hit us with lashing rain and a force 9 wind. I thought it was a squall, but not a bit of it. This was the weather for the whole night. It just went on and on. At times, gusts reached 48–50 knots and the seas got very rough.

By now we were about 10 miles north-east of Fécamp, tired, wet and hungry. The options were to make for the harbour, run up channel to Dieppe, or even go back to Brighton. We chose Fécamp.

Riot was sailing well with little weather helm and though we were having to work hard we felt confident we could make it. It was tack, tack and tack again. By now I was on the helm, Chris and John on the sheets, assisted by Jennie and Helen tailing lines. Bob, meanwhile, calmly called out the bearing and distance to our target. Reassuringly, we were getting closer. Green seas were pouring over us from time to time, seeking every crevice in our oilies and flooding the cockpit. We were a good team, we knew each other well and as we clawed our way nearer to Fécamp our spirits rose. We were going to make it.

Finally, we weathered Cap Fagnet, but needed to put in yet one more tack to make the harbour entrance. As we came round onto port tack we became aware of four boats on starboard tack bearing down on us. I was in an awful dilemma. Did I turn further to the right and risk a collision with the nearest boat, or go back onto starboard and head in again? I chose the latter. We had, however, seemingly made enough ground to lay the harbour entrance. We were going to make it.

But within 150 metres of our target, I looked to starboard and saw an appalling great wave. The next moment we'd been knocked down on our beam ends. I was under water and washed off the helm. Helen grabbed my leg as I started to go overboard and the whole world was chaos.

Riot was lifted sideways, like a cork, by another great wave and hurled onto the shore with a grinding crash. This must have been about 0130. There was a long, long pause of stunned silence as the sea washed us in towards the rocks east of the harbour, a place known as the Trou au Chien, with an evil reputation for claiming sailors' lives.

Helen recovered first and shouted to Bob to send off a Mayday. Helen and Chris found the flares and fired off two, as people on shore were not certain where we were. John got the main down to reduce windage. Jennie was below in the flooded cabin doing 'subaqua salvaging' of wallets and other small and important items. I launched the liferaft. Fortunately, we didn't use it, for amongst the rocks in the huge seas it would have been torn to pieces. Shortly afterwards, it turned over, punctured and sank.

No one panicked. A shocked silence descended on all of us as we waited for rescue. We could see the lights on the shore beneath the towering cliffs about 80 metres behind us. Suddenly, to our amazement, a swimmer in a wetsuit appeared through the surf among the rocks and came to the stern of the boat. How he managed it, I shall never know. Not only did he do so once, but he came back five more times. Tough, brave, strong? You name it, he deserved all the superlatives I can think of. I'm a Francophile till the day I die.

We were warned to stay put. The currents were too fierce to attempt to swim ashore on our own and the combination of rocks and sea would grind us to mincemeat. One by one, with the aid of a line, we were hauled ashore, helped by our rescuers, members of the Sapeurs Pompiers of Fécamp. First Jennie, then Helen, Chris and Bob were taken off.

One of the Frenchmen came back to tell John and me that it was too dangerous to continue. By this time, about 0400, the tide was well up and the waves were breaking over us. The boat was also breaking up on the rocks. The Frenchman told us a helicopter was on its way, though we didn't understand this last bit. Neither of us thought much of staying on the boat at this stage. By now the sea was up to my chest, the hull under my feet had broken away and every wave washed my feet out horizontally. I was tired and cold. I didn't think I was going to last. The Frenchman realised this and jerked his thumb towards the shore, seized my harness and we pushed off into the sea. He swam strongly. I tried, but my foul weather jacket and boots made it difficult to do more than flounder.

I swallowed plenty of sea water, but suddenly, blessed relief, there was shingle under my feet. Hands grasped me and I was hauled up on the beach, flat on my back. I looked up at a ring of faces. 'I'm all right!' I told them. Two strong men helped me to my feet and supported me on either side for the 200-metre trudge along the shingle.

Among the helpers on shore were Jonty and Viki Layfield, who had taken part in the race and got there before us. They had raised the alarm when we were wrecked and later helped us all on shore, Jonty heaving us up the steps to the ambulances when our weary legs would no longer support us. Viki got our wet clothes off us and wrapped us in blankets. It was a huge relief when she told me John was safe.

John had a long and very lonely 20 minutes wondering what was going to happen to him, with the waves coming ever higher. Fortunately, he managed to secure himself to the lifelines and grabbed an extra lifejacket, just in case he had to chance his life in the sea and rocks. Suddenly, he was aware of a tremendous noise and thought the adjacent cliff had been brought down in the storm. A bright light appeared from above. The helicopter had arrived. Down came the crewman. John, with his army training, knew just what to do. Up went his arms, down went the strop around his chest and he was airborne. The pilot showed consummate skill in the appalling conditions.

The staff at Fécamp Hospital soon had us warm and comfortable from the effects of hypothermia. That night, the fate of 50 yachts in the race was unknown. Mayday calls were received and caused the French Coastguards to impose radio silence. It was not until noon the following day that the whereabouts of all the competitors in various Channel ports had been established. Several yachts were towed into Fécamp and St Valery by local lifeboats. Six yachts sought refuge in Dieppe.

I and my crew reflected on the fact that you never know how wonderful and generous people can be until some moment of awful and dire need. None of us will ever forget Les Sapeurs Pompiers Fécampoise: Jean-Claude Confourier, David Levasseur, Phillipe Fiquet and Phillipe Duvivier. We also owe a great debt of gratitude to Viki and Jonty Layfield for help, reassurance and kindness. Dany Prevet, a citizen of Fécamp and honorary member of Sussex Yacht Club, visited us, attended to our concerns, arranged the washing and drying of our clothes and devoted her entire weekend to helping us, finally driving three of us to Le Havre to catch the ferry home. Oliver, John's brother, drove the remaining crew, as well as lending clothing and raising morale.

Finally Navigators and General Insurance settled my claim in full, with promptness, and I can buy another boat and get back to sea. The sooner the better! I'm glad to say that we all feel the same.

From *Yachting Monthly*, September 2000

Lessons learned

- ✐ No matter how benign the weather forecast, always monitor it. You just never know.
- ✐ No matter how well your boat sails, go for the safest option and head away from bad weather.
- ✐ Off a lee shore make sure you have searoom, especially in bad weather.
- ✐ Don't let thoughts of crossing a race finish line blind you to dangers.
- ✐ We were asked to monitor VHF channel 72 and not use it as a chat channel. But no weather reports were given on this race channel.
- ✐ With hindsight, I should have monitored channel 16 as well.

3 Mayday for *May Bee*

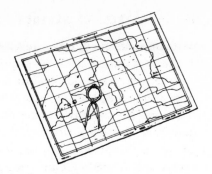

Yacht *May Bee* (Rustler 31)
Skipper Gordon Stanley
Crew Barry Thunder, Jenny Warmsley
Bound for Gosport, Hampshire for northern Spain
Date of loss June, 1994
Position Some 25 miles north-west of Cape Finisterre.

Bound for Spain across Biscay, the Rustler 31 May Bee *was rolled over by a freak wave and dismasted. Crewman Barry Thunder recalls the drama and helicopter rescue of the three crew.*

It had been a dream to take a two-month cruise visiting new and warm places. The plan was to sail south to Spain and then west to the Azores, returning home via the Isles of Scilly. The crew of three comprised Gordon Stanley (48), skipper and owner of *May Bee*, a Rustler 31, his sister Jenny Warmsley, a teacher, and myself. All old schoolfriends, we had sailed together since our early twenties.

Gordon, an experienced engineer, spent four years fitting out *May Bee* in his engineering shop in Chertsey, Surrey, sometimes helped by me. Wherever possible, the work was done to ensure extra strength and durability.

By 4 June 1994, we had sailed the boat from her home base in Gosport to Falmouth Marina and spent a weekend provisioning. We visited Falmouth Coastguard Station to check weather conditions for Biscay, and two days later said tearful goodbyes to our respective families and cast off for Spain.

The first couple of days were an unpleasant beat, but during the afternoon of the fourth day the wind rose to gale force. In the night it was up to force 9 and we were down to a scrap of headsail. We estimated the waves were 4m (13ft) high. Dawn revealed a wild seascape of white-topped waves as seas continued to build during the morning, the northeasterly wind gusting from 45–50 knots. The sound was a constant shriek and it was a great relief when it dropped a little to about 35 knots.

Despite the conditions, the boat was handling well, responding fairly quickly to the wheel steering. With the sun low in the sky, you could tell when a big wave was approaching, as it blocked out the sunlight, leaving everything in shadow. Our speed was about 4 knots. We managed to maintain our course, depending on whether we were surfing down a wave or holding the boat up in the big gusts.

Since the weather forecasts sounded no worse, we decided we'd carry on to our preferred port in Bayona, rather than fight our way into La Coruña. Next day, day five, we were well into the shipping lanes off Cape Finisterre and got a weather check via VHF from a passing American warship. This confirmed our decision to carry on, since we were only about eight hours away from reportedly calmer conditions on the sheltered side of Cape Finisterre.

Gordon and I were elated with the way *May Bee* was sailing. She took little water over the side and did not feel pressed in any way. Nevertheless, a warp was readied to stream over the stern as a drogue if the yacht's speed increased unacceptably. We each took spells of 30 minutes at the wheel throughout the day. By the afternoon, I was at the wheel, Gordon was off watch, sitting in the cockpit, and Jenny was resting below. Gordon and I were both securely clipped on. *May Bee* was surfing down the face of another wave and as I was correcting the boat near the bottom of the trough. Gordon called, 'Look out, here comes a big one.'

Then I was under water. There was a sensation of being pulled along in the boat's wake. I have no memory of how I was plucked from the wheel, since I was certainly holding on very tightly. A desperate need for air drove me to fight my way to the surface, and then I saw *May Bee* lying dismasted a few yards away. We later discovered one of the yacht's safety harness fixing points, a U-bolt of 5mm stainless steel, had sheared off as though the 'U' had been hack-sawn away.

My first thought, looking at the mast in the water, was 'how do we got that back up again?' Then logical thought took over as slowly, but surely, I pulled myself along the rigging back to the boat. I had no sensation of fear. I wasn't aware of feeling cold, or of the sea being rough. I wasn't alarmed when I realised how difficult it was to get back on board. Gordon was calm and efficient. He found my harness line, made it fast to the compass binnacle and rolled me safely back on board.

Gordon, who had been looking astern at the time, said that *May Bee* had been hit by a second wave, immediately behind the wave we'd surfed. She had been knocked over to starboard through 180°, the mast snapping off at deck level, with the heel fitting completely shattered. But the boat quickly righted herself.

As *May Bee* was knocked down, Gordon had remained in the cockpit, but as she righted herself, he was sucked into the sea, still clipped to the port side cockpit U-bolt. This was fortunate, as it kept his head above water and, since the guardrail wire had been cut by the shrouds and a stanchion had been swept away, he managed to clamber back aboard.

Jenny, down below, had been thrown around the cabin but emerged from the hatch and was able to collect lifejackets for everyone. A Mayday was sent out and the EPIRB switched on. But as there was no mast, and therefore no aerial, the first distress call was never received.

We started to clear up the debris. The main compass had been washed away, but strangely the lifebuoy holder, which was only lashed on with thin line, was still in place, although somewhat bent. A 23 litre (five-gallon) emergency water bottle, securely lashed under the mainsheet fixing point and binnacle stand, had been ripped away, breaking lashings and a 6mm polypropylene rope.

I found the pump handle and began to pump the bilges. During the roll-over we reckoned some 320 litres (70 gallons) of water had been forced through three ventilators. Waves were still breaking over the boat, but otherwise she remained relatively stable.

The biggest danger was the threat of the mast punching a hole in the hull as it was held against the starboard side by stays and shrouds. One of the port side shrouds had hit the four-man Beaufort liferaft on the coachroof with such force that it had sliced into the hard plastic of the canister like a cheese cutter. Gordon had to use brute force and a hammer to extricate the shroud.

Seeing a tanker quite close and apparently heading towards us, we fired two parachute flares and an orange smoke flare. But the tanker continued on without seeing us. During the next 30 minutes we spotted two or three other tankers, but felt it unwise to waste further flares since they were quite far away. Gordon continued to cut lines to the boom and release more shrouds. We thought about using the mast as a drogue but decided to let it go.

The final stay to be released was the forestay. In such a precarious position, it was difficult and dangerous for Gordon to cut. With the weight of the mast and sails hanging on it, he was conscious of the threat of a whiplash effect when it was finally released. It took a lot of effort to remove the final quarter inch of the clevis pin from the fitting.

With all the rigging gone, the boat was much easier to handle, lying a-hull to the waves. We all sat together in the cockpit deciding what to do about the lack of a VHF aerial. Gordon started to jury rig an aerial, using 3m

(10ft) of wire and the diesel tank dipstick and sent off several Maydays. I continued to pump. We were concerned about Jenny, who was gradually becoming colder. She seemed confused and in a lot of pain. She kept holding the EPIRB and asking if her children were all right. Was it some reaction, possibly due to delayed shock? When the yacht had been knocked down, Jenny had hurt her neck and arm. However, what we didn't realise was the full extent of her injuries. (It was later discovered that she had fractured her spine.)

Down below, the cabin was covered in mayonnaise from a broken container. The GPS was still functioning, but despite heroic efforts, Gordon was unable to start the engine.

Fortunately, one of our VHF distress calls had been heard by the tanker that had failed to see our flares. The transmission was very broken, but we believed she was heading back towards us.

We were still very concerned about Jenny. By this time she couldn't move her left arm and was in a lot of pain. We clipped her lifeline to the binnacle stand. I was still pumping and calling out orders, and I remember Gordon shouting at me that if I didn't shut up he would throw me back into the sea again.

The tanker was now only about half a mile away, but despite being given our GPS position, he could not spot us through the breaking seas. It was then that we realised how big the waves were.

Hearing the tanker captain on the VHF telling a helicopter rescue pilot that he couldn't see us, George fired off orange flares and parachute flares. These the tanker eventually spotted. A fishing rod, with a pair of Jenny's red thermal longjohns attached, acted as a flag signal and more flares were set off to pinpoint our position for the helicopter. Some failed to ignite, while the wind strength burnt others like oxyacetylene torches. Gordon burnt his hand and had to throw one flare into the water.

Finally, the helicopter was overhead and we could see how hard it must be to fly in 40 knot winds. A line was dropped, which landed on the bow. Gordon took a flying leap to catch it and then the winchman, complete with flippers, dropped into the sea.

Unfortunately, he came up on the port side of the yacht where the life-lines were still intact and got caught up in the wires. Managing to free him-self, he then began to attach Gordon and Jenny into a duel harness. Meanwhile, two tankers took up station to windward giving us a lee. Large waves made it difficult to stand. Jenny and Gordon began their ascent, but, after moving only a foot or so, they were dropped back on deck.

It was decided that the safest way to lift them was for them to jump into the sea and be winched from there. But when Jenny's lifejacket failed to inflate she disappeared under the waves. Gordon managed to push her up to the surface and they were lifted another few feet before dropping back into the sea. Then they were dragged along the waves before being safely hoisted.

It was my turn next. I not only had the grab bag attached to me, but also had Jenny's handbag round my neck. Summoning all my courage to go overboard again, I jumped with the winchman and felt my lifejacket ride up over my face. I had not tied it tight enough. As the lift towards the helicopter began, the air was pushed out of my lungs and I seemed to be swinging into nothingness. Suddenly I was safely inside the helicopter, reunited with Gordon and Jenny. Wrapped in warm blankets, we were still anxious about Jenny's neck.

On landing at La Coruña, Jenny was taken off to hospital in an ambulance, while Gordon and I had warm showers and were given smart new blue flying suits to wear and various forms to fill in. We phoned home to break the news to our wives. Later the helicopter pilot and his wife found us accommodation in the centre of town.

The local Lloyd's agent was notified of our accident and subsequently alerted shipping and the local fishing fleets. *May Bee*'s last position had been some 25 miles north-west of Cape Finisterre. We had been so near the protection of the lee of the cape, yet so far. Lloyd's felt there was a reasonable chance the yacht might be found and salvaged.

Thanks to the grab bag, we had money and credit cards and were able to go shopping at C&A for new clothes next day. In hospital, Jenny was laid out flat, encased in a neck brace. Her injuries were serious. She had a fracture to her sixth vertebra, compounded by a crush injury to the radial nerve down the left arm. This in turn caused the loss of sensation to the index and third finger, as well as some reduction in the muscle power of her left arm.

Some days later, Gordon got permission for Jenny to be flown home on a stretcher. With three return tickets (cheaper than singles) we all headed off for Santiago Airport, Jenny in an ambulance. The final hurdle was that the airline insisted on six more seats being paid for (the length of the stretcher was nine seats) before Jenny would be allowed on board. Two hours of argument followed, with Jenny left sweltering in the ambulance in the full glare of the midday sun. The money still had to be paid, despite the fact that the plane was nearly empty.

At Gatwick Airport, staff arranged for a special lift vehicle to take Jenny's stretcher out through the catering loading door and the local ambulance service drove us to East Surrey Hospital, Redhill, where we were reunited with our families.

In Spain we had time to talk, think and reflect. One thing we agreed on was our strong desire to go back to sea and try to do the trip again.

Footnote

Some days after returning home, Gordon received news from Spain that a fisherman had found *May Bee* 300 miles from where she had been abandoned. She was towed into La Coruña. Gordon flew out with the loss adjuster. The yacht's interior had been stripped, apart from the engine and two anchors. Even the saloon table, cabin heater and stove had been unbolted. The hull was badly damaged and the yacht declared a total loss by the insurers, with no salvage money awarded to the fishermen.

Jenny made a good recovery, but still has no feeling in two fingers.

From *Yachting Monthly*, February 1997

Lessons learned

Barry Thunder describes how one of the yacht's safety harness fixing points, a U-bolt of 5mm stainless steel, had sheared off 'as though the U had been hack-sawn away, U-bolts can have a nasty habit of fracturing. The reason is simple, according to Jeremy Rogers, a well-known boatbuilder. 'A solid looking U-bolt may conceal a narrower gauge threaded end, because the screw thread has been machined out of the original thickness of the bolt. So, for example, a 10mm U-bolt may have a puny 6mm thread below deck. If you're worried about yours, look for U-bolts with the deck-plate welded on rather than a loose fitted one. The welded plates are best.'

Dismasted and with no VHF aerial, the crew found that their first distress call was never received. Fortunately, the skipper was able to jury rig an aerial, using 3m (10ft) of wire and the diesel tank dipstick and sent off several Maydays. An emergency VHF aerial would be advisable in most other cases.

Liferaft stowage is always an important topic. In the case of *May Bee*, one of the port side shrouds hit the four-man Beaufort liferaft on the coachroof with such force that it had sliced into the hard plastic of the canister like a cheese cutter.

Barry Thunder also relates how he jumped into the water with the winchman and felt his lifejacket ride up over his face. He had not tied it tight enough. In these circumstances the use of a crutch strap is shown to be essential.

4 The sinking of *Galway Blazer*

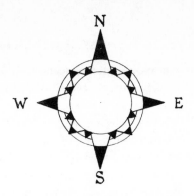

Yacht *Galway Blazer*
Skipper Peter Crowther
Bound from Plymouth, England, for Newport Rhode Island, as a solo
   competitor in the 1996 Europe 1 Singlehanded Transatlantic Race
Date of loss 24 June, 1996
Position 49°41'N 20°33'W

*It was 1900 on Monday 24 June 1996, and I was aboard the vast 300m (985ft)
container ship* Atlantic Compass *heading for Halifax, Nova Scotia. Why? That
morning I had been aboard my own yacht* Galway Blazer *competing in the tenth
Singlehanded Transatlantic Race, Europe 1-STAR.*

It had been a normal night on board – I didn't sleep too well, but it was
the first blow. I put two reefs in each sail and the boat was comfortable
and going in the right direction. I must have slept a little, for I dreamt of a
shallow man-made reservoir next to an old aerodrome and the reservoir
workers reprimanded me for putting debris in it from the dinghy; and yet
there were hundreds of rats in their control tower and they kept getting
into people's clothes.

I got up about 0600, made myself a coffee and noticed that the turbine
from Walter the water generator had disappeared and reminded myself
to get a new one sent over from Ampair. The solar air vent was letting
in water – another reminder to fix it. There was plenty of juice in the
batteries and I tried to get Portishead between the chats, but to no avail.
I put *Galway Blazer* time back to GMT, ate a banana and planned to
have grapefruit later and rice salad for lunch. I read a bit of the post-war

history of England. Annie the Aries was steering well. I was not in much of a hurry, but at about 0930 it was time for the vitamin pills and cleaning teeth.

I was standing by the chart table when we slid off a wave, hitting the starboard side, aft of the mast, with a horrendous thud. It was as if an invisible shoulder had charged at a door and burst it apart. There, up by the frame which goes under the bed, a torrent of green water poured in. I knew at once there was no way of stopping this miniature tidal wave, given the sheer power behind it.

I fumbled like hell to put out a distress call on the SSB radio. I gave position, name and 'abandoning ship!'. The water was almost to my knees and surging through the boat.

I grabbed a container of water, and a thermal top, which I put on, plus waterproofs. I should have grabbed a bag with passport and money from above the chart table. I should have closed the saloon doors to the cockpit, to stay afloat longer. I should have said goodbye. I should have turned off electrics.

Instead, I grabbed a penknife, always open and by the hatch, plus a portable VHF radio and GPS, and then went up through the hatch aft to get the EPIRB. I wanted the EPIRB in the liferaft and not on the boat. I activated it and carried everything to the Tinker liferaft dinghy, inflated, thank heaven, up forward between the masts.

I cut the restraining ropes, and also the foresail sheet which was in the way. The bows were already down and almost under water, the transom in the air slightly.

I shoved everything under the deflated canopy, and sat on top, soaked and trying to prevent the dinghy from getting caught between the lifelines, knowing I had to get free of *Galway Blazer*. I drifted off the starboard side, avoiding the slapping mainsail. That's how low the boat was in the water.

Then I got under the canopy and bailed with the bucket to get the water out, before inflating the canopy and getting the sea anchor to work. The instructions were still on board *Galway Blazer*, which was a little way away, sails touching the water and transom a little raised, the wind generator and the Aries working. I looked again between surges and only the mast tops above the reefed sails were visible as she chose where finally to head downwards to rest 49°41′N 20°33′W.

Thank you for all those wonderful years of sailing.

I was completely soaked. No socks or seaboots. My waterproofs were lying in the bottom. It was time to take stock. I checked that the EPIRB and the VHF were working. The GPS batteries were low. There was plenty of food and water. I tightened the dinghy's bow flaps to stop the waves coming in and also the stern ones, just in case of capsize. I decided to look out every so often but I had no watch and no way of knowing the time.

I put on wet waterproofs. My thermals would dry out. I decided to wrap my feet in a space blanket and stick them inside a waterproof bag when they became cold. The liferaft was very claustrophobic. Enclosed, with no horizon, and bobbing about is a recipe for seasickness, but so far I felt fine. I had some water, a tot of whisky, another recipe for seasickness, and an oatmeal biscuit. Very, very dry, sticking to the top of my mouth.

Between sponging sessions, which took up a lot of time, I decided to lie down with my bum on one canister, my hips on the centre seat, and the top of my body on another canister. I tried to catnap, hood pulled over my head to stop any water going down my neck. With eyes closed the motion got better. I thought I heard a plane, but looked and saw nothing. It was too early anyway. I mentally prepared myself for at least a night afloat.

It must have been the roar of a breaking wave. Later, I heard the same roar again, but saw nothing. I decided to let off a flare anyway. It was a very old flare and didn't work. Most of the new ones were still on *Galway Blazer*. I threw the flare away. The next one was up-to-date and worked. I saw a Nimrod plane and contacted them on my hand-held VHF. I told them who I was. They asked if I was the only person aboard. They told me that a vessel was on its way, 20 miles from me (or was that my imagination?) and stayed in contact between me and the ship's Master, which helped. Then I saw the vessel looming out of the mist straight ahead of me, some 2½ miles away.

The weather was getting worse. Fantastic guidance was shown by the plane as the ship, *Atlantic Compass*, came slowly to windward of me and stopped. I later learned that she used her bow and stern thrusters to get close to me.

A line was thrown and I scraped down the side of the ship and tied it on the thwart. I was pulled to a doorway 3m (10ft) above the water. It was difficult to get out of the stern of the dinghy. The canopy was rigid. I thought of cutting it, but I was not safe yet and water was slopping over the transom.

A rope ladder was thrown down and a rope with loops. I went for the ladder. Unfortunately, my right leg was behind the ladder against the hull and the other was around the front. It was the wrong way to climb. I swivelled round and moved my feet. Left one first, automatically, like learning to dance as a teenager. And then through the door, thanking faces and climbing up and up through the cargo decks. I arrived at the ship's bridge, dripping water. I thanked the Nimrod crew. My liferaft was still bobbing about far below, EPIRB turned off by me, confirmed. The VHF was still on. It didn't matter. *Atlantic Compass* told me it was not able to pick up the liferaft.

I was taken to a cabin. My clothes, all I had, were taken away to be washed and dried and I was given a pair of overalls. Then I talked to my wife, Alix, and the girls. That was worth surviving for and we shared our grief over the loss of such a happy and beautiful boat.

Footnote

Peter Crowther (50), Devon pub landlord, arrived home to a hero's welcome at the Green Dragon, Stoke Fleming, near Dartmouth, after landing in Nova Scotia, minus passport and money. It had been his fifth solo transatlantic race, his fourth in *Galway Blazer*, the 12.80m (42ft) whale-backed junk-rigged schooner which he had owned for 23 years. Designed by Angus Primrose, she was built in 1968 for Cmdr Bill King, who circumnavigated in her. Crowther has written a book on the yacht's chequered history: *Single-handed Sailing in Galway Blazer* published by Waterline.

From *Yachting Monthly*, October 1996

Lessons learned

Having a 'grab bag', or 'panic bag' and a well-rehearsed 'abandon ship' routine is essential. So catastrophic was the collision damage to Crowther's boat that, with water already up to his knees, he had only seconds to grab a container of water and thermal top, plus waterproofs, before abandoning ship. On the way out he also managed to grab a penknife, 'always open' by the hatch, plus, more importantly, hand-held VHF, GPS, and EPIRB. He left behind passport and money, as well as seaboots and socks. The instructions for the Tinker dinghy/liferaft were also left aboard the sinking vessel, along with most of his new distress flares.

In an ideal world, we would all rehearse our safety procedures. Deploying equipment, such as liferaft, flares, drogue or parachute anchor, even on a calm day, as a practise run for a real-life disaster scenario, or for heavy weather, ensures a degree of familiarity and confidence.

Crowther found that the batteries for his hand-held GPS were running low. Always carry spare batteries in the 'grab-bag'.

The importance of having a hand-held VHF is demonstrated by Crowther's ability to talk to the pilot of the Nimrod aircraft who co-ordinated the rescue that saved his life.

5 A short race across the Atlantic

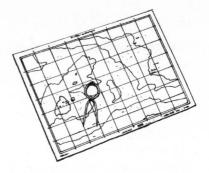

Yacht *Ana* ex *Modi Khola* (a water-ballasted Phil Morrison design)
Skipper Jason Baggeley
Bound from Plymouth to Newport Rhode Island
Date of Loss June 2000
Position Mid-Atlantic

Jason Baggeley had spent the last two years dreaming of, and preparing, for the Europe 1 New Man Star Singlehanded Transatlantic Race from Plymouth to Newport Rhode Island in June 2000. Twelve days out from Plymouth disaster struck.

Three weeks before the start of the race I arrived in Plymouth having bought and refitted the old *Modi Khola* for singlehanded sailing. *Modi* was well known on the short-handed racing scene, having competed in three double-handed Round Britain races. Designed and built in 1989 by Phil Morrison, she was incredibly advanced for her time, with curved decks, improved aerodynamics, and water ballast. No faster 30-footer has been built for offshore racing, as evidenced by her unbeaten record in the 30ft class. This speed came at a price, as Phil had not built in any comforts – she was a very wet boat to sail, and physically demanding.

I had named her *Ana*, after a dear friend who died of cancer aged just 32. I made several changes to the boat, including putting in a saildrive engine, to replace the old outboard, and totally upgraded the electronics with new Raytheon instruments, Yeoman Sport Plotter and SSB receiver, as well as installing a deck hatch in place of the normal companionway that had always let in water. I also put in a seat at the chart table – the only seat on the boat, and one I knew I would spend a lot of time in.

The week before the start was excellent fun as I met up with old friends and made new ones. With only one crew member per boat you don't get the little crew groups associated with normal racing, instead everyone drinks together. *Ana* was looking great and ready to go – this race is more fun if you are prepared, and have the time to watch all the 'pros' rebuild their boats.

I had not raced singlehanded before, and once the buzz of the start had died down and few boats could be seen it was time to relax and settle into a routine. I had made a last minute change to my game plan to follow the rhumb line, instead of the Great Circle route, as I was concerned how far south the icebergs were. I had no radar, and the idea of icebergs and fog over the Grand Banks had little appeal.

Four days into the race we got the first gale. It was expected, but going upwind into a gale in such an extreme 30-footer is not much fun. It was, in fact, the first time I had used my trysail in anger. I quickly developed a routine of catnaps, food, housework (bucket and sponge), navigation and steering. The gentle Atlantic swell and settled winds of fairytales never developed, so I had to change sails, alter water ballast, and tack more often than my body thought appropriate. Generally everything worked well. My early problems concerned the autopilot – the mountings for the tiller drive (I had one each side) both collapsed in the first four days, even though they were epoxied in. I managed to rig a repair, but was surprised at the loads, and often had to re-secure them. Then on day 10 one tiller arm just broke in two.

The weather was very variable with lots of fronts coming through – a general description would be 'miserable'. There was a massive amount of rain, and I didn't see the sun or stars for nine days. The wind continued to be variable – reefs and water ballast in and out, in and out. I spent lots of time at the chart table trying to get weatherfaxes etc. I got very lonely and missed friends and family; because I had a limited budget I had no two-way communications, so I didn't know how I was doing. This sometimes made motivation a problem . . . but then that's what singlehanding is about and I'm a stubborn and competitive sailor.

One of the reasons *Ana* had such a good record is that she has been pushed hard by her various owners. But for this race I had to take a different approach – there are no stopovers and 2900 miles of beating is more than most boats do in several years, let alone 20 days. As a result, I had a golden rule: reef as soon as you think about it; shake it out half an hour after you think about it. My tactical requirement was always to be on the making tack. At times, this meant several tacks in an hour – hard work, as I would transfer all my water and food to the high side each time.

Day 11 was a defining point. I was approaching the halfway mark, and ready to celebrate with a bag of sweets from my sister and a double ration of chocolate from Fortnum & Mason (a present from Mary Falk who held the class record of 19 days). Although I didn't know it at the time, I was leading my class, and in front of many larger yachts. But in the early evening the barometer started to drop fast. We were going downwind with poled-out No 3 and one reef in 20 knots true wind, and I decided to steer for a while to try and get the best out of the waves. Within half an hour the ride was getting too exciting with the wind increasing and backing. Time for another reef.

The next ten minutes were hectic, I dropped the No 3 and stowed the pole, put a reef in, got the No 4 on deck – put it back and got the storm jib, put the third reef in the main, put the storm jib up, dropped the main. I decided that I had enough sail with only the storm jib. The trysail wasn't needed, as I now planned to lie a-hull for the night as the wind had increased to a steady 55 knots plus and was now on the nose. My 2300 log entry shows the pressure at 1001, and falling fast, down from 1014 at 1400. I spent the night in a bunk with a space blanket over my oilies, trying to rest. The noise of wind, rain, hail, and the sea was amazing. A fellow competitor, over 100 miles to the south, saw gusts of 62 knots during the night.

At 0550 the next day I was sitting on the cabin floor mopping the bilges when *Ana* was knocked over by a wave. The floorboard I was sitting on hit me on the head, as did a can of food. As we righted it became clear that the mast had hit the water, but that no major damage had been done. Inside, things were a bit of a mess though. *Ana* had an angle of vanishing stability of 127° – I think we used at least 120 of them.

I went on deck to drop the storm jib. The wind was incredible, blowing steady white streamers off the waves, which were only 12–15ft high but steep and breaking. As I was sorting the lines, I saw a large wave begin to break above us and grabbed the lifelines. Again, we were knocked down. The boat came over me and I was dunked up to my chest – I was rather annoyed as these clothes had been fresh on the day before and still had four days to go.

At this stage I thought things were getting a bit serious. One knockdown could be considered unfortunate, two was a bit much. I wanted to improve the boat's angle to the waves and put out a form of sea anchor – two kites on long lines from the main anchor and line. It made not a jot of difference. While I was below cleaning up, we got hit again.

My memory of this one is a bit vague, linked, I think, to a new bruise on the side of my head. But this knockdown dismasted the yacht. As I started to cut away the rig I realised that maybe I had lived in Scotland long enough to become a native – I was trying to save blocks and lines rather than cut them away. I finally got the rig away, but was on my last hacksaw blade.

Waves continued to hit the boat hard, but no longer capsized her. I went below and started to bail, getting most of the water out before sitting down at the chart table to have one of my sister's flapjacks and some water and to take stock. I was in the middle of the Atlantic, but still had plenty of food and water – so maybe I could get home under jury rig. Whilst thinking about this I realised more water was coming in. That was the deciding factor.

With heavy heart, I set off my EPIRB and rewired my Satcom-D which had come adrift. Almost immediately my radar alarm went off. I set off a rocket flare, which vanished about 10 feet above the water, not to be seen. The conditions were still poor and I didn't know how anyone could spot me. When things improved, I planned to rig up the spinnaker pole with a radar reflector and strobe light and to lash my Dayglo orange trysail across the deck.

I soon realised that the radar alarm was reacting to the EPIRB and turned it off. I tried to settle into a routine of bailing every 15 to 20 minutes and resting in between. I was aware that I could have quite a wait and had to be careful not to get dehydrated.

I regularly gave out a Mayday on the VHF, but held little hope as I had cut the emergency aerial when I slammed the hatch shut to avoid a breaking wave. In between bailing and sending Maydays, I started to read the history of Shackleton. The first page dealt with the loss of the *Endeavour*; I thought it would give me hope since, in the last gale, reading about Willy Kerr and his latest adventures in his Contessa 32, *Assent*, had been a great source of encouragement. I was on page three, and about to start my next round of bailing, when I thought I heard a voice on the VHF. I was right. I made contact with the tanker NCC *Baha*. Before then I had imagined all sorts of voices, including the sound of RIBs (rigid inflatable boats) coming alongside.

Within two minutes of making contact, the ship had a visual fix on me – I quietly congratulated their lookout and helm as well as staff at the Marine Rescue Co-ordination Centre (MRCC) Halifax for such an accurate search pattern. Meanwhile, I was still at the chart table desperately trying to do up my Musto survival suit (undone for a call of nature) and get on deck. As I appeared on deck, I saw a bright orange chemical tanker 400 yards away – a wonderful sight indeed; they may not be the most beautiful of ships but they have a fairly low freeboard – during the whole episode my greatest concern was the transfer to the ship as I saw this as the most dangerous part. As the ship manoeuvred I sat in the cockpit crying and patting *Ana*, saying 'I'm sorry, I'm so sorry darling' – it was all I could do.

The master of the ship, Gwyn Armitage (British) brought his vessel alongside to the weather side of me – my engine actually started, although it lacked power, and my rudder was damaged. A line was attached under the guidance of Ivar Glesnes, the Norwegian mate, and Gary Rodaway, the British chief engineer – who grabbed me by the scruff of the neck and hauled me over the handrail from the netting.

Ana had swung away from the ship and was now being towed backwards. The line was cut and she was left to it – I lacked the courage to go and look at her. I was worried that she would be a danger to others, as her five buoyancy tanks would help keep her afloat for a while. But the master did not want to have to turn around again in those conditions – once had been more than enough. I understand, though, that the Inmarsat-D stopped sending a signal fairly shortly afterwards.

My rescue ship was a Norwegian registered chemical tanker on transit to Stockholm, nine days' sail away. The Master and engineer were extremely good company, and I feel it important to say how it has changed my view of ships – although I don't think they are converted to the yachties' cause yet.

At no stage was I made to feel that they had lost time because of the rescue – in contrast to many stories of ships being keen to plug straight on.

The first phone calls to my family were very emotional, and followed by a cup of tea and a shower – I had a number of bruises, cuts and strains but nothing serious, although I was worried about the lump on the side of my head.

Written specially for *Total Loss* by Jason Baggeley

Lessons learned

The rescue services were fantastic, MRCC Halifax sent a Hercules aeroplane to look for me, and made contact with the nearest ship by telex – they were most professional throughout. It is good to know that when you set off a distress beacon a well oiled process swings into action. These points are well worth noting:

- ⚡ Storm sails should be coloured high-visibility orange.
- ⚡ Make sure your EPIRB is registered to your yacht. Mine was, although at first it was reported as belonging to another competitor. If it is correctly registered to you it helps people know what they are looking for, and to establish if it is a false alarm or not.

☞ The deck should be a bright colour – white hull and grey decks are very hard to see from a ship in those conditions. It was my storm jib, floating off the bow, that was seen. It might not look good in the marina, but a bright orange foredeck would make all the difference.

☞ If your self-steering has a tiller arm then have more than one point to mount it.

☞ Take lots of hacksaw blades – I was on my last one.

☞ Two-way communications, such as Inmarsat Satcom-C would have made a huge difference – to know someone was coming and not far away would have been great. (SSB is now less useful following the closure of Portishead.)

☞ My roving bilge pump was a godsend – especially good for shallow-bilged boats.

☞ A space blanket will only last a maximum of two nights – I had not used my sleeping bag that trip because of the amount of water taken on board, and slept in oilies or survival suit.

☞ My kettle was secured in a deep baking tray with shock cord – it still flew out. On most boats the gimbals would not hold much – if you are next to a hot kettle it can be very dangerous.

☞ A radar transponder would make locating you easier. It bounces off the ship's radar. I did not know about them before I took part in a safety drill on board the *Baha*.

☞ Keeping calm is the important thing to do. At least at first, as you know there is so much to do. It is worthwhile taking a few minutes to think through the job list and what tools you need, and to establish a routine. Make sure you continue to eat and drink – a little often will keep you fitter and better able to cope.

I have no doubt many people will say that this experience only happened because I was racing an unsuitable boat. *Ana* was only 30 feet long; she weighed only 2500 kilos, and had a big rig and deep fin and bulb etc, but she was a very seaworthy yacht. I personally have sailed over 5000 miles in her in all conditions, and she has revelled in them. She was built of cold moulded mahogany with glass, and was all curves – she generally went through waves creating very little resistance, and was remarkably strong.

The rig survived two good dunkings, and I believe the only reason I had the difficulties was a rapid change of wind direction as a front went through – the boat changed its aspect to the waves, and I guess their nature had changed with steeper breaking faces. The Master of the *Baha* has said that they experienced steady force 10-plus winds throughout the night, and the low deepened to 980, having started life the evening before at approximately 1014. It continued on its merry way until it found John Passmore (see story on page 93) a few days later off the Shetlands. I was simply in the wrong place at the wrong time – right in the middle of a quick forming deep low.

Now I just have to find another boat for the race in 2004 – unfinished business.

6 Fastnet Rescue

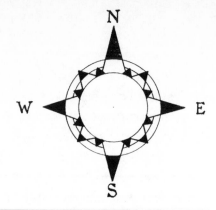

Yacht *Griffin* (Offshore One-Design 34)
Skipper Neil Graham
Navigator Stuart Quarrie
Mate Peter Conway
Crew Four students from the National Sailing Centre, Cowes
Bound from Cowes to Plymouth, racing round the Fastnet Rock
Date of loss 14 August 1979
Position approximately 40 miles SE of the Fastnet Rock

This description of events preceding the loss of Griffin *was written by her navigator, Stuart Quarrie, and because the subsequent rescue of* Griffin's *crew from their liferaft was such a remarkable feat of seamanship, I have also included part of Alain Catherineau's account of how he and the crew of* Lorelei *saved lives.*

We expected a gale during the race – the Met office had forecast one – and we just hoped to be going downwind when it arrived. Rounding Land's End in almost calm conditions we discovered a short in a lighting cable which had drained the batteries – 'someone' had turned the isolator to 'both' during the night and this meant we couldn't start the engine and only had minimal electrics. It had been impossible to get all the charts we really wanted, owing to a strike in part of the Hydrographic Department. This meant we were short of large-scale charts of Southern Ireland, and those which we had were mainly metric charts but with no colour – very difficult to interpret, especially with a torch.

By the time we got the 0015 forecast on the night of the storm, we already knew we had a blow on our hands. We had progressively gone down from close reaching under spinnaker through No. 2 and No. 3 jibs and reefing the main as the wind came up from just before dusk. As the forecast time approached we were still racing – with Pete and Neil putting the third reef in while I steered. The mouse, which we had put in for reefing the third deep reef, had come adrift and the operation took about half an hour – by this time we were also down to storm jib.

I asked one of the crew to take the forecast since I was busy, and I could hardly believe it when he said SW/NW 10–11, possibly 12! Unfortunately, he had not taken down the time period for the veer to NW, so we didn't know how long the southwesterly would last.

After that forecast we decided to stop racing and I was asked to decide whether to run for shelter or stay at sea. Not knowing the Irish coast, and being hampered by lack of some charts, I wasn't able to tell that Cork was a possible refuge even in a southwesterly; and, not knowing the timescale for a veer, I didn't want to close the coast. We therefore opted to stay at sea. We reduced sail to storm jib only and found that with a maximum allowed IOR storm jib we surfed and planed in a manner difficult to control, and therefore went to bare poles.

With three crew below and four on deck we then sorted things out and I tried various different helm positions in the hope that we would be able to lash the tiller and all go below. We were quite happy for about 20 to 30 minutes with the helm pushed moderately hard to leeward, until an exceptionally big, unbroken wave rolled the boat. It is worth noting that those waves that had already broken didn't appear to be dangerous as their crests were mainly foam.

At this stage I was thrown from the boat and my harness hook – which had been clipped to a stanchion base – opened out to leave me 'free swimming'. This was at about 0130. I first thought of my life insurance then I miraculously saw a high intensity lifebuoy light 20 or 30 metres away. I swam to it and found the whole boat upside down with the light still in its clip. Neil Graham swam out of the cockpit air-gap and we talked somewhat inanely on the back of this upturned 'whale', until another wave finally rocked her upright.

After a head count – with everyone OK – we tried to take stock of the situation. It appeared that the boat was awash to the decks with the cabin almost full to the washboard level, and after a brief attempt at pumping, Neil decided – after talking to Pete and me – that it would be prudent to abandon ship in good order, rather than wait for her to start going down.

I must say that at this stage I was in shock to some extent; I had been so sure I was dead just minutes earlier and therefore didn't take as full a part in the decisions as I might have done, but I did agree with Neil.

We launched our Avon eight-man raft with no real difficulty and, taking the yacht's flare pack, abandoned ship into the raft. We couldn't find a sea anchor – whether by stupidity or not we will never know. We arranged ourselves around the raft to try to give it stability. We let off just one parachute flare, more as a gesture than anything else, and settled back to wait for daylight. After about 30 minutes a big wave rolled the liferaft upside down, ejecting two crew as it did so. While righting the raft we lost its canopy, and so after that we were like an open dinghy and up to our armpits in water.

At this stage we realised that one crewman, who had been below, hadn't got an oilskin top on and he was in fact semi-comatose with hypothermia within about 15 to 20 minutes.

After less than half an hour in the open raft we saw the masthead light of *Lorelei*, and the rest of the story belongs to Alain Catherineau . . .

We were racing with 50 knots of wind, using the No. 4 jib and with three reefs in the Hood mainsail. At about 0200 (French time), 14 August, we were sailing at 310° at 90° degrees apparent wind, our speed was considerable and below decks there was a constant impression that we were surfing. Thierry, my first mate, was at the helm, taking great pleasure in the almost effortless sailing; the boat was standing up well and quite stable. Towards 0230 we were 30 or 40 miles from Fastnet and well on course. After about a mile we set the star-cut; shortly afterwards, with an apparent 30 or 35 knots, we replaced this, first with the No. 2 and then with the No. 4. For about an hour we passed many boats, both windward and leeward of us.

Suddenly we were astonished to see a red parachute flare about half a mile downwind. I donned my harness and rushed forward and, with the help of Marc and Gerard, hauled down the No. 4. I had been prepared for this: the wind was remarkably gusty and our anemometer was recording up to 60 knots. Thierry and I decided to get closer to the red light; with three reefs in the mainsail it was easy for us to steer towards it. After failing on the first try, we finally went about. We were heading roughly south, Thierry still at the helm, when we saw a rocket or a red hand-held flare (I can no longer remember which). We could not see the source of the light, only a red halo that was visible from time to time above the waves. I asked Thierry to stop heading towards the glow and ease off by about 30°; we had no idea what sort of boat we would find. Some hours earlier we had met *Rochelais*, a rusty French trawler from La Rochelle, a most impressive sight. For some reason I thought that the crew in difficulty now was on a fishing boat.

We were very comfortable below deck; however, on deck, we would have lost two or three crewmen had not our harnesses been well-fitted. We were still heading towards the light when we saw two smaller lights above something dark; these were in the same wave and about 50 metres downwind. It was a liferaft. Some way farther on we turned and headed towards the liferaft, our mainsail at three reefs. We came three metres upwind of it, the same distance away from it and at a speed of about three knots. One of my crew threw a rope to the liferaft, but it would not reach. Two of the liferaft's crew hurled themselves towards us in an attempt to catch the hull; instead they fell into the sea and were hauled back by their colleagues.

I decided to take over the helm. I felt it was possible to save these men as long as I was at the helm and an integral part of my boat. I know *Lorelei* (a Sparkman and Stephens-designed She 36) very well and can often demand and get – the impossible. I started the engine and hauled down the mainsail. The engine is a 12hp diesel, but the propeller has automatic variable pitch which gives maximum power very quickly and greater than normal acceleration and deceleration. After seven or eight unsuccessful attempts I finally managed to come about and headed into the wind. During this time we had covered some distance. We were heading south, in total darkness, in search of the red light. Suddenly we saw it. I turned again – an easier job than it had been the first time – and cautiously headed towards the red glow, which lit up the surrounding blackness whenever it became visible. I turned to the north and crossed at about four or five knots. I approached the liferaft and aimed *Lorelei* straight at it when we were about 25 metres away. I threw the engine into reverse in the last few metres and, thanks to *Lorelei*'s propeller of variable pitch, she drew rapidly to a halt, stopping within a metre of the liferaft.

Thierry and Marc each threw a line to the raft and the crew hauled themselves alongside *Lorelei*. I felt dead. There was some confusion on the liferaft as the crew leaped to catch hold of our ropes or deck. One or two climbed aboard easily; three more remained in our stern on the aluminium toe-rail. I suddenly noticed that the liferaft was drifting away from us with two of the crew still on board. Luckily, one of them managed to grasp a rope that had stayed on board and pulled the raft back alongside. A few moments later the liferaft drifted away, empty. The end of the rope had not been made fast. I stopped the motor for safety and some of my crew helped two men climb aboard and three or four more of us at the stern helped the remaining three. The first few castaways were already in the cabin; there were only two left in the sea and we were having difficulty getting them aboard.

I sent the fit members of the liferaft crew to help out on deck. I was holding on to one who had been under the counter with only his head above water. He was one of the few to have a harness and I managed to pass a rope through it and then over the pushpit. In this way I lifted him out of the water. However, the harness slipped over his shoulders and I had to release him into the water again. Philippe was holding him by his T-shirt, the only garment he had. Finally, helped by his fellow English crew members, the castaway was rescued from the waves. He was heavy and it took five or six heaves on the ropes to pull him into the cockpit.

In the cockpit his leg became trapped between two ropes, but we soon released him. The most injured member of the English crew was forward but there was still one more in the sea. I can no longer remember how we finally rescued him. I think that *Lorelei*, crossing the waves, heeled on the right side, sometimes very severely, so that we could grip the last castaway and haul him in a few centimetres. He was stiff with cold and could not help us rescue him. Soon he was in the cockpit surrounded by his rescuers. I realised that there was something wrapped around his head; he was being strangled by a cord on his T-shirt. I pulled at it with all my strength and it finally snapped. He was taken into the cabin.

It was about 0400 by then. An Englishman came out of the cabin and warmly shook my hand in thanks. All seven of his crew were safe; it was a happy moment. Thierry and I were in the stern. We hugged each other fiercely: we had succeeded.

From *Roving Commissions* (Centenary Edition, 1979),
published by the Royal Cruising Club

Lessons learned

A crew member aboard *Griffin* transcribing the radio weather forecast 'unfortunately', as navigator Stuart Quarrie relates, failed to note down the time period for the storm force wind veer to NW, so no one knew how long the southwesterly winds would persist. The crew also discovered a short in a lighting cable which had drained the batteries – 'someone' had turned the isolator to 'both' during the night and this meant they couldn't start the engine and only had minimal electrics.

Another problem that revealed itself later was that it had been impossible to get all the charts they really wanted, owing to a strike in part of the Hydrographic Department. Thus they were short of large-scale charts of Southern Ireland. When the strong winds came, Quarrie, hampered by this lack of charts, and not knowing the Irish coast, wasn't able to tell that Cork was a possible refuge even in a southwesterly; and, not knowing the timescale for a veer, he didn't want to close the coast. *Griffin* therefore opted to stay at sea.

When they abandoned the yacht for the liferaft, Quarrie was thrown from the boat and describes how his lifeline harness hook – which had been clipped to a stanchion base – opened out to leaving him 'free swimming'. Another crewman, who had been below, and hadn't got an oilskin top on was semi-comatose with hypothermia within about 15 to 20 minutes. Even when off-watch in extreme conditions it can pay to wear proper clothing. The safety harness of another crewman slipped over his shoulders when the rescuers tried to get him aboard *Lorelei* and he had to be released into the water again. A modern-day harness/lifejacket with a crutch strap solves this problem. The crew of the RORC boat *Griffin* may well owe their lives to the fact that the French yacht *Lorelei* was able to use her engine –a 12hp with variable pitch propeller –to manoeuvre alongside their liferaft before taking them all aboard. The automatic variable pitch gives maximum power very quickly and greater than normal acceleration and deceleration.

7 Capsize! How I lost *Gulf Streamer...*

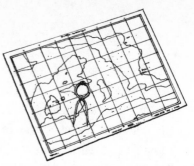

Yacht *Gulf Streamer* (trimaran)
Skipper Phil Weld
Crew Bill Stephens
Bound for Plymouth, England, from America
Date of Loss 27 April, 1976
Position 38° north by 64° west in the Gulf Stream

Grandfathers are normally past the age for spills and thrills in the ocean, but not Phil Weld. In this extract from his book Moxie, the American Challenge, *the 65-year-old adventurer who shattered every previous record with his victory in the 1980 Observer Singlehanded Transatlantic Race, crossing in under 18 days in* Moxie *his trimaran, describes how he spent five days trapped in his previous trimaran,* Gulf Streamer, *when she capsized on the way to the start of the previous 1976 OSTAR.*

The irony of losing *Gulf Streamer* in the Gulf Stream still makes me wince. It had been in a mood of celebration racing to Bermuda that I'd chosen the name. To pay tribute to this elemental force had seemed the friendly thing to do.

When planning the voyage to England for the 1976 OSTAR, it never occurred to me to regard the Stream as anything but a beneficent force that would hasten us on our way. It would sweep us past Florida, once we'd made our way from St Petersburg to Key West, at 4 knots. From Cape Canaveral, we'd follow a Great Circle to the Scilly Isles. This track would cut north-east inside the Stream's curve. We'd rejoin it east of New Jersey, somewhere north of Bermuda, to allow it to keep us warm and boost us on our way to Plymouth.

The low coast of America disappeared in the sunset on the afternoon of Tuesday, 20 April, 1976, as *Gulf Streamer* cantered along at 10 knots in a light southeasterly. The stern, relieved of the weight of the diesel engine, had risen two inches to give her a new lightness of foot. In light air, it could mean 8 knots instead of 7. Both the boat and I felt up for the race.

A new antenna rigged from the port spreader captured the Coast Guard's new sequence of voice broadcasts of North American weather. All through Sunday, 25 April, as we ran almost dead before a freshening southwesterly, it warned of a new gale centre over Cape Sable, Nova Scotia. It forecast winds from 25 to 35 knots and waves to 20 feet as far as 450 miles from the centre. Our position midway between Cape Hatteras and Bermuda came within that circle.

Bill Stephens, my 21-year-old shipmate, from Birmingham, Michigan, helped me to tie in a second reef before it got dark. By Monday's dawn, continuous streaks of foam were showing in the wave troughs. Time to drop the main. Under staysail only, it required constant attention at the wheel to hold the course without flogging its 300 square feet in accidental jibes. All through the day, the seas built up. Between wave crests, the surface took on that creamy look that indicates force 9 – over 47 knots.

'I'm rapidly gaining respect for the power of the Atlantic,' Bill remarked mid-morning. His offshore sailing had heretofore been in the Great Lakes.

Frequent checks on WWV, the government station broadcasting from Fort Collins, Colorado, at eight minutes past the hour, indicated that the gale centre, per the prediction, was moving north-east, as were we, but much faster. As it out-distanced us, conditions would steadily improve.

'Bet on the wind's veering north-west tomorrow,' I said. 'Then look for six days of perfect reaching to England.'

So dawned the fateful morning of Tuesday, 27 April. The wind had veered. We'd come over to the port jibe. During my watch from 0500 to 0900, the seas had notably decreased. It seemed prudent to put the helm under the control of the electric autopilot, while I took a sun sight through the patchy clouds and plotted our position.

I was using an old small-scale chart that showed this was the sixth time in two years that *Gulf Streamer* had been within 300 miles or less of this intersection of latitude and longitude, 38° north by 64° west: eastward from Gloucester to England, May 1974; St Martin to Gloucester, April 1975; back and forth on the Bermuda race, June 1975; Gloucester to Puerto Rico, December 1975. Like Old Home Week!

When Bill came on deck to take over the watch, we remarked upon the abating seas and noted that our speed had dropped to 8 knots. 'If we were racing,' I said, 'we'd be putting up the main.' But we agreed in the interest of rest and comfort to postpone this until I came on watch at 1300.

I went below and kicked off my boots for the first time in 36 hours, hung up my harness and oilies, and prepared for a nap. My bare feet tucked into the sleeping bag, my head pillowed in the outer corner of my berth, my knees wedged against the canvas bunk board, I felt utterly content. I munched a RyKrisp.

Bill had impressed me as an alert helmsman more than once in the past ten days. I could see him through the companionway checking the Tillermaster autopilot. I hadn't the slightest worry, only a small guilt that, had I been solo racing, my lot would have been less easy. I took out *Can You Forgive Her?*, the first volume in an Anthony Trollope six-pack that my mother had given me for Christmas, and was in the middle of the first sentence when I heard Bill shout, 'Look out!'

A second to rise up. Another to swing my legs off the bunk. Four seconds. Bill's next agonized cry coincided with the cracking, clapping sound of flat surface slamming water with maximum impact. Cracker boxes, dishes, cups, books, came tumbling over my ears. Water, sunlit and foam-flecked, poured through the companionway.

Even as the mast must have struck the water, and *Streamer* lay like a wing-clipped swan on her side, I still felt confident that the immense strength and buoyancy of her outrigger would be able to heave her upright.

'This just can't be,' I thought.

A second shattering smack. Then gently, as the mast subsided below the surface, the bunk revolved upward above my head. I stood calf-deep in water on the cabin ceiling. All was suddenly quiet except for the water gushing through from the cockpit.

Panic for Bill seized me. The trapped air was being compressed upward against the bilge by the rising water which had yet to reach the level of the cockpit sole. I wanted him clear of the cockpit. He put his head into the rising water to swim down beside me but had to withdraw to unhook his safety harness. Then he swam down inside.

Ten, twelve, fifteen seconds might have passed since his shouted warning, surely less than thirty.

I remember the smell of damp Naugahyde, the plastic fabric sheathing the underside of the bunk cushions. As the outstretched arms of the outriggers assumed their upside-down position, their buoyancy took over part of the support of the main hull, now resting on the flat surface of the main cabin top. The water level had stopped rising at about our belt line. The last temperature reading had shown 68°F. As the sea surged both fore and aft and crosswise inside the hull, the sun shone through the glassfibre, causing the interior wavelets to twinkle merrily.

Bill and I discussed the air supply and agreed it was adequate. We both seemed gripped by the same icy calm. 'Well, I'm sorry if I dumped your boat,' said Bill. 'But I don't feel guilty because I know I did the right thing.'

'I know you did,' I said.

'I'd been looking ahead. I turned around. This wall. Forty feet high. I had two crests just off the stern. I kicked Tilly clear. Grabbed the wheel and pulled her off with all my weight. Three spokes. I thought she'd come back until I saw the mast hit the water. Then the second crest hit us.'

'I could see you hauling on the helm,' I said. And with few more words we got down to the business of survival.

Multihull designer and sailor Jim Brown, who had questioned the survivors of *Meridian*, a trimaran that had capsized off Virginia in June 1975, had told me the key: 'The hulls will float high. Don't rush the vital items into the vulnerable liferaft. Safe your energy to live aboard upside down.'

From the welter of objects surging in the waist-deep water we grabbed first for the three radio beacons. We tucked them with the two sextants, the almanac, the navigation tables, a pair of pilot charts, the first-aid chest, the waterproof metal box of flares, into the shelves and corners most nearly high and dry, in this topsy-turvy world. The crown-jewel safekeeping spots were the underside of the chart table and the two bins for cleaning materials beneath the stove and galley table. Here, safely wedged, we found the two-gallon jerry can of emergency water.

Now came the urge to communicate with fellow men. As I'd planned with Jim Brown, I unscrewed, from what was now 'the overhead', the through-hull fitting for the log propeller, just forward of the mast and of the midships bulkhead. Through the two-inch hole I could see blue sky. I'd punctured the seal of our air cushion. Would the escaping air cause the water to rise? We thought not and it did not. The craft's inherent buoyancy from her Airex sandwich construction, together with the four airtight compartments in each of the outriggers, provided us with what would prove to be raft status of indefinite duration.

Into the little window on the world, I thrust the rubberized antenna of the oldest of the three beacons and set it to pulsing.

Next we had to cut a hatch through the keel to the outdoors. It took three hours to complete the fourteen-by-eighteen-inch aperture. First a drilled hole. Then enlargement with hammer and chisel to make a slit admitting a hacksaw blade.Then a pruning saw with a curved, coarse blade to lengthen the slit on one side. My talk with Jim had prompted me to tuck these tools for safekeeping beneath the chart table. We repeated the process at three subsequent corners. It was tiring, this reaching overhead to saw. Glassfibre dust got in our eyes. Mounting claustrophobia kept us hard at it until finally we'd hammered the rectangular panel free.

Once again we could look out into the real world, and a sombre sight it presented: grey sky, grey water; squall clouds all about on the horizon, but nary a ship. Here and there bits of Sargasso weed.

'We're in or near the Gulf Stream,' I said.

'The nearest shipping lane?' Bill asked.

'About 30 miles south-west of here the pilot chart shows a junction point. But I think we shouldn't plan on a quick pick-up. Let's think in weeks. Not hours or days.'

Looking out of our hole in the hull, I saw the big red spinnaker clinging to the aft end of an outrigger. However did it get there? It takes the weight of a man to force it bagged through the forward hatch. Only then did we note how empty the cabin had become of floating debris. Investigating the head, we saw that the hinged hatch cover had opened under the pressure of water on its 'inside' surface. Through that two-foot-square opening the hungry sea had sucked seven-by-three foot cushions, sailbags bulky as barrels, boots, clothing, pillows, bottles, cans, fruit, anything that floated.

We began then to retrieve whatever we could grab and to dive for heavier items lying on the cabin's former ceiling, now its floor, or caught in bunk or locker corners. I dived five times to grope for and find the pistol-grip hacksaw and extra blades that I'd taped inside three waterproof bags and secreted in the aft starboard locker where it could have been reached from outside after capsize. Triumph!

I'd bought three extra sets of these to present as boat-warming presents to the skippers of the three 31-foot Newick trimarans fitting out at Vineyard Haven, Massachusetts, before their 500-mile qualifying solos for the OSTAR. All during Monday's gale, I'd worried about them and thanked my stars that I had more boat under me than they. As it turned out, all made uneventful fast passages to England.

Outside, the sea remained too rough for us to want to venture out onto the keel to commence cutting through to the aft cabin where we knew we'd eventually find food aplenty. Both encased raft and deflated dinghy remained beneath the cockpit seat, now upside down.

First night adrift

Bill waded to the forepeak to fashion us a dry lair on the underside of the bow deck. Though it was dark and narrow, with the one remaining bunk cushion as a base, and the new staysail and light spinnaker to use as coverlets, he made us a bed just clear of the water.

'The first night will be the worst,' I said. We discussed strategy. Protection against cold and wet came first. We calculated that we had a liquid supply for three to four weeks. Juice in cans of fruit and vegetables to be salvaged later would stretch it out.

The underside of the chart table formed a mini-quarter-berth, more nearly high and dry than any other place inside. I stuck it out there for two hours, then gave up when a cramp knotted my thigh. Sucking wind as I lowered myself into the waist-deep water, I lunged forward to join Bill. Flecks of phosphorescence gave our cabin the eerie glow of a darkened discotheque, 'Davy Jones's Hideaway'. My left leg went down through the hatch to the open sea. I checked my descent by clutching the toilet seat dangling overhead. I muttered an oath.

'You all right?' from Bill, deep back in his den.

'Yes, but I just lost the bottle of bourbon,' I had to confess. My lurch had dumped it from my oilskin pocket. It was a dreary moment.

I crawled inside beside the daggerboard trunk and stretched out on the bunk cushion. As the hulls pitched slowly to the ocean's rhythm, the water ebbed and flowed up my trouser legs. My shoulders, resting against Bill's knees, felt him shivering.

'Tomorrow we make a hammock,' he said.

Second day adrift

At first light we shared a can of orange juice. Even if we'd had food, I doubt we'd have eaten anything.

From its bag came the never-used staysail, reserved for the race. Neither of us could bear to hack at the pristine Dacron so we gathered it at the corners – as one would knot a handkerchief headdress – and hoped for the best. Every 20 minutes one of us would squirm shoulders through the lookout for a scan. We agreed that the wind and the sea had dropped. From a skein of wires suspended from the chart table's instrument panel, we retrieved the bubble compass from the RDF set and established that the hulls lay on a north-south axis athwart the wind with waves still coming from the west.

Gingerly, I folded back the sodden pages of the *Nautical Almanac*, noted the declination of the sun for 0400 GMT, Wednesday, 28 April, mentally calculated the sextant setting for a meridian crossing of the sun at latitude 38°30', and settled down to pounce on 'noon' like a duck hunter awaiting dawn in his sneak box.

Squall clouds rimmed the north horizon. Sargasso weed floated in the cabin. A Portuguese man-of-war had hung itself up in one of the wing nets. The water felt warmer than the air. The sea was smooth enough to go 'on deck'.

'Time to tackle that hole to the aft cabin,' Bill said. He wriggled out, humped himself aft along the keel to a point we'd agreed on over the engine bed, and set to with a will to saw slots through the inch-thick keel, laid up of layers of solid glassfibre, hard as steel. Bill kept at it for two hours. Two slits athwartship, through the tough spine of the keel down to the foam sandwich, testified to his zeal. Having earned a rest, he took to the hammock and I took his place astride the keel. It was slippery and sloped down toward the stern. I had to grip with my knees, as if riding bareback on a horse that's stopped suddenly to crop grass. At a fraction of an inch a minute, the slit lengthened. I drilled, chiselled, and hacksawed four corners. When it was almost too dark to see, I knocked off. Only one side of the rectangle remained to be cut in the morning.

Second night

I tried to leave the hammock to Bill and stretched out in the forepeak. More water had settled way up in the bow so that it continually rinsed me, first down the collar, then up the crotch. Bill insisted I join him. We lay head to feet. I actually slept fitfully, despite the frequent splashes from below. But at Bill's expense, I fear. The bulk of the sail had bunched up on my side, leaving him slung lower and less protected. He didn't sleep until daybreak, when I returned to my hacksaw.

Third day adrift

The sea was down. Only a gentle westerly riffled the surface. Pink in the east. Blue sky above. Using a fresh blade, I attacked the last 18 inches with vim. A final hammer-whack broke out the V-shaped segment. Bill heard my gleeful call and stood in the lookout prepared to receive each recovered item. We'd rehearsed the priorities.

Four cases of tins had stacked themselves on the underside of the bunk projection – high and dry as if placed there by a grocery clerk.

Then through the hole to Bill's outstretched arms went a five-gallon jerry can of water, three lifejackets, two radar reflectors, a horseshoe life ring, floorboards, strips of batten, the rubber survival suit, a sleeping bag, a tool box. I emerged with a can of chicken stew and a can of corn. We breakfasted astride the hull. The roofs of our mouths were unaccountably tender.

Refreshed, Bill took charge of rehanging the hammock. Working down from the head of the sail to a point where its breadth would then span the gap between the bunks, we measured off a further seven feet, and sliced through the Dacron. We cut more lanyards, drilled more holes. Stretched taut by the bolt rope on one side, by rolled cloth on the other, at last there was a proper litter. A length of anchor warp, pulled tight beneath, provided a fore-and-aft dividing ridge and extra security. So absorbed were we that I missed my noon sight.

We rested in the late afternoon sun, squeezing water from the down in a sleeping bag, scanning the horizon, and planning for the morrow.

'We need a way to get from the hammock to the lookout without getting soaked,' Bill said. 'And tomorrow I'll unscrew the big cabin mirror, break it up and glue pieces with epoxy to the hull. We need more ways to attract attention.'

He had stuck a six-foot aluminium extrusion, a spare for the jib-furling system, into the daggerboard slot and had wired the metal reflector to its peak. But the first of three beeping beacons had exhausted its battery some time the night before. We agreed to husband the expensive unit with the capacity to receive and transmit voice as well as beep, for moments when planes might appear overhead.

'Every helicopter in Vietnam carries one,' the boat show salesman told me. Pilots with whom I'd checked it at both Boston and Beverly airports considered it good. We even had an extra battery for it. The less costly beeper-only beacon would remain in reserve. Its test light failed to blink but because it was brand new, we had a right to think it would work.

Third night

The hammock, though vastly improved, lacked room for two to sleep. Inadvertent jostling kept one or the other awake. Wavelets from below splashed up water that pooled in the hollows. By using my end of the damp, down sleeping bag to cover my nose, and exhaling forcibly, I generated enough heat to forestall shivering.

At dawn we agreed hereafter to split the dark hours into two five-hour shifts, sundown to midnight, midnight to light. Off watch in the hammock, on watch in the survival suit.

Fourth day adrift

I rose first, made a bad guess on an unlabelled can: cold watercress and lentil soup. Bill began to make a 'crawlway' to get from the hammock to the lookout without getting wet.

Soon we'd unscrewed the seven-foot mahogany planks that served as the outer edges of the forward bunks. We cut one into two-foot lengths. Into one end of each we drilled a hole. We screwed down the outboard ends to the hull, then lashed the inboard ends with wire to holes drilled in the reinforcing of the daggerboard trunk. Thus they served as the trestles in a swinging bridge. Twisting the drill chuck a quarter turn at a time by hand (the rusting handle turned hard) had chafed the soaked skin of our fingers so they were painfully raw.

While I took the noon sight, Bill tackled the adhesion of the broken mirror shards to the flanks of the main hull, well forward, and aft by the rudder.

About 1500, basking in the sunshine and holding damp sweaters to the light westerly, Bill spotted a ship's bridge just appearing from north-east.

The flare sequence was an orange, a big parachute rocket, then the small rocket and the cartridges for the signal pistol. Our logic: first an attention-getter, then the big one to mark us by, then the smaller ones for follow-up.

'Perfect angle for visibility.'

'Let's hold back till they're within two miles.'

We each took a sizeable hunk of broken mirror and practised bouncing the focus of the sun in the west toward the approaching vessel whose white bridge and three buff cranes were now visible.

Now the orange flare was stripped of its protecting tapes, the 'scratch-to-light' directions reviewed.

'Two miles? Okay. Now.'

The hot magnesium sputtered. It was plausible that the torch, held high for nearly a minute, could have been seen by an alert lookout.

'I believe they've altered course.'

'Now for a rocket.'

First I tried one dated 1971, expecting a dud, and it was; then one of the five fresh ones.

'Point downwind . . . press the lever firmly.' Up, up, 300 feet. High in the sky burst a pinky-orange ember that floated slowly down, in perfect view of any watcher on the bridge, now well within a mile.

'They've slowed down.' We fired the small rocket with the pistol.

'They've got to see this mirror. See it bounce on the bridge.'

We called 'Mayday!' on the beacon that had a voice transmitter. There was the odd chance that the ship might monitor its aircraft frequency. We waved orange towels. Now she was broadside.

'She's going to drift down on us.'

'She's going away.' The last of the three cartridge flares in the pistol packet proved a dud. What a fraud.

'They just had to have seen us,' said Bill, momentarily enraged.

'Maybe we only thought they slowed down,' I said. Disappointment engulfed us. We shared an inch of bourbon from the remaining half-bottle and a can of stew.

Fourth night

A coin toss gave me first watch. At sunset I pulled on the survival suit over oilskins and sat snug where I could catnap and peer around the horizon every 20 minutes. It was comforting to hear Bill snore. Solo, the hammock worked.

I reviewed our state. My reading had buffered the impact of the ship's failure to see us. Dougal Robertson, the Baileys, *Meridian* – all had shot flares for several ships that didn't stop before, at last, one did. By the law of averages, over a period of weeks in this busy area east of Norfolk and New York, we were sure to be sighted. We had food and water to wait it out for at least five weeks. We could now manage to stay dry and out of the wind. There were no signs of the hull connections weakening. We'd ration our flares, watch for planes on which to use the beacon.

My only haunting worry: my wife, Anne, had a ticket for the plane to England on 16 May. By then we'd be overdue. We just had to be picked up in the next two weeks. But until then, it was comforting to know that no one was worried. When the handle of the Big Dipper stood erect, I swapped places with Bill and slept like a felled ox till dawn.

Fifth day

A half-can of juice, a can of stew. The warming sun had Bill down to bathing trunks and safety harness while he stood barefoot on the underside of the bunks with a screwdriver, scratching 'SOS' in four-foot-high letters into the bottom paint.

We'd agreed on today's goal: rest the hands, dry out the clothes, settle in for a long siege. But the ship-miss had Bill restless.

I tore some pages from the back of a used notebook to make a log. On one sheet I mapped our position showing Bermuda 325 miles south; the Azores, 1700 miles downwind, downstream to the east; Nova Scotia, 300 miles north; Nantucket, 350 miles to the west.

'I'd vote to head for the coast and lots of ships,' said Bill. 'If we had a stretch of good weather, we could make it in nine days rowing in the dinghy.'

We exhausted the possibility of sawing off an outrigger and, with the raft and the dinghy to support the arms, converting it into a proa. At the rate our saw blades and other tools were turning to rust, we'd have lacked the equipment. Besides, to have violated the integrity of our raft would have been an act of desperation.

We agreed to forego as futile further discussion of leaving the ship for at least another week.

We decided to use up the canned and bottled liquids before calling on the seven gallons of water, our most easily managed drinking supply in case we took to the dinghy.

'Look, jet,' Bill said, grabbing for the transmitter, and pointing to a contrail travelling towards New York.

'And there's another,' I said, pointing south-east at one homing on Washington. Two planes at once after four blank days. Unnerving. We fumbled with the antenna before extending it all the way for a sure transmit. The encounter with fellow man, even 35,000 feet away, left me tingling. Petrels dabbling their feet in water, dolphins bounding, small fish swimming about in the cabin, all represented planetary life. None set the pulse pounding like that white trail in the sky saying People.

'Well, now we've had a practice run with a ship and planes,' said Bill, 'maybe we score next time.'

'It'll not be till the seventh ship,' I said.

He retired for a nap while I, in the late afternoon sun, tackled the pulpy wad representing the complete plays of Shakespeare. Whole folios of the least-read chronicle plays remained intact. *The Tempest* had taken a beating. Here was intellectual nourishment for many weeks. Lovingly I pressed pages one by one in the fold of a sun-dried towel. My spirits soared.

'Another jet. Eastbound.' On with the beeper. Then: 'Mayday, Mayday, Mayday! Capsized trimaran *Gulf Streamer*. Estimated position thirty-nine north by sixty-four west. Please report us. Over.'

I paused to listen for a reply and to let the beeper pulse a minute, then repeated the message. There was time for four sequences before the trail vanished on its way to Europe.

At sundown Bill got into the suit and I hit the hammock for four hours' sound sleep.

Fifth night

'Ship's lights. Coming from the south,' Bill called. He was astride the keel by the time I'd wormed my way to the lookout. 'What luck. I'd just put my head down for a nap when this big wave smacks me in the face. I sat up again to dry off and there she was.' Bill was jubilant.

Ship's lights they were. Now we could see red and green running lights as well as the white lights bow and stern.

'First we'll give 'em an orange flare.'

It burned hot, glowing much more impressively than in the daytime. Bill held it high in the suit's rubber mitten while I readied the 'chute rocket.

'Now for the big one.' It soared magnificently.

'He's blinking. Let's give him a white one to home on.'

In close succession, we lit two whites and an orange. Each brightly illuminated the three hulls and the blessedly calm sea surrounding us. Now the ship had halted 100 yards upwind. I scrambled forward for two life vests hanging from the hammock and urged Bill to get out of the suit, which was too heavy for climbing ladders.

As the ship drifted closer, we could see men readying a cargo net and a figure on the bridge directing a searchlight on our hulls. I had only time to tuck passports, wallet, and letter of credit into a sleeping-bag sack, hang it around my neck, and crawl out.

In big white letters on her lee starboard side, I read *Federal Bermuda*. The rungs of a rope ladder stood out against the mesh of a net as the vessel nestled gently along the outrigger.

'Nip up, lads,' a voice called from the deck.

Hand over hand, first Bill, then I, scrambled up the swaying ladder and swung ourselves over the rail onto the steel deck. Concerned British faces came out of shadows created by the glare of a floodlight.

'The master asks do you want to salvage anything?' asked a big blond-bearded man in a heavy white turtleneck sweater.

'No, thanks. Not a thing,' I replied.

'Pity we're a container ship,' said another voice. 'We have no crane.'

From the living quarters in the superstructure at the stern, a bare white deck stretched 250 feet to the stem. We were guided to the bridge, where we shook hands with the skipper standing at the wheel.

Master John 'Tony' Stapleford, Norwich, England, shone a floodlight down on *Gulf Streamer*'s upturned hulls. The letters SOS, the orange flag, the radar reflector, the two holes, the rudder aloft like a mizzen sail . . .

'The poor dear,' I said aloud, and my eyes filled with tears.

Extracted from *Moxie –The American Challenge*, by Phil Weld published by Little, Brown & Co with kind permission of Phil Weld's daughter Eloise Hodge and the *Moxie* Copyright Trust.

Lessons learned

Advised by multihull designer Jim Brown, Weld knew that the hulls of a cap-sized trimaran would float high. 'Don't rush the vital items into the vulnerable liferaft. Save your energy to live aboard upside down,' Brown told Weld. *Gulf Streamer*'s inherent buoyancy from her Airex sandwich construction, together with four airtight compartments in each outrigger, provided 'raft status of indefinite duration'.

As Weld had planned with Jim Brown, he unscrewed the now 'overhead' through-hull fitting for the log impeller, and through the two-inch hole, a 'window on the world', he thrust the antenna of one of the three emergency beacons and set it to pulsing.

Jim Brown had also prompted Weld to tuck emergency tools for safekeeping beneath the chart table with which to cut an access hole through the upside-down hull. 'It took three hours to complete the fourteen-by-eigh-teen-inch aperture. First a drilled hole. Then enlargement with hammer and chisel to make a slit admitting a hacksaw blade. Then a pruning saw with a curved, coarse blade to lengthen the slit on one side.'

Next, he and his crew, Bill, unscrewed the big cabin mirror, and broke it up and glued pieces with epoxy to the hull as another way to attract the attention of rescuers. Crewman Bill, stuck a six-foot aluminium extrusion, a spare for the jib-furling system, into the daggerboard slot and wired the metal reflector to its peak.

Bill also used a screwdriver to scratch 'SOS' in four-foot-high letters into the bottom paint of *Gulf Streamer*'s hull. Sensibly, they both decided to use up the canned and bottled liquids before calling on the seven gallons of water, their most easily managed drinking supply in case they had to take to the dinghy.

8 Capsize of *Rushcutter*

Yacht *Rushcutter* (30ft Harmonic class sloop)
Skipper Anthony Lealand
Crew Annette Wilde
Bound from Wellington, New Zealand to Sydney, Australia
Date of loss 19 April, 1978
Position 190 miles west of Auckland, New Zealand

Annette Wilde and Anthony Lealand, both from Christchurch, New Zealand, had undertaken to deliver the 30ft Rushcutter, *a boat of the Harmonic class, to Sydney for her owner. They had examined her in Wellington and considered it was a reasonable proposition to sail her the 1200 miles across the Tasman Sea. Anthony Lealand tells the story:*

The disaster really started when we spent 10 days waiting around for a chart, which the Post Office lost, and our beacon battery, already a year on order.

When the new battery arrived, our beacon refused to light its test lamp, but after a day of tests and phone calls to Auckland it was decided that the beacon worked, although the test lamp was at fault. I made a little test unit to take with us for future checks, and this was heat-sealed in polythene bags along with our over-age batteries which still tested 'good'.

We had stripped our own yacht *Valya* of all her navigational equipment, our sailing necessities, and a good selection of tools, and with this ponderous load of excess baggage we flew to Wellington on 3 April, leaving a friend to live in our house, water our cat and feed our plants.

Rushcutter had not been sailed seriously for a year, so right away we had a year's accumulation of rust and stiffness to set to rights. Owner Charles Troup had left us a detailed list of things he knew of to attend to and, with what we considered necessary, it was 11 days before we were ready to clear.

We started with a morning's work cleaning out a bilge full of engine oil, dropped by a recently broken oil line. I regarded this as very important for there was no depth to her bilge and it would need only a splash below to have the whole slimy lot swilling around above the cabin sole.

At the masthead I found the reason for the jib halyards needing a winch even to move them. Severe corrosion of the alloy sheaves was bulging the ³⁄₁₆in stainless sheave box. To remove the sheaves was difficult for the mast fabricator had bolted the sheave pin in and then welded on mounting flanges, completely blocking the pin's removal.

I did not understand the reason for the severe corrosion until we found the alloy sheave had a bronze bearing. Aluminium in contact with bronze and salt water is severely corroded – a fact well known since 1895 when *Defender*, an America's Cup yacht, was built with bronze hull and aluminium topside plating. She was broken up after six years, so severe was the action.

Our next surprise was to find the available replacements constructed in the same way. Oh well, we greased them well and considered that they would last the two weeks to Australia.

A day at Shelly Bay slipway saw *Rushcutter* fitted with ply deadlights and a spare rudder. The shipwrights and manager took an interest in the work and we were able to get through a long list of minor items, leaving finally with a big handful of assorted nails and a spare sheet of ply for luck.

We had lashed down the liferaft aft in the cockpit. Over this, on a board, athwartships was our new Sestrel compass. The board was held by headless screws so it could be pulled away should we want to get at the liferaft. *Valya*'s chronometer seemed to like its new lodgings, and for the first time in its life settled to a steady rate. We were in some difficulty over our emergency aerial, a 13ft-long helical whip we had made in Christchurch. This had been lost in transit, but Ted (Annette's brother) brought it down just in time for our safety inspector's visit.

Wellington Customs were kind enough to come to the marina to issue our clearance, which made departure easy. It is a nuisance to have to clear from some foul commercial berth with piles a boat length apart.

As we beat out of Wellington, we marvelled at the improvement in the mast, now solidly wedged. Her mast, stepped through the deck, had been rubber wedged on our sail some days before, and shook about in a lively manner. Of course the solid wedges now rendered the bendy mast gear inoperative but did mean we no longer had 6ft of unstayed mast thrashing about below.

We were perhaps an hour late catching the tide at Sinclair Head, but with full main, a fresh southerly, and an indicated 8 knots, we felt more than happy.

That is till I went below and found all our clothes, bunks and sleeping bags sodden. In the beat out of Wellington the deck joints of the inboard chain plates had obviously hosed water everywhere. It continued to leak even now, running downwind. Murmuring rude words I climbed into the pipe berth, still in my waterproofs, which we were to wear till rescued.

This was my first acquaintance with a pipe berth, and I found it a damn good bunk, even though *Rushcutter*'s were a little narrow.

Annette was tight-lipped about the wet below. She feels that boats with deck leaks just ought not to be allowed. I suppose we were rather spoiled on *Valya* with no deck leaks and a diesel heating stove to dry our gear while off watch.

Rushcutter hustled on, a delight to sail. Occasionally, the full quarters would catch on a wave, but she needed no more than a firm hand to bring her back. There was no sign of loss of control.

By now life below was pretty foul. The main hatch was a cunning contrivance of the cabinetmaker's art, for surely no shipwright could have made it. Every slosh that landed on it was delivered below by the hatch's forward slope to dribble across the deckhead, fill galley lockers, soak the charts and eventually wipe out the beacon receiver. What the hell, the sailing was good!

On Sunday, *Rushcutter* was changed to cutter rig, using the storm jib as a staysail. The sheet from this ran through roller-bearing blocks to the tiller's windward side and was balanced by a red rubber tube from leeward. She steered herself well, though as the wind drew aft, the staysail would have to be backed. Self-steering by this method seems to have a lot in its favour, not least of which is rapidly learning about the balance and steering of the boat. It will not, of course, put you about or hold you on a course with an unbalanced rig while you change sail. But it is very powerful with a breeze in the open sea.

Monday night saw a rising easterly wind which soon had us clearing the deck of lashed-down sails and, for the caution of it, putting the deepest reef in the main. Just as well, for the easterly had us swishing along in perfect control, dodging breaking seas in the confused turmoil that the rapidly rising wind caused. *Rushcutter* sometimes banged solidly up forward, but she had thumped more heavily beating out of Wellington, so we felt no worry.

Charles had mentioned he felt it unwise to let her thump, but to reduce sail when we had such good control seemed a pity. We had good visibility with a near full moon behind clouds. By the time the moon was setting the wind was dropping, which was just as well for it is less funny to dodge seas in the darkness.

By dawn the wind was light and the seas pleasantly regular. We jilled along quietly that day, doing a lot of sleeping but confident that *Rushcutter* was more boat than she perhaps looked. The cabin was pleasantly dark too, for as the easterly had risen I had whipped out the deadlights and spiked them on with three-inch roofing nails. It seemed a little dramatic and I wondered how I was going to explain the splinters to Charles.

The seas that came rolling in from the south late that day had me thinking we needed even less sail than the deep-reefed main. As the trysail had only a little less area than the main reefed, I hanked on the storm jib. This proved a dubious arrangement. Hanked on the topmast stay, and so having a very long sheet, it vibrated badly, shaking the whole rig, and unless the wind was taken a long way round on the quarter, it would bang from tack to tack with great wrenching thumps.

But now the wind was so strong that we were overpowered and broaching badly on the crests. The storm jib came down, leaving us still overpowered by the yacht's windage alone on the crests but dead and down to 3–4 knots in the troughs. Big seas filled the cockpit. We had never taken serious water from astern into a cockpit before, but, as other commentators have said, in the conditions in which it comes aboard, it is thrown out just as quickly. Which was just as well, for *Rushcutter* had a large cockpit.

By midnight I was worried. The wind was from the south and steady Storm Force, but seas came from WSW and SE as well. They were each about 20ft high with the top six feet breaking, which it did fairly frequently. *Rushcutter* was piggishly slow to answer in the troughs but a handful on the crests.

Around 0130 on Wednesday morning I asked Annette to send out a PAN PAN call saying that if we did not call up within 24 hours it could be presumed we were in trouble. Unfortunately, it was just past the silence period. Indeed, the set did not load up well, no doubt as a result of the salt water sloshing over the deck, aerial lead-in, and lower backstay insulator.

At 0140, as *Rushcutter* slid off the back of a southerly wave, broaching a little to port, from the port beam came a classic breaker. *Rushcutter*, dead in the water, would not turn and to my surprise rolled right over. I came up on her port side, my lifeline taut at water level, to see her floating high and very stable upside-down. My lifeline was short to avoid being flung some distance and injured. Now as *Rushcutter* settled I was slowly spending more time under water and as my knife had been flung from around my neck, I knew that shortly I would drown. I rapped on the hull for Annette but heard no reply. At this moment, Annette was contemplating a tedious wait for a silence period when *Rushcutter* started pouring the contents of the lockers over her and she saw the whole cabin slowly revolve around her. Water gushed in the gap between the washboards and hatch slide, and perhaps through the ventilator and where the mast was.

She scrabbled at the hatch trying to open it and get out, but the water was soon over her head as she bent to it. Hearing my rapping she saw the water rolling about, and with a quick understanding of the situation blundered back and forth in time with the water, till a good roll built up. *Rushcutter* came up so fast I did not know what had happened till I found myself in the cockpit roaring for a knife to release myself from the tangle of sheets, halyards and safety harness. Annette was similarly yelling for me to open the hatch and let her out. In her hand was the carving knife which had jammed the hatch.

We turned to find the mast gone at deck level, about two feet of water below, and the liferaft in its slick glassfibre case surging alongside. It was agreed in an instant not to waste time getting it on board, for it was a six-man raft weighing well over 100lb, and I would have had to go into the water to get a line securely around it. At any instant we expected to be slammed again; *Rushcutter*'s stability and self-righting were seriously in doubt now she had taken so much water below.

We pulled yards of string from the liferaft, till it popped open and was full in an instant. Annette leapt in gratefully, for although totally in control she had been thoroughly freaked when trapped below. I cut free our water bottles and bag of emergency gear, passing these to Annette, who lashed them into the liferaft. One bottle had been holed, and so I left it. There was another below but the boom of a nearby sea had me in the raft in an instant. The line was cut, *Rushcutter* went behind a wave and we did not see her again.

Inside the raft we had to shout to make ourselves heard, for the canopy flogged with an insane rage. Its door, something one would hesitate to fit to a pup tent, could not be closed properly, for the foolish, stiff plastic domes just kept popping open.

Then a great crushing roar slammed us into numbness. The raft was very full of water, on its side, and the door torn. By moving our weight inside we righted her and then bailed, using a cut-open gallon water bottle. We had poured its contents into the 5-gallon bottle, which was not completely full, purposely so that it would be easy to handle and float.

We had just finished stabbing holes and lashing the door shut when we were hit again. This time the canopy burst open on the opposite side. Again we bailed, stabbed holes and lashed, and again we went over.

This time the raft stayed upside-down. Annette did not know where she was and I was spluttering in the little air under the raft trying to get my arm out of one of the rope handles. Annette decided which way was up and told me to cut the rope. The water-activated light inside the raft must have been obscured by the torn canopy. Without this light we would have been totally lost in the black tangle and drowned blindly.

Diving outside the raft, I did not think of anything tied to that rope. It must have been very dark now for I did not see the raft's waterballast bags whose existence I knew of. Instead, I clawed my way on to the bottom, holding handfuls of the rubber, put my feet in the girdling rope and threw myself backwards. Annette slid in as the raft surfaced, awash, and bailed till I could be dragged aboard safely.

At this stage the canopy had pulled away completely from the raft, the glue line having failed. We were not flipped again, just filled by roaring seas. Perhaps the loss of the canopy contributed to our stability.

Dawn brought us the sight of huge seas marching from the south, and still small steep cross-seas making crests tumble and break. With light we felt we had come out of a minute-to-minute survival situation, and started to make things shipshape. It was then I saw our five gallons of water had gone, cut away by me when I freed my arm.

With our weight at one side of the raft, it took up an attitude with the remains of the door side of the canopy across the wind. We, in the lee of this, had tightened up all our belts and buckles and with an aluminised plastic foil blanket around us were reasonably warm.

It was impossible to keep the raft dry; sloshes and occasional big seas came on board, slamming the canopy tube down on us. I had the beacon out, tied to my wrist, and we kept a constant lookout for breaking seas. I folded the aerial at any hint of one, for aerial length is critical for transmission of a signal.

I doubt that we could have survived the night had we been alone, or with anyone else but each other. There were so many occasions when we had to know exactly what the other was doing without even talking or with just a few brief words.

We sat in silence, from time to time bailing as seas hit, and licking the salt splashes off the beacon's aerial insulator. From time to time the wind would rise, and in an instant the wavetops would be hissing and breaking.

Around 1000 (a guess, for we had no watch), I saw a vapour trail overhead. Annette, who had lost her glasses, could only just see it. It cheered us greatly.

Lunch was tinned peaches. And I can thoroughly recommend them. Easy to swallow, sweet and wet. Later we tried a lifeboat biscuit. Scientifically designed they may be with no protein and high in calories, but they are such a foul brew, forming a great sticky glob in our mouths, that we gave up eating them.

Early that evening I snapped out of a doze to see a flashing red light above us in the sky. But by the time I had a red parachute flare in my hand, I could not see it. Surely I had seen it? Perhaps I had seen a star scintillate strongly.

Some time later Annette woke me to point out another flashing red. If she, without glasses, could see it I was convinced, and I had two parachute flares fired before I realised the plane could be 20–30 miles away as it was fairly low on the horizon.

Annette slept now and I held the beacon as high and as far out as I could, keeping it away from the salty wet canopy which would absorb the signal. Every time the tattered canopy started to shiver with a rise in the wind we both felt a sick apprehension that it would continue to rise, treating us to another night of breaking seas.

Dawn brought considerable cheer to Annette for she recognised a stable Tasman sky. It also brought me water, which I was craving. We had caught a little water in the showers the previous day, about a quarter cup each. Most had been wasted in waiting for the salt to be rinsed off the canopy. Torn and tied as the half left was, it caught water rather well.

Anyway we punctured the first of our six-pint tins of water, drank, and then spent about half an hour devising a way of holding the rest so it did not spill. The beacon we lashed to the canopy support tube.

I had been having hallucinations for some time and we decided that I was dehydrated, not because of lack of water but because of all the salt I had drunk while admiring *Rushcutter*'s underwater sections.

We had not drunk much in the last couple of days on *Rushcutter*, for it had really been too rough to bother fixing the innumerable cups of tea I normally fill my day with. So it was with the measured precision of a drunk that I carefully knelt up to listen to a plane sound I heard. I decided it was the wind.

Fish had been bumping under the raft, so we set to trailing a lure and then pulling it in with inviting tugs. From time to time I checked the beacon's output with our tester, finding the needle still flicking high.

I had to put a strong conscious effort into ignoring flaring red and blue blobs which crossed my vision. Even the shiny black raft floor was bad to look at, reflecting a writhing image of the sky.

Annette was still her quiet self, not even very hungry or thirsty. Our next can of peaches was again a winner, but the fishing was not going too well. We could not have eaten the fish had we caught it, for fish is very high in protein, needing lots of water to digest. We were going to just suck the juices out for water.

It was just when the sea around the raft was starting to resemble a marine safari, for there were so many fish, that Annette heard the low throaty roar of a real piston and propeller aeroplane. We could not see him, low though he was, because of the cloud and blinding sun, and after our last waste of flares we were excessively cautious. Then, sighting the Orion, we had smoke and parachute flares ready for his next run.

Leaving us marked with a sonar buoy and smoke candles, the Orion went to fetch a Japanese refrigerated freighter, the *Toyu Maru*, which was 20 miles off. They were alongside us in an hour and a quarter, crossing very close upwind of us, with a ladder and boarding nets out. The raft leapt over the bow wave, leaving us wishing we had lifejackets for this last bit. I grabbed a thrown monkey's fist and twirled it on to the raft, Annette meanwhile held her weight central in the raft to stop the floor bulging up and sucking the raft down, which happens when flexible rafts are towed.

Thumping into the ship's side threw me on to the ladder, which I started to climb, my legs hardly able to support my weight. Below me as I climbed I could see Annette climbing too.

From *Sea Spray*, June 1978

Lessons learned

Skipper Anthony Lealand describes his exemplary preparations before setting off on the delivery trip from Wellington, NZ, to Sydney, Australia, in *Rushcutter*. Working from a detailed list provided by the owner 'it was 11 days before we were ready to clear.' *Rushcutter*'s shallow bilge meant he had to work hard to clean out engine oil which, in bad conditions, would 'need only a splash below to have the whole slimy lot swilling around above the cabin sole'. At the masthead he found severe corrosion of the halyard alloy sheaves –caused by a bronze bearing. 'Aluminium in contact with bronze and salt water is severely corroded.'

The yacht was fitted with ply deadlights and a spare rudder. They left 'with a big handful of assorted nails and a spare sheet of ply for luck'. When, later, the wind increased, Lealand 'whipped out the deadlights and spiked them on with three in-roofing nails. It seemed a little dramatic and I wondered how I was going to explain the splinters to Charles.'

When the yacht rolled right, over Lealand's lifeline, which was short, to avoid being flung some distance and injured, meant he found himself 'slowly spending more time under water and as my knife had been flung from around my neck, I knew that shortly I would drown'. A handy, available knife, is essential in these circumstances. When *Rushcutter* righted herself, Lealand found himself in the cockpit roaring for a knife to release himself from the tangle of sheets, halyards and safety harness. Mercifully, Annette was able to hand him a carving knife.

Soon they took to the liferaft: a six-man weighing well over 100lb. Not surprisingly, without the weight of six people, they were flipped. Liferafts are designed to be stable when used to capacity. For two-handed cruising, a six or eight-man liferaft is as much of a liability as six people in a three-man raft.

Rushcutter had been well prepared for her voyage across the Tasman Sea, and when she had to be abandoned, Anthony Lealand cut free water bottles and bag of emergency gear, passing them to Annette, who lashed them into the liferaft. Of the items of food contained in the emergency kit, Lealand comments on two:'Lunch was tinned peaches. And I can thoroughly recommend them. Easy to swallow, sweet and wet. Later we tried a lifeboat biscuit. Scientifically designed they may be, with no protein and high in calories, but they are such a foul brew, forming a great sticky glob in our mouths, that we gave up eating them.'

9 So near and yet...

Yacht *Merlan* (43ft Bermudian sloop)
Skipper WL ('Lance') Curtis
Crew Keith Douglas Young, Eric Walker, Brian Shaw
Bound from Georgetown, Tasmania, to Geelong, Victoria, Australia
Date of loss 16 January, 1949
Position on rocks off Phillip Head, near Melbourne

Merlan had competed and been just beaten into second place in the Sydney–Hobart race of 1948. For the race she had a crew of nine, but only three of them, together with an additional volunteer, were left to sail her back to Geelong. The voyage of 250 miles across the Bass Strait is described by Keith Douglas Young:

We left Georgetown at the mouth of the Tamar River, in Northern Tasmania, at about 1330 on Friday, 14 January. Not, as events later proved, a particularly auspicious day on which to have sailed. The weather forecast promised a good voyage . . . fine weather with southerly winds veering to south-east, which would give us an easy run to the Heads. According to the radio reports, all barometers in Tasmania were rising; and with the weather seemingly assured, we felt no forebodings as we set out under full sail on what should have been a simple and speedy passage of one and a half to two days, for the approximately 250 miles distance.

Fine weather stayed with us for the first day. We made good time with a favourable wind and a gentle swell which set the reef points jigging against the inward curve of the sail. The smooth racing hull of the *Merlan* porpoised forward in a series of powerful lunges while the towering mast described a pattern of arabesques and circles against the sky. It was perfect sailing weather.

The log reading after the first 24 hours showed us to be considerably more than halfway home. However, during the afternoon of the second day our barometer began to fall, slowly at first, but with increasing rapidity as evening approached. At the same time a dirty black scud began to build up in the sky. The almost hourly stream of planes which had been in sight as they sped overhead were lost to view in the rapidly forming cloud-wrack. These planes, in addition to relieving that sense of mid-ocean loneliness and isolation, had served as a good check on navigation. It was comforting, however, to be able to hear them still.

By midnight Saturday our glass, which had been steady at 30.05, had dropped to a menacing 29.5 and showed signs of falling still further. A good fresh breeze was blowing, but at that time not yet strong enough to cause us any real discomfort or worry. *Merlan*, still under full sail, was giving a good account of herself, although solid water and spray were being hurled aboard in some of the gusts. It was obvious to us that the worst was still to come.

We carried on under these conditions for a further hour or so, when it was decided to take the mainsail off altogether and set the storm trysail. This was accomplished without much difficulty as the wind lulled temporarily while we were shifting sails. Hardly had we made everything secure when it really began to blow. The advance-guard of the gale, as forecast by the rapid and steep fall of the barometer, finally menaced our ship.

Shortly after the gale struck we sighted our first light on the Victorian coast. This was identified as the Cape Woolamai Light. Here it became necessary to change course to the west in order to stand up to the Heads. Our position was confirmed some little time later when the unmistakable 22½-second flash of Cape Schank was sighted in the murky distance.

By this time the wind had veered round to the west. We decided to get away from the land and stand in once more in the morning. With the night pitch black and the coastal lights periodically blacked out in driving rain squalls, it was scarcely a safe risk to approach the land too closely.

There was no rest for any of us that night. Those who tried to snatch a little sleep found it almost impossible to wedge into a bunk securely enough to avoid being pitched out as *Merlan* fell heavily off some of the more precipitous seas. In addition, it had become bitterly cold and all our clothing was thoroughly saturated. It was impossible to prepare any sort of hot meal or drink. The best we could do was to snatch a handful of biscuits, an orange or an apple and perhaps a bit of chewing gum. I had quite a battle keeping my cigarettes and matches dry, but succeeded by wrapping them securely in a spare oilskin.

It was a thoroughly miserable night. Next morning found us under trysail and jib ploughing through a lumpy grey sea with the wind coming in gusts and sometimes petering out altogether before coming in just as freshly from another quarter.

We were still, at this time, some considerable distance offshore and making slow progress under reduced sail. Again we changed course to make directly for Port Phillip Heads, whereupon the wind began to build up until in a short time it was blowing half a gale directly out of the west. This was rather disheartening, as it meant we had to drive *Merlan* right into the teeth of the wind under trysail, not a particularly efficient sail at the best of times.

By midday the wind had mounted to full gale – about force 10 or 11. Some of the gusts we estimated at from 70 to 75mph, a figure which was later confirmed by Weather Bureau observations made at the time ashore. This state of affairs prevailed for the next few hours, during which we tried to battle our way to the west under the inefficient trysail. Then the wind helped us by backing to the south'ard so that we eventually found ourselves making heavy going against a full sou'westerly gale along the Victorian coast between Cape Schank and the Heads.

Huge seas rolling up Bass Strait were making it difficult and dangerous for those of us who found it necessary to remain on deck. In spite of efforts to ease her over some of the worst of the seas, our decks were being continually swept. There was hardly a moment when the self-bailing cockpit was free of water; for as fast as it could drain the contents of one sea another would pour aboard. Much of this water was finding its way below, where, to add to our troubles, both pumps had gone out of action. Soon the water below reached a level several inches over the floorboards and it became necessary to bail with a bucket, which we continued to do for the ensuing several hours.

In the early afternoon of Sunday it was decided to take in the trysail. Even that small patch of canvas was more than the boat could safely stand. With an almost continuous series of breaking seas hurling themselves feet deep across the decks, this was a hell of a job.

Blinded and almost choked by the tumultuous waves, Lance, Brian and I clawed our way forward where, on looking aloft, I was somewhat startled to see the mast trembling and vibrating like a plucked harp string. We returned to the cockpit for a trick at the tiller. At the end of an hour it was time for another spell at the bucket. To our dismay, the water was gaining on us and was starting to splash up over the mattresses on the bunks. It was now a matter of getting into shelter quickly, or having the boat founder under us.

It was too late to turn back and run for shelter at Flinders or anywhere in the lee of the Schank. Heaving-to was also out of the question, owing to the size and force of the seas. With the deadness of the sloop occasioned by the terrific weight of water in her, there was always the danger that they would overwhelm us.

Merlan had behaved magnificently in all that we had come through, and any boat less honestly built would, I am convinced, have foundered long before. But there is a limit to what even the best craftsmanship in wood can stand, and it was apparent that *Merlan* was tiring. The bucket bailing was by far the worst of all our previous ordeals. Not only did the bucket become progressively heavier as it was handed up full each time, but the crew handling it had to brace themselves against the unpredictable dips, lurches and wrenches of the yacht.

Meanwhile, under the single jib, we had gradually closed the land until *Merlan* was not more than a mile or two off shore. The height of the seas and the flying spray was such that we could catch only brief glimpses of the nearby coastline. By mid-afternoon we estimated that we could be only a short distance from the Heads. We expected the entrance to be hazardous, but our condition was such by this time that it would have to be attempted in spite of the risks.

At about 1600 I wedged myself securely against the boom and strained to catch an identifying glimpse of the shore. At the moment I was about to give up, I caught one brief glimpse of the white shaft of the Lonsdale Lighthouse on the western side of the Heads. This momentary peep was sufficient to give us a bearing, and on checking our position we discovered we were about a mile due south of the Heads. It was a simple matter then to ease our sheets and begin the run for the Heads and what we earnestly hoped would be shelter, safety and rest.

As we drew closer to the entrance we could see the tidal signal flying from the yardarm of the Lonsdale Light. It informed us that the tide was adverse – that it was ebbing. There was no turning back. We would have to try and force our way through. The regular steamer channel in the center of the Rip was a churning, boiling maelstrom in which I am convinced no small boat could possibly have lived. Further to the east lay the dreaded Corsair Rock, unseen in the welter of white water that was the Heads, but still a lurking menace. Our best, in fact our only plan was to carry on as we were – as close as possible to the Lonsdale side.

With gigantic seas sweeping up under our stern as we stormed along on a northerly course, we were picked up and literally hurled ahead at terrific speeds as we skated on the crests of some of the waves. A breaking sea would almost certainly have meant our end; and though many times it did look as though we might be overwhelmed by water hurtling up astern, none broke upon us.

The next greatest danger was the possibility of a broach, and this actually happened during our hazardous dash through the Heads. I found myself grabbing for grip on something as *Merlan* was picked up by a monster sea charging up astern and hurled ahead at a speed we estimated to be in the vicinity of 15mph. As the yacht began to slide down the almost perpendicular slope of the wave to the great bulk of water which had forced its way below, all ran to the nose of the boat. This, of course, left the helmsman with no control and we had a ticklish minute before the yacht was brought back on her course. But this single broach, as it turned out later, had been sufficient to bring us within the orbit of the Lonsdale reef, quite lost to view beneath the boiling surge. Next moment we struck the reef! It was a mortal blow for *Merlan*. That much was obvious after the first shock. I was standing at the foot of the hatch with a just-filled bucket which I was about to hand up to Brian. To the accompaniment of a horrible grinding sound I was pitched the full length of the cabin, where I picked myself up, dazed and shaken, with the bucket still in my hand. The dreadful tearing, rending, crunching sound as the yacht drove on the rocks is something quite impossible to convey.

Picking myself up I began to fight my way to the hatch and escape through an indescribable confusion of sodden sails and clothing, charts and navigation instruments, mattresses and tins of food which had been flung out of burst lockers. My one thought, I suppose naturally enough, was to get on deck.

Just as I reached the foot of the hatch (about five seconds after the initial shock) *Merlan* struck again. Once more I was hurled the length of the cabin, to end up even more bruised and battered at the foot of the mast. A second time I clawed my way through the hatch just in time to see and feel a really terrific sea lift *Merlan* bodily and hurl her forward on to the reef. Brian, who had apparently secured a firm grip on something substantial, seemed to be all right. Eric, tightly lashed in the cockpit, had likewise emerged unscathed, though the heavy bronze fitting at the rudder head had snapped completely off, leaving him with the now useless tiller in his hands.

But we did appear to have one casualty. At the moment of impact Lance had been flung violently against the doghouse at the after end of the cabin and his face was a mass of blood which poured from a nasty gash near the bridge of his nose. The effect was pretty ghastly. Apart from the shaking up and a few bruises and scratches, I seemed to be in working order.

The jib had blown itself out at the moment we struck. After a moment Brian and Lance went forward to lower it. However, they found the halyard in such a tangled mess that they were forced to abandon the attempt. In the meantime I had returned below, where I managed to retrieve four life-jackets. We put them on. Just as well we did, for beyond doubt those lifejackets saved our lives in the struggle which was to come shortly afterwards.

Within minutes, a large crowd of holidaymakers had begun to gather on the shore about half a mile away. There was, of course, absolutely nothing they could do, but we must have provided them with an interesting spectacle. The keeper of the Lonsdale Light had witnessed the entire happening and had telephoned at once for the lifeboat stationed at Queenscliff.

Before long the lifeboat appeared, but because of the tremendous sea running, the adverse tide and the treacherous currents and tide-rips it could not be brought close to the wreck. At that moment things never looked more hopeless. We held a bit of a conference to decide what our best course of action might be and whether we might, by our own efforts, save ourselves. It was clear to us that so long as the gale prevailed there was absolutely no hope of a boat approaching us. It seemed, therefore, that we would have to take to the water and try to make for the lifeboat cruising up and down about a quarter of a mile away in the lee of the reef.

It was now about 1700 and since the tide appeared to be at low water slack we determined to make our effort before darkness set in. On the cabin top was a small plywood dinghy. Though none too optimistic about its chances of supporting the four of us in the waters swirling and boiling over the reef, we did hope that it might perhaps carry us some of the way. It did – about six feet. We had barely left the stricken *Merlan* when our cockleshell dinghy was swamped and we were left struggling in the powerful, sucking tide-rip.

Within seconds the seas had taken complete control and we had been swept dozens of yards apart. The same gigantic wave which had engulfed our tiny dinghy seemed, once it had us firmly in its grasp, to sweep each one of us in a totally different direction. Then began what was really a nightmare struggle before the eyes of some hundreds of people.

We had swamped in one of the labyrinthine channels of the reef, a channel though which a vast volume of water was swirling at a terrific pace. I began swimming as desperately as possible, but like the others, was entirely at the mercy of the currents. The most fortunate of the four, I managed to crawl through a mass of slimy kelp on to a more solid portion of the reef. Actually I crawled part of the way on to the reef three times, only to be washed off by seas sweeping across. But on the fourth attempt I contrived to hang on. Clinging grimly to the reef for a few minutes to catch my breath, I recovered some strength. Then began a staggering walk to the leeward side where I knew I would once more have to take to the sea for a swim to the lifeboat. Before doing so I turned to see how my shipmates might be faring.

I was elated to see Brian dragging himself on to the reef, but was quite alarmed to see Eric and Lance, supported solely by their lifejackets, being swept out past the wreck into a position which seemed fatal. Then, as I watched, Eric was swept by a wave into a favourable current and began to approach the reef. He began to struggle once more and by dint of furious efforts was at last able to clamber on to the water-swept rocks. Somewhat later, Lance, nearly spent, made it also.

By this time a group of Queenscliff fishermen had succeeded in launching a dinghy and by a marvellous combination of seamanship and courage had brought the boat right up to the reef from which we had expected to have to make another swim to the waiting lifeboat. One error of judgment, one unpredictable sea sweeping aboard their dinghy, and they too would have been struggling for their lives.

It was a comparatively simple matter to pile into the dinghy, a solidly built 15-footer, but there was still the dangerous quarter-mile pull to the waiting lifeboat. The seas had not abated, and with eight men aboard even a 15-foot dinghy is somewhat crowded. But our rescuers displayed faultless seamanship; we got a line to the lifeboat and were hauled alongside. In a matter of moments we were wrapped in coats and blankets and a man-sized pannikin of rum was thrust upon each of us. First aid was applied to our cuts and scratches received on the boat and more especially from the jagged rocks on the reef. And so we were rescued.

From *Yachting*, October 1950

Lessons learned

The importance of preparing hot food in advance, perhaps in a Thermos flask, when bad weather is expected, is underlined when Keith Douglas Young describes the barometer dropping to 'a menacing 29.5' on Saturday night and later says 'it was impossible to prepare any sort of a hot meal or drink. The best we could do was to snatch a handful of biscuits, an orange or an apple and perhaps a bit of chewing gum.'

Having an effective, self-bailing cockpit, with ample drain holes, is also demonstrated when Young says 'there was hardly a moment when the self-bailing cockpit was free of water; for as fast as it could drain the contents of one sea another would pour aboard'. Much of the water found its way below, where, with both pumps out of action, it was soon over the floorboards. Despite bailing with a bucket for several hours the water was soon splashing up over the mattresses on the bunks.

It was now a matter of getting into shelter quickly, or having the boat founder. The terrific weight of water in the sloop made her unresponsive and the danger that seas would overwhelm them came true when they made for Port Phillip Heads with a fast ebbing tide. 'As the yacht began to slide down the almost perpendicular slope of the wave to the great bulk of water which had forced its way below all ran to the nose of the boat ...' This single broach was sufficient to bring them near the reef, where the mortal blow was struck.

Luckily, Young managed to get below to retrieve the lifejackets which saved their lives in the struggle that followed. Again, in such adverse conditions it is sound seamanship to insist the crew are wearing lifejackets before it becomes necessary.

10 Sea dark, sky crying

Yacht *Ecureuil Poitou Charentes 2*, (60ft cutter designed by Jean Berret with a canting keel (a beam of 17ft 8in and a draught of 14ft 10in)
Skipper Isabelle Autissier
Bound from Cape Town to Sydney
Date of loss 28 December, 1994
Position 920 miles south south-east of Adelaide

Isabelle Autissier, the only woman competing in the 1994–95 BOC Challenge Round the World Singlehanded Race, was forced to abandon her crippled yacht deep in the Southern Ocean, plucked by helicopter at the limits of rescue services.

It took just a split second and an unavoidable slam on the port side for Isabelle Autissier's dreams to suddenly come toppling down around her. A rigging screw on her yacht's main port shroud failed and the mast collapsed over the starboard side, snapped at the base.

It was 2 December and the 38-year-old French yachtswoman, a marine science professor and engineer, was halfway between Cape Town and the Kerguelen Islands on the seventh day of the second leg of the BOC Challenge Round the World Singlehanded Yacht Race.

Her 60ft rocket ship *EPC2* had streaked away down the Atlantic from the September start in Charleston, South Carolina, America, to win a decisive victory in the first leg of the race, leaving the men, her follow competitors 1200 miles astern battling in her wake for second place.

Now she was the southernmost boat in the fleet of 14 reduced from the 18 competitors that had begun the epic race.

I felt like I had been hit in the stomach. I thought 'No. Not this. Not here.' It was already over for me. 'But what was the use of yelling, shouting and crying for a victory that was completely lost?' Isabelle asked herself.

She sent a message to Race HQ in Charleston: 'Dismasted. No danger immediately.' She was 1,200 miles from Cape Town, and lying at 48°52'S.

There was no time to waste. A mast can become a horrific hammer of carbon fibre threatening to puncture the hull of a yacht. The winch at the foot of the mast was already starting to smash a hole in the deck. With hacksaw, pliers and a knife, Isabelle scrabbled about on her knees cutting away the rig as the yacht rolled. She tried to save the boom, but it broke, dragged down by the weight of the mainsail.

Ninety minutes later, she had cut away most of the rig and stood on the bare deck of her yacht. She had one complete spinnaker pole and half of a broken one.

'There are 5000 miles left to Sydney. I feel so much like crying for my lost hopes. But this is the way racing goes.'

Fellow competitor David Adams, 65 miles away, diverted to her position, sailing at 11 knots in storm-force winds. All day long in rough sea conditions and strengthening winds, Isabelle worked to set up a replacement rig. In an eloquent message to her supporters in France, she described her plight: 'Thirty knots of wind, sea dark, sky crying. I'm working to clear off the deck and see what I can do. There is almost nothing left on deck. Nothing left of my dream. But I won't think about that now. I am safe . . .'

By evening she had managed to put the small pole at the mast foot, ready to use it as a support for raising the main 9-metre pole as her replacement mast the next day.

Out of the mist and the darkness that night appeared the ghostly silhouette of David Adams' *True Blue*. He swept past riding the ocean swell under three reefs. Adams was a close friend as well as fellow competitor. More than anyone else in the race he would understand the emotional turmoil Isabelle was suffering.

As Adams passed to leeward, Isabelle could see his silhouette on deck.

'How are you Isa? Can I help?' he shouted at the shadowy figure of Isabelle on deck waving a torch. The mastless boat was, in Adams words, 'rolling her guts out'.

'No Dave, just think about me. It's just so good to see you that's all. Good luck. Have a good race, see you in Sydney,' she yelled back.

Adams stayed on station for a while. Conversation was impossible. They could only talk in bursts of shouting. They switched to 'talking' for a while on their laptop computers, via Satcom-C.

'There was nothing I could do. There was no way Isabelle was going get off and no point in my hanging around. If you accept outside help you are disqualified,' said Adams afterwards. Soon his blue hull faded away in the darkness.

But he was deeply affected. 'Isabelle didn't need my help so I carried on. But for two days I couldn't get anything together.'

For Isabelle, too, it was hard to keep up her spirits. 'Everything tastes like ashes and I am physically and morally exhausted. What is the point in continuing a race already lost? But I already know I will carry on because one cannot quit like that. I am in the race until I cross the finishing line, no matter what it takes.'

As she slept that night it was blowing 40 knots and *EPC2* was drifting due south of two remote island outposts: Marion Island and Prince Edward Island. Coast Guard officials in South Africa had been notified and had an aircraft on standby alert.

'Perhaps the Indian Ocean doesn't want me,' thought Isabelle as she lay in her bunk. She had suffered a dismasting four years ago on this same leg of the BOC Challenge, south of Tasmania. On that occasion, the mast broke at the first spreader and she fashioned a jury rig and sailed into Sydney Harbour to step a new mast. She gained many admirers by going on to complete her circumnavigation.

At the crack of dawn next day, Isabelle began work afresh on erecting an emergency mast. Using her small 5-metre broken spinnaker pole, with a halyard rigged from the top, she raised the 9-metre pole.

'I am forgetting about the second leg. My goal is to arrive in Sydney with enough time to make preparations to start leg three with the others.'

Under two tiny headsails, Isabelle set course for Kerguelen Island, a remote French outpost some 1200 miles away that was home to weather and scientific research stations.

Two days later, when the sun was out, she worked to reinforce the base of her new mast with epoxy glue and carbon fibre. She wound a length of small diameter rope around the mast and glued it together to add thickness at the foot. In the damp conditions, to help it dry, she made a tent around the mast and used her small emergency generator inside to add warmth. *EPC2* was averaging four knots and was expected to arrive at Kerguelen Island in 13 days. Sources in France found a replacement mast for her yacht on Reunion Island that was shipped to Kerguelen on a French cargo vessel.

Two weeks later, sailing under jury rig, Isabelle, dubbed 'Isabelle the Incredible', arrived at Kerguelen Island eager to re-rig her yacht with the replacement mast.

It was snowing hard and the winds were over 40 knots as *EPC2* was towed into the protected harbour by a French scientific vessel conducting studies in the Antarctic region.

After a three-day stop at Kerguelen, Isabelle had converted *EPC2* from a single-masted sloop into a double-masted yawl, using her spinnaker pole as a mizzen mast. Her new 13-metre main mast was from a much smaller Figaro Solo yacht and a set of sails had been donated by French yachtsmen Philippe Poupon and Pierre Follenfant.

On the 20th day of leg two, Isabelle reported: 'I'm now at sea again. Everyone has been wonderful. Now I'm heading for Sydney as fast as I can.' Her new rig gave her the ability to fly 70 square metres of sail on an upwind heading and 153 square metres for reaching and running. Position reports showed she was averaging over nine knots. Under her drastically shortened emergency rig, Isabelle reeled off a remarkable 24-hour run of 229 miles.

But 12 days later on 28 December, the 32nd day of leg two, Isabelle was averaging eight knots under bare poles with the wind howling around her at 60–70 knots. The yacht had been laid over twice, creating chaos in the cabin, but things seemed to be holding up reasonably well. She tried to sleep on the cabin floor to avoid being thrown from her bunk.

'The crests of the waves were a beautiful sight, but a worrying one,' she said. 'Around noon the wind eased slightly and it was time to put up the storm jib.'

But she was concerned about her small makeshift mast. Before she put the sail up she wanted to finish a small repair job in the yacht's aft compartment. It was a decision that probably saved her life.

The wind was gusting and had changed direction as the storm system moved on causing the swells to combine into monstrous seas. She was at the back of the yacht in the narrow tunnel-like passage which linked the main cabin and the watertight aft compartment containing the yacht's steering systems.

'It was then that I heard it coming ... like a powerful locomotive. I instinctively crouched down. I knew it was going to flatten the boat.' A rogue monster wave crashed over the yacht, launching it through a semi-pitchpole, end-over-end. At the same time the yacht did a corkscrew rollover through 360°. She was thrown onto the roof, choked by a rush of ice cold water. 'I could feel it rolling. I fell on the bulkhead, then on the ceiling, then on the other bulkhead. When I opened my eyes the boat was full of water. If I had been on deck I would have been washed away. It was very great for me that I was not there.'

The whole incident had lasted not more than 20 seconds. Isabelle crawled out of the tunnel and was speechless at what she saw. The yacht's cabin roof above the navigation station and her living quarters had disappeared. There was a gaping hole of five square metres where the carbon fibre coachroof had exploded under the water pressure. All she could see was forbidding grey sky and the sea washing in as waves continued to sweep the deck. The air pressure had plucked a lot of loose items out of the yacht in the rollover. The devastation was as sure as it was complete.

'I was standing in water with equipment floating around me. The batteries and generator and other electrical equipment were submerged. I was lucky. Everything that was at the navigation station was sucked out of the boat. If I had been sleeping or at the chart table, I would have been washed away . . .'

On deck, most of *EPC2*'s jury masts and rigging had been swept away by the ocean. Isabelle's world had literally turned upside down 920 miles south-south-east of Adelaide. The boat was very low in the water, almost half submerged. She had to act quickly.

'A second wave would definitely finish us,' she thought. For two hours she bailed out as much water as possible using a bucket and stretched a sail over the gaping hole in the cabin roof, using a salvaged spar as a ridgepole for her makeshift 'tent'.

'All the steering systems were gone. The tiller had come away under pressure, leaving a hole which was leaking water into the once watertight rear compartment.'

The water temperature was freezing and the current was taking Isabelle further south, away from the nearest land. The air temperature was only 5°C with the wind chill factor sending even that plunging to -15°C. At first she thought she might try to go on. Her defiant optimism told her she might somehow rebuild the jury rig. Slowly reality dawned as fatigue took over. The steering system was destroyed. She was exhausted from sailing for three weeks with a jury rig.

'With the state of my boat and my personal state I knew it would not be safe to try and get to Sydney. I had to save what could be saved.' Two hours after the rollover, and for the first time in her seafaring life, Isabelle took out her distress beacons, two Alden 406 EPIRBs, and as night began to fall she switched them on.

'The small lights began to flash and up there in the stars the satellite picked up my call.' she said.

Like all yachts in the BOC Challenge, Isabelle had two emergency beacons, a liferaft and survival gear in case she had to abandon her yacht in extreme conditions. 'When I switched on my EPIRBs I was quite confident of my rescue. I knew it was a good system . . . I had never used it before, but I have seen it working for other people. It is an incredible organisation,' she told reporters later.

Both EPIRBs were triggered just before six in the evening Sydney time. Ashore, BOC Challenge staff alerted by a satellite ground station immediately went into their well-rehearsed emergency procedures. An anxious message was relayed by Peter Dunning from Race HQ in Charleston: 'Isabelle, do you have problems? We have a 406 EPIRB alarm from you. Please let us know, Pete.'

Search and rescue operations were co-ordinated by Australia's MRCC in Canberra, while in France Isabelle's family were notified.

The BOC Challenge has a history of fellow racers coming to the aid of competitors in distress. In this instance, Nigel Rowe, more than 250 miles away on board *Sky Catcher*, received a message from Race HQ: 'Once more we need your help. Two EPIRB 406 alerts from Isabelle. Not responding to Standard-C polls or messages. Please be on standby. Please cease easterly progress until we sort this one out.'

Nigel, battling against survival conditions himself in the same low pressure system, was hove-to in 50–60 knots of wind with huge breaking seas and damaged self-steering.

At Royal Australian Air Force bases near Sydney and Adelaide, flight crews were scrambled on long-range aircraft. A military search plane was on standby to fly to the yacht's last known position at first light next day.

As darkness fell on that first long night at sea, Isabelle, realising how far from land she was, knew that no rescue bid would be attempted until the next day. The forward watertight compartment, where her sails were stowed, was the only area on her stricken yacht not submerged in water and not structurally compromised. It was there that she sought refuge.

Lots of things had disappeared in the waves. The aft compartment was full of water and she didn't know if the rudders had gone because she had to shut the watertight doors to keep the boat afloat. She gathered clothes, food and survival gear, including a hand-operated desalinator for making drinking water, and moved into the forward compartment.

After the rollover this was to be her home for the next three days. She changed into her one-piece survival suit to try and conserve body warmth in the chilling conditions and wrapped a reflective foil space blanket around her.

It was a sleepless night for BOC race officials, as well as those on duty at Race HQ. All efforts to contact Isabelle by satellite messaging and long range radio had been in vain. From the slow drift of the EPIRB signals they knew something was badly wrong. Was Isabelle still with the yacht or in her liferaft? Or had the yacht sunk, leaving only the beacons afloat to transmit their bleak alarm?

Early next day a C-130 Hercules aircraft left Adelaide at 0400 on a mercy mission to find Isabelle and her yacht. The plane carried an extra passenger, Serge Viviand, head of Isabelle's shore support crew. The plane, equipped to drop liferafts, handheld VHF radios and other survival gear, took four hours to reach the search area after a refuelling stop in Tasmania.

By dawn, Isabelle was already awake with the cold and had started work to clear the deck of broken rigging and spars ready for any rescue operation. She was tired and staggered around as the mastless yacht pitched and rolled in the heavy Southern Ocean swell. Suddenly she heard a distant rumble and looked up to see a plane flying overhead.

At around 0900 the plane had reached the search area. But sighting Isabelle was not easy. The positions given by the two distress beacons on board *EPC2* were sometimes as much as nine miles apart. And to make things even harder, from the skies above, the white deck of the stricken yacht was invisible against the backdrop of breaking wave crests. It took an agonising two hours and 50 minutes before the Hercules confirmed a visual sighting of the yacht. Isabelle on deck jumped up and down and waved to the search plane to show that she was uninjured. She was reported to be 'fit and well' and 'very near the location that her distress signal had begun transmitting'.

It had been an anxious 18-hour wait before the world knew that Isabelle Autissier was alive and still aboard her yacht.

'When I heard the plane it was great moment for me,' said Isabelle. 'Communication was impossible because my radio was out of action. I sobbed with emotion.'

From the time they arrived, the Royal Australian Airforce never left Isabelle. Having found their needle in a haystack, they didn't want to risk losing her again. Military aircraft relayed every few hours and remained on station, like guardian angels, keeping a watch over her and monitoring the yacht's drift. The Hercules took some three hours to fly to her position and was able to stay four hours before flying back to refuel. An Orion PC3 anti-submarine aircraft also remained on vigil during daylight hours.

The rescue planes tried to establish voice contact to get details of her physical condition and the extent of onboard damage. But Isabelle's own emergency hand-held radio, even in its waterproof bag, had been flooded and rendered useless. At the same time the Australian Navy frigate, HMAS *Darwin*, was despatched from Fremantle, Western Australia. It was not expected to reach Isabelle's position for four days, on late Sunday afternoon. A Seahawk helicopter was despatched from Albany to rendezvous with the frigate and join the rescue mission.

With only visual contact possible with Isabelle, the Hercules plane, flying low over the water at 200km per hour, made precision drops of liferafts and supply canisters loaded with survival items, including flares, water and a handheld VHF radio.

Knowing that Isabelle was unable to manoeuvre the yacht, the pilots and crew invented a new system. They dropped two plastic canisters strung together with a floating line. The plan was that the canisters, dropped upwind of *EPC2*, would drift down towards the yacht and float either side of the hull with the line snagging on the yacht's keel to stop them drifting past. The first drop missed the yacht. On the second the rope broke and the canisters were lost in the heavy swell and gusting winds. Eventually, Serge

Viviand, on the same Hercules that had spotted *EPC2*, reported back to the BOC Challenge that an 11-person liferaft containing a handheld VHF radio had been successfully dropped in the 50-knot winds and gigantic seas. Isabelle had managed to secure it alongside the yacht. The liferaft was inflated and 'the yacht was bobbing around like cork', said Viviand. 'Both *EPC2's* masts were down, though a portion of the main spar was secured on deck.'

'The pilots' skills were amazing,' said Isabelle. 'What they could do dropping me things at high speeds just above me was incredible ... through a large hole at the rear of the plane I could see small figures moving.'

Frustratingly for the rescue crew, Isabelle did not realise that the liferaft contained a radio for her to make contact with the plane's crew.

By now the rescuers and Isabelle had worked out a kind of system for communicating. If they wanted her to come on deck they would pass over very low 'making one hell of a noise!' If they wanted to drop equipment they would first drop smoke markers to calculate the drift and wind direction. The crew of the Orion aircraft tried signalling by Morse and hand to tell Isabelle that the liferaft contained a radio. The second afternoon after being sighted, Isabelle located the radio and made voice contact with the crew of the Orion.

For the first time she learned that HMAS *Darwin* was en route to her position, having recalled its sailors from their Christmas holidays. She was also told of plans to lift her off her yacht by *Darwin's* on-board helicopter in two days' time.

She told the rescue plane that the rear compartment of *EPC2* was flooded and she had lost all steering capability. She added that she had plenty of food and water in her stores. The RAAF Orion PC3 aircraft crew arranged a regular radio schedule with Isabelle.

While Isabelle faced a wait of some 40 hours, she also started to come to terms with the impending separation from her yacht which had become such a part of her life after three years of work and thousands of miles.

December 31 bought mixed emotions. Relief that rescue was imminent, for she had been told that she would be lifted off her yacht by helicopter early that morning. Sadness that she was leaving her yacht. But she was overjoyed to hear that a salvage attempt was going to made from Hobart to recover *EPC2*.

In one of the last drops from the plane there were two apples and a carefully packed beer for New Year's Eve 'celebration'. They also dropped two new EPIRB beacons so that before abandoning her yacht, she could activate them to assist the salvage ship in finding *EPC2*. The signals would last a maximum of 60 hours, probably less as the cold temperatures drained the lithium batteries. It had taken nearly three hours for search aircraft to find *EPC2*, so what chance did a salvage vessel have, with its much more limited field of vision as sea level?

Isabelle's last night on board was strange, damp and cold. 'A New Year's Eve in the darkness of the sail locker, wrapped in a rescue blanket.' She took photographs of herself and the damaged yacht as a final remembrance.

As dawn lit up her dark world another low, noisy fly-past bought her up on deck. The wind was blowing 20–25 knots. A new noise filled the sky. 'At sunrise I heard it coming. It happened very quickly.' A Sea Hawk helicopter was hovering over the area which she had cleared on deck at the front of the yacht. She activated the EPIRBs.

'An incredible acrobat was hanging from a rope. He made it onto the deck and put a harness around me and we were winched back up together.'

It was 0659 Sydney time on New Year's Eve. Three days after the rogue wave had overwhelmed her yacht, Autissier suddenly felt a great pang of sadness as she looked down on the heaving deck of *EPC2*.

'This is the first time I had to leave my boat. It was very difficult. The yacht represents three years of my life, thinking about and preparing for the BOC. After the first leg everything was so wonderful for me. I had a big lead. But I have done a BOC before. I know what can happen. But this time the Indian Ocean was very tough for me ...'

Within 30 minutes the helicopter had landed on HMAS *Darwin*, which turned towards Adelaide with an ETA of midday 2 January.

In a ship to shore call to the BOC Race office in Sydney, Isabelle said she was feeling good. 'I am dressed like a sailor in the Australian Navy,' she said. 'The colours are good for me.' The colour of her fleet air arm jump suit was grey. She was not quite in mourning.

On board she showered, ate and slept deeply. Some 24 hours after she had been airlifted aboard, she boarded the helicopter again as the warship approached the Australian coast and was flown to Edinburgh Air Force Base near Adelaide, where she stepped on to dry land for the first time in 37 days. Her smile and expression of relief said it all.

'I am here because of you and I will never forget that,' she told her rescuers. She was re-united with her shore crew, wearing a T-shirt which bore the legend: 'I spent New Year's Eve with 200 Aussie sailors'. She had finished the race with only 'my wet passport and my wet credit cards'.

So ended one of the most dramatic rescues in the history of ocean yacht racing as the courageous Frenchwoman twice lost the rig from her yacht in one leg and then found her life in deadly jeopardy. The incident graphically demonstrated how fate and fortune could single out even the best prepared yacht in the race while others less well prepared survived to sail on.

Extracted from *The Loneliest Race*, the story of
the 1994–95 BOC Around Alone Challenge, by Paul Gelder,
published by Adlard Coles Nautical

Lessons learned

Many lessons would be learned from Isabelle's rescue. Most important was the question of making a yacht more visible to searchers. The white deck of *EPC2* proved almost invisible against the breaking waves. Having a yacht's deck painted in a bright, visible colour, or having a sheet of fluorescent material that could be tied to the deck to make sighting easier, would be a necessity in future.

Petuna Explorer, a deep sea trawler, left Hobart on New Year's Day, having been commissioned by the insurers of *EPC2* to search for the drifting yacht. But days later the salvagers reluctantly announced they had given up the search, believing the 60ft yacht had either sunk or drifted too far south towards the Antarctic, beyond the range of a feasible salvage operation.

By the time the BOC fleet had left Sydney for the next third leg of the race questions were asked in Parliament about the cost of rescuing Autissier from her stricken yacht. The bill was 5.8 million Australian dollars. Thirty one personnel had been recalled from leave for the operation and the country's defence assets were used for a total of 224 hours. Senator Jocelyn Newman asked: 'Why hasn't the Government inquired about the insurance held by Ms Autissier and the race organisers to defray at least some of the not inconsiderable cost? The BOC race involves millions of dollars' worth of yachts and sponsorships and is contested by professionals. It is only reasonable that professionals would take all possible precautions and some responsibility for their actions,' added the Senator, no doubt thinking of Blondie Hasler's entreaty that singlehanded sailors should hazard no rescuers but 'drown like gentlemen'.

When the Australian media questioned the cost of the rescue, Isabelle responded: 'Maybe I am not worth a million dollars . . . I don't know. I cannot say anything about it.'

John Hornby, chairman of the Safety Committee of the Yachting Association of New South Wales, wrote a letter with the counter argument: 'It's high time the myth concerning the cost of search and rescue is laid to rest. We, the taxpayers, already own the planes and ships and pay the crew's wages ... the only real cost is fuel, stores and liferafts. The incident should be treated as a hands-on exercise for the services concerned and is better than playing "war games", the cost of which is never questioned.'

11 Oopsie Daisy!

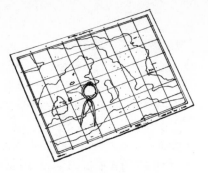

Yacht *Lazy Daisy* (29ft 6in Catalac catamaran)
Skipper Lionel Miller
Crew Bruce Rankin, Bill Tulloch, Charlie Tulloch
Bound from Inverness to Kinghorn, Scotland
Date of loss 24 October, 1980
Position off Rattray Head, Scotland

Lazy Daisy had left Inverness at 1345 in good weather on a day in late October 1980, bound for Kinghorn on the north bank of the Forth, some 250 miles away.

We quickly settled into a three-hour watchkeeping routine. The weather remained fine and the wind gradually strengthened until we decided to put in a reef just before sunset. The sea was steadily becoming lumpier and all except Bruce began 'calling on Hughie' from time to time, but without too serious an effect on performance. The boat was making excellent progress and we were in good spirits. Mine were improved still more when I caught Bruce retching and attempting to spit to windward (ex marine engineers are not used to being sick, unlike us family sailors).

Bill and I left Charlie and Bruce in charge at 0200 and got our heads down for a highly appreciated rest in warm sleeping bags. The noise below was continuous and the boat felt like an old car being driven fast on a rough track but we were tired and pleased to pass the responsibility to the other watch for a bit.

We were roused from our wet sleeping bags by a shout from Bruce: 'Your watch.' As we came on deck we could see that we were rounding the corner at Kinnards Head and the NE force 6 was giving us a broad reach as we turned south. The sea was a sailing man's dream with big rolling seas swept with silver grey spume under a brilliant cold full moon. Unfortunately, our

stomachs were unaffected by the beautiful scene and we both moved quickly across to the leeside to be sick. That chore completed we all got busy to
dowse the reefed main and open out the roller jib. Bruce, off watch after
three hours on the helm, disappeared below to make himself a thick cheese
butty and Charlie fastidiously removed his boots and jacket and climbed in
the still-warm quarter berth. My watchmate, Bill, decided to call the
Coastguard on VHF to report all's well (a task which my stomach would not
allow) and then came back on deck. The boat was handling well as the wind
came aft and we had obviously seen the last of beating for a bit as we turned
ever further towards the south.

We were making great time and had actually caught the last of the south-
going tide round Buchan Ness over six hours ahead of our planned time.
Bruce and Charlie had debated whether to go into Fraserburgh, but the look
of the harbour entrance in the offshore seas, plus the excellent chance of
getting round on the favourable tide, persuaded them to press on. I was well
pleased with the way things were going and handed the helm to Bill for a
spell. Lying in the cabin out of the wind I was reasonably warm and comfortable and I wondered whether to get my exposure suit and wellies on,
but the thought of going and searching in the forward cabin hanging locker
was not appealing. After ten minutes or so the motion altered and I suspected an increase in wind. Out on deck again Bill suggested reducing sail,
but I wanted to keep the speed up so as to get well clear of the strong tidal
area before the tide turned north. I therefore took the helm to assess the
situation. We were doing 6–8 knots SE with an apparent wind speed of 25
knots from the north under full jib. The boat was certainly flying along but
the heel was not excessive and with the wind so far abaft the beam I felt
quite content. The waves were now giving us some fast sleigh rides as we
boiled along and, despite the darkness and cold, at 0530 we were having a
great sail.

Suddenly I found the boat going downhill at an alarming angle, the high
flared bows were almost under water despite their enormous reserves of
buoyancy and the hulls vibrated with a deep humming sound as we tore
through the water at 12 knots plus. This was unexpected and rather frightening. Bill again looked at me to see if we should reduce sail, but I felt the
problem was the size and steepness of the wave rather than the wind forces,
so I turned the boat so as to present her port quarter to the seas, which did
not look any bigger than previously. Down below, Bruce lay awake listening to the crashing and banging of the waves against the hulls. He did not
like the sound of our speed as we tore down the waves, and his cheese sandwich was not helping either. Charlie on the other hand was sleeping the
sleep of the just – just off watch.

Bill suddenly noticed that the dinghy, which we carry hooked to the aft rail, had come untied at one end. He knelt on the seats and leaned over the rail as he struggled to bring it inboard. I hoped that he could manage to tie it on again successfully, as it would be far too cumbersome to have lying around inflated in the cockpit. It was difficult to concentrate on the problem whilst steering because of the need to keep a watch on the waves coming up astern.

Looking round now, all thoughts of the dinghy problem vanished. The wave coming up now was very big, perhaps 30ft, but the threat of destruction was in the 5ft-high breaking crest which was commencing its avalanche down the long slope towards us.

This was obviously a 'survival wave' for our boat with its large open cockpit and lovely big windows. I shouted a warning, and then concentrated on holding the boat on course to take the sea on the quarter, but it was impossible. The stern was smashed round and we were hit almost broadside by many tons of water travelling at 20–30mph. The enormous thrust of the impact lifted the boat into a vertical position and the press of water under the bridgedeck completed the capsize in a matter of 2–3 seconds.

Below, Charlie awoke in mid-air as he flew towards the ceiling. Hitting it, he expected to fall on the floor, but instead the floor fell on him, followed shortly by a lot of ice-cold sea!

Meanwhile, in the other hull, Bruce felt a mighty lurch and heard the loudest cacophony it is possible to imagine, as bottles, pans, plates, tools flew across the boat and smashed into the windows over his head. Tonic and lemonade bottles exploded and several knives and forks stuck into the hull after falling the full width of the boat. Bruce thought, 'He's been and gone and done it' as the cabin rotated around and things crashed down towards him.

Outside, Bill was flung across the cockpit as the boat accelerated sideways and lifted. He distinctly remembers the blue flash as the batteries shorted out, and then we were both in the water under the boat. I thought 'when the boat sinks, we will all drown' and reckoned we had about 15 minutes left. Bill swam under the cockpit seats to the outside but my brain had begun to work again and I realised that the boat might not sink after all.

Inside the boat, Charlie picked himself up off the ceiling and made his way forward through the waist-high water and debris whilst his mind grappled with the problem of finding the way out. 'Up' was now down and 'right' had become left. The normal route out to the cockpit was turn right, up steps on to the bridgedeck and right again. The new route in the cold wet darkness was left, downwards and left again. Pursuing this course, he came across Bruce who was attempting to find the door catch. Eventually, Bruce found the knob, opened the door an inch or two then pushed it wide as the pressure equalised.

On the other side of the door I had heard Bruce and Charlie talking and swam over to help open the door and to advise them that we might be better off inside the boat rather than outside. They came out and we started to discuss whether to go outside or not, when suddenly the air under the cockpit disappeared into the hull via the open door and the floor of the cockpit came down to push our heads under water. That curtailed the discussion and we all dived towards the outside.

Bill, of course, had been outside for some minutes and, ever litter conscious, had tidily collected a floating fender and lifebelt and put them into the dinghy, which had luckily come unhitched from all its fastenings, except the painter, and lay bobbing happily at the stern. He had just climbed in when our three heads popped up and we realised that we had all come through our the first test.

Once we had all got in the dinghy and saw that the boat was not going to sink immediately we decided to climb onto the bridgedeck and take the dinghy with us. Unfortunately, the dinghy was impossible to untie and none of us had a knife. Luck was on our side again, however, because the painter broke as we climbed out and we soon gathered on the bridgedeck with it. The waves occasionally washed through between the hulls but although we had no way of tying on, it was quite easy to stay put and the hulls broke the force of the wind.

Exposure was now the problem, particularly for Charlie who had taken off his windproof jacket and boots when he went to bed. We all huddled together against the windward hull, which made a good windbreak.

Ashore we could see the lights of civilisation, but we knew that it could be a long time before we were spotted or even missed after our reassuring radio check. Time passed rapidly, although we began to ache from standing in one spot and to shiver from the cold. A grey dawn broke and we could see that though the tide was carrying us north, the wind was pushing us inshore slightly. Another hour and we could see that we were drifting towards a long shallow bay fringed by sand dunes. We decided to beach through the surf in the dinghy as the big waves could have easily rolled and smashed the cat on top of us.

About half a mile off the beach the wreckage began to drag on the bottom and our drift slowed. We launched the dinghy and began paddling with our hands downwind towards the breakers. The waves were piling into magnificent combers as they swept in and at first we dreaded the thought of eventually entering them. After almost half an hour of exhausting paddling, however, we were disappointed every time one missed us and we had to paddle some more.

We developed a technique to prevent capsize in the breaking crests. We all threw ourselves sideways towards the breaker as it struck and after a while we were able to judge quite well just how hard to thrust to remain on an even keel. Obviously our second moment of serious danger was imminent and we all wished each other luck every time 'the' big one bore down on us. After a while we began to feel a bit stupid at this abortive ritual and so we yelled at the waves to come and get us. Eventually, one heard and it impressed us considerably as it mounted and surged towards us. It broke and swept down on us head high in a mass of frothing foam. Bruce and Bill were pushed forward by the impact and the rope Bill was holding broke. Charlie and myself at the front were thrown back by the acceleration and then we were off. The dinghy (just 9 ft long, completely full of water and four grown men) picked up to full speed to match the wave and wriggled like a live thing beneath us. Our heads and shoulders emerged from the foam and we shouted with the exhilaration of surfing at 20 knots in towards deliverance. The surge carried us as though we were an underwater bobsleigh and we covered the 200 yards into the beach in less than half a minute.

Will we buy another multihull? Most definitely – a monohull would certainly have been rolled 360° and might have sunk with the loss of all hands.

From *Clyde Cruising Club Journal*, 1981

Lessons learned

Lazy Daisy was a Catalac catamaran, modified by having 7ft by 12in keels fitted to her hulls. It is very tempting to say that, in this case, the catamaran was capsized because of her excessive speed. But no one can be sure what would have happened to her had she lain a-hull. Lionel Miller seems to have been unaware of any risks and remembers that 'the waves were giving us some fast sleigh rides as we boiled along; despite the darkness and cold, we were having a great sail'. Then the warning came: 'Suddenly I found the boat going downhill at an alarming angle, the high flared bows were almost under water, despite their enormous reserves of buoyancy, and the hulls vibrated with a deep humming sound as we tore through the water at 12 knots plus.'

Miller also recalls lying in the cabin out of the wind. 'I was reasonably warm and comfortable and I wondered whether to get my exposure suit and wellies on, but the thought of going and searching in the forward cabin hanging locker was not appealing.' Perhaps, like the rule of thumb on reefing, the time to act in such circumstances is when you first think of it. Exposure to the elements became a problem later on.

For *Lazy Daisy*, with her large open cockpit and big windows, the avalanching wave that capsized her in a matter of seconds was not survivable. But for offshore passage-making, when extreme conditions can catch you out, a surveyor would undoubtedly look closely at the method and speed of draining the cockpit, as well as recommend carrying plywood storm shutters, with an internal strongback, to bolt over the biggest ports.

The other lesson underlined was the importance of a yachtsman's knife. When Miller and his crew took to their rubber dinghy, the dinghy painter proved impossible to untie and none of them had a knife. Fortunately, luck was on their side when the painter broke.

12 Surviving Hurricane Assault

Yacht *Island Princess* (48ft Bermudian ketch)
Skipper Barry 'Finbar' Gittelman
Crew Michael Munroe, Bob Harvey, Matthew 'Doc' St Clair
Bound from Marathon, Florida, to Belize, Central America
Date of loss 6 August, 1980
Position approximately 40 miles S of Santiago de Cuba

This account of the loss of the ketch Island Princess *is based on the comments of her skipper and crew, linked together by SAIL reporter, Bob Payne.*

*I*sland Princess was being sailed from Florida to Belize by a delivery company based in Key West. The yacht was a strongly built wooden ship with two-inch planking that had been refastened prior to the trip. Both masts had been removed and checked, all standing rigging replaced and the engine put in 'top running order'; so that Gittelman could say: 'She was in just about perfect condition. And as far as equipment goes, I would say we had a full complement of the very best safety gear available.'

Among that gear was a four- to six-man Givens Buoy Liferaft with a water-ballasted stabilisation chamber. The skipper and two of the three-man crew were experienced offshore sailors, but the fourth man, 'Doc' St Clair, was making his first deep-water passage. However, *Island Princess* had two characteristics that were to prove fatal to her. Her internal ballast was in the form of lead pigs and her companionway hatch was offset to starboard, which meant that if she were knocked down to starboard that hatch remained under water for a long time.

Gittelman and his crew had given thought to the possibility of encountering a hurricane, and they had chosen the much longer route round the eastern end of Cuba, instead of heading directly across the Gulf of Mexico and down the Yucatan channel because the former route offered more chances of shelter in hurricane holes.

Island Princess left Marathon on 27 July, but the first word they had of Hurricane Allen was on Sunday, 2 August, when WWV weather reported that a low had developed into a tropical storm, had officially become a hurricane and was moving west on a course that would probably take it south of Jamaica.

Bob Harvey remembers hearing a report on 4 August that said the storm would pass south of Jamaica and had been downgraded. Those aboard *Island Princess* heaved sighs of relief. What they didn't know was that at that very time Allen was taking a jog that would put them directly in its path. Nor did they know that it had been downgraded from Category 5 only to Category 4. Being caught in a Category 4 rather than a Category 5 hurricane would be rather like being hit by a train that has slowed to 60 miles an hour. As it turned out, the hurricane was soon to be upgraded again. Munroe said: 'At 1000 on the fifth we sighted a grey wall of clouds. But we weren't worried, because from the reports we'd been getting we thought it must have been a local depression.'

As the wind and seas increased they decided to put a reef in the main, but by the time they were through reefing they knew they didn't want the main at all. Slowly they began to suspect the truth. What they were experiencing was the front edge of a hurricane.

'My thoughts at that point were that the hurricane was still probably going to pass south of us,' said Gittelman. 'I reasoned that the best thing to do was turn to the north; first, because we wanted to avoid the centre, but just as importantly, if we did get into it and were dismasted or anything like that, we would be driven down on the north coast of Jamaica. And the north coast of Jamaica is a rockpile.'

By sunset the wind had reached 50 knots out of the north-east and was building fast. The seas were 10 to 15ft high. The *Island Princess*, with her engine turning over slowly in forward, was close reaching under a tiny forestay sail.

Gittelman was at the wheel; Harvey and Munroe sat with him in the cockpit. They all wore lifejackets and safety harnesses. In the dark, Harvey had rigged safety lines all over the boat so that there would always be something to clip on to, and he had crisscrossed the cockpit with heavier lines so that if the boat was knocked down no one would have far to fall before he could grab hold of something. St Clair was below in his bunk, seasick.

Just before 2200 Harvey went below to listen to the weather report.

When he came back he said things sounded bad and were going to get worse. The wind was already blowing over 100 knots. At midnight the forestay sail blew away.

'Even then I don't recall being particularly worried,' Gittelman recalls. 'Even under bare poles she felt stable and the engine was driving her to windward controllably. I told myself that it was blowing like stink, but I'd seen it bad before, and we could get through this. We just had to grit our teeth and do it.

When the wind got up to somewhere around 125–130 knots, the boat was still stable. The seas were ugly, but they weren't that high, maybe 20 to 25ft, because the wind was blowing the tops off them. The boat would rise up and be stable at the top; then she'd come back down and rise again. We were real happy with her. I was just hanging on, gritting my teeth, pretty well all consumed with driving the boat. I had little else on my mind.

Then it got up to somewhere around 150 knots – I'm guessing at this point – and I'm saying to myself: Jesus, I had no idea it could get this bad. But it can't get any worse, so all we have to do is hang in there.'

And then it did get worse.

About 0300 Gittelman began to have doubts. The boat didn't feel stable any more. In fact, all 30 tons of her were being lifted off the crests and thrown sideways into the troughs. Gittelman thought it was time to try trailing warps.

Clipping into the safety lines, Munroe and Harvey crawled forward, taking about ten minutes to get from the cockpit to the rope locker, and dragged all the anchor lines aft. They streamed them over the stern, along with all their chain and a 45-pound anchor. How long that took they have no idea. 'Nobody was stopping to make log entries,' Gittelman said.

'It took me about two or three minutes to realise it just wasn't going to work,' Gittelman said. 'She was doing 8 knots and was broaching, rolling her sides under. She was squirrelly as hell, and we were getting pooped. So in a relatively smooth patch we brought her back up into the wind and dragged all the lines back aboard.'

How they managed such a mammoth task under those conditions, even they are not sure.

'All I know is that anybody who says he can't do something never had it standing between him and survival,' said Harvey.

'She did all right for another half-hour, but then things got worse,' Gittelman commented. 'And at that point I couldn't tell how much. It was beyond my comprehension. I've been 20 years going to sea, and I just couldn't imagine these things were possible.'

When they were first knocked down, St Clair was still below and, in-experienced sailor that he was, still not sure how bad things were. Half an hour earlier Harvey had come below and told him to get into his foul weather gear, lifejacket and safety harness because the boat looked as though she might not have long to live.

'He didn't sound like he was kidding,' St Clair recalls, 'so I got up.'

When St Clair was dressed he got on the VHF and started calling for anybody who might be listening. He told them who they were and their approximate position, and that they were experiencing hurricane-force winds and didn't know how much longer they were going to be afloat. He did that for four or five minutes but got no response.

'Then I told myself it couldn't be that bad or they would have called me. So I lay down again. About the time I got stretched out good the boat suddenly slammed over and everything on the starboard side fell straight down. I was standing on the port side of the cabinhouse watching a two-foot-high geyser of water coming in the porthole. I couldn't believe it. I had to touch that geyser to convince myself it was there. As soon as I was convinced I knew it was time to get my fanny on deck.'

On the way out he grabbed two things: his good-luck hat and a rigging knife on a lanyard, which he slipped round his neck. As he bolted through the companionway he mockingly chided the rest of the crew for the mess they had made of the inside of the boat.

Then he looked around at what was outside and almost went into shock. In the orange glow of a sky lit with sheet lightning, he saw the boat lying on its side with water halfway up the cockpit. Gittelman was hanging off the boom gallows, screaming something to Munroe and Harvey, who, covered with lines, were on the high side of the mizzen, with their feet dangling down into the cockpit. Water, glowing orange from the lightning, moved horizontally through the air. Waves struck the boat from all directions. The noise of the wind had gone beyond loudness; it was simply a 'dull white sound'.

In the next 20 minutes the *Island Princess* was knocked down three more times. The crew would be swept over the side to the end of their safety harnesses; then they would drag themselves back aboard, only to be swept over once again. They were constantly swallowing sea water. Water was coming in the boat's engine air intake, her portholes and her companionway.

On the fourth knockdown – which was to starboard – her ballast shifted, putting the companionway under for good. Three or four minutes later the glow from a submerged but still burning decklight was all that marked the spot where she had slipped beneath the waves.

'When Finbar yelled for us to abandon ship,' said St Clair, 'I suddenly realized that this was no movie, so I kicked the liferaft free and fired the bottle to inflate it.'

The raft inflated upside down. St Clair and Munroe scrambled onto its upturned bottom and fought desperately to push it away from the boat, which was flailing at it with the wildly rolling mizzen mast. St Clair thinks that may have been when he broke his ribs; but he isn't sure as he wasn't aware of the pain until several hours later.

Meanwhile, Harvey and Gittelman were fighting desperate battles of their own. For what almost proved too long, Harvey couldn't get to the end of his safety harness to unclip himself from the sinking boat. He finally had to unclip from his end, and – attached to nothing – leap for the raft from the mizzen. Only a fingertips grab by Munroe prevented him from being swept away. Gittelman, it seemed to St Clair and Munroe, who watched him from the overturned raft, had decided to go down with the ship.

'I'm not sure what possessed me,' Gittelman said. 'But I just sat at the wheel and tried to steer the boat. It was already under water, everybody else was on the raft. I was clipped to the raft's painter. But I tried to drive.'

Perhaps the boat slipping beneath him finally convinced the skipper to abandon the helm and jump for the raft.

'As soon as I climbed onto the bottom of the raft I realized that something was tangled with it and that the boat was pulling it down. I needed a knife, but couldn't get to mine because it was inside my foul weather gear. So I shouted for a knife and before the words were out of my mouth, Doc slapped his into my hand. The blade was already open.'

'I'd lost my good-luck hat in the first five minutes,' said St Clair, 'but that knife saved our asses.'

Once the raft was free of the boat, a wave crest immediately flipped it right side up and the ballast chamber filled. Everyone scrambled through the opening in the canopy.

Gittelman's order to abandon came at approximately 0415 on Wednesday, 6 August. By comparing weather service advisories with the *Island Princess*'s position, which was between Port Antonio, Jamaica, and the extreme south coast of Cuba, it appears that the four men took to the raft in 175-knot winds.

They had no way of estimating the wind strength, but they do remember that the wind-driven spray sounded like buckshot hitting the canopy and that the 30ft seas were cresting and breaking on them from all directions.

'Every time one of those 30-footers decided to collapse on us it would fill the raft with water and drive it so deep that my ears popped,' said St Clair. 'At that point we would have to push down with our feet and up with our hands to make an air space at the top of the canopy. We were constantly up to our necks in water, and there were even fish swimming around inside the raft. The only thing that helped us to realize we were still alive was a little light glowing at the top of the canopy. '

It was around this time that Gittelman, who is slightly claustrophobic said: 'To hell with this; I'm going outside where I can breathe.' The others made sure he didn't go.

Despite the buffeting they were taking and despite their skipper's claustrophobia, the crew felt that once in the liferaft they had it made.

Harvey said: 'Once the ballast chamber filled, which didn't seem to take any time at all, the raft settled right down. You'd feel it pitch over when we were hit by a wave, but as soon as the pressure came off it would come back up again. It was like being in a womb. We were floating around in there, sometimes with our feet off the bottom. We didn't feel comfortable, but we did feel secure.'

Soon after they had entered the raft, the roaring and frothing suddenly ceased. The seas stopped breaking, the wind subsided, and in the darkness overhead the men could see broken patches of sky.

They were in the eye of the hurricane.

Gittelman said: 'We could hear the roar recede into the distance, and then there were five or ten minutes of perfect silence while we just sat there staring at each other.'

St Clair can still remember how the others' faces looked drawn, tight, and with eyes that were big and glistening, and he is sure that his face looked the same. He also remembers saying: 'Finbar; this is another fine mess you've gotten me into!'

Fifteen minutes later the storm was upon them again. They described its approach as sounding like that of a thousand freight trains: 'But we don't know what it looked like; nobody volunteered to look out.'

At about 0600 the sky started getting light, but St Clair remembers: 'I didn't want it to, because I was afraid of what we would see. But I finally pulled down one corner of the Velcro – and wished I hadn't. Waves were collapsing on top of waves that were collapsing on top of waves. Everything was grey and white and screaming. It was insanity.'

But then they discovered a new problem. Munroe had begun to throw up blood. Later, Gittelman – seasick for the first time in his life – would follow.

St Clair had charge of the survival kit, in which he found a knife, six ten-ounce cans of water, two cans of candy and other survival rations, a fish line and hook, a first-aid kit, a whistle, six hand-held flares, eight small pen-type flares, a signal mirror, a repair kit, a sponge, and four or five packs of soggy tissues.

Harvey observed: 'If we needed papier-mâché for anything, we would have had plenty.'

In addition, St Clair had three more pen-type flares that he'd been carrying with him since his days in Vietnam. The raft also contained two paddles, a sea anchor, a life ring, a pump and a two-part EPIRB, with the battery pack separate from the transmitter. The wires between the two had pulled out, making the EPIRB inoperable.

'I opened two cans of water and let everybody drink a fair amount,' said St Clair. 'We'd all swallowed a lot of salt water, and the kidney and liver damage that can result from that is no fun.'

While Munroe and Gittelman rested, Harvey and St Clair spent much of Wednesday hanging out of the opening in the canopy with the paddles, trying to keep the opening to leeward of the breaking seas, which even after the wind subsided remained large and dangerous. Occasionally, Harvey would remove his seaboots and bail with them. 'The raft kept filling, but at least we were doing something.'

On Wednesday the raft's two inflatable ring sections began to separate from each other. Using line from the sea anchor, the men lashed them together again.

That evening they drank two more cans of water; and St Clair, noticing signs of hypothermia, encouraged the men to huddle against each other for warmth.

'We were experiencing cold and little pains,' he said. 'Every time we'd get the water fairly warm from our bodies and start to doze off, a wave would come in and make it cold again.'

Thursday, before daylight, the hallucinations began. St Clair saw what he thought were the lights of Jamaica. He was picking out street lights and cars driving along the shore. 'There it is, guys, we've got it made; it's right there – look. ' The others looked and saw nothing there. Harvey heard a dog bark and people talking. Munroe saw comic books.

Later, St Clair spent much of the day talking to a bird that had landed on the top of the canopy. 'The bird was real,' said Gittelman. 'But it couldn't talk.' That afternoon they drank their last can of water and, because Munroe's condition seemed to be worsening, they gave most of it to him.

St Clair recalls: 'At that point I took one long look at Michael and told myself he would be dead by that time tomorrow. He was starting to get incoherent. His eyes were sunken in. I've seen men like that before; just one step away. And that would be it. He was going to be the first. Finbar had been throwing up a lot of blood, too, so I figured just from blood loss alone he would go next. I had some broken ribs; that made me the next weakest, so then I'd go. And Bob would probably go just from the psychological shock of watching us three die.'

Harvey, however, had no intention of seeing the script played out that way. He'd slept most of the day so that he could stay awake through the night, when he figured they'd have the best chance of signalling any ships they spotted. That's how he came to be staring through the canopy opening at about 2200 when a light appeared on the horizon. He watched it for a while; then, in a low voice, almost without emotion, he announced: 'There is a ship.'

Instantly, the other three were at the opening. As soon as they all agreed that what they saw was a ship and not a low-lying star, St Clair fired four red flares, one right after the other. Then he lit a hand-held flare. Harvey, who knew Morse code, began to signal with the flashlight. Among other things, he signaled 'SOS' and 'Out of water'.

On the bridge of the Norwegian tanker *Jastella*, the second mate spotted a red pinpoint of light to the north. At first he thought it might be a light-house on Cuba, but his chart showed that light to be white and 40 miles away. He figured that it must be a fishing boat. Then he saw a blinking white light; somebody was trying to signal him. He picked out the word 'water'. He tried the radio and did a radar sweep. Nothing. It had to be, he reasoned, a raft.

Two days later, the crew of the *Island Princess* were in hospital in the Cayman Islands – the *Jastella*'s destination – and after a week's stay, they were home again in Key West.

Afterwards, Gittelman said: 'It has played on our minds, sure; but we are sailors, and it won't keep us from going back to sea. What we'll do is go back with a few lessons learned. We learned about liferafts, about survival, and we learned about what it takes to sink a boat. But most of all we learned where not to be when. We learned to stay the hell out of the Caribbean during hurricane season.'

From *SAIL*, February 1981

Lessons learned

In such extreme survival conditions the lessons learned aboard *Island Princess* and the liferaft are somewhat unique.

When the wind reached 50 knots, Harvey rigged safety lines all over the boat , making sure there was always be something to clip on to. He even crisscrossed the cockpit with heavier lines so that in a knockdown the crew could grab hold of something.

When the wind got up to more than 100 knots and all 30 tons of boat was being lifted off the crests and thrown sideways, Gittelman thought it was time to try trailing warps. But after dragging all the anchor lines aft and streaming them over the stern, along with all their chain and a 45-pound anchor, he realised it was not going to work, and they dragged them all back aboard.

Abandoning ship, St Clair grabbed two things: his good-luck hat and the rigging knife on a lanyard, which he slipped round his neck. Once again the importance of a knife was demonstrated. 'I'd lost my good-luck hat in the first five minutes,' said St Clair, 'but that knife saved our asses.'

As Gittelman tried to abandon ship, he found himself trapped, clipped to the liferaft's painter. 'I needed a knife, but couldn't get to mine because it was inside my foul weather gear. So I shouted for a knife and before the words were out of my mouth, Doc slapped his into my hand. The blade was already open.'

The crew of *Island Princess* were rescued by the tanker *Jastella* only because Bob Harvey, who knew Morse Code, 'began to signal with the flashlight. Among other things he signalled SOS and Out of Water.' The second mate aboard the tanker 'saw a blinking white light, someone was trying to signal him. He picked out the word "water" . . . It had to be, he reasoned, a raft.'

The boat's downfall, literally, was her internal ballast , in the form of lead pigs, plus the companionway hatch, offset to starboard, so that in a knockdown to starboard the hatch was under water.

13 'I am not going to die!'

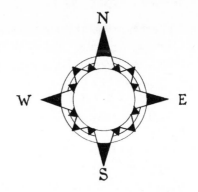

Yacht *Lottie Warren* (27 ft Heavenly Twins catamaran)
Skipper John Passmore
Bound singlehanded and non-stop around Britain anticlockwise
Date of loss June, 2000
Position 80 miles north-east of Shetland

These were not the records I was looking for as I set out to sail singlehanded and non-stop around Britain and Ireland: The lowest barometer reading for June since records began in 1871 – 966 millibars. The highest recorded windspeed for June, also since records began; sustained 40-50 knots; gusts up to 96 knots. And finally the third record to turn the whole project into a sort of sick hat trick: the first recorded capsize of a Heavenly Twins catamaran.

It goes without saying that if I had known I would meet these sort of conditions, I would never have set out. That if I had suspected I was about to be engulfed in Scotland's own version of the 1987 'hurricane', I would have sought shelter in the Shetland Islands. But that is with hindsight.

When I sailed out of the River Deben ten days earlier it was with 'reasonable confidence', as I told the local television reporter. As it happened, anyone who witnessed the start would probably not have put money on me getting out of the river at all: In the euphoria of waving to all my well-wishers, I put *Lottie* aground on the Deben Bar. Like all the best boats she shrugged off the incompetence of her skipper and floated herself off as if to say: 'Let me take care of this. You get on with the PR.'

And for the next week she demonstrated to me why this Pat Patterson design has been such an enduring success for so long. Without the weight of a family of four and all their belongings – without the hundredweight of Lego and 200 books – she flew.

With a northwesterly force 4–5, we were doing a sustained 6.5 knots with bursts up to 8 knots, and in a 27ft boat designed for maximum accommodation; and the accommodation was amazing. I sat at the saloon table with my laptop computer in front of me, enthusing about the sensation of sitting on a pebble that some youthful giant has sent skimming across the surface of the water. Then, since all this was taking place on an even keel, I would leave the computer sitting flat on the table and connect it to the mobile phone with the aerial on the top of the mast and fire off reports by e-mail to *The Daily Telegraph*.

It was while I was doing this that, I received an e-mail from Mike Golding, automatically forwarded by his press office as he nursed a damaged *Team Group 4* through a viciously low depression in the Europe 1 New Man Singlehanded Transatlantic Race.

Conditions, said Mike, were atrocious – and this from a man who had sailed three times round Cape Horn the wrong way. The unusual low featured again on the long range forecast after the 0535 shipping bulletin on the Saturday morning. It would bring gales to North West Scotland on Monday or Tuesday. On Monday or Tuesday, I planned to be off the coast of North West Scotland.

It was fortunate that I was not in a race. All I had to do was get back by the beginning of July for the church fete, the cat's kittens and a weekend in Paris. And so, when I reached the top of the Shetlands, I stopped. I sorted out my long warps, re-read Pat Patterson on the management of catamarans in gales and waited to see which quadrant of the west the unpleasantness would be coming from. If there was to be any north in it, I would duck back down the East Coast. Anything else would see me running off towards Norway.

After 24 hours, during which every fishing boat in the Shetland fleet came to see whether I wanted to be salvaged, the Coastguard shipping forecast gave the definitive SW force 9. Ideal, I could get some westing before it arrived. It was while I was on the way that I heard my last Coastguard broadcast which had now become: "SW storm force 10, soon.'

Suddenly time seemed to stop as the significance of that cheerful Scottish voice came crashing down on top of me. I had never been in a force 10. What I did know was that I had no business to be in one. I knew that very soon I would be in a survival situation and everything depended on how well I managed my boat. If I had wanted to end my long-distance sailing career with a flourish, I was certainly getting the opportunity. The storm arrived with unhurried deliberation. When progress to windward started to put a strain on the boat, I hove-to.

This is stage one on the guru Patterson's storm management manual. Since I knew that we would soon reach stage two, I went straight into it while the wind was only 25 knots and I could walk around the deck without being blown off. I organised 100 metres of 14mm anchor warp in a bight from starboard bow to starboard stern. In the middle of this bight was attached a 25-metre length of 16mm plaited warp with a car tyre on the end. Then I handed all sail and trussed up the main like a mummy. *Lottie* settled immediately broadside to the seas and began to bob up and down like a little duck. Now monohull sailors may be horrified at the idea of lying beam on to breaking seas but they have deep keels which bite into the still water below the surface and 'trip up' the boat as the moving crest presses on the hull. That is how they get rolled. A catamaran with no keels behaves like a raft and is simply swept sideways but stays upright. As the wind increased that is exactly what happened. We lay like this for 24 hours and it worked.

Every 20 minutes or so I would go on deck to check for chafe and shipping. I wore, next to the skin, a Montane Interact thermal suit and on top of that Helly Hansen's Aukland gear. I cannot praise either highly enough. Best of all, I had Dubarry's Gore-Tex boots which I had been wearing for 24 hours a day over for ten days, only needing to change my socks once.

Gradually the windspeed crept up and up. Pat Patterson offers a third and final stage in his book. This is for conditions of force 10 and above. The point at which to make the change is when the impact of the waves from abeam becomes what he calls 'shock-like'.

Once or twice I suspected we had received such impacts – a loud bang, with small items being thrown across the cabin. Then, in the space of five minutes, it happened three times – culminating in the pot of spare light bulbs being shot across the 14ft cabin as if fired from a catapult. Very carefully, slithering about the deck on my belly to reduce windage, I transferred the bow line to the port stern. Obediently *Lottie* swung to present her stern to the seas. I switched on the autopilot again and she set off NNE at six knots.

It was, of course, the wrong direction and something of a disappointment after the two knots drift I had logged while we lay beam-on. But compared to the sensation of calm now, we were going with the storm, instead of trying to resist it; what did that matter? For half an hour, I watched the seas and the compass. The boat was sailing fast and straight under bare pole. I went below for a biscuit and a glass of pink grapefruit juice. It would have been helpful, at this point to have had another forecast. The barometer had stopped falling but I was appalled to see it reading 769 – I had never seen it that low before.

If the depression was tracking NE, then presumably the wind must veer at some point. But I was not getting forecasts. When I set out I reasoned that I had four sources of information: Coastguard on VHF – now out of range. Navtex –the aerial connection had shaken loose and the motion was such that four attempts to re-make it had all ended in failure. I had a radio cassette player, but in this kind of weather the two Aerogen wind generators set up such an electronic howl that I couldn't hear a word. Finally I had been presented with a Freeplay wind-up radio. I was thrilled with this. There was something wonderfully wholesome about earning your episode of the Archers by grinding a handle for 60 turns. Yet what possesses anyone to manufacture an expensive radio with wonderful tone and AM and FM –not to mention two short-wave bands – and then not include Long Wave?

I cannot say if things would have been different if I had known that the wind shift was imminent. Certainly I imagined that when it came I would have half an hour before the difference in the wave pattern would be significant. I set the kitchen timer for 20 minutes, backed it up with the loudest alarm clock out of the Casio catalogue and lay down to sleep. Later the helicopter pilot was to tell me that with windspeeds at this level, the wave pattern would change within five to ten minutes.

All I knew of it was when I awoke to the insistent hiss of rushing water as *Lottie* – still steering the original wind direction – began her broach. I saw the bulkhead start to cartwheel. Small items began to cascade from cave lockers. 'Oh,' I said. 'She's going over.' I was, at the time, extremely calm. I suspect this was because up until now everything had gone according to plan. Somehow I imagined this was just another development and I knew what I had to do. First the EPIRB: It was already flashing as I took it from its bracket in the cockpit and brought it into the starboard hull, tied the line to the toilet pump and pushed it out of the head window. Next the liferaft. This was when I first began to get frightened.

The liferaft was in a valise and stowed in the starboard aft cabin. I had thought about tying off the static line, but worried that if it should shift and fall off the bunk, the thing would inflate. Also, in fog, I might want to keep it in the cockpit. Now I did need it, I looked into the aft cabin and saw the hatch wide open. I hoped that the liferaft had not simply dropped out and gone spiralling down to the seabed, complete with line. I dived under the water and began to search. I found the dingy floating in its bag. I found my beloved sextant, the boards I had made for blocking up smashed windows, the brand new Autohelm, which Raytheon had lent me in case I should need it. But the liferaft? No. In the time I could hold my breath, I just could not find it. And besides, it seemed logical that it had indeed dropped out of the hatch.

This meant the best option was to stay inside the hull. Thinking of Tony Bullimore, I wedged myself clear of the water and tried to think of anything else I could do. I was surrounded by apples. I picked up one and bit into it.

It turned out to be an orange. I have no idea how long I was in there because after a while sensations took a while to register. One of them was that I was now in the water, not because I had moved but because the boat had begun to settle. Then I realised that I was breathing very fast. Of course: I was using up the oxygen in this confined space. I made plans to get out. Now which way should I turn when I got out of the hatch? My befuddled brain just couldn't handle this one at all. In the end I knew I had to go for it while there was still enough good air around to make a deep breath worthwhile.

I think I even told myself 'Go!' and I was out, losing my lovely boots instantly, dropping the flare canister straight away – but popping up next to the rudder. In no time at all I was standing on the bottom of the bridgedeck, holding onto the starboard keel. And there I knew I had to stay. When the first really big wave hit me, swept my feet from under me and left me in the middle of a breaking crest holding on by my fingertips, I knew I was in real trouble.

In all the survival manuals I have ever read it tells you that the single most powerful tool in your possession is your mind. You must never, ever – even for the tiniest moment – remotely consider the smallest possibility … of not coming through alive. This was kind of difficult at the time – partly because during that last morning I had been taking photographs in the cockpit and kept wondering why the flash was going off. But it was not the camera flashing. It was the EPIRB. I had sat on it and set it off. Reasoning that it had only been activated for a few seconds, I switched it off again and broadcast a 'false alarm' message on VHF. Now it was transmitting in earnest, I wondered whether there was someone down in Falmouth saying: 'Oh that's just the false alarm, don't worry about that one.' But that, as I say, was not to be considered. Instead I concentrated, wave by wave, second by second on holding on, thinking of Tamsin and the children and shouting at the sky: 'I am not going to die. I am coming home.'

The estimate is that I was in the water – both in the hull and on top of it – for between two and three hours. When the Coastguard helicopter arrived, it took maybe another ten minutes to find a calm enough slot to come down below the 30-metre maximum wave height to get me off. That seemed like the longest time. But once a magnificent and very brave man called Peter Mesney had swung down on his line and literally plucked me to safety, I was hardly able to speak and shaking uncontrollably.

They flew me to the Murchison oil platform and treated me for hypothermia. It seems almost unreal as I sit here writing this looking out over the garden to a tranquil River Deben while little Theo points to the Montane suit on the line and says: 'Daddy was upside down in that.' Meanwhile, the telephone keeps ringing and the postscript continues to be updated. Premium Liferaft Services say the EPIRB was accurate to within

100 metres only because the Americans have now unscrambled the GPS signal. Also, they believe the liferaft is still aboard. It was not designed to sink at all, but to float so that it can be fitted to a hydrostatic release. Maybe if I had taken a sea survival course, I would know things like this. Shetland Coastguard ring to say that an anchor handling vessel has located *Lottie Warren* but must remain on station, what do I want to do about this? I call Pantaenius (I would suggest the only appropriate insurance company for the singlehander) and say I had been planning to sell the boat anyway and would be happy to agree a total loss.

From *Yachting World* August 2000.

Lessons learned

After talking to the helicopter pilot, I assumed that a wind shift had set up an immediate cross-sea which pushed the boat beam-on to a breaking crest – and then acted as a stumbling block to prevent her from surfing sideways. However, Pat Patterson the designer of the Heavenly Twins catamaran disagrees. He believes this was a case of the boat surfing before an uncommonly large wave, rounding up when the autopilot failed to correct in time and then capsizing from a combination of kinetic energy caused by the sudden deceleration from 14 knots and the absorbed energy from the wave itself.

His advice is that a multihull must not be allowed to surf in such conditions. Certainly I knew this. When I went below, the boat was running steadily at six knots and since she did not normally surf at speeds under 12 knots, I assumed this was a good safety margin. However I had already seen one very large wave and should have realised this was merely the first rather than the exception.

At any event, I should have been at the helm – after all, I was well-rested from lying beam-on to a warp as the storm reached its crescendo. Meanwhile, in the light of my experience Pat tells me he is going to buy himself a parachute anchor. I had thought about getting one myself but could not justify the expense for one last trip at the height of the British summer. Don't you just love hindsight?

Finally, never forget that the single most powerful survival tool in your possession is your mind. You must never, ever remotely consider the smallest possibility of not coming through alive.

Part two:
Faulty Navigation

Keelson II, *Hugh Cownie's Vancouver 32 lost on a reef off the Caribbean island of Nevis.*

14 The fatal reef

Yacht *Nainjaune* (35ft Super Sovereign ketch)
Skipper Peter Middleton
Bound from the Carribean for Mayaguana, at the eastern end of the Bahama chain
Date of loss 23 February, 1977
Position off the coast of Mayaguana, Bahamas

Peter Middleton, a retired airline pilot, had sailed since 1949 on the basic principle that 'a sailing boat is an aeroplane tipped on its side'. Here he recalls the last moments when his blue water cruiser ran hard aground on a coral reef in the Bahamas.

The Harbourmaster stuck a label, reading 'Welcome to S Caicos', on the coachroof, gave us a sleepy smile and ambled back to his comfortable basket chair on the verandah of the sun-soaked, harbour office. 'Goodbye, Captain, and have a good trip.'

We had come a very long way, just the two of us, five months out from England in our 35ft ketch *Nainjaune*, along the lazy man's route to the West Indies. The longest passage had been the 23 days from Gran Canaria to Barbados. We had wandered from Barbados to Bequia, at the north end of the Grenadine chain, then through the islands, until we fetched Antigua for the traditional English yachtsman's Christmas. We were on our way to Fort Lauderdale in America to enter the Intracoastal Waterway.

Re-orientating ourselves from the high-sided Leeward Islands to the almost totally flat Caicos proved difficult. We had got used to seeing targets from 20 to 30 miles away. If not the actual land, you could nearly always see the cloud cap sitting on top. But Caicos was only a few feet out of the water and had no telltale 'lid' on it.

Our next port of call was to be Mayaguana, right at the eastern end of the Bahama chain. We expected a two-day passage, and we had sufficient stores and water from our previous trip to cover this twice over, so we had no worries on that score. The only doubt that nagged was this change from high land and deep water to flat land and shallow water.

In the pilot books I had read that you need a crewman up the mast to watch ahead for the discoloured water which marks the coral lurking only inches under the surface. And the positions of these reefs are not always marked accurately on the charts.

One up the mast, one on the wheel, and one keeping an eye on the navigation should be the minimum crew for Bahamian waters. We were, therefore, one short. But we had met several American crews on their way east, who told us that on no account should we bypass the delights of the Bahamas. Just one Englishman, who had sailed for many years in the area, had warned us not to try it with such a small crew. We should have listened.

Needless to say, as we prepared to leave Caicos, I had forgotten all about this. I was more concerned with the decision whether to cross the Caicos Bank, in about 12ft of water, or sail outside it, in deeper water. Even when I went forward to get the anchor up I had still not decided. For once, the sky was covered in high cirrus, and looked very flat. The sea lacked colour and the sand bottom was featureless and dead. These things generated a strange feeling of doubt, and I opted for the longer passage in the comfort and safety of deeper water.

At 1030 on 22 February, 1977, we sailed clear of South Caicos, towards Mayaguana, on what turned out to be *Nainjaune*'s last voyage.

Taking the outside passage meant leaving South Caicos in a northeasterly direction, supposedly into empty ocean. A glance at the chart, however, will show that you can't sit back and wait for the ETA to come up. There are several extensive reefs unpleasantly close to the track – some of them out of sight of land, all of them unlit. Since the trip will take about 24 hours, clearly some of them will threaten you after dark.

I am talking about a time long ago, before Decca became common in small boats, before the days of satellite navigation, a time when offshore navigators used the sextant, the hand-bearing compass, and the eyeball almost exclusively.

On this occasion, visibility was good and the islands we were leaving were in full view. In fact, the log shows that we were still taking bearings of identifiable objects seven hours after we left. In this time we had cleared most of the Caicos reefs, and the course had turned northwesterly to miss another offshore reef. Now it got dark, stars were covered, and we proceeded on dead reckoning.

Our extremely rugged windvane gear had taken us right across the

Atlantic almost without a human hand on the helm. It was steering us now, through the dark night, leaving my wife free to cook and sleep, and me free to navigate and keep a watch – not that there were any ships in this area to watch for. However, wind changes resulted in course changes, so that a regular look at the compass was essential. We had become so used to this efficient and uncomplaining helmsman that it was easy to forget who was doing all the work.

While we were bowling along at 4–5 knots, I had time to decide on several imaginary turning points, all designed to miss various reefs by a good margin. But one reef remained a threat, and I estimated that we should be on it before dawn, so at 0230, after a lot of calculation, I wrote in the log a memo, for whoever should be on watch at the time. It read: 'Assuming one knot current on to dangers, when log reads 124, STOP, and wait for daylight.'

Duly, at 0430, with the log reading exactly that, we hove-to on port tack, drifting slowly south. I went to my bunk and left Val to stare into space and wait for the first tinge of dawn. It says in the log: 'Stars at 0520' – the time at which you can expect to see the fading stars and the dawn horizon at the same time, enabling you to use the sextant for a three or four star shot. Such a shot takes some time to work out, but gives you a fix, as opposed to a single position line. On this occasion, a fix was what we needed.

By 0645 we were once again under way, having plotted our star fix, and worked out an ETA to sight Mayaguana. All seemed well. The only remaining reef was a few miles off the island, the dark night was over, the worries behind us, and through the sun was not actually shining, the light was improving and the sky clear.

Just after midday, the south-east point of Mayaguana appeared as a very thin line on the horizon; the sort of line which leaves you wondering whether it really is land, or just a bit of haze in the distance. No point in reaching for the hand-bearing compass. It was much too early to identify anything. We would not be there for another three hours.

As the time passed and we approached nearer to the island, some detail began to appear. We knew there was a large American tracking station on it, left over from the moon-landing. It was reported to be inactive and occupied by a caretaker. But its position on the chart was uncertain and the height of its buildings and aerials was unknown. This made such information practically useless in trying to measure our distance-off by horizontal or vertical sextant angle.

About 1430, we were sailing along the south coast of Mayaguana, still seemingly about 10 miles off, for what we could see of the land was very low on the horizon and without any detail. I went to the chart table to look for clues, and as Val was on watch in the cockpit and the vane gear was doing the steering, I called to her to come down and look at the chart to explain what I was hoping to see.

'Before you come below,' I said, 'can you see any white water, discoloured water or anything which looks like coral?'

'No sign,' she replied, and I stuck my head out of the hatch to make sure. The sea was smooth, its colour was deep, dark blue and the sun was shining. No thought of imminent disaster.

About 30 seconds later the boat seemed to hesitate under our feet. It was like the first shake of an earthquake, giving warning of impending disaster. The stunned silence was followed by a noise like a massive tree being felled, a tearing, rending, ripping, splintering noise, which brought our hearts jolting into our mouths. It took a fraction of a second to realise that the ship had juddered to a dead stop.

We bolted for the cockpit and stared in astonishment. How could this happen to us? We, the experienced long-distance sailors, were hard on a reef. We could see the three feet-long jagged blades of stag-horn coral only one or two feet under the water.

The mast was still standing, and immediately we lowered all sail straight on to the deck. Then to the engine, to see if we could back off. Engine started – into reverse. Clanking noise of bronze on coral – propeller gone. To the wheel – perhaps if we hoisted a genoa she could be turned? Wheel jammed. Looked over the side and saw pieces of rudder floating past, in a slight current – towards the reef. Wind and current behind us – not a hope.

There was no help in sight. No buildings on the shore. No passing ships. No fishing boat to tow us off. And slowly, relentlessly, the hull started to lift on the swell and crunch down on to the reef, port side first, then starboard – heavily, and fatally, the sharp and jagged coral pounded at *Nainjaune's* teak planking, as she rolled 30° either side on her lead keel. With each little sea breaking she was pushed further up on to the reef. Our hull had seemed so strong – 1½in thick in places, and backed by oversized frames. She was wedged where she had come to rest, after ploughing like an ice-breaker through 50ft of stag-horn coral; the channel she had cut dead straight and very deep. She took some stopping that boat, but stopped she was.

The immediate panic died down, and I got out the portable Callbuoy, set it up on 2182kc, pulled up the retractable aerial – and it broke off. I sent a distress message anyway, but was certain no one had heard it. Next, an orange smoke signal; I lit it on the foredeck, downwind, and the lurid smoke drifted low over the water, parallel to the shore. Watching the land through binoculars for a possible reply, I could see nothing but scrubby bush and a thin strip of sand. No people, no houses, nothing.

It was now about two hours before dark, and a decision was needed: should we spend a night being pounded to splinters on this reef, or should we abandon ship and row ashore? Frankly, it didn't seem safe on board. Already the planking was starting to split, and the shaking of the hull made it difficult to move about without being thrown off. There would certainly be no rest on board, and if she fell apart during the night, we should have trouble reaching an unlit shore.

The beach was more than 2½ miles away, north of us, and the trade wind just north of east, so it would be a cross-wind row; it would take at least an hour, and there was the risk that the wind, plus any current, might take us right round the western end of the island and out to sea. Then we should indeed be lost. It would be dark soon – better get started.

We inflated the liferaft from the foredeck, where there was some shelter from the breaking seas. The dinghy was also inflated and the two boats tied together. We collected valuables and necessary paperwork, sextant, chronometer, money, alcohol and some food, two water containers, medical box, camera, passports, etc, and secured them in a waterproof holdall. Dragging this load up the perilous sidedeck and dumping it in the boats was extremely risky, for anyone falling over the side would certainly be crushed by the hull on its next roll.

With Val in the liferaft and me in the Avon dinghy, we shipped the oars and cast off. In fear and trepidation we floated across the ugly, sharp coral, in water only a few inches deep, expecting the boats to be ripped to pieces on every swell, but thankfully we reached the deeper waters of the lagoon undamaged. Looking back, we had a dismal view of our lovely ship in dire straits, her sails draped anyhow on the rocking decks, and the ensign still flying on the stern, being savagely smashed to pieces on the reef.

We got to the shore just before dark, hauled the two boats up the narrow strip of beach, and congratulated ourselves on our survival. Then a quick look around disclosed a row of posts, each one numbered, apparently marking an underground power cable. Weary, and not too sure of finding anything, we followed these along the beach. Nothing but scrub and sand in one direction and still nothing. Darkness fell suddenly, as it does in the tropics; we were utterly alone, and a little afraid.

We made our home, as best we could, in the liferaft, and dined off ginger biscuits and a slug of Scotch with the moon and Venus bright in the night sky. Light was provided by putting the liferaft's seawater batteries into a jug of seawater, but this only served to underline our isolation. Throughout the long night, we both woke every 20 minutes or so, wondering whether this was all a bad dream, and believing that we were still at sea, rolling up the miles towards America. But when daylight came, there we were, still sitting in the liferaft on the beach and our yacht gone.

After breakfast (more ginger biscuits and Scotch) we set out, this time with more determination, to find civilisation. Walking up the beach we discovered a pair of blue plastic fenders which looked vaguely familiar. So they should; they were our own, blown ashore during the night. *Nainjaune* was out of sight over the horizon – out of sight but not out of mind, for we had loved her dearly. It took all of that day and a lot of exhausting walking through the bush to find other human life, and at one time we were convinced that the island was uninhabited. But we did eventually make contact. We spent a week on Mayaguana, where there was one other white man, and Val was the only white woman. That was an experience not to be missed – but that's another story.

Apart from the boat, the worst of our various losses was, surprisingly, our visitors' book. It contained the names of all the people we had met on this voyage, like-minded people engaged on an adventure like ours, with whom we would like to have kept in touch.

The voyage from Hamble to Mayaguana was 5700 miles, and since then we have owned two more boats and sailed another 11,000 miles. Although you could say that 23 February, 1977 was not our day, it did not put us off sailing. But eventually, at the age of 70, after 40 years' cruising, I sold our latest boat and 'swallowed the anchor'.

From *Yachting Monthly*, September 1994

Lessons learned

Our distance-off was wrongly judged as we were used to high islands. Mayaguana is only a few feet high and I thought we were at least 10 miles off.

We should not have approached coral with such a small crew. From sea level, changes in the colour of water are hard to spot. Someone should have been up the mast. Calm weather meant that there was no white water breaking on the reef, to mark its position, though it was visible from the landward side.

The timing was wrong. You should approach coral with the sun behind you. It was 1500 and we were heading north-west, almost dead into sun.

While we were considering how to measure distance-off, we should have disconnected the windvane gear and hove-to.

The fact that the echo sounder was running at the time was not a lot of help, because (as I now know) the wall of the reef is almost vertical from a depth of about 100ft. For this reason, an anchor put out astern would not have pulled us off.

If there had been a powerful motor-boat waiting for us when we hit (some chance), this might have dragged us off the reef backwards. She might then have been beached inside the lagoon, and since the damage would have been less, she could have been patched up without heavy lifting gear. We might then, hopefully, have sailed her on her own bottom to Miami.

We had done so much work on *Nainjaune* during the long voyage, that the 'Work to be done' notebook contained only one entry – 'oil port toe rail'. Small comfort that when she sank she had never been in better condition.

15 The Loss of *Keelson II*

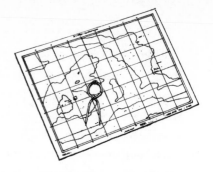

Yacht *Keelson II* (Vancouver 32)
Skipper Hugh Cownie
Crew Sue Cownie
Bound from Trinidad to Tortola in the British Virgin Islands
Date of loss 11 December 1999
Position Off the island of Nevis

A year after the launch of Keelson II, *our Vancouver 32, in 1985, and a month after our retirement, my wife, Sue, and I sailed out of the Solent for the Caribbean and ports in between. Nearly 14 years later we swam from our cherished Caribbean home, and left her wrecked on a reef off Nevis.*

We left Trinidad in light airs and had to motor towards our destination, Tortola, in the British Virgin Islands, some 500 miles away. Caribbean cruising had persuaded my brother-in-law to ship his yacht from Greece and we were sailing with him and his wife to greet its arrival. After two windless days and nights under engine and with little prospect of wind, we ran short of diesel; it was touch and go whether we had enough to motor to the island of Nevis. Unwisely, in the event, we abandoned our non-stop voyage to buy fuel in Martinique.

Hurricane Lenny had gone the wrong way, travelling eastwards instead of westwards. Lee shores became weather shores. Swells, as high as 30ft off some islands, caused considerable damage to westerly facing harbours and installations from the south of Grenada to St Maarten, where, we were told, several yachtsmen had been lost.

We sailed into Anse Mitan, a popular anchorage opposite Fort de France in Martinique, to find that the recently rebuilt marina and fuel jetty was totally destroyed. The tourist beach, usually decorated with topless ladies, had no sand and was deserted. Its many restaurants and bars were nearly all derelict.

After refuelling in the small marina at Fort de France, we set out to resume our sail northwards to the Virgin islands but, ironically, were ambushed by a tropical wave with 40 knots of wind and big uncomfortable seas. A night in Portsmouth, in the north of Dominica, seemed preferable to continuing on a night sail in such awful conditions. So we altered course and, in the blackness of early evening, crept into the anchorage for supper, hoping for a good night's sleep.

Once again we set sail for Tortola. After passing the Saintes in glorious sailing conditions our guests decided that they should fly to Tortola as they were running out of time for the arrival of their yacht. So we diverted to the unaccustomed luxury of the marina in Pointe a Pitre in the south of Guadaloupe. Sod's Law ruled that we should be weather-bound there for some ten days, by far the longest time we had spent in a marina since 1986. We endured and too frequently succumbed to, the temptations of delicious French cooking.

On a beautiful morning we set off, intending to spend a couple of days in the Saintes, one of the loveliest anchorages in the Caribbean. But the weather was so good we decided to carry on northwards, again towards Tortola. Well offshore we lost the protection of Guadaloupe and began to have a pasting from high north-north-easterly winds and sharp seas over a sizeable swell. These conditions were not for us so we altered course to regain the protection of the island to spend the night in Deshaies, a popular anchorage on the north-west coast. In the lee of the island one is normally motoring in calm seas, but not on that evening. We had a strong current against us, a heavy swell and continued strong winds. Never before, on several passages along that coast, had we seen such conditions so close inshore.

Even knowing the entrance quite well, we had a few uneasy moments until we saw the anchor lights of yachts. To our delight, our anchor held at the first attempt and we enjoyed relaxing in the cockpit over a beer, relieved to be safe and comfortable for the night. Our intended one night stay lasted three because of persistent large swells from the north and heavy winds and seas.

David Jones, the Caribbean's omniscient tropical weatherman, forecast a window for the weekend of the 11–12 December, with the threat of deteriorating conditions thereafter. So, after George's ham-net forecast had confirmed David's, we left Deshaies on the morning of the 11th and had a superb sail northwards, passing the sad sight of Montserrat with its terrible destruction from the active volcano. Yellow dust from the lava flow whirled over the once picturesque town of Plymouth, where we had anchored a few years before.

Because of an adverse current, it was getting dark when we came under the lee of Nevis. We calculated that, with similar unfavourable currents, a non-stop sail northwards would mean arriving off Tortola in darkness the following evening. A night at anchor off Charlestown or Pinney's Beach would allow us a leisurely meal and a good night's sleep to fortify us for a day and night passage the next day to arrive off Tortola on the Monday morning. And then nature intervened.

On our passage northwards we had seen a bank of cloud ahead. This was lying in ambush for us as we came under the protection of the island. The quarter moon was obscured and it began to rain. We were well offshore when, to our surprise, we saw through the glasses a well-lit dock with a ship alongside. In the poor visibility we wondered whether an unknown current had quickened our progress towards Charlestown.

The Garmin GPS showed us to be close to its latitude. We altered course to investigate but, as we closed the coast, saw that this was not the jetty we wanted. Because of the poor conditions and our failure to identify any navigation lights, we decided to stay where we were. I tried to anchor to the north of the jetty, but, unknown to us at the time, the bottom had been recently dredged and was hard; two attempts failed to set the anchor.

Slowly we resumed our way northwards, much closer inshore than we had planned, in search of Charlestown, which we knew must be close. The recently corrected Imray Iolaire chart showed a light to the south of Fort Charles and another marking the Charlestown jetty. We searched hard for the former without success; it was when we were looking for it against the background of shore lights that we struck the bottom.

There was quite a heavy swell running. One minute a wave would lift us clear of the reef only to dash us down again the next. I put our new Yanmar engine full astern each time the swell lifted us, expecting to get free and return to deeper water the way we had come. But as we rose, the swell drove the boat relentlessly shorewards until the seas were breaking over us.

We immediately recognised we were in trouble and put out a PAN PAN. A local radio operator responded and relayed our call to the Coastguard who could not help as their vessel was being refitted in St Kitts. Captain Greene, master of the Nevis-St Kitts ferry, offered help but, when told of our position off Fort Charles, decided that he couldn't hazard his vessel in such shallows, or his crew at night in such surf. We received one radio call from a cruising yachtsman at anchor off Charlestown to tell us that we were going aground, but that was too late. We were already aground.

Nothing else was heard from the anchored yachts, although I am sure that a couple of stiff-bottomed dinghies with moderate sized engines could have saved us if they had responded to our distress call. We were only about half a mile from the Charlestown anchorage.

After some two and a half hours the Coastguard and the police, who were by now above the beach, advised us that, as nothing could be done to help us and with our lovely yacht in danger of being swamped or worse, we should consider abandoning ship.

Sue distinctly recalls the solemn message from the Coastguard: 'We urge you to remember that your priority should be the preservation of life rather than property.'

'You bet,' Sue had hissed under her breath.

With our starboard toe rail under water, the decision was made and, with heavy hearts we donned our lifejackets, unfastened our lifelines, climbed over the rails and slid backwards into the sea. We swam only a few strokes before feeling the reef under our shoeless feet. As we struggled ashore, the breaking surf and undertow tried to prevent our advance but, by walking sideways on to the swell, we made slow progress, the ship's papers, passports and Sue's credit cards dangling in bags strung around our necks.

Helping hands stretched out to pull us from the surf onto dry land and we were quickly whisked away to the police station. There, with the Caribbean dripping from our sodden clothes and bodies, making pools on the office floor, we had to attend to first things first – the completion of entry formalities, though our passports were too wet to be stamped. Once all this had been attended to, a kindly policewoman lent Sue a diaphanous dress –many times larger than her usual size –and a pair of large flip-flops. A young policeman lent me underpants, a jazzy shirt and shorts, also with some flip-flops. He wanted me to keep them all when I returned them a couple of days later.

We were lucky and were relatively unharmed physically, although devastated mentally. Sue was bruised from being wedged against the chart table during her time on the radio. She had also been unlucky enough to tread on a sea urchin while wading ashore.

Brian David, the Commissioner of Wrecks, arrived and could not have been kinder. It was a Saturday night and, with the official work completed, I mentioned with some feeling that we could do with a drink. After I had explained that we didn't mean tea he, with Captain Greene, took us to a local watering hole where the lovely owner refused to accept payment for generous tots of Black Label and local rum. Seated at the bar, Mr Walters, a friend of both Captain Greene and Mr David, offered us accommodation at his holiday apartment block on Hilltop. We arrived to find a clean and comfortable bed for the night and a television set to help to distract us from our disaster. Captain Greene, who had accompanied us, took our wet clothes for washing.

Early the following morning Captain Greene stood off the reef in his ferry. In a dory three of his crew took us alongside our stricken yacht so that I could recover some cash and basic clothing. But the surf was so heavy the dory was swamped and nearly capsized. I found oily water up to the chart table and this, on my bare feet, caused me to slip, making movement difficult. I just had time to grab some money and a few clothes, but no shoes; I tried to unfasten our new Autohelm autopilot but was urged to get in the dory before it capsized. It was heartbreaking to feel our lovely yacht being dashed on the reef and to abandon all our possessions.

The police later told us that by midday the boat was cleaned out of nearly everything, Some items were of little worth, but of great sentimental value; even the running rigging and ground tackle had been taken.

An American yachtsman, Steve Macek, who had heard of our plight, came to see us and was almost in tears as we told him our story. He told us that a Brazilian yacht and later a large new Oyster also found themselves at the same point where we were. They were luckier as they had grounded in daylight and had escaped with relatively minor damage. The following day he went aboard the *Keelson II* and managed to retrieve our precious but sodden visitors' book.

On the Monday I asked Mr Walters for my bill for the two nights stay and good food, but he wouldn't hear of accepting a cent. We moved to a seaside hotel near Charlestown to be close to faxes and shopping. There, the owner volunteered us a highly discounted daily rate.

The kindness and friendliness of the Nevis folk has to be experienced to be believed. Admittedly we had lost all our possessions to looters but, sadly, an abandoned yacht would be looted in Devon or Cornwall, or indeed, anywhere else in the world.

In Charlestown we received many words of commiseration from shop-keepers and local passers-by but, surprisingly, none from fellow yachtsmen we saw wandering the streets. This touching kindness was not confined to the black population. The American owners of the exclusive Hermitage Inn invited us to a delicious family dinner, accompanied by fine wines.

On the Sunday morning, after our visit to the yacht, Brian David took us to his office to telephone our daughter who was able to contact our insurance brokers the following day. They could not have been more helpful: they arranged for a surveyor to fly in from Antigua and he inspected the wreck two days later. Mr David also drove Sue to the hospital where her painful and now swollen foot was treated.

Thankfully, Sue's credit cards were able to equip us with shoes and other essentials, such as our flight to Antigua, from where we could fly home. And in Antigua those cards were more than essential. We had lost our air tickets with the boat. Although our return booking to London was clearly shown on the airline's computers, both at the airport and at their St John's office, and despite their having had permission from London to issue copies, the staff insisted on our paying £800 for tickets home. This has since been refunded. But without credit cards we would have been in real trouble.

Now we ask ourselves what comes next? Do we buy *Keelson III* in our seventies? Two days ago we had decided definitely against it, but in the next morning's post came the Ocean Cruising Club's Newsletter. It reminded us of our lovely friends in Trinidad and of happier times; we both doubt whether we want to cut ourselves off yet from the cruising way of life.

From *Yachting Monthly* June 2000

Lessons learned

Even with a recent Imray Iolaire chart, do not rely on it. Chart A25, corrected to December 1999, shows three lights that have not been functioning for many years. The commercial jetty which was completed some time ago is shown as being 'under construction'. Even Doyle's excellent 1998/1999 *Cruising Guide to the Leewards* refers to the jetty as being 'planned'. It was this jetty that had attracted us shorewards. The 2000 edition of Doyle's book showed the jetty.

Nevis seems to be about half a mile north of where the chart shows it to be. Chart errors are known to exist for all the Caribbean islands but it bears repeating that great care has to be used when employing GPS for pilotage.

We had a 'panic bag' below the companionway, but this was designed for an offshore escape to the liferaft. It was of no use to us in our predicament.

Always have your ship's papers, passports, credit cards, any return air-tickets, and some money in a waterproof bag that can be grabbed in an emergency and dangled around your neck when swimming.

Approaching Charlestown from the south in the dark, the tall mast of the radio station topped by a blue light is an excellent landmark. Just don't close the shore until this has been passed.

We had been insured with the same Lloyd's underwriters since buying our first yacht in 1981. They settled for the full insured value. Chopping and changing one's insurance company to save a few pounds could prove expensive.

Most important of all, be sure to sail with as competent and as brave a wife as mine.

Footnote

Willie Wilson, Managing Director of Imray, said: 'There is always a time lapse between verifying corrected information and updating a chart. Our Caribbean charts, in particular, warn about not relying on lights. Chart A25 carries a further caution about running close inshore at night on this particular stretch of the coast.'

16 *Song* – the final episode

Yacht *Song* (26ft hard-chine, twin-keel sloop)
Skipper George Harrod-Eagles
Bound from England to Australia
Date of loss 19 January, 1982
Position on Roncador Reef, E coast of Puerto Rico

George Harrod-Eagles set out, singlehanded, from Lowestoft, Suffolk, in the summer of 1981, to sail the 26ft hard-chine sloop Song *back to his native Australia.* Song *was a smaller version of the Maurice Griffiths-designed 31ft Golden Hind class. Her auxiliary engine was an 8HP two-stroke Stuart Turner. Harrod-Eagles left Santa Cruz, Tenerife on 3 November, 1981, bound for the Bahamas.* Song *reached Barbados in 42 days and Christmas was spent in Carlisle Bay. There followed a week in Fort de France, Martinique, before leaving for Fajardo, on the east coast of Puerto Rico on 14 January, 1982.*

I laid course hard on the wind for St Croix, our first landfall, some 300 miles to the north-west. With no possibility of a sight, beacons not working, and the extremely poor conditions, there was little sleep for me. *Song* was making a fair amount of leeway, being closehauled, so I was unable to point up enough to make St Croix, and that landfall was abandoned in favour of Punta Tuna, the second option, which was now preferable since strong northerly winds would put us on a lee shore if we attempted the passage to windward of the Island of Vieques.

As I was unable to obtain a sight, it was fortunate that the beacon at Punta Tuna was operational, and gave me a bearing down which I could run until I was able to pick up the light. In the early hours of the third morning this light came into view and was positively identified. I had made landfall on the extreme south-east corner of Puerto Rico.

This portion of the Puerto Rican coast lies in a roughly north-east south-west direction, the distance from Punta Tuna to Fajardo, our destination, being 38 miles. The wind, as we neared the coast, was lighter than before and about NNE. A big swell, caused by several days of northerly winds, made more tedious the long tacks needed to traverse this coast. Navigation was complicated by the Island of Vieques, with a long unmarked spit protruding from its south-western extremity, far out into the passage between it and the Puerto Rican coast; and by the dearth of navigational aids in these waters, which abound with natural hazards.

Song crept through the passage de Vieques, progress further slowed by the wind becoming light and uncertain in direction. It was time to make a decision, keeping in mind the golden rule of reef-strewn waters, *do not sail at night*. I weighed the odds of reaching our destination before darkness. The choice lay between finding a suitable anchorage (hazardous, in view of the uncertain weather, no information as to the holding quality and the horrible consequences if we dragged), turning around and running back until there was enough searoom to stand off (the safest course, but one that would make pointless all the hours spent getting this far), or continuing towards our destination.

It was early afternoon and warmth in the sun shining through great blue rifts in the cloud cover was a scene to grace the cover of a glossy brochure advertising the delights of the Caribbean. But I was about to enter an area with few navigational aids, with islands and unmarked reefs on either side. The mile or two between them was a very small distance, particularly once darkness fell. A decision had to be made, and I chose to go on – a fateful and perhaps imprudent decision in view of the contrary winds and the slowness of our progress, but one prompted by the desire to end this tiresome passage.

To assist progress I started the engine and ran at half throttle. I motor-sailed past Roosevelt Roads, the US Naval Base, and as we cleared Punta Puerca and the Isla Cabeza de Perro, the wind, no longer diverted by the land, and unaffected by the small islands and reefs in its path, reverted to NNE about force 3. The swell was still with us, and I estimated about a knot of tide against us, a factor which, with no information about the tides and currents hereabouts, had not entered into my calculations. Nevertheless, Fajardo and the Isleta Marina were visible, and slowly becoming clearer, as we continued to tack, heading for Isla de Ramos and the last buoy before Las Croabas, on the north side of the Bahia de Fajardo and some five miles distant from Isla de Rumas. As we passed this rocky island with the most difficult miles of this passage still to be traversed, the sun was already low over the mountains of Puerto Rico, the shadows growing longer, and the outline of Isleta Marina's two islands becoming difficult to distinguish from the darkened hills behind them. I realised I was unlikely to make the anchorage before darkness. I took a bearing of the buoy lying behind us, close to Isla de Ramos, and one on the buoy ahead near Las Croabas. These were the only lit buoys in the area that would be visible and if we could stick to these bearings we ought to be well clear of reefs, particularly the long reef guarding Isleta Marina, named El Roncador, The Snorer.

The difficulty of keeping one light in view among a confusion of unrelated lights and the bright glow from the shore is well known. Not surprisingly, as night descended with tropical swiftness, the light astern became impossible to see, leaving me with no reference except the buoy ahead, the light from which I could see reasonably well. To continue tacking in the Stygian darkness that now surrounded me was plainly foolish. I lowered all sails, and continued under engine, keeping the light from the buoy ahead. The shore lights of Punta Gorda ahead, and those of Isleta Marina to port, were partially obscured, but coming more into view as we plodded on into the blackness for, with the stars obscured by the overcast, the only light was from the distant shore.

I was stowing sails and watching for white water with the echo sounder registering 30ft and the lights from the complex on Isleta Marina in plain view off to port. The depth on the echo sounder plunged to 15ft then up to 20ft, the chart indicated a number of relatively shallow spots, and I thought to check to see if I could relate our position to the charted depths when the echo sounder plummeted to five feet and immediately the boat struck, crunching and bumping half a dozen times before coming to a stop.

There was a horrible, cold, heart-sinking moment of realisation, before I reacted and put her hard astern, hoping that she would come off: a forlorn hope, for the tidal set which had by its invisible and unknown presence put us up on the reef was, aided and abetted by the strong swell, acting on our bows, pushing them round, pivoting the boat on the stern, which (being the deepest part) was stuck hard, forcing the bilge plates against great jagged coral heads, which were crunching and grinding in a horrifying way against the hull.

The swell, now that we were aground, was lifting the boat up and bumping it further on to the reef. Clearly I had to get an anchor out and try to pull us off. The inflatable dinghy was unlashed and inflated, and the anchor got ready, but the tide was falling and what was a swell now became breakers. Great rolling walls of water were roaring down upon us, lifting *Song* and smashing her down, with shuddering impact, onto the cruel coral, amid great clouds of spray and solid water which broke over the boat continually. Obviously *Song* could not take much of this pounding, and I think it was then I knew she was doomed.

I do not think I can describe the sickening despair I felt at that time; the self-recrimination, followed by intense feelings of being terribly alone and forsaken. It is an awful thing, the knowledge that all you have striven for, over so many months, is being destroyed while you are impotent to prevent it. The continued pounding of the hull and the bilge plates against huge coral heads was not long in taking effect. Within what seemed no time at all, but must have been an hour or more, during which, wet through and continually pummelled by the breaking waves, I struggled to get all in readiness so that I could kedge the boat off, she heeled sharply to port and water appeared with a rush inside her. She settled on her side and, as the port bilge plate had broken, it was now just a matter of time.

What difference it would have made I am not sure, but only the shortage of time and the lack of equipment prevented me from cutting off the bilge plates before I left England. Not to offset the effects of striking a reef (I had not envisaged that problem) but because, having read accounts of attacks by killer whales on sailing boats, I thought them an invitation to disaster, should a whale decide to attack head on.

It was time to call for help and the US Coast Guard was contacted on VHF radio (not without some difficulty). Details of the situation and position were given, and an assurance received that assistance was forthcoming. Whilst I waited, I gathered essentials, wading waist-deep inside the boat in the dimming glow of the overhead fluorescent light, transferring books and equipment to the crowded but still dry starboard-side lockers and shelves. I was thrown violently off balance as each wave, striking with thunderous impact, lifted the boat and let it fall back again. The tide, ebbing fast now in the darkness, revealed a foaming expanse of white water informing me, too late, of the implacable El Roncador.

Several hours elapsed as I waited for the Coast Guard. Inside the cabin, the light had winked out some time earlier and I was in total darkness. Incessantly soaked with spray, I remained in the cockpit, with some difficulty because of the acute angle of heel, wet, cold and bedraggled in spite of the relative warmth of the water. The wind had dropped with the outgoing tide, and was now gentle from offshore, conveying the cinnamon scent of the land. I sat in silence, lost in my thoughts.

At last there appeared a fast-moving light searching the area of the reef, but away to the north-west. Concluding it to belong to the Coast Guard, I flashed a Mayday with the torch I always kept in the cockpit. This soon brought a response, and the light described a wide circle to the north, flicking from side to side, gradually approaching until it was I saw a large inflatable powered by two outboard motors, and crewed by four men in the uniform of the US Coast Guard. They hailed me, while still a considerable distance away, to ask if I was the originator of the Mayday. They would not come closer than about 20 yards, requesting that I use the dinghy to traverse the now smaller, but still formidable, waves that were breaking onto the reef.

Taking with me only my valuables, and a sailbag containing dry clothing, I launched the dinghy on the port side, and clambered aboard. I cast off and rowed around the stern to face the waves, taking great pains to keep head on to them, for a broach would have tumbled me out into the jagged coral, with terrible injuries. There was now little depth of water covering the reef, giving me great cause for concern, should the fragile bottom of the dinghy be caught and rent upon the coral.

The dinghy bottomed each time the water receded, but was lifted up once more with each new breaker as it roared in, high upon the crest, enveloped in spray and solid water. I rowed as hard as I could to keep head-on to the waves. Perhaps ten minutes passed between leaving *Song* and reaching the quieter waters clear of the reef, but they seemed endless minutes, calling heavily on my physical and mental reserves. Once aboard the Coast Guard boat, the dinghy was made fast astern, jumping and rearing in the wake as we made for the shore at high speed. I was exhausted and drained, the image of *Song*, as we abandoned her, lonely and forlorn, lying on her side like a seabird with a broken wing, still imprinted on my mind.

A mere half-hour later we were nosing into Puerto Chico, and I was put ashore and taken to the Coast Guard station at Cabo San Juan, where hot showers, coffee, and dry clothing were made available. After going through the usual formalities, I discussed my position with the Coast Guard men, who thought that, with the improving weather, the swell should diminish enough to allow us to approach the boat from the inside of the reef, to salvage what we could. But they advised me to make the attempt at first light, for there were scavengers who knew the reef intimately and would soon take advantage of my misfortune.

I accepted the good sense of this advice, and relied further on the good nature of these kindhearted men; some phone calls and a ride back to Puerto Chico brought from his bed Carlos, who runs the diving shop there, and an agreement that he would run me out to the reef in the morning. A visit to the Water Police who are stationed at Puerto Chico, and an explanation of my circumstances and fears, produced complete indifference to my plight. It was past midnight when I returned to the Coast Guard station, spending the remainder of the night in fitful sleep.

The morning dawned bright and clear, with a light wind from the NE. In Puerto Chico, I found Carlos and his charming wife, June, waiting for my arrival. They made me welcome, with sympathy for my loss and offers of whatever help they could give. Leaving my meagre possessions with June, we boarded the 18ft aluminium open boat used by Carlos in his diving business. He informed me that El Roncador was not a place to which he would take any of his clients. On average five boats were wrecked there each year. This number included several small coasting vessels. It was a dangerous and poorly charted place.

With *Song's* dinghy in tow we made the half-hour run out to the reef. Our approach was on the lee side, where although we would have to cross the full width of the reef, the waves would have spent most of their energy. We dropped anchor in a few feet of water onto white sand, and prepared to row the dinghy across to where *Song* lay on her side, still shuddering as each wave lifted her; but now the sun was shining and the seas moderate. Progress across the reef was slow and it was not until we were quite close that I saw something was wrong. Where was the boom with the main sail stowed upon it? Where were the genoa and working jib I had left lashed to the pulpit? With a sinking feeling, I scrambled on board to discover the full extent of this second catastrophe to overtake us.

The boat had been stripped of everything easily removed from on deck and below. Sails, anchor, rope were gone, lockers rifled, empty spaces only remained where once had been the VHF radio, tape recorder, short wave radio, camera case with all the lenses and film, clothing and equipment. In their search for valuables, the thieves had swept books from shelves and emptied the contents of containers, all of which had been still quite dry, into the swirling waters, invading the boat, turning them into sodden pulp or shattered pieces. Saddest of all was the loss of my sextant and my log book, with its record of the memories of my grand venture. I think then I reached the depths of bitter despair, looking into the chaos and destruction wrought upon my boat. I pitted myself against the sea and lost, but it would have been better had the boat sunk in deep water and everything been lost, than to have my boat thus defiled by such human dregs.

From *Lowestoft Cruising Club Journal*, 1982

Lessons learned

As George Harrod-Eagles unashamedly admits, his decision to sail in to an area with few navigational aids, with islands and unmarked reefs on either side, and with darkness falling, was 'a fateful and perhaps imprudent decision in view of the contrary winds and the slowness of our progress'. Not unnaturally, perhaps, it was prompted by the desire 'to end a tiresome passage'.

The lack of information about tides also stacked the odds against him. Finally, the well-known difficulty, even to experienced sailors, of keeping a lit buoy in view among a confusion of unrelated lights, as well as the bright glow from the shore, certainly did not help. 'Not surprisingly, as night descended with tropical swiftness, the light astern became impossible to see,' recalls the skipper.

After *Song* had struck the reef off the coast of Puerto Rico, Harrod-Eagles successfully contacted the US Coast Guard on VHF radio, but they still had the problem of locating him in intense darkness among dangerous reefs.

'At last there appeared a fast-moving light searching the area of the reef, but away to the north-west. Concluding it to belong to the Coast Guard, I flashed her with the torch I always keep in the cockpit. This soon brought a response.'

So a torch, as well as a knife, are essentials to have at hand on your person, or in the cockpit.

17 Last time over

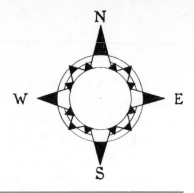

N
W   E
S

Yacht: *Northern Light* (45ft Colin Archer type gaff-cutter)
Skipper Lt Cdr James Griffin RN
Crew: Ann Griffin
Bound from Horta, Azores to Gibraltar, Spain
Date of loss 10 September, 1982
Position on Spanish coast, 6 miles S of Cadiz

Lt Cdr James Griffin and his wife Ann had lived aboard Northern Light *for 22 of the boat's 52 years. After four years pottering around the Bahamas and the coast of Florida, the Griffins had decided to sail back to Europe. In this personal account Ann Griffin tells what happened after they left the Azores.*

Northern Light is a 45ft Colin Archer type gaff ketch, with 15ft 6in beam and 8ft 6in draft, built of 2½ inch Burma teak, copper sheathed, 52 years old, but good for our lifetime. One of our four daughters, Heather, was itching to push us out and buy her off us, but after living in her for 22 years no way would I give her up.

We were almost at the end of our fourth Atlantic crossing, only 100 miles to our destination – Gibraltar. I looked around at our beautiful ship – we had never had a house or a car – our transport was bicycles and they were lashed to the guardrails. We had survived Force 9, gusting 10, on August 28–31, during which time we were hove-to and had been carried 60 miles to the south by leeway. No hope now of seeing Cape St Vincent and creeping round the corner to anchor and recover. During the blow a new steel strap holding the crosstrees to the mainmast had snapped seven out of its eight stainless steel bolts and was hanging down swinging back and forth, threatening to fall on our heads at any moment. It had sawn through the topsail and jib halyards, and was now threatening the main. We had fitted rigging screws inside the shroud lanyards and all of them had broken their fittings, making it impossible to climb the ratlines and secure the wretched thing, nicknamed Damocles. We were sailing at one knot under mainsail and staysail; we had lost the mizzen gaff jaws in the blow, and the mizzen and the jib were our main driving sails. Jimmy had spent the day repairing seams on the mainsail – the Terylene had stood up to seven years in the tropics, but the stitching hadn't. Everywhere I looked on deck we needed repairs, but there was nothing wrong with the hull, thank heavens.

The wind was dying, but there was still a heavy swell. It had been north-east or east all the way across from the Azores. Only enough fuel was left to get us in the last four miles to enter harbour. No sign of shipping, but there should have been; another frustrating night ahead.

It had been a hasty crossing to Bermuda from Florida, then a glorious 19 days for the 1850 miles to the Azores, light favourable winds, fantastic sunrises and sunsets, and starry and moonlit nights we would never forget.

Jimmy and I had taken her across the Atlantic in 1974, having left behind all four daughters, now married, but as we were now aged 62 we thought it prudent to invest in a new autopilot. It left us very low on cash, and one day out from Bermuda it packed in. We were watch and watch about for the rest of the trip. We don't carry a radio or liferaft, or any aids to navigation, apart from a sextant, but had lots of flares and a nine-foot ply and glassfibre dinghy.

It had been so hazy that sights had been unreliable for the last two days, but the log was accurate and we were allowing for a half-knot current carrying us into the Straits – the charts and the pilot book said it was so. Just after sunset we saw a ship, and during the night 21 went past us, heading due east . . . we must be near. The ninth dawned heavily overcast – no sights today. At last the wind went south-east . . . we should go north-east. At midday we were suddenly over green water with a fishing boat visible a mile away. A check with the chart revealed where we should have been, on the Banco de Trafalgar, but no sight of land eight miles away. The wind pulled round and went west at last – and we were able to sail direct towards Gibraltar. At 1930 we saw a lighthouse flashing twice every six seconds and went wild with delight . . . we had done it, after 20 days at sea. We celebrated with a cup of tea! We'd be in Gibraltar before dawn, God willing. We got to the lighthouse, but where the heck was Tarifa light? We looked at the lights on the shore – far too many of them, unless Tarifa town had changed a lot in nine years. Feeling very uneasy we put on the engine and hauled off. Shortly after we struck rock and stuck.

The rudder broke off with the first impact, and jammed the propeller. For the next three hours we banged every five seconds. For the first two hours she held, during which time we sent up 20 flares, and signalled with the Aldis lamp to every car that stopped to have a look. Then the water crept over the floorboards and started to beat the pump. I sat on deck in a state of frozen shock, trying to stop three terrified cats from jumping over the side, watching and waiting with the signalling lamp to shine on our sails when help arrived. Nobody came.

Jimmy collected ship's papers and passports; we launched the dinghy, and then he said: 'I'm sorry, darling; it's time to go; if we wait she might fall on the dinghy.' I couldn't believe it; we had been on coral reefs in the Caribbean and always got off, but they were soft by comparison. We put the cats in a sack, and rowed clear, then let them out.

Jimmy rowed two miles inshore, then two miles along through breakers trying to find a beach. We saw a lit one . . . how I got through the surf I'll never know . . . I slipped on rock, but held on; we got the dinghy ashore and tried to capture three soaking wet and petrified cats.

We had landed on a top-security Naval beach. We had left the engine and bilge pump running, cabin and deck lights on. The navy hadn't any English, we hadn't much Spanish, but found we were in Cadiz. We found out later there had been Force 6 and 7 easterlies in the Straits of Gibraltar which had stopped the south-going current. The bank had been the entrance of the Guadalquivir River and the lighthouse had been the Santa Caterina, flashing twice every seven seconds. The Spanish Navy was very kind, gave us cognac and coffee at six in the morning . . . water was running all over the floor from our soaking wet clothes. They offered showers and breakfast, but we were anxious to contact Lloyd's and help.

Jimmy himself is a marine surveyor for Lloyd's, and for the last four years had been working as such for the Bahamas Government. We got to town (two cats in a box, the other one on my lap), and spent three hours trying to get things organised, but as there wasn't a British Consul in Cadiz, went on to Algeciras. After a little difficulty we found a pension that would take cats; sent cables to the girls, and collapsed into bed, cuddling cats.

We were lucky . . . we had each other, and the clothes we stood up in, but oh! the heartache of leaving behind 40 years' diaries and photographs, to say nothing of all the letters the children and grandchildren had written us. The tears came in the middle of the night when the shock wore off. Next morning, down to the ferry to go to Gibraltar – but they wouldn't take the cats. Over the next day *Northern Light* came off the reef and drove herself onto an army firing range: a salvage team went down . . . they could get her off without any difficulty when we could get the army to stop firing.

We were only insured for total loss, but we would have used our life's savings to get her back. It took five days to get permission, by which time vandals had been aboard, stripped her and taken the bronze strips off our 32 decklights. The water inside pushed them out and she was held down.

The weather deteriorated on 19 September – my birthday – and the answer came that salvage was impossible. At this time both Jimmy and I broke down, but fortunately our eldest daughter, Geraldine, had come over with her fourth child, and that helped. Next day Jimmy went over to see *Northern Light* for himself, and said his own farewell.

Now the tears have stopped; it's only material things we have lost – we must find another boat, and get the cats back ... they are in a kennel in Spain. We are in Gibraltar with our daughter. We'll never get another boat as beautiful, but nothing will ever take away the memories and we were lucky to own her for 22 years.

Extracted from an account by Ann Griffin

Lessons learned

James Griffin and his wife Ann had invested in an autopilot for *Northern Light*, but one day out from Bermuda it had 'packed in', so they had stood watch and watch about for the rest of their voyage across the Atlantic, and now they were within 100 miles of Gibraltar and perhaps very tired.

'We don't carry a radio or liferaft, or any aids to navigation, apart from a sextant.' But the trouble was that it had been so hazy that sights had been unreliable for the last two days ... but the log was accurate and they were allowing for half a knot of current carrying them into the Straits – the charts and the pilot book said it was so ...'At 1930 we saw a lighthouse flashing twice every six seconds and went wild with delight ... we had done it after 20 days at sea. We got to the lighthouse, but where was Tarifa light? Shortly after we struck rock and stuck.'

It's a classic error to make the evidence before your eyes fit your assumptions. Entirely understandable in this case, since only the difference of a second lay between the light characteristics.

They found out later that there had been force 6 and 7 easterlies in the Straits of Gibraltar, which had stopped the south-going current. The bank had been the entrance of the Guadalquivir River and the lighthouse had been the Santa Caterina, flashing twice every seven seconds.

18 A gaffer's grave

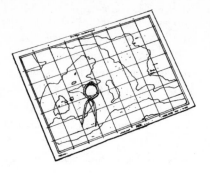

Yacht *Quiver* (21ft 6in gaff cutter)
Skipper Michael D Millar
Crew Richard Penn
Bound from St Peter Port, Guernsey to Lannion Bay, North Brittany
Date of loss 4 June, 1971
Position NE side of Les Triagoz Rocks

Michael Millar, a past President of the Old Gaffers' Association, accompanied by his grandson as crew, left Chichester Harbour on Saturday, 29 May, 1971, with the intention of attending an Old Gaffers' Rally in Braye Harbour, Alderney, later that weekend. Millar had owned Quiver *for 16 years, and Richard Penn had sailed with him for almost as long.*

Quiver *was thought to have been built in Cowes in 1895 and was probably converted from an open boat around 1920. Late in her life she was fitted with a small inboard petrol engine. Because of contrary winds, they did not cross to France directly, but called first at Yarmouth, Isle of Wight, Poole, and Lulworth Cove, where they spent the Sunday night. After setting out on Monday morning to sail to some Devon port, the wind became favourable for a Channel crossing and they set course for Alderney, arriving in Braye Harbour early on Tuesday morning (too late for the Old Gaffers). They moved on to Guernsey after hearing a forecast that it would soon blow from the north-east. Two frustrating days were spent in St Peter Port, which they left on Friday morning.*

We decided to head for Lannion Bay in the eastern end of Morlaix Bay; it appeared to have easy access by day or night (we should probably arrive in the dark, and those French leading lights are terrific), and was reputed to be good holding in firm sand. It promised a cosy anchorage on a weather shore. Furthermore, it was downhill all the way. We did not then realise how steep that hill was to be.

The direct route from St Martin's Point (SE corner of Guernsey) took us between Les Sept Iles and Les Triagoz, two of the reefs lying off the Brittany coast, then between Les Triagoz and Ile Grande, the latter being on the 'corner' of Morlaix Bay, there being a safe gap of over three miles between the two. However, this course (240°M so far as I can remember) was dead downwind, and as the wind was a bit fresh for spinnaker work for a crew of two, it would have meant a very tiring day at the tiller. So we decided to make a dogleg of it, and steer due west until the DR put us north of Les Sept Iles, then due south until we found them. This worked very well, enabling us to keep the headsails drawing all the time, especially when the wind fell light during the afternoon, when we shook out the reefs and changed up from No 2 to No 1 jib.

During the afternoon we saw a French fishing boat executing some alarming manoeuvres, and stood by to take evasive action in view of the stories one has heard of yachts being 'attacked' by such vessels; however, it seemed that she was only locating and picking up her pots on the Banc des Langoustiers, and we were able to exchange cheery greetings as we passed them.

Soon after dark, we picked up the Les Sept Iles light where expected, and, crossing this with a radio bearing on Les Roches Douvres, got a satisfactory fix which showed we were back on our rhumb line.

Being quite happy with the fix, we altered back to the original course of 240°M, and in due time picked up the light on Les Triagoz, where expected, fine on the starboard bow. We were now sailing on a dead run, boom to port and staysail goose-winged to starboard. The log was giving us 5 knots, the fixes indicated that we were making good 3½ knots, which confirmed the rather meagre information gleaned from the charts and tidal stream atlas that there was a 1½ knot head tide. This tide was supposed to run till about 0400, dropping to about one knot in the last hour.

Until about 0130 the sky was clear though the visibility was still apparently poor, and a brilliant moon, three-quarters full, moved steadily round until it was right in our track. If only it had stayed there ... but it was not to be. Some heavy cloud came up from the south, across the wind, and blotted everything out, leaving us with nothing but the two lighthouses.

By 0200 we had drawn abreast of Les Sept Iles, and I had a feeling that we were being set somewhat to the SE towards the outlying dangers at the western end of that reef. I therefore altered course more westerly, until the Les Triagoz light was just open to port, for about half an hour, and until I was satisfied that we were well clear of Les Sept Iles. I then altered back about double the amount until Les Triagoz was well open in the starboard rigging; a quick check on the chart confirmed that at 3½ knots made good (and nothing had changed to alter this), we would clear the eastern tip of the Les Triagoz reef by about ¼ miles, a comfortable margin. At about 0300, I was just contemplating resuming the compass course when *Quiver*, with a resounding crash, stopped dead.

There is, of course, no excuse for wrecking one's ship on a well-charted reef, especially when one can see two lighthouses and has a commanding wind. There are, perhaps, reasons. I will suggest three. The first is that during that last hour we had done the full 5 miles over the ground; in other words we had lost the 1½ knots head tide which we had been experiencing, and which we should have had for another hour at least. One can only assume that it was masked by the reef into whose shadow we had sailed; there may even have been a counter-eddy: at any rate we were undoubtedly 1½ miles further on than I thought we were. The second reason may have been that I made my detour by eye on the lighthouse, rather than on compass courses – not very seamanlike. The third reason was undoubtedly because it was 3 o'clock in the morning. We both felt wide awake, and were thoroughly enjoying the ride. I was (thank God) at the helm myself, while Richard was below planning the next move. But at that hour one is not at one's brightest, we may have been taking careless bearings, plotting carelessly, or simply doing our sums wrong; we shall never know, as the deck log and chart went down with everything else.

After the initial impact, which probably broke the stem and certainly opened up the hood ends, *Quiver* shook herself free of the half-tide rock she had struck, luffed a bit, and went charging off again into the dark. She took a great tombstone square on the bowsprit end, and again stopped dead; in the dim light from the cabin one had the feeling of being in a flooded graveyard, with great slabs of granite sticking up all round, and the water boiling on unseen tombs beneath. She swung round, hinging on the bowsprit, until the port bilges found some of these on which she then pounded for several minutes. We let go all sheets to try to take some of the weight out of it, but the swell kept her pounding until she finally slid clear in a northerly direction. To keep her quiet (and reduce the frightful din of flogging sails), we furled the jib and backed the staysail, leaving the main sheet free; thus hove-to, she fore-reached at about a knot in water which within a few yards gave a depth of 35 fathoms. We had hit the top of a 200ft cliff.

A quick look below revealed a hopeless situation; Richard was already on the pump, but the water in the cabin was rising at an alarming speed. Water was gushing in both sides of the stem forward, under the port bunk, and again under the cockpit. It would not have been easy to try to deal with one puncture in force 5 on a pitch black night in a fair old seaway; four or more holes were out of the question – we had to abandon.

While Richard set about releasing the dinghy (9ft Nautisport, fully inflated, upside down on the coachroof), I started in on the flares. My main armament was some seven or eight of the 'Roman Candle' type; they burn a steady red flare in your hand, while throwing up a succession of red balls to a very satisfactory height. They all went off beautifully, and the display must have lasted at least four minutes, possibly longer; the only snag was that there was no audience. The mainland coast was a good three miles off, but the visibility was much less than that; I felt sure that the lighthouse should be keeping a watch, but at 0300 . . . ?

We started loading up the dinghy: oars, rowlocks, pump and bailer. Food? We found a big plastic gash-bag, shoved in cakes, biscuits, tarts, and tied a knot in it. Water? It was all in the tank, with a tiny galley pump and no container to hand. At that moment, six long-life milk cartons conveniently floated out of their locker, in they went; what next? I grabbed my wallet and travellers' cheques; personal kit – one large travel bag each. Next? My second bag, with all the ship's and personal papers – in it went (it wasn't until two hours later that I realised that it was the wrong second bag; all I saved was a lot of useless hardware).

By this time the water was over the cabin bunks, slowing down a bit as it had more room to spread out, and the relative buoyancy increased, but still rising visibly. We grabbed a few more bits and pieces, but then decided we had better get out in case she took a wave into the cockpit and plunged suddenly. We had been something over ten minutes, probably about quarter of an hour, from the first impact. After we let go, *Quiver* went on fore-reaching in a northerly direction, while we started drifting rapidly WSW. The direct cabin light disappeared quite quickly over our limited horizon, but the glow from it on the sails could be seen for another five minutes or so as she sailed sluggishly into the darkness. Then she just disappeared.

I won't go into all the sordid details of the next ten hours. It was a hell of a long time. Every quarter of an hour or so a wave would sweep right over us, to make sure we were kept as cold and wet as possible. We bailed it all out again, though there was not really much point. We never saw a suspicion of land or vessel the whole time. Cramp was rather trying.

I found that I had in my pocket my plastic hand-bearing compass. It was comforting to confirm, by sighting up wind, that we were being blown WSW, and that therefore France lay somewhere to leeward. I tried rowing, but found that I could not do anything very effective, except in short bursts which were very tiring. I felt however that I had to try to do something useful, so kept gently paddling across the wind in a generally southerly direction, thereby reducing the possibility of missing France altogether. We decided that we really did not know what the tide might be doing to us. Even if we had managed to grab any charts or pilot books which were floating around in the cabin, they would have dissolved before we could have made any use of them.

Sometime about midday, Richard declared that he had been watching for a timed quarter of an hour the same two slag heaps directly to leeward. Unlike all the other land we had been imagining, they were still there. They could only be Ile de Batz. Soon they joined up and became a proper island, with the cliffs above Roscoff appearing opposite. Then a buoy went past, obviously the landfall for the Roscoff channel. Things were looking up . . . or were they? As the actual coast became visible, it was increasingly apparent that it was very knobbly; the lighthouse in the channel had spray bursting 20 to 30ft up it; what would happen when we got in amongst that lot? I decided to try to row across our track sufficiently to guide the dinghy into the Roscoff channel, in the hope that we might be able to pop into the harbour as we went past, or at least find a lee behind it.

Just as I started the lighthouse-dodging operation, I saw the bows of a vessel pointing at me from windward. Digging in my bag, I found a large yellow towel which we hastily lashed to an oar, and which Richard waved vigorously aloft, while I resumed rowing, trying to dodge being flogged in the face by the wet towel. The *langoustier*, for such it was, altered course away from us to keep to his channel, and we quite decided that he had not seen us. Then figures appeared on deck; the ship stopped, turned, and slowly took up station to windward of us; a rope was thrown, we were hauled alongside. The rolling of the ship made getting aboard relatively easy; you step on the rubbing strake as it rolls down, then you are catapulted over the bulwarks as she goes back. They gaffed our gear with an outsize boathook, then hauled up the dinghy as well.

After that life became somewhat more civilised. The crew took us down to the aft cabin, stripped us off, and delving into their own bags, found enough spare clothing to kit us out warm and dry. They brewed coffee and laced it with rum; they found some hard tack and butter, chocolate and fags; they did it all with great good humour; one can ask no more of any man.

We were not, as we thought, bound for Roscoff, but for Mogueriec, some five miles further west. *Le Rayon de Soleil* (she was the only sunshine we saw that day) was heading for home and Sunday dinner, and the tide being right, was taking the short cut inside Ile de Batz; otherwise . . .

On arrival at Mogueriec, we met our host for the first time; he had been at the helm hitherto. M Jean Baptiste Le Bihan is a great powerful jolly man, *patron-pêcheur*, a man of substance, and with a great heart. Initial difficulties over language soon became easier, as he has acquired some English from frequently marketing his catches in Cornish ports.

Our first visitor was the *douanier* who took one look and decided he was not interested in us. Then came a gentleman who introduced himself as of the French Navy. He was subsequently described in the local newspapers as *syndic des gens de mer à Roscoff* and *l'administrateur de l'inscription maritime de Morlaix*. We never did discover which hat this M Balcon was wearing that day, but he made the civilised suggestion that it would be more comfortable if he were to interview us with a glass in our hands, so we adjourned to the local cafe. Having satisfied him that *Quiver* was not a danger to shipping (he must have been Receiver of Wrecks as well), he undertook, after making his report to his own authorities, to notify the British Embassy in Paris; they in turn reported to the Foreign Office, who telephoned Richard's parents with the true story of what had happened, thus forestalling the inevitable inaccurate press reports.

Meanwhile, Mme Le Bihan had gathered up all our wet garments, plus our saturated baggage, shoved them into the boot of her car, and taken all home. There she rounded up some neighbours, and they spent the whole of Saturday afternoon and evening feeding it all through the washing machine, hosing out our bags, spreading out all our other bits and pieces to dry. Sunday she spent drying and ironing, so that by Sunday afternoon we had the whole lot back, ready to pack.

Now came the embarrassing bit. We had no passports, therefore my travellers' cheques were useless. We were rapidly eating our way through the few francs I had forearmed myself with at the local hotel. I could not get any more money till I had a passport; I could only get a passport in Paris; how to get the fare? I offered Baptiste (as our host is known to his friends, amongst whom I now count myself lucky to be numbered) some English money, knowing that he frequently visits British ports, but he would have none of it; we might well need that before we got home. He would buy our rail tickets; and he did just that at 6 o'clock on the Monday morning, after driving us 20 miles into Morlaix to save a taxi fare.

After sorting ourselves out in Paris, we duly obtained temporary passports; then, liberty at last, some money! An evening in Montmartre was indicated, and enjoyed.

We caught the night ferry back from Dunkerque to Dover, where, just to rub things in, the ship went aground while turning to back into her berth. We were rather glad to get home.

From the *Old Gaffers' Association Newsletter*

Lessons learned

Quiver, like two other shipwrecked vessels in this book, *Song* and *Northern Light*, was lost because of erroneous estimates of tidal currents. Such mistakes are much more likely to be made at night than during the day when, except in fog, there will be so much more visible evidence by which to assess drift or leeway.

Michael Millar talks about a clear sky with a brilliant moon, three quarters full, which helped. 'If only it had stayed there . . .' he says. Heavy cloud came up from the south and blotted everything out, leaving us with nothing but the two lighthouses.'

He was happy with the fix he obtained from Les Sept Iles light and the one on Les Roches Douvres, and altered *Quiver*'s course. But later he had a 'feeling' that they were being set to the south-east and altered course again. 'At about 0300, I was just contemplating resuming the compass course, when *Quiver*, with a resounding crash, stopped dead.'

He suggests three reasons. The first is that he had lost the $1\frac{1}{2}$ knot head tide which he should have had for another hour at least. He wonders whether it was masked by the reef into whose shadow they had sailed; 'there may even have been a counter-eddy'. At any rate they were $1\frac{1}{2}$ miles further on than he thought. The second reason 'may have been that I made my detour by eye on the lighthouse, rather than on compass courses – not very seamanlike.' The final reason is that at 3 o'clock in the morning, even though they both felt wide awake, 'one is not at one's brightest, we may have been taking careless bearings, plotting carelessly, or simply doing our sums wrong; we shall never know, as the deck log and chart went down with everything else. . .'

When they had to abandon *Quiver* in the middle of the night, Millar and his grandson were not well prepared, but then *Quiver* was only sailing between Guernsey and Brittany and they were no more than three or four miles offshore. But the importance of a well-prepared 'grab bag' or 'panic bag' is demonstrated.

The water was all in the tank, with a tiny galley pump and no container to hand. Fortunately, 'six long-life milk cartons conveniently floated out of their locker'. Into a second bag, Millar put all the ship's and personal papers. Two hours later he discovered it 'was the wrong second bag; all I saved was a lot of useless hardware.'

After deciding to abandon ship, Millar's immediate concern was to get out of *Quiver* and into the 9ft Nautisport dinghy, which, fortunately, had been stowed fully inflated upside down on the cabin top.

He also had to signal their distress. His main armament was some seven or eight hand flares. 'They all went off beautifully, and the display must have lasted at least four minutes; the only snag was that there was no audience.' The importance of keeping in hand a flare for 'a last chance' cannot be under-estimated. Flares are one of the many ways in which distress can be signalled, but they cannot always be relied upon, even when in date.

19 *Chartreuse* on the rocks

Yacht *Chartreuse* (31ft cold-moulded half-ton sloop)
Skipper Paul Newell
Bound from Cowes in a singlehanded race around the Isle of Wight
Date of loss June 26, 1993
Position The inside passage between the celebrated wreck of the *Varvassi* and the Needles.

The problem with sinking is that it has the tendency to ruin your day completely. It doesn't do much for the rest of the week either. You don't normally sink on your doorstep, so there is quite a lot of travelling to do and much to sort out: salvage, hauling-out, damage assessment, insurance forms, washing gear that has been salvaged, finding somewhere to store it away from sticky fingers (and the moment there is a wreck, sticky fingers are never far away). The list seems endless. And all the while you are still trying to come to terms with the awful truth that you sank your boat whilst trying to perform a manoeuvre that you have done many times before. That's what happened to me.

There is so much to learn in a very short space of time, and no textbooks to swot up on. The whole experience is new, horrible and most unwelcome.

The first mistake of the day was not to switch off the ignition after stopping the engine prior to what promised to be an exciting single-handed Round the Island Race. I settled down to a crisp beat with a flattened mainsail and No 3 genoa. The Needles were rounded at 0710. I didn't get any further. Mistake number two had just manifested itself with the biggest collision bang I have ever heard. The boat stopped. I didn't. I hit the companionway bulkhead, via the mainsheet track and runner winch, shoulder first. This is what comes from taking the inside passage between the celebrated wreck of the *Varvassi* and the Needles.

A loud rush of water behind me suggested that I should have seen whatever I had just hit, but it was Richard Burnett in *Albatross*, two boat lengths back, making an impressive U-turn, who saw that there appeared to be no gap. A cursory glance below was more than enough to tell me that water above the floorboards within 10 seconds meant swimming lessons in the near future. Sinking on the spot was not going to happen straightaway and I reckoned I had half an hour to save the situation.

A beach, preferably with sand and no tide, was needed. Scratchell's Bay was too rocky and Freshwater Bay too far. Alum Bay was not too far (at least in a homeward direction), had a sandy bottom and no tide. I had to tack the boat. I didn't know what I'd hit, but I hoped I didn't hit it on the way back.

The spinnaker pole was in the water, but I couldn't leave the helm as other competitors were turning the corner. I was asked if I was okay and shouted: 'NO, I'M SINKING!' and bore away round the inside of the Needles. The boat already felt heavy, but speed was still good at 6+ knots.

I grabbed a red rocket flare. Caps off. Operate pin. Pin comes away in hand. Useless. Grab another. Caps off. Rocket canister slides out of plastic casing and falls into cockpit. This is really useless. Grab red hand flare. Bet this doesn't work either! It did and it was hot. 'Hold at arm's length,' said the instructions. They were not kidding.

A small fishing boat arrived. I could see it was too small really to help, but might take some gear. They were not interested in saving equipment but told me to 'abandon ship'. I told them 'No chance!' A big fishing boat, *Diana C*, turned up, offering a big tow rope, which I gladly took and tied to the stemhead as boat speed was down to 4 knots and the point of the bow was now at water level. I was only halfway there and I wasn't going to get much further without outside help. The stern was now too far out of the water to steer and the mainsail was making the boat trip over herself by driving the bow down. I lowered the sail and tied it to the boom, and then secured the boom to stop it disappearing when the boat sank. This was now inevitable as the beach was still too far away and progress was getting slower.

I couldn't get the No. 3 down as the bow was 4ft under water. I went below and grabbed a bag of dry clothing. There was so much to save and no time to do it. I threw a bag into the cockpit and climbed out. It was a climb, too, as the boat now took a big surge forward in a downward direction and I could see water at the windows.

I grabbed my car keys and wallet from the companionway locker on the way out and put them in my zip-up jacket pocket. A second big fishing boat turned up full of day-trip fishermen. I passed them a bag of clothes and a bag of food and drink. I tied the tiller off amidships, fitted the washboard and pulled the hatch shut. I coiled down a few ropes that had got their tails overboard, picked up the self-steering gear, climbed over the pushpit and walked along what was now a horizontal transom then climbed on board the fishing boat just as water started to flood the cockpit.

I was transferred almost immediately to the Yarmouth Lifeboat, where I had a first class view of *Chartreuse* as her transom disappeared under water. And that was that.

I've written it fast because it happened fast, or at least that was the way it seemed to me. The whole thing took just over 35 minutes. I know that some boats go down in seconds and others take forever, but those 35 minutes for me went all too fast. I couldn't get enough done.

Some boats go down with no one else around, which must be horrendous, but I was lucky to have boats around me at the time and they were able to help me. I am very grateful for that, but the feeling of helplessness was almost too much to bear. I knew she was going to sink right from the start and nothing I could do was going to stop her, and yet I worked harder to try and save her than I have ever worked before. I hadn't managed to get right in to the beach but 200 yards off wasn't too bad. The water was only 12ft deep and the bottom was mostly sand. This was my worst nightmare come true.

From the lifeboat, I was transferred to *Diana C. Chartreuse*'s transom was just under the water so we manoeuvred alongside where I was able to re-board, taking one of his anchor lines, and making it fast to a stern cleat. The anchor was then streamed offshore for about 300ft to stop *Chartreuse* from moving about too much, as the wind had got up to a good force 5. The No. 3 was still set and showing. The boat had settled on the bottom in an almost upright position, although with only the bow and keel actually on the bottom. It was then decided to go to Yarmouth to try and get some help in the form of Bembridge salvage expert Martin Woodward. The tide was too low to get out of Bembridge that evening and he was already committed to another job, so he left first thing on Sunday morning.

In Alum Bay next morning, strops were put round *Chartreuse*, air bags attached and inflated and at 0910 she was on the surface once again. The tow to Yarmouth was slow, which allowed two big pumps to be put aboard. There was a large hole in the bow below the waterline. It was too big for the pumps to keep up with the flood of water. So we found the cockpit cover as it passed us in the swirling water below decks and fitted it over the hole from the outside, tying it tight to the stemhead and stanchion bases. This made it an easier job for the pumps to win the battle. As the water went down, I disconnected the electronics and passed them to Martin to put into fresh water straightaway with the hope of salvaging them, but it soon became obvious this was a waste of time, as mistake number one reared its head. With power going through them at the time of sinking all the circuits had burnt out; this included all of the engine electrics as well. The terminals and most of the wiring just fell to bits as soon as they were touched. The insides of all of the 'magic boxes' were in a similar state.

By the time we reached Yarmouth, the boat could be kept afloat as long as the pumps were kept going. The tide by this stage was on the flood and the men at Harold Hayles's yard were put on standby to get her out at the top of the tide. Meanwhile, she was berthed alongside the Harbourmaster's office, where I started unloading sails, anchors, sheets, bunk boards, floorboards and anything else that had been washing about down below. They were taken home and rinsed with fresh water. The more gear that I took out, the more damage I found. The hole in the bow was caused by the boat nose-diving into the seabed all night, but at some stage she had heeled well over to port and had taken a severe bashing on her port side right back as far as amidships. This could be seen from the inside with planking burst inward between the stringers. An immense amount of sand that had come aboard through the bow hole was sucked out via the pumps and a rupture in the hog could be seen. The keel had been driven backwards and the aft end upwards had burst the hog and broken three of the six keel-bearing frames.

Chartreuse was fitted on to a cradle at Hayles and lifted out of the water. I could see the damage to the keel. The leading edge, about halfway up, had been the point of impact; as a result the steel casing had buckled to about 1ft back and the leading edge itself was off centre by about 1½in over a distance of 2ft. A rough guide as to how so much damage was caused by such a light boat is the pinpoint impact load formula of Mass x Velocity (squared). *Chartreuse* weighs about 2.75 tons. Therefore 2.75 tons x 7.25 knots = 19.94 x 19.94: 397 tons. I know that this is not a truly scientific way to work it out, but it does give a guide as to the sort of load that a boat has to put up with when grounding at speed. The insurance company declared *Chartreuse* a 'constructive total loss' and made a reduced offer if I wanted to keep the boat.

This was accepted, and not long after I towed the whole lot by road to A A Coombes's yard in Bembridge where restoration work began.

From *Yachting Monthly*, September 1995

Lessons learned

Don't go for the inside gap round the Needles as it is exceptionally difficult to judge the distance (as one yacht demonstrated in a later fully crewed Round the Island Race).

✐ Don't forget to switch off the engine ignition; if there's time, isolate the batteries by switching them off too.

✐ Try not to panic because you won't get anything done.

✐ The importance of a grab bag, even on short trips, was driven home graphically that day. If you have time before sinking, grab the following: car keys (there's a lot of travelling about to do when you finally get ashore); wallet (you can be sure you'll have to buy something ashore, even if it's only a bus fare to get to your car); dry clothing (if you've stayed calm so far, a degree of shock will set in and you will get cold quite fast); something to drink, because you'll be very dehydrated and that comes over you all of a sudden.

✐ I should have used the time before *Chartreuse* sank more constructively. The No. 3 genoa should have been taken down at the earliest opportunity. It would have meant a lot less damage to the topsides. I could have removed the electronic navigation boxes so I only had to buy the connecting wires and not the whole system. I'm glad that I tied the mainsail and boom down and tidied the boat up a bit, as they would have got in the way of the salvage team under water.

✐ I often 'play' with my boat –crash-tacking, heaving-to, sailing her backwards, making her turn the tightest possible corners under sail or power. As a result, some of the manoeuvres that I did on that fateful morning were automatic.

Paul Newell subsequently competed in the 1995 crewed Round the Island Race and was fifth overall and first in class. He sailed dinghies from childhood and joined Ratsey & Lapthorne as an apprentice sailmaker in 1971 and raced quarter-tonners, half-tonners and one-tonners. He competed in the 1977–78 Whitbread aboard *Condor.* In 1986 he started his own sail loft, Paul Newell Sails, in Bembridge and in1988 bought *Chartreuse III*, a cold-moulded half-tonner designed by Hugh Welbourne.

Part three:

Failure of gear or rigging

No bilge pump is as effective as a frightened man with a bucket.

20 Four pumps – and still she sank

Yacht *Mariah* (86ft staysail schooner)
Skipper Ed Clark
Crew Bruce Paulsen, Chip Williams, Beth Brodie, Jimmy Joner, Jay Linsay,
  Elisabeth Storm
Bound 'south from City Island', New York State, USA
Date of loss 26 October 1980
Position approximately 200 miles SE of Cape May, New Jersey

Mariah, an Alden-designed staysail schooner, was built in 1931, and her owner, Ed Clark, wanted her down south for the winter of 1980–81. They left City Island, New York, at 0100 on the morning of Thursday 23 October, having 'flushed out the bilges, using every pump on board – to see that each was functioning properly'. Bruce Paulsen relates the subsequent events:

The night was cold, but crystal clear. The huge clock at the Watchtower Building read 44°F at 0600; a beautiful day, with crisp Canadian air and north-west breezes. Both Bendix and NOAA predicted good weather with a slight trough developing over the middle Atlantic region which could produce some storm activity, but nothing serious. We were not worried since we would be well east of any trouble.

At 0900 we left Ambrose Tower to starboard and were joined by a family of sparrows. The wind was north-west at 15 knots as we broad-reached under full sail. Beth set our course at 140°M, which would take us out across the Gulf Stream. We had a beautiful day of sailing, but by evening clouds began to roll in, and the wind picked up. It was time to shorten sail, so

Jimmy and I furled the flying jib, while Ed and Chip double-reefed the main. This left us a bit under-powered but made for a manageable, balanced rig. After a chicken dinner and a brief sip of Jay's renowned homemade wine, we broke into watches.

Jay and I were on deck as the day came to an end. The clouds continued to build as we looked to the west. 'There'll be no sunset tonight,' I told Jay. By 1900 the wind began to veer and increase. At 2000 we dropped the main staysail. The wind, now 25 to 30 knots, swung around to the north-east. We had trouble holding course at 140° and headed down to 160°M. At 0400, we spotted a school of porpoises which lifted our spirits on a cold, grey night.

The wind increased as daylight approached, and continued to shift to the right; by 0600 it was straight out of the east at about 35 knots. The sunrise was a brilliant red; the sparrows had disappeared. Friday was cold and unpleasant, as the wind kicked up to 40 knots, and veered south of east. *Mariah* was working hard and began to leak, which was hardly unusual for a boat of her age. By afternoon our small seven gallons-per-minute electric pump had trouble keeping up.

Mariah had four bilge pumps aboard; besides the electric pump there was a Whale Gusher on the deck. Its capacity, however, was only about a quarter of a gallon per stroke. Then, there were our big guns: a 50-plus gallons-per-minute Jabsco that ran off the Lehman diesel, and a 75-plus gallons-per-minute firehose/bilge pump that ran off its own one-cylinder diesel mounted in the lazarette. Either could handle any kind of problem. Both had functioned properly ashore. I had said with pride to visitors, 'If we have anything aboard *Mariah*, it's bilge pumps.'

By 1900 Friday we were leaking badly enough to engage the Jabsco. Ed turned over the diesel, and flipped the pump. It worked for a minute or two, but then grew hot and stopped pumping altogether. He took the pump apart and discovered the impeller had been completely destroyed. We inspected the intake for pieces of debris, but the fine screen was still intact. Confused but undaunted, we scraped out all the remnants of the old neoprene impeller, making sure to leave the cylinder perfectly clean. Ed then installed a spare impeller and reassembled the unit. By the time the pump was back together, however, the water in the bilge was over the level of the belt that drives the pump, causing it to slip around its pulley whenever the pump was engaged. Before we could operate the pump, the water level had to be reduced. We then began the gruelling process of bucket-passing which was to last for the next 30 hours.

Beth, Jay and I bailed for about half an hour before the water level was low enough to try the pump again. Ed cleaned the belt with degreaser and once again cranked over the diesel. As before, it functioned for a minute or so before growing hot and stopping completely. Jimmy began pumping the deck pump, but its small capacity made it relatively useless. The rest of us kept bailing with the buckets.

Still not overly worried, we had yet to engage the automatic-priming, one-cylinder diesel, our USCG-approved monster pump. However, once turned on, it would not prime, perhaps because of the 10-foot waves. Jay, who knew pumps, assisted Ed, but after repeated attempts, it still would not hold a prime. By 2400 the decision was made to head for New Jersey and safety. We could still keep up with the incoming water, but we had no pumps. We were 300 or more miles from Bermuda with the wind south-east at 40 knots and increasing. Beating and bailing for three or four days did not seem particularly inviting. Cape May, however, was about 200 miles to the north-west. We could perhaps pick up some gas-driven pumps there and then continue. At 0100, Saturday, we gybed and began to run with the seas at 290°M. We kept bailing.

The wind increased to 50 knots, and squalls were frequent through the night. Seas grew to 20 feet or better, leaving both Jimmy and Elisabeth incapacitated by seasickness. Bailing was constant and unbearable, thanks to a break in the main fuel line leaking diesel into the bilge. There was no time for rest, and daybreak brought no relief.

By 0600 the water was a foot over the floorboards. Something had sprung, and it was getting difficult to keep up. At this point, the first of a long series of Maydays was sent, and the tanker *Navios Crusader* relayed our message to the Cape May Coast Guard. At 0830 the Coast Guard informed us that an aircraft was on the way to drop a 140 gallons-per-minute bilge pump. The news gave the whole crew an emotional lift – the cavalry was coming over the hill. At 1030, Beth, manning the radio, told us that an aircraft was near.

We expected a helicopter, but a huge C-130 transport plane appeared instead. Slightly taken aback, we hoped they were good at high-speed air drops. Our only sail was the double-reefed main staysail, which gave just enough steerage to manoeuvre in the mounting seas. I tried to keep *Mariah* heading 300°; the plane would make its final approach on the reciprocal course. After several practice runs, the pilot approached with amazing speed; we watched anxiously for the drop, but nothing happened. Then Ed spotted a bright orange parachute about 200 yards behind us, to weather. Recovery was impossible, since we could not head upwind. The C-130 headed back to Elizabeth City, NC, for more pumps and would not return for four hours. For the first time, we realized we were in danger of losing the schooner and possibly our lives.

Shortly, the Coast Guard informed us they had despatched the 210ft cutter *Alert* to our position. The 30ft seas, however, were keeping her under

10 knots, and she was over 100 miles – 10 hours – away. At noon, two of the main staysail seams blew out, and within minutes the sail was in ribbons. Now running under bare poles, we were pushed by waves as big as houses. Steering was difficult and tiring as the waves continued to mount, yet it provided the only relief from bailing.

At 1430, the C-130 reappeared. This time the orange drum containing the pump was dropped about 300 yards ahead of *Mariah*. I steered toward the drum, visible only every two or three waves, and finally it appeared on the crest of the wave ahead of us. Ed gaffed the parachute which immediately began to tear. The drum submerged as the pressure on it increased, and finally broke away. Strike two.

Another pump was dropped well ahead of us, and once again I pointed *Mariah* toward it. The trail line was difficult to spot in the foamy sea, and once we saw and gaffed it, it was too late. There was no loop in the end of the line; it slipped off into the sea. Strike three.

At 1600 the C-130 departed, telling us an H-3 helicopter was on the way with more pumps, and that another C-130 would circle us until he arrived. *Alert* was getting closer, and the merchant vessel *Dorsetshire* was standing by. By now, however, we had bailed for about 20 hours, and the diesel fumes had formed a thick haze over the knee-deep water in the bilge. Diesel coated everything in the cabin, and the floorboards on the leeward side were floating. Exhaustion was setting in. We were losing ground quickly.

The radio chattered again; it was the Coast Guard telling us that the helicopter had been delayed and would not arrive until 2200, four hours away, and we received a message from *Alert* that due to our rapid forward progress, even under bare poles, she would rendezvous with us around the same time. Perhaps our long-awaited pump would finally make it. Meanwhile, we kept working. Ed stopped to rest for a while, knowing that one of us would need to be fresh when the pumps arrived. With Beth on the radio and Jimmy doubled over with pain, that left three of us to bail and steer. Seasickness could not hold us back; Jay vomited into the buckets as he dumped them overboard.

At 2145 the helicopter arrived. The winds were up over hurricane force with waves well over 40 feet. I brought the boat up as close to the wind as possible, about abeam to the seas. The water in the saloon was chest high, and the heavy maple floorboards began to slam around, tearing apart the interior. The lee rail was down, with only three feet of freeboard on the cabin port and side. In the pitch dark, the helicopter had trouble manoeuvring around our 86ft mainmast, and after half an hour backed off and radioed that instead of lowering a pump, he would begin evacuation procedures. We still wanted a pump more than anything else, but were obviously in no position to disagree.

We were told to inflate our Avon liferaft, which Chip had readied, to place two people at a time into it, and trail it aft. Elisabeth, not a sailor, was overcome with fright, so the captain decided to put her and Jimmy into the liferaft first. Ed streamed the raft out behind *Mariah*. The helicopter's huge floodlights illuminated the monstrous waves as the basket bounced across the water and the liferaft. Jimmy strained to grab the basket, but half an hour passed before he got a good grip and helped Elisabeth into it. Overall, it took nearly 40 minutes for both to reach the helicopter.

As Ed hauled the raft back into the boat, a gust of wind flipped it over, partially filling it with water. He brought the raft upright and alongside, however, and Jay and Beth prepared to jump in. Before they could do so, a huge wave broke over the boat, knocking both of them over the lifelines. Ed hung onto Beth and hauled her aboard, and, Jay, thanks to his safety harness, was brought back aboard. Once the wave had passed, we saw that the top ring of the liferaft had deflated. Beth, back on the radio, told the pilot of the fate of our liferaft. We were then told that the operation had to be abandoned, but that the cutter *Alert* was standing by to complete the evacuation.

Our batteries were long since dead, and the wave had drowned the generator that had been running a single light bulb that was our sole means of being identified. As *Alert* steamed straight for us in the darkness, Ed searched the wreckage below for *Mariah*'s flaregun. He found it and fired when the cutter was about 150 yards away.

Below, I grabbed my wallet and car keys. The cabin was a mess. No one had bailed since the helicopter arrived, and all the floorboards were floating; they had destroyed most of the interior. Diesel fumes filled the air; I got out as quickly as I could.

Meanwhile, *Alert* launched a 19ft, hard-keel Avon inflatable with two frogmen aboard. They brought it quickly alongside *Mariah*, and we all jumped on as quickly as possible – Jay head first. *Mariah* had only three feet of freeboard on the windward side, and the leeward rail was awash. We hoped she could make it through the night.

By 0030 we were safe and sound aboard *Alert*. The captain, Commander Armand Chapeau, informed us that we were to stand by the schooner through the night, and perhaps, if she was still afloat at daylight, a pump could be taken aboard and we could take her in tow. But around 0130 *Alert* received orders to hurry to another distress call to the south-east. *Reliance*, another 210ft cutter, would proceed to *Mariah*'s last known position to search and perhaps take her in tow. But 24 hours of searching proved futile. *Mariah* surely went down during the night.

The schooner was lost; but we still didn't know how lucky we were. Later we learned that the storm of the weekend of 25 October claimed many boats and many lives; it was vicious, unpredicted, and caused extensive damage and losses all along the north-east seaboard. *Mariah* was not her only victim; another was the 33ft *Demon of Hamble* with her owner, Angus Primrose, the noted English ocean racer and designer of *Gypsy Moth* in which Sir Francis Chichester had sailed alone around the world.

Every time a storm of such intensity strikes, all of us on the water learn many lessons, most of them the hard way. Questions are raised about sailors and their equipment. Why is it, then, that a main chapter in almost every sailing disaster story is pump failure?

From *Yachting*, August 1981

Lessons learned

No doubt Bruce Paulsen considered he had done his homework so far as the pumps aboard *Mariah* were concerned, since before setting out to sail her south from City Island, New York, he had 'flushed out the bilges to see that each was functioning properly'. *Mariah* had no less than four pumps on board. 'Besides the 7 gallons-per-minute electric pump there was a Whale Gusher on the deck ... Then there were our big guns: a 50-plus gallons-per-minute Jabsco that ran off the diesel engine and a 75-plus gallons-per minute firehose/bilge pump that ran off its own one-cylinder diesel mounted in the lazarette.'

Despite all this, the 50-year-old *Mariah* was soon in difficulties, because when she began to work and leak in a 40-knot wind, the 7 gallons-per minute electric pump could not keep up, and when they 'turned to the engine-driven Jabsco, it worked for a minute or two, but then grew hot and stopped pumping altogether'. It was discovered that the impeller had been completely destroyed. By the time they had installed a spare impeller and reassembled the unit, the water in the bilge was over the level of the belt that drives the pump, causing it to slip around its pulley whenever the pump was engaged. To reduce the water level so they could operate the Jabsco pump, they began to bail with buckets – and continued to do so for the next 30 hours. But the Jabsco impeller once more burnt out. The monster firehose pump was supposed to be self-priming, but 'perhaps because of the 10ft waves', it never did, so they kept on bailing.

All of which lends support to the saying that 'no bilge pump is as effective as a frightened man with a bucket.'

It has been estimated that a two- or three-man team working flat-out can take some 200 gallons an hour out of a boat by bailing with buckets. This rate of transfer could not be matched by a relay of people working a single pump. Des Sleightholme, former editor of *Yachting Monthly*, once carried out a 'live' experiment by opening a 2½in skin fitting in a 24-footer, and found that she took in 40 gallons in 2½ minutes – just about matching the capacity of most large diaphragm pumps.

The planes attempted to drop pumps to them by parachute but they could not head upwind to the first. The second orange drum containing the pump appeared on the crest of the wave ahead but when they gaffed the parachute it immediately began to tear and the drum submerged and finally broke away. The third pump was dropped successfully well ahead of them but the trail line was difficult to spot in the foamy sea as there was no loop in the end of the line; it slipped off into the sea.

By the time the helicopter arrived, the winds were up over hurricane force with waves well over 40ft and the water in the saloon was chest high, with heavy maple floorboards slamming around, tearing apart the interior. The conditions even caused the top ring of their liferaft to deflate.

21 The wicked old *Martinet*

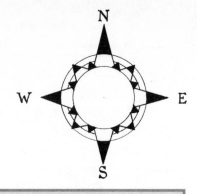

Vessel *Martinet* (99 tons ketch-rigged 'boomie' barge)
Skipper AW ('Bob') Roberts
Crew Jerry Thomason (mate), Freddie (third hand)
Bound from Swanscombe, Kent to Norwich, Norfolk
Date of loss February, 1941
Position in Hollesey Bay, off Aldeburgh, Suffolk

Many sailing barges were lost during World War II, most of them by hitting mines laid in the Thames Estuary; but one barge, the Martinet, *foundered in rough seas off Aldeburgh in the winter of 1941. Bob Roberts was skipper at the time, and they were bound for Norwich with a cargo of cement intended for use at one or other of the air-fields then being hurriedly built in East Anglia. The trouble really sprang from the fact that sailing craft were not, at that time, permitted to proceed after dark – which in February meant a short sailing day. Consequently, instead of reaching Yarmouth by midnight on the second day out, Roberts had to anchor the already leaking barge off Orfordness in rising wind and sea. Bob Roberts takes up the story:*

Having got the *Martinet* off to her anchor in the morning I hastened ashore to Gravesend, where I had to clear out of Customs and get my secret documents from the Admiralty office. The mate and third hand were left to batten down the hatches, scrub round and get the barge ready for sea.

We had a new third hand with us this time, a young barge-mate out of the river craft who was waiting to take a berth in a motor ship. He was a good seaman and did his job without having to be told what to do. That is a great thing about men in sail who are any good – they don't need telling when there is a job which obviously wants doing. They just go and do it.

We sailed out of Sea Reach at the crack of dawn and made a splendid run down-Swin and over the Spitway, coming abreast of the Naze in the late afternoon. By this time our lovely west wind had all but disappeared and in its place came a doubtful breeze from further south. There were threatening clouds driving over us and the mate and I discussed the advisability of going into Harwich for the night.

The *Redoubtable*, a big Mistley-owned barge – one of the finest wooden sailing vessels on the coast – went scooting over the Stone Banks under our lee and I had a good mind to follow her. But the tides were such that we should not be able to get out of harbour in the early morning and therefore should fail to make Yarmouth before the next night.

After we had weighed up all the possibilities, I let the *Martinet* run on down to Hollesley Bay and anchored under the highest part of the Whiting Sand. That was about five o'clock. I did not like the way the wind was freshening, but it was just one of those chances forced upon us by the wartime anchor-at-night regulation. We could have been in Yarmouth by midnight under pre-war conditions.

I was somewhat alarmed when we came to pump her out before going below for our evening meal. There was a lot of water in her, much more than I had expected. But we sucked her out and then fell-to round the cabin table. While we thus gorged upon the mighty mound of hash the cook had prepared, the mate, who sat next to the bulkhead dividing the cabin from the hold, said that he thought he could hear a lot of water slopping about. We removed a piece of the bulkhead under the mate's bunk and looked into the well. The water was almost on the floor of the hold – and we had sucked the pumps only ten minutes before!

We left the meal half-eaten and hurried up on deck. We got both the big pumps aft working and the three of us settled down to regular spells, two pumping while one rested. After half an hour of this I went below to see how much was left in her. To my horror there was no difference – if anything, she had more water in her than when we had abandoned our meal and re-started pumping.

It was pitch dark now and there was not much hope of finding where the leak was, especially as the barge was deeply laden. I had a look round with a torch, but apart from an old leak in the counter (on which a shipwright had spent an entire day recently without making the slightest improvement) I could not find any place bad enough to warrant all this pumping.

There was only one thing left to do – pump all night and get her into some sort of harbour – anywhere – as soon as it was light. In these ominous times all the beaches were mined as a defence against the probable invader and it was not possible to save a vessel in distress by beaching her. She would only be blown to bits if not first sunk by a salvo from the shore batteries. And all the harbours were bolted and barred at night by defence booms and nets. So there was nothing to be done except try and keep her afloat with the pumps until daylight allowed us to make a move.

Eleven o'clock. The pumps were just about holding their own. Then the starboard one choked. Frantically we took it to pieces and lay flat on the deck, the seas breaking over us and washing through our clothes, to reach down the pipe in a desperate attempt to clear it. Each of us had a try in turn but the stoppage was down in the very bowels of the ship. In the end we had to resort to a small pump in the hope of our being able to stick to the ship until daybreak. I was becoming doubtful. In fact, it was not very pleasant blundering about below decks up to my knees in water and knowing that, being cement loaded, the ship might take a sudden plunge to her doom.

Each in turn went below and put his personal belongings into kit bags, finally bringing up a stock of hard biscuits, condensed milk, corned beef and the usual items that ship-wrecked mariners endeavour to have beside them. It was no good taking any chances. She might not last until morning.

She sank so low in the water that eventually the tops of the pumps were submerged. It was half-past two. We were wet through and the wind seemed very cold. We could feel sleet driving above the spray. Pumping was no longer of any use – or even possible.

A gloomy trio, we mustered aft under the lee of the wheelhouse. Our prospects were dark indeed. If we took to the lifeboat and lived through the breakers in the bay we were faced with the risk of landing on a steep shingle bank down which the pebbles and stones rushed at amazing speed with each recoiling wave. It was a bad place to try and beach a small boat. And even if we succeeded in getting ashore we should almost certainly be either shot by the soldiers on guard or blown to smithereens by a land mine.

For two hours we hung on to the side of the wheelhouse, cold, tired and hungry, wondering how long she would last. One more inspection below brought me to a decision. There was so much water in her that she might sink at any moment, though she might wallow in a half-sunken state for many hours, as wooden vessels often do.

We lit a rocket but it misfired, hit the mizzenmast and went straight down into the sea. We tried another and were more successful. It soared skywards in a graceful arc, leaving a trail of sparks behind it. Immediately afterwards we lit a flare so that if anyone on shore had seen our rocket they could then determine the position of our vessel by bearings. It was half-past four. I hoped that the coastguards at Orfordness would see our signals. At least we were advertising the fact that we were in trouble. I felt bound to do that as the lives of the crew depended on my action. Whatever risks I take myself, I was in no way entitled to gamble with other people's lives.

Our supply of signals was limited, so we waited 20 minutes before we again sent up a rocket and a flare. This we continued to do until about eight o'clock, when the dim streaks of dawn could be seen over the North Sea.

The *Martinet* was practically awash. Only her proud head and shapely counter were above sea level. I estimated, although I could not be certain, that since she had not already gone down she would last several hours more.

It was the third hand who first saw that our salvation was at hand. His keen young eyes spotted something bobbing up and down in the white capped seas to the eastward. It was the Aldeburgh lifeboat coming to our assistance.

Now that help was near I felt a grim reluctance to leave the ship. I imagined that the old devil in her was laughing at me. Apart from that, the *Martinet* had been my home for practically two years, and I had grown fond of the old vessel in spite of her bad reputation. And although I had decided that the time had come to abandon her, there lingered within me a dim spark of hope that perhaps she might be saved. Common sense told me that her days were about to end, but I could not bring myself to realise it. But there was no holding back now. The lifeboatmen were shouting to us to get ready to jump as they manoeuvred to bring their craft alongside.

It was not an easy matter for the coxswain to take us off the *Martinet*, half-submerged as she was, rolling heavily and with the seas breaking right over her. He brought his boat round in a wide sweep under our port quarter, but at that moment the barge took a wild sheer away from him and the gulf between us was too far to jump.

We hung on while the lifeboat motored down to leeward again and at the second attempt she rose on a sea and almost landed on our deck. As she crashed into our bulwarks Jerry and the third hand slung their kitbags into her and jumped. As she descended into the hollow of the sea I followed them and we all landed in a heap in her cockpit.

The coxswain had come alongside on the tideward side of the barge to make sure of getting us off and he had some difficulty in getting away from the stricken vessel. With three sickening jolts the lifeboat struck the *Martinet* and the seas descended mercilessly on both the rescuers and the rescued. At last the little boat's head was pushed clear and she plunged out to windward.

'Which of you be the captain?' shouted the burly, red-faced coxswain, shrouded in dripping yellow oilskins.

When he had identified me we had a brief conference on the fate of the *Martinet*.

'You 'adn't reckoned on tryin' to save 'er?' asked the coxswain with a forlorn hope of profitable salvage.

I looked over at the *Martinet* and shook my head. Her midship decks were no longer visible above water, even when she rose on a crest, and she had that unnatural, out-of-time motion which spells the doom of a vessel in distress.

'She won't last long now,' agreed the coxswain. 'She's too far gone. We'd better leave 'er and get you chaps ashore. Go t'hell if you don't look some'ut wet and cold. This 'ere sleet don't 'elp, neither. Where's that there bottle of rum, Horace? Open 'er up. Them biscuits, too.'

As we chugged northwards to Aldeburgh, running before the wind and careering giddily down the steep-sided seas, the crew told me their story.

The Coastguards at Orfordness had seen our rockets and had telephoned to Aldeburgh. The lifeboat crew were called from their beds at five o'clock in the morning and they hurried down to the beach. There was a heavy sea breaking onshore and there was no hope of getting the biggest lifeboat afloat because an enemy air attack had damaged the slipway the day before.

The only thing they could do was to try and haul off the little 'summer' boat, as they called her. This boat was designed for minor rescue operations in fine weather and was hardly fit to be launched in a winter's gale. But these Suffolk men are a hard lot, and although there is no harbour at Aldeburgh to shelter them from onshore winds, they have never failed to go out in answer to a call for help. Waist-deep in the icy water, with the blinding sleet driving almost horizontally, they struggled to get the little cockleshell afloat. Three times men and boat were flung back on to the shingle beach but at the fourth attempt they got her off and drove her out through the breakers.

They deserved that rum.

'Go steady with that bottle, me lads,' laughed the coxswain. 'Don't forget the shipwrecked mariners.'

By the time everyone had had his turn with the bottle it was empty. By a nice piece of judgement there was just enough left in the bottom for the last man, the entire operation taking not more than three or four minutes.

When we arrived off Aldeburgh beach the coxswain told me that there was a boom defence and minefield between us and the shore. He would not be able to beach his boat as he would in the ordinary way. She would have to be brought broadside to the breakers to get in through the narrow gap and round the inner shoal.

'You'll get a wet shirt when she hits,' he warned us.

As she struck the beach the seas broke right over our heads and the boat all but capsized. I found myself sprawling in the backwash and some soldiers ran down into the water and dragged me up. Jerry and the third hand were wading ashore, hauling their sodden kitbags after them.

Ten minutes later we were having a hot bath in a waterfront hotel. The people on shore had everything ready for us – dry clothes, hot food, hot whisky and cigarettes. They are accustomed to playing host to shipwrecked mariners in Aldeburgh.

After we had eaten I telephoned the Orfordness Coastguards and they told me that the *Martinet* was still visible, wallowing half-submerged in a heavy sea. The wind was of gale force and they did not think she would last much longer.

A few hours later she sank. That was the end of the wicked old *Martinet*, last of the 'boomie' barges.

From: AW Roberts, *Coasting Bargemaster*, 1949 Edward Arnold & Co

Lessons learned

The nightmare scenario of blocked bilge pumps is graphically described by Bob Roberts. When the starboard pump choked they 'frantically took it to pieces and lay flat on the deck, the seas breaking over us and washing through our clothes, to reach down the pipe in a desperate attempt to clear it. Each of us had a try in turn but the stoppage was down in the very bowels of the ship.' Many boats have sunk because the pumps got blocked by floating debris – sometimes it's labels washing off cans of food or charts and books turning to pulp.

When it came to firing distress flares there were also lessons to be learned. They lit a rocket but it misfired, hit the mizzenmast and went straight down into the sea. The next was more successful and soared skywards. Sensibly, immediately afterwards, they lit a flare so that if anyone on shore had seen their rocket they could determine the position of their vessel by bearings. And since the supply of signals was limited, they waited 20 minutes before again sending up a rocket and a flare. They continued to do this until dawn, when the lifeboat appeared. Conserving your flares for a second, or last, chance is a vital consideration in these circumstances.

22 The end of an OSTAR

Yacht *Livery Dole* (35ft trimaran)
Skipper Peter Phillips
Bound from Plymouth, England to Newport, Rhode Island, USA, in the 1980 Observer Singlehanded Transatlantic Race
Date of loss 28 June, 1980
Positio: 42° 20′ N 54° 10′ W (approximately 700 miles E of Newport)

Livery Dole *was one of the 88 starters in the 1980 OSTAR race, in which trimarans gained the first five places. But Peter Phillips, a police sergeant from Plymouth, was not so fortunate.* Livery Dole *was sponsored by a charity in aid of needy children, and she had been 21 days at sea.*

I have just over 700 miles to go to the finish. By 0500 the wind is up to about 35 knots and I have three reefs in the main and the No 2 jib. *Livery Dole* is not at her best. She is doing 6–7 knots but slamming and dipping the lee float well under the water. The weather float is another problem. The seas are so big that every now and again a wave hits the up float with alarming force.

Not much later, I have the fourth reef in the main and the storm jib, and I have got the speed down to 4–5 knots. I shall try and hold at that but as *LD* is such a lightweight trimaran I may have to run off under storm jib or heave-to for a spell. The seas are the biggest problem. I reckon they are 12 to 15ft with heavy breaking crests. It's about 0600 and I look up on deck. Not much different. I then hear a roar behind me and I look back to windward. There is a big wave, much bigger than the others, coming towards me with a vicious, already breaking top. It hits the windward float and throws it in the air. The tri is virtually standing on its starboard float with the mast along the surface of the water. I am convinced we are going right over and will capsize. The wave picks up the main hull and then moves upright but the down float goes on up and the windward float gets slammed back down on to the water to windward with an almighty crash. I hear a crack and to my utter surprise the whole front section of the windward (port) float has just snapped off and is gone. The wave crashes on through and we are nearly capsized again.

We are still afloat, but for how long? She is sailing on the good float but slamming so badly I ought to heave-to, but I cannot because the other float will fill and capsize us. The windward float and front crossbeam are taking a terrible bashing. The seas crash into the open end and put undue pressure on the crossbeam. The broken edge is right at the crossbeam and the bolts are beginning to tear out. If the remainder go, the float will come off and fracture at the rear beam by pressure alone. There is little doubt: I am in trouble.

I start to get things organized in case I have to leave the tri, but almost immediately there is a crack and part of the front crossbeam is broken off by another wave. I go on deck and cut the liferaft straps and pull it out ready to go if need be. The problem is that I cannot launch the raft at this speed, about six knots again, but I cannot reduce too much for fear of a capsize to windward by wave action. I tune my radio into 2182kHz, the distress frequency, ready for use. The front end of the port float is breaking away from the beam. I broadcast a Mayday and give my position several times. Fortunately my navigation is up to date and I reckon my position to be 42°20' North and 54°10' West. I get a part confirmation from St Lawrence Coastguard that they have got my message, but they want the name of the yacht and the nature of the trouble. I give it to them and repeat the position.

Suddenly the lee (down) float is pushed up by wave action. The open end of the windward float digs into the water and we stall. We begin to capsize to windward. I grab the emergency beacon from my bunk and jump up through the hatch. We are gradually going over to windward.

I throw the liferaft over the side and operate the 'panic' button on the Argos satellite transmitter. The tri is almost over. I climb up and jump over the side into the water near the liferaft, hanging on to the emergency beacon. The mast hits the water, momentarily stops, and then carries on going. Then it's upside down – completely inverted. The whole process has taken only seconds.

I grab the liferaft painter and pull it several times. It inflates right way up. I put the beacon inside and get in myself, leaving the liferaft painter still attached to *Livery Dole*, which is still floating, but low in the water. The damaged float has already torn itself off and is attached just by the bracing wires. I try several times to get into the tri through the safety hatch to get more food and water but the big seas break and wash me off. It is obvious that with these seas I am not going to succeed. I make my way back to the liferaft and get into it. I set the emergency beacon going and put it in the water on its line. The pulsating light is operating well and that makes me feel a whole heap better. If a search does get under way soon and my position is correct it will help them locate me. I close the canopy on the liferaft to conserve body heat as hypothermia and exposure are the real killers in situations like these.

I decide that I will stay in the liferaft attached to the tri for as long as is possible. If people are searching it will give them a bigger target to look for. She looks in a terrible state and I feel very sorry about what has happened and for all the people that have been involved in the project from beginning to end. I was doing well and it should have never ended like this.

I decide to wait until the weather moderates and then try to gain access yet again. I get most of the water out of the liferaft and curl up on the floor for a bit of wet and uncomfortable sleep. I wake up after maybe a couple of hours; I don't really know as I didn't even have time to pick up my watch from the chart table.

I look out and there is a problem. The starboard float has completely snapped off with most of the crossbeams and the main hull has gone deeper in the water by the escape hatch. The seas are no better but I am going to have another go at getting in before I am unable to reach it at all.

I pull myself in and climb back on the bits of crossbeam – there isn't much of them left – but try as I may I cannot get to the hatch, I just get washed off every time by the seas. I eventually get back into the liferaft somewhat exhausted by the effort.

About an hour later I hear an aircraft. I look outside and see a Search and Rescue plane flying straight for me. What luck, and so soon. He flies over the top and straight on. I watch for him to turn but he goes out of sight and I am puzzled. I wait for him to return but no such luck. He should return if he is homed on to the beam from the emergency beacon. The beacon is lying around the back of the liferaft so I pull it into sight. The flashing light is NOT working. No wonder the plane went on. I pull the beacon in, check the battery connections and everything. It looks okay but is not working. Just my bloody luck – my Mayday was received, the plane is there but he has no beacon to home in on. Visibility is not good and I doubt that he will see me from the air.

I take stock again. Without the beacon they will have difficulty in finding me and it will take a lot longer. I am going to have to last without the food and clothing, but I will stay attached to the tri for as long as is possible, to aid identification. *LD* is now lower in the water.

Later the visibility improves – I have no idea of the time but it is still light. The tri is very much lower in the water and the main hull is trying to roll over. I cannot risk staying attached any longer so I cast off and gradually drift away from it with the wind. I have never seen such a sorry looking mess, and yet to me it was a beautiful-looking craft. I gradually lose sight of it in the swell and I am pleased when I can no longer see it.

The weather has eased, as is always the way. The swell is still large and I cannot see much chance of being spotted, particularly from the surface, but I hope and get ready to spend a cold wet night in the raft. Funny thing, I haven't noticed the lack of food and water yet. I shut up the raft and try to sleep to conserve energy. I hear aircraft and look outside. There are two Search and Rescue planes flying in circles not far from me. They are about 50ft off the water and obviously conducting a visual search. I am elated. Their circles are coming closer to me all the time. As they reach me they pass over several times and show no signs of having spotted me. I can't let the chance go. I get three red flares ready and wait until one of the aircraft is flying straight at me. I light all three flares at once and stand up and wave at them. Nothing and then YES – something is dropped from the plane. It hits the water and goes off; a smoke marker. He has got me. I suddenly feel on top of the world. The plane approaches again, very low this time. I wave and can see the pilot wave back. It is a Canadian plane and I notice that the other is American. More smoke markers around me and I begin to feel secure and relieved. Even if I don't get picked up for a couple of days it doesn't matter. I can wait.

The American plane begins a long run in and makes a drop. As the items hit the water two dinghies inflate about 600ft apart and joined by a floating line. I am going downwind towards the centre of the rope. A great drop by the pilot. Packs are floating attached to the dinghies. They are obviously survival packs and I presume it means that there are no ships immediately to hand and I am in for a wait.

I decide to help things along and paddle my way towards the rope. I eventually reach it and pull myself along and secure my liferaft to one at the end of the line. I pull in the survival pack containing space blankets, water and sweets and begin to get myself sorted out for a stay. The plane still circles around replacing the smoke markers, and it is comforting to have him there.

Later I look up and see a ship approaching. This is great. I am not even going to have to spend a night in the raft. I can hardly believe my luck. As it comes closer I see that it is a container ship well loaded. It slows up and then comes forward until the bow protruder picks up the rope between the two rafts only feet away from me. Lovely positioning. This brings my raft alongside the starboard side of the ship. It isn't rough but in the liferaft I am moving up and down quite a bit. The scramble nets are in position near the stern and ropes along the side. I learnt later from the Captain that the ship's boats were crewed ready for use if needed. I catch hold of one of the ropes and begin to pull myself along the ship's side. The gangway is being lowered ahead of me and that looks like a very civilised way of going aboard. Someone is at the bottom of the gangway ready to help. I approach slowly because of the up and down movement. There are lots of people to help. The liferaft comes up, one step and I am on the gangway. The man at the bottom catches hold and pushes me past him, and in seconds I am on deck and it's all over.

From *Royal Naval Sailing Association Journal*, Autumn 1980

Lessons learned

On the subject of multihulls in heavy weather, the late Rob James, author of *Multihulls Offshore*, considered it is best to keep sailing as long as possible, 'as I am firmly of the belief that it is the correct thing to do, even to windward'; but he also added: 'The most likely event that may cause one to give up the effort, is damage.'

This is what seems to have happened to the *Livery Dole* on her way to Newport, Rhode Island. Peter Phillips reported 'doing 6–7 knots but slamming and dipping the lee float well under water. *LD*, as he says, was 'such a lightweight trimaran'. The weather float was another problem. 'The seas are so big that every now and again a wave hits the up float with alarming force.'

Having taken the fourth reef in the main, so that speed was reduced to 4–5 knots, a wave much bigger than the others, with a vicious, already breaking, top hit the windward float and threw it in the air. The tri was virtually standing on its starboard float with the mast along the surface of the water. Phillips was convinced the tri was going right over. He heard a crack, and to his utter surprise the whole front section of the windward (port) float snapped off and was gone.

It is worth noting that several accounts in this book blame extraordinarily large waves with breaking crests for their disasters. There are some waves which are of a size and shape such that there is no defensive tactic which would prevent them from rolling or severely damaging a yacht caught in their path.

Livery Dole had a safety hatch in her main hull, and after taking to his liferaft Peter Phillips tried to use the hatch to enter the cabin to get more food and water, but big seas washed him off. Abandoning ship in a hurry after the capsize, he only had time 'to throw the liferaft over the side and operate the panic button on the Argos satellite transmitter.' Fortunately he had already broadcast a Mayday on the 2182 kHz distress frequency, and this, together with the use of flares, resulted in his eventual rescue. He was lucky his Mayday got through, so that he was able to give an accurate position, since his EPIRB failed to work and he had no food or water in the liferaft.

Wisely, he decided to stay in the liferaft attached to the trimaran for as long as possible to give SAR a bigger target to look for. But when the tri was lower in the water and trying to roll over he could not risk staying attached any longer and cast off, drifting away with the wind. When two SAR aircraft were flying overhead, Phillips got three red flares ready and lit them all at once, standing up and waving them. Luck was with him, again, and it worked. Usually it is better to leave an interval of a few minutes.

23 The death of *Banba*

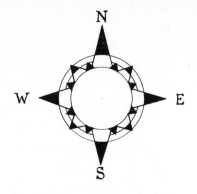

Yacht *Banba IV* (38ft gaff-rigged cutter)
Skipper Malcolm Robson
Crew Merrill Robson, Tex, Hank and John
Bound from Cape May, USA, to Sark, Channel Islands
Date of loss 6 July, 1969
Position approximately 1200 miles E of New York

This laconic account by Malcolm Robson, and the one that follows by his wife Merrill, tell how they lost first Banba IV *and then the* Maid of Malham.

*B*anba IV was a 20-ton cutter designed by Fred Shepherd and built by the Whitstable Shipping Company in 1911. Malcolm Robson and his wife Merrill had left Annapolis, Maryland, towards the end of June, after giving *Banba* a very thorough refit, including 'new rigging, all running gear replaced, sheets turned end-for-end, new bowsprit rigging, new parts for the vane steering, scrubbed and painted and sails strengthened. Fuelled up to the eyebrows, watered and victualled for five men for eight weeks, for the non-stop voyage to Guernsey, about 3500 miles.'

At midday our new crew arrived, three husky American yachting types between 17 and 24, and an hour later off we went, through the Chesapeake and Delaware Canal to Cape May, our jumping-off point.

Armed with a five-day forecast of Atlantic weather from the US Navy, it was unfair of the gods to send us east winds for three days. What could we do except battle on, southward? Runs of 20, 70, 50 miles a day weren't going to take us home at record speed! The next day it blew. Not the ocean winds we had had on the southern route westward, but good old North Sea wet'n-windy force 7-plus and 10ft swells into the bargain. Then it stopped. Yes, dead calm and poor old *Banba* stumbled down holes in the ocean, crashed into solid walls and skidded into mountains. And all with sails lowered and the engine using precious fuel just to keep her head to the seas. When eventually the winds came they were force 1, but from the north. On for an hour, force 8 from the west, then another day of dead calm. This continued for five days and we gloomily watched our fuel dwindling until in the end we stopped the motor and drifted.

It was about here that we knew that the bread was mouldy, so every loaf was unwrapped and dried in the fitful sun. Not serious though, as we had plenty of nosh aboard and water for 75 days. About here, too, the port forebrace parted with chafe and the yard fell on deck. Again not serious as later that day we put her on a reach and were able to send a man up the mast for repairs.

So far, so good; and the crew were in good heart. By 5 July we had nearly 900 miles on the log and only a quarter of the fuel used. 'Pity about the fuel,' I thought, as after the 23rd sail change, the squaresail tore from yardarm to yardarm. Heigh, ho, we have plenty of spare canvas aboard, though stitching would be impossible until the weather moderated a bit. It was reefed, too.

It was that evening that we first noticed that something not altogether right was happening to the mast. We could hardly set up the starboard runner lever, the backstay was too tight. Too tight? Now I know *Banba* would much prefer a docile cruise around Brittany than these antics in mid-Atlantic, but I thought of her wrought iron framing straps, the 4in by 5in frames, the oak planking and more. Besides, she wasn't making any water, except through the decks above our bunks, so I puffed away the cloud no bigger than a man's hand. But when, the following day, the mast must have been a foot out and it took two men to flip the runner lever over, I thought again (strumming a top E from the backstay) and decided that either the mast step had moved or the tongue at the foot had broken off. *Banba*'s mast, of solid pine, is 52ft long, and weighs half a ton and is held up with massive ⅝in shrouds, forestay and topmast shrouds, but the thought of this stick waving about in a force 9 breeze was a cloud a bit bigger than a man's hand.

So we hove-to under tiny staysail immediately and considered the situation. Newfoundland was 450 miles and against the prevailing winds, and on the starboard tack, dangerous for us. The Azores were some 1100 miles away and very far south of the sailing ship-recommended track, and against the prevailing wind for the last part. Bermuda was 700 miles upwind. Total fuel about 90 hours in calm, was say 270 miles at half speed. Total Trinidad rum: about three cases; say your prayers, lads, and away with prohibition!

We had seen several ships along this Atlantic highway, though by now we were a little to the south of the main steamship tracks, and I had a small secret thought that ... well. But what a decision! To carry on. IF the wind didn't exceed, say, force 7? We read the US pilot chart for this July and it showed us 1.5 gales above force 8. IF the swell-after-gale wasn't as bad as we had already had? IF we could hoist sail properly ... so many ifs. Or to abandon *Banba*. With the round trip almost complete? With our home for a year to go to the bottom? Six hundred charts, instruments, clothes, tools, nautical books, everything? What about this funking lark, too?

All day I turned over the problem, sitting mostly in the cockpit being rained upon, until about teatime I spied a large freighter a mile away to windward in the grey murk. The problem solved itself. I called the crew aft, read them chapter 23 of *Hornblower*, put on lifejackets and sent up a red flare.

'Passports and money only,' I said, starting the engine. For nobody would have a second chance once near the freighter, it would be 'Jump' and then would come the crashing of rigging, splintering of planks, etc.

With the exception that my trousers fell down at the critical moment, all went well: the ship made a lee and I brought *Banba* alongside the scrambling nets. The yacht alternately smashed into the vertical walls or rose and fell crazily ten feet or so. But we all made the deck and willing hands rolled us over her rails. I staggered to my feet and counted the heads, five, and looked back to see *Banba* rolling her decks under 50 yards away. Her engine was still running in astern gear and within a few minutes she was lost in the driving rain.

From *Ocean Cruising Club Journal*, 1970

Lessons learned

Perhaps the best lesson to be gleaned from the late Malcolm Robson is his ability to retain a sense of humour and perspective faced with so many unsumountable problems.

He seemed to have done everything he could. Fifty-eight year old *Banba IV* was given a thorough refit for the non-stop voyage to Guernsey of about 3500 miles. But the five-day forecast was a work of fiction. They had a bit of everything thrown at them: east winds for three days, a North Sea wet'n-windy force 7-plus, 10ft swells, dead calms, a force 8 from the west ... 'Poor old *Banba* stumbled down holes in the ocean, crashed into solid walls and skidded into mountains. And all with sails lowered and the engine using precious fuel just to keep her head to the seas.'

It was thought that either the step of *Banba*'s 52ft-long mast of solid pine had moved or the tongue at the foot had broken off. But still Robson described half a ton of mast waving about in a force 9 breeze as 'a cloud a bit bigger than a man's hand' and he hove-to under staysail to consider the situation.

With 'so many ifs' over whether to abandon *Banba*, Robson spent all day turning over the problem, until he spied a large freighter a mile away to windward and took the seamlike decision.

24 What went wrong?

Yacht *Maid of Malham* (48ft Bermudian sloop)
Skipper Malcolm Robson
Crew Merrill Robson
Bound from Galapagos Islands to Marquesas Islands
Date of loss 1973
Position 7° 48′ S, 110° 57′ W (About halfway between Panama and Tahiti)

Maid of Malham was designed by Laurent Giles as an ocean racer for John Illingworth and was built by King & Sons at Burnham on Crouch in 1936. She was very different from Banba IV, *but her fate was the same.*

L et me give you the facts. Halfway between Panama and Tahiti *Maid of Malham*'s rudder came adrift at the foot, and, though we could steer, the Pacific came in through the trunk, with only Merrill and me to pump it back again every hour or two. We bore away under a small jib only in the rumbustious SE trades for two days, and discussed survival with more than just academic interest. Our landfall in the Marquesas was 20 days away; the Galapagos Islands were 1000 miles back, upwind, upswell, upcurrent; the Pacific Routings showed shipping to be as good as non-existent. Thinking about the inflatable liferaft made morale, if possible, lower. At this point – over to Merrill:

I was baking bread. Malcolm was working out his morning sight. Finished, he went on deck, gave a roar: 'a ship'. I thought he was joking, there never was a ship. Then I looked at his face, near tears of relief. Hurrying below. 'The flares.' 'I've been dreaming about this, the million to one chance.' Bang. Bang. Two red Very lights soar up. 'Are they slowing down?' 'Can't tell.' 'What nationality?' 'Port something ... London.' 'Yes, they're turning. Thank God.' 'Down with the jib, ready with the sheet?' The engine starts but oh dear ... 'Don't forget the wheel's disconnected.' 'It's the tiller – you work the controls.'

'Get some stuff together, there may not be much time. Where's that sail bag?' 'In the booze locker stopping the rattle.' Now then. Passports, ship's papers, money in that box. Into the bag with it. Oh, there's that photo. Tear it off the bulkhead – the lovely ones of the children. Now the small clothes locker. Thank goodness I had put shore things in a plastic bag for dryness. 'Malcolm, put some shoes on. Have you got your specs?' 'I'll bring life-jackets.' In the flag locker. Put mine on then help Malcolm with his. Nearly alongside. Lovely big ship, grey and red. Rails lined with people. They've thrown down a warp. Round the anchor winch and make fast. What's that fellow with the walkie-talkie saying?

Near enough now. Malcolm bawling: 'We're making water. Can you take us two on board?' Talk. Shout. Crash against ship. 'What's your weight?' '15 tons.' 'We have crane to lift 25 tons.' 'Malcolm, he says they might lift us on board.' 'Our draught is 8ft and the mast 65ft. It's going to be a job, but we'll help.' Down snakes a pilot ladder. 'Can you let down a line for this bag?' Catch it now. No panic, it's over. Tie it firmly, proper hitch. Over the side, no matter if it trails in the water. 'Up the ladder, Merrill.' Slow now. Wait until the *Maid* is at her highest point. Then up, no hesitating. Nearly there. My leg hurts, must have scraped it. The top. Willing hands, jump down on solid ground. Steel. Malcolm next. 'Come this way to the Captain.' Walk. People. Grim faces. Cameras. 'Welcome on board!' 'Lord, how we feel for you.' 'Are you all right?' Four long flights to the bridge. Out of breath. Shake hands. Malcolm talking ... four, five officers. Captain and Chief Engineer having second thoughts of lifting operation. Crew might get bashed about. Must take out mast first. Operation scrubbed. Malcolm going down ladder for more salvage. Sack on heaving line. Water sloshing in cabin. There he is in cockpit, jolly good, sextant, chronometer. Wonder if he has remembered second sextant we bought from Canal pilot? What's he holding? Hand-bearing compass. Come up. Don't wait too long, they're casting off the *Maid*. Long warp trailing astern, that's bad, could get in ship's propeller. Our *Maid* won't leave, she hugs the ship. That crosstree is going to spike a porthole in a minute. Lord, how it's scraping. What a noise, scattering paint. Now both spreaders broken, poor *Maid*, what an awful end. Doesn't she look long and slim from so high up, never seen her from here before. There's the jibstay gone, still she won't leave the ship. Seems to be sucked in close, though the ship is going slowly ahead. Right under the stern, can't bear to look at her.

'No, we don't carry a transmitter, what's the point? The range is so small when you are on the oceans.' 'Our guardian angels certainly were hovering when this ship chose to be in the same spot of water at the same time.' I can't see our boat any more; oh yes I can. There she is rocking about, getting smaller. She's low in the water. Poor, lovely, *Maid of Malham*.

From *The Cruising Association Bulletin*, June 1973

Lessons learned

Halfway between Panama and Tahiti with *Maid of Malham*'s rudder broken at the foot and the Pacific coming in through the trunk, the Robsons were fortunate to find a rescue ship in an area where shipping was rare.

Looking back to 30 years ago we can appreciate how vastly different our sailing now is from the tough game it was then – satellite and radio communication, EPIRBs and many other facilities – have vastly improved our chances of survival in cases of emergency. But none of these things has altered the fact that the same difficult decisions have to be made today that skippers have faced since sailing began.

25 The tri that broke up

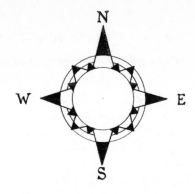

Yacht *Triventure* (29ft Islander trimaran)
Skipper John Nicholls
Crew Malcolm Beilby
Bound from Aldabra Is, Indian Ocean to Lourenço Marques, Mozambique
Date of loss 11 November, 1969
Position Mozambique Channel, Indian Ocean

John Nicholls has described the loss of his 50ft ketch Heart of Edna *on a New Guinea reef in 1979, in several accounts published in magazines, but it was his friend and crew member, Malcolm Beilby, who, ten years earlier, had told the story of Nicholls' previous loss of the trimaran* Triventure. *Nicholls built* Triventure *in a backyard in Sydney in the early 1960s, and for a year after launching her he sailed around Sydney Harbour and the nearby coasts. In 1968 he planned to sail the trimaran back to his native England.*

The first leg, 'with three friends on board, was a leisurely voyage up the resort-studded Queensland coast and across the Coral Sea to Port Moresby', where Nicholls met Beilby, who agreed to join Triventure *as crew as far as Durban.*

From Port Moresby the voyage continued via Timor, the Christmas and Cocos Islands, the Seychelles, Aldabra Island and then south into the Mozambique Channel, where their troubles really started:

The opening act of *Triventure*'s tragedy began on John's 29th birthday, Friday, 31 October. We'd hand-steered through a quiet night and in the morning a southerly breeze began to pick up. We set Angus up and went below to sleep.

Just before midday, *Triventure*'s motion and the wind noise awoke us to freshening conditions with black clouds and rain ahead. By 1400 the wind working against the current had whipped up a nasty, steep sea and we were slogging into it under reefed main and working jib.

At 2000 John had just relieved me on watch when we heard a loud, sharp crack. A torch search failed to reveal anything wrong in the main hull or the wing decks, and we tried to convince ourselves that it must have been caused by some small floating object that had been thrown against the hull. But ominous creakings became apparent and persistent and John took a torch into the port float to investigate. Watching from the cockpit it seemed an eternity before he emerged and when he did his words dropped the bottom from my stomach.

'Get the sails off her!' he shouted. 'The float's coming off!'

Together we had the canvas down in seconds and *Triventure* lay beam-on to the seas and rode them like a raft while John, with characteristic calm, prepared a cup of tea.

The plywood main spar in the forward edge of the wing deck, he explained, had broken inside the float where it butted against one of the major bulkheads. The bulkhead also was broken, and water resistance against the fin was flexing the float outwards away from the main hull. With the sails off, the stress would be minimised and he proposed G-clamping the broken frames to hold them overnight until repairs could be made in daylight.

We fished four clamps from the tool box and John took them into the float, while I packed a haversack with tinned fruit and prepared some water bottles in case we had to take to the raft.

John was amused by my dire interpretation of the situation and assured me that leaving the boat was the last thing in his mind. Then he climbed into his bunk and went to sleep. Lucky him. I lay awake for hours listening to the creaking of the fractured plywood.

In the morning the wind had dropped a little, but the sea was still steep. Seasickness repeatedly forced John from the cramped confines of the float, but he bolted strutting either side of the broken spar and bulkhead and we set about getting *Triventure* under way again. The outer shrouds, from the float gunwales to the masthead, were disconcertingly slack, a sign that the mainspar was no longer straight, but there was nothing we could do but take them up and hope for the best.

Under sail the severity of the damage was more obvious. With the port float to windward we could see the gunwale rising and falling as the float flexed in and out on the edge of the wing deck.

The first night after the break was spent hove-to under reefed main, but the next day, Sunday, the weather eased and on Monday we were becalmed again. We awoke after an afternoon sleep to find half a dozen large dorado and twice that number of sharks circling the boat. The dorado refused to take a hook and John spent a futile half-hour hanging over the side trying to shoot one with his speargun. When an evening breeze got the boat moving again the sharks lost interest, but the dorado stayed with us and through the night they cut phosphorescent streams through the dark water as they paced *Triventure* towards the African coast.

We decided to abandon plans of making Lourenço Marques and to head instead for Inhambane, a Portuguese port several hundred miles north and correspondingly closer to us. Inhambane is situated eight miles up a wide tidal estuary, which we reached late on Tuesday afternoon and anchored about six miles from the town. Not knowing what to expect, we sat on deck that night and speculated on the significance of the distant lights, and John, an unseamanly teetotaller, dreamt of Coca-Cola. In the morning we battled up to the town against a very strong tide and anchored about midday off a long wharf.

Remembering our difficulties in Portuguese Timor, we were surprised by the affability of the Inhambane harbour authorities who quickly cleared us to go ashore. The harbourmaster himself drove us to a timber yard and advised us where to get supplies.

Inhambane was quite a surprise. We expected a dusty, one-horse, one street town and found instead an extensive, substantial town with lawns, trees and sidewalk cafes along the main thoroughfare. My chief recollection, however, is of alarmingly high prices. In the five days we were there we spent more than $US60 on a minimum of timber, glue and a modest amount of supplies.

Through the days John laboured in the oven-like confines of the damaged float, reinforcing the broken bulkhead and mainspar and securing the inside planking of the float hull back to the stringers and frames from which it had pulled away.

I attended to minor jobs about the boat and got the stores and water aboard. In the evenings we'd go ashore and join the citizens at the cafes or stroll along the front. In this fashion the days slipped quickly by and though we did not realise it, the good weather was passing with them.

On Monday morning, 10 November, we went ashore early to clear our papers and get a weather report before sailing but the harbourmaster, who had agreed to translate the previous night's forecast for us, was not in his office. His deputy handled the paperwork but when the harbourmaster had not returned more than an hour later we decided to snatch what was left of the ebb tide and take a chance on the weather. As it was the tide turned before we were halfway down the estuary and as *Triventure* battled against it, it became sickeningly apparent that the float was still flexing badly.

We reached the open sea in the late afternoon and John entered the float but could see nothing working there. Evidently the main spar break had been the primary trouble but fixing it had done nothing for the weakness that had developed inside the wing deck itself between the float and the main hull. John accepted the fact with fatalistic resignation and decided to press on for Durban 400 miles south. But his plans, shaken by the first troubles, had now come crashing down around him. Ahead had been another year of cruising and the hope that successful completion of his voyage might help him win sponsorship for an attempt in the Singlehanded Transatlantic race. In Inhambane he thought his repairs had removed the threat to his boat and future but now he was faced with the certainty that *Triventure* could not be taken past Durban.

Meals at sea are usually looked forward to as highlights of the day but tea that night was a bleak affair.

Overnight our luck finally ran out. The wind picked up steadily from the south and the reaction on the current quickly resulted in a steep sea. By dawn we were hove-to in a 40-knot gale and it was worsening.

At 0700 the rending sound of tearing wood told us the end had come. We scrambled from our bunks and into the cockpit to see the port float, fortunately to windward, swinging up and down through almost 60° as though on a huge hinge along the edge of the wing deck.

John put up the jib, and I eased her away in an attempt to run west for the coast which we knew could not be far away; but it was apparent as we gathered forward speed that the float was tearing off even more quickly. In no time the arching stanchions crushed and flung the glassfibre dinghy overboard from its chocks on the wing deck, and as we put *Triventure* back on to the wind, the float came away completely. While I held the boat into the wind John cut the guardrail wires between the cockpit pushpit and the float stanchions. But he could make no impression on the port outer shroud, the only thing now keeping the float beside us. Tethered by that, the float plunged wildly up and down, smashing into the remains of the wing deck, and we feared it would push a stanchion through the main hull.

Luckily the chain plate pulled out first, and the float swirled away astern as I put the helm over to head for the coast again. Now all the strain was on the port inner shrouds, and as John ran forward to attend to the jib they gave way. The mast and sails came down on him and he disappeared beneath them.

One moment *Triventure* had been gathering speed and the next she was lifeless and wallowing with her spars and canvas half overboard.

For an instant I thought my companion was overboard too. I think I stood frozen until he freed himself from under the mainsail. Most other things of that morning I can remember with crystal clarity but actually seeing him emerge from the tangle on deck, I cannot. Certainly he was on his feet before I had moved from the cockpit.

Amazingly, he was unhurt. The mast had actually hit his back, throwing him to the deck, but the starboard stanchions and guardrails had checked its fall and prevented it from pinning and crushing him.

Now things were right out of our hands. Together we attempted to drag the mast back on board, calculating that its weight lashed down on the starboard float top would hold the float down and prevent the boat from flipping over to port on the backs of the waves. But in the pitching seas the mast's weight was too much for us. We could not get it fully on board, and instead lashed it as best as possible diagonally over the cabin top with the end hanging over the starboard side.

Below, the cabin was a shambles and every violent lurch made it worse. The wind was already easing and few of the waves were now breaking, but every so often a white top would slam into the port beam and push *Triventure* violently to starboard. Then she would lurch alarmingly to port as the crest passed beneath.

John was thinking as clearly as ever though when he suggested breakfast and, on the understanding that he wouldn't be too demanding, I put the kettle on and buttered some bread. I was passing him his second slice when he looked around the crushed weathershield and spotted *Slavisa Vajner* looming past not 400 yards away.

Breakfast was forgotten as we waved from the cockpit but it seemed the tanker had not seen us as she steamed majestically past. The first flare was blown into the water, the second was a dud and John was preparing the third when we saw the ship turning slowly to starboard. Back she came, this time so far upwind that only her superstructure was visible. As she went by, two smaller ships came into sight and away to the west the coast was visible.

John considered taking a gamble on being washed ashore, but we decided against it when we found the radio, with its aerial down, could not contact the tanker which was obviously making rescue preparations. The 70,000-ton ship was manoeuvring to be directly upwind of us when she lost forward motion. The 40 minutes that preceded our pick-up was necessary to switch the single big diesel engine from the crude oil used at sea to the fuel oil used in manoeuvring.

A couple of hundred yards away two rope ladders dropped down her towering side, and as we bumped alongside down came throwing lines and a hawser. John made it fast, then followed me up the ladder clutching his typewriter and precious *Times Atlas* under one arm. Then, barefooted on the slowly rolling steel deck, we found ourselves skating helplessly to either side as we attempted to follow a crewman to the bridge where Captain Uros Lombardic was waiting. In good English he offered to hoist *Triventure* on to his deck but explained 15 minutes would be needed before auxiliary steam could be raised to power the winches. John, considering the risk to crewmen, decided against it. Instead, he asked for time to go back aboard and get off what he could. The Captain agreed, and we returned to the rail where John donned a safety harness and went down the ladder.

I took pictures from the rail, then followed him down. He was at work in the cabin when I reached the deck and noticed the float bow cracking under the pounding against the steel plates alongside.

'Hurry it up! She's breaking up!' I yelled in alarm, and panicked us both. We grabbed the bare essentials, bagged and sent them up on the heaving lines, and cast *Triventure* off.

Then, as the tanker slowly gathered way, we paced *Triventure* along its deck and she fell astern looking like a crippled seabird exhausted and helpless on the water.

'I can always build another,' said John as we stood at the rail watching and filming until his yacht was lost to sight among the swells.'

From *Yachting Monthly*, July 1970

Lessons learned

As Rob James pointed out in his book *Multihulls Offshore*, written just before his death, multihulls gained a bad reputation, in the 1960s in particular, because a lot of amateur-designed and amateur-built craft foundered, causing unwanted and unwarranted adverse publicity for multihulls in general.

Nicholls built his *Triventure* in a backyard in Sydney in the early 1960s and planned to sail her home to England. When the plywood main spar in the forward edge of the wing deck broken inside the float, together with a bulkhead, Nicholls tried G-clamping the broken frames to hold them overnight until repairs could be made in daylight. Further repairs were made ashore, but they left without a forecast – 'to snatch what was left of the ebb tide and take a chance on the weather.' As it happened, the tide turned before they were halfway down the estuary and, as *Triventure* battled the tide, it became apparent that the float was still flexing badly. The decision to press on for Durban, 400 miles south, proved unwise. Overnight, their luck ran out. The wind picked up steadily from the south and the current resulted in a steep sea. By dawn they were hove-to in a 40-knot gale listening to the rending sound of tearing wood which told them the end had come.

Part four:

Failure of ground tackle or mooring lines

Bob Robert's 27ft gaff smack snapped her anchor chain on the Pacific island of Cocos.

26 A gallant Dutchman

Yacht *Maaslust* (45ft yawl-rigged boeier)
Skipper John P Wells
Crew Margaret Wells, Frank Philips, Freda Philips; children on board: Peter
  Wells (22 months), Nichola Philips (12 years)
Bound from Deauville, Normandy, to Langstone Harbour, Hampshire
Date of loss 29 July, 1956
Position off Selsey Bill

This account of the loss of Maaslust, *one of the Dunkirk Little Ships, is by Margaret Wells, whose 22-month-old son Peter was on board at the time.* Maaslust, *a boeier, was built of steel in Holland in 1923. Having left her mooring in Langstone Harbour on 20 July, 1956, she made an uneventful night passage to Cherbourg. Visits to St Vaast, Isigny and Ouistreham followed, and by the end of the week she was in Deauville:*

It is very difficult for me to write of preceding events when my mind's eye can see nothing but the picture of a gallant Dutchman, *Maaslust*, abandoned to fight a losing battle against fantastic seas; but this is to be an account of the happiness she gave us during her last weeks and a requiem for her brave spirit.

Neither John nor I had been very keen on the idea of Deauville and Trouville, knowing that all 'the best people' go there and feeling that it would not be our 'cup of tea' at all. However, we were favourably impressed and unhappily allowed ourselves to be talked out of our plan to make Fécamp on Saturday and to return to Shoreham on Sunday. Had we not succumbed to the fleshpots, how different would be the ending of this story!

However, it must be admitted that we thoroughly enjoyed ourselves, meeting by chance old friends from Le Havre and being hospitably entertained by them and by the Monks. We visited the casino, where we gained entrance to the Inner Room without even our passports. We basked and bathed to the music of the orchestra at the swimming pool, we shopped in the market and bought presents in the sloping streets. On the first evening I had surpassed myself by producing a dish of *moules* which were voted nearly as good as those in Cherbourg.

Having been lured to remain in Deauville, neither John nor I was anxious to move, and so we did not entirely regret the falling barometer, suspecting that our departure would be delayed by weather conditions. However, by Friday the glass had steadied, the thundery atmosphere had passed and we decided that, subject to a satisfactory weather report, we would set sail for England on Saturday afternoon. On Friday evening John radioed Niton, requesting a report from Dunstable for 1100 next day, together with a long-range forecast for the Channel area. The message came through at 0900: southerly wind, force 1–2 veering westerly, and increasing to 4–6 on Sunday evening. This obviously gave us no excuse to tarry, and Saturday morning was spent on a provisioning orgy in the market.

We had arranged to refuel at 1400, and were more than annoyed to find the fuelling wharf abandoned and no one at all interested in telling us where to find the attendant. It was here that a factor arose that was for us to have fateful consequences. The skipper believed in having ample reserves of fuel at all times, and this rule will never again be relaxed. But time was passing and, having waited for the attendant for over an hour, there was no immediate prospect of receiving our expected replenishment. We had on board fuel for four to six hours' running in case the wind failed. So, impatient to be on our way, we cast off from the wharf and made sail. But had it not been for intransigence at the fuel depot we should, no doubt, have brought the ship safely to port at the end of our journey.

We eventually left Deauville-Trouville at 1500 on 28 July, immediately meeting a lumpy sea. The weather was fine and the wind free, but the sea, meeting *Maaslust*'s plum bows, knocked her way off. John had to be talked out of a farewell visit to Le Havre. We blamed our late visit to the casino the previous night for our unwonted lack of enthusiasm for the homeward journey, and turned our eyes resolutely from the coast of France – more's the pity.

Being a great believer in the nourishment of the inner man, I made a gargantuan stew on the way out and Freda was the only one who did not partake to capacity. She, perhaps wisely, preferred Dramamine. I took the first watch from 2100 to 2300 and did not enjoy it. It rained, and the seas made the old girl extremely heavy on the wheel – one moment's lapse of

concentration and she would do her best to gybe. The breeze was not excessive, however, and there was nothing to indicate that we should turn back.
We had a little trouble with the diesel's water pump, and the man off watch
had to keep an eye on the gauge in case the filter clogged again – we motor-
sailed to help her through the waves. At 0100 on Sunday 29 July, we took
the staysail off her because it was doing no good and at 0400 the first reef
was taken in. From then on conditions deteriorated rapidly. The increasing
SW gale brought squall after squall and the seas rose higher. We had long
abandoned the idea of making Shoreham, since the entrance is a nasty one
in any weather, so we headed for the lee of Bembridge Ledge. It was soon
necessary to take in the second reef, and she still made seven knots, with
seas 12–14ft high to surmount. We watched the two 12ft dinghies with
anxiety as comber after comber crashed down upon them, but their grip-
ings held them firmly against the davits. Twice seas filled the mainsail and
Maaslust lay right over, but up she came again like the gallant fighter she
was. The scene below decks was indescribable: the stove jumped its gimbals,
the cutlery broke out of its locker, crashing to the ground with devastating
noise; the saloon table lifted itself bodily, abandoned its weights and came
to rest, none too gently, upon my recumbent form; the combined radio and
television set took charge; in fact everything that was not screwed or bolted down became a potential menace.

Small Peter slept peacefully enough until the vessel first lay over, when
he became a little frightened and, once awake, very seasick. He needed a
prolonged cuddle to calm him but eventually resigned himself to the dou-
ble-cabin berth with Freda and Nicky, where the three of them shared their
misery with mute stoicism. Poor Freda, who feels sick at the suggestion of
a ripple on the water, was heroic, for when the whole mattress rose up and
landed half on the floor, she wedged herself against the bulkhead to hold
the children in. It was indeed hellish down there, but, even so, those below
had little idea of the seriousness of the situation with which we were faced.

After settling Peter and stowing and wedging all that I could in the
saloon, and having parted company with the stew, I went up into the wheelhouse to survey the scene. One has read of the icy hand which grips one's
vitals in moments of dread, but although I have had several hazardous
occasions at sea I had never felt it before. The sight of the waves, 30ft from
base to crest, green-grey and streaked with spume and sand, was for the first
moment truly petrifying. Later there was no room for fear, although one
accepted the fact that survival was unlikely. I remember a feeling of thank-
fulness that the three of us would be going together, regret that Peter had
seen so little of life, sorrow for our parents, and regret about our dogs and
our lovely home, but no fear of the end. Perhaps our sensibilities were
numbed by the physical battle in which we were involved, for, discussing

it later, we found that we had all reacted in the same way.

By 0900 it was evident that our hopes of finding a lee under the Isle of Wight were groundless; in fact we were now in a far worse situation, for the seas were steeper and closer together. Before we reached the forts the tide turned to the eastward against us and, despite all that Frank could do at the wheel, we had soon driven past the Nab towards the lee shore of Hayling. It was impossible to keep the vessel head to the seas, for they came so rapidly that she could only take every third one, the others breaking over her with 6ft of solid water upon the decks. She could not free herself of the weight of the first before the second was upon her, and the side decks were perpetually awash, but still she rose. The backlash of the wheel was so great that Frank refractured an old wrist injury (we knew nothing of this until later) and it was physically impossible to stand on deck against either the wind or the sea. I doubt that the three of us would have survived had it not been for the high bulwarks and stout handrail, for in such weather lifelines were quite ineffective. Near the Nab the parrels of the double-reefed main-sail began to go, and a rent started in the leach, so we decided to take it off her. To do so I had to let go the lee signal halyards against which the gaff had fouled, and they blew out of my hand to stream away like wire at 60° from the mast. Shortly after this the mizzen blew out – the heavy canvas tearing down like calico. We now depended for our lives upon the gallant Porbeagle engine with its limited fuel supply.

When we were a few hundred yards off Hayling shore we let go both our anchors, one a 2cwt CQR, the other a 2cwt fisherman. As the fisherman bit in, the chain vibrated so violently that the whole forepart of the ship trembled and in a few minutes the claw stopper jerked off and the whole chain went over the side, leaving the CQR to take the strain alone, until its chain also parted under water with a crack like a whiplash. At this moment I yelled to John to hold on as an enormous comber came crashing down on us on the foredeck; I was to leeward and clung to the binnacle bolted through to the deckbeams below. It came away in my hand as the sea hit us; and it, the kedges on deck and John came down upon me. We can only ascribe it to a miracle that I ended up under the dinghy, which must have risen to receive me, surrounded by clutter, but unhurt with the dinghy's keel pressing the back of my thigh. But with its weight supported by the combing I was extricated from this uncomfortable situation before the next ton of water descended.

By now Frank had won sufficient offing to pass the Chichester Bar buoy and there was a rapid consultation as to the advisability of trying to make the harbour. Seas mountains high were breaking upon the Winner Bank and we realised that one touch and the children at least would be doomed. Our chances of getting through were, to say the least, remote, even at full throttle. So we decided not to risk it. John and I turned our attention to the engine bilge, which had taken a lot of water through the wheelhouse doors and a loose skin fitting. The bilge pump was not man enough for the job and priming it was virtually impossible with the motion of the ship, so we set to with a bucket and basin, bailing alternately. The engine was partially submerged by now, the water slimy with diesel oil and green paint from a tin which had burst asunder, and as it surged from side to side great spurts flew up into our eyes from the belt pulley driving the dynamo. We cannot speak too highly of that beloved machine, newly installed and greatly prized as it was. We certainly owe our lives to it and would like to thank Parsons of Southampton for the craftsmanship which enabled it to chug faithfully on even after we had abandoned ship. We hope that another Porbeagle will grace the new *Maaslust* when we have her.

By the time we had bailed out the engine bilge and repaired the skin fitting, Frank had got us past the Mixon Rocks. At odd moments we had been sending up rockets and handflares with little hope of attracting attention – visibility was less than 100 yards because of the height of the seas, the tops of which were broken into a welter of flying spume – and we sent one up for luck to a vessel to seaward of us. At this moment the after end of the rudder parted, the vast iron girth snapping off like tin. We realised that there was little now to do but to keep the water out and hope as the beach at Selsey drew nearer. I went below to look at the main bilge, which needed attention but was not alarmingly flooded. As it was of steel, we had always kept it bone dry and had omitted to test the pump, which not unnaturally refused to function now. Accordingly I spent an unhappy time bailing into the galley sink and being sick. Freda and the kids looked as if they were past caring, until an enormous jolt shook them to life. My immediate reaction was that we had hit a buoy (of all things, in those waters!) and I prepared to bail harder in case we had sprung a leak. I could hardly accept the fact that it was actually the lifeboat.

My only recollection of the next few minutes is of the sight of Peter, suspended in nothing but his pyjama top over the seething water, as John handed him across to our rescuers. My bare feet were slippery with paint and oil so that I came a cropper on the lifeboat deck, knocking myself out momentarily on a cowl, and the next thing was the incredible sight, which I shall never, never forget, of our beloved vessel battling there alone. I could not believe that we had actually left her, and even now, in spite of everything, I wish we hadn't. It was desertion of a faithful friend, and, though human life is infinitely valuable, we shall always feel remorse, knowing as we do now that the wonderful old lady did not give herself over to the whim of the seas, but fought on for many hours after we left her.

Who knows to how many anxious hearts she brought relief and joy, at the darkest period of the last war, bearing home husband, son or loved one. One of the 'Little Ships,' she bore the proud battle honour, 'Dunkirk, 1940'.

Footnote

The rescued crew of another vessel *Bloodhound* were already aboard the Selsey lifeboat, so that by the time a third rescue had been made and the crew from the yacht *Coima* had been taken on board, the small hold was crammed with seasick bodies for the four long hours it took to reach and enter Portsmouth Harbour.

That same night, John and Margaret Wells went to Shoreham to contact their insurance broker, feeling sure that *Maaslust* would already be ashore and might be salvaged, even though her engine had been left running to keep her head to the seas when they had abandoned. On the Monday, hoping against hope, they scoured the coast between Selsey and Newhaven and found nothing, but at Littlehampton they learned that the Dutchman had been seen lying off at 1000 on the Sunday and had looked as though she was waiting for the tide to come in. She was seen again, 'clawing out to sea'. Lloyd's List gave her as being afloat on Monday morning – but after that – silence.

From *The Little Ship Club Journal*, 1956.

Lessons learned

Maaslust was not a motor-sailer in the modern sense, but even devoted owners of such traditional Dutchmen would not claim that these picturesque flat-bottomed craft sail well to windward. So, when a sequence of gear failures occurred while they were near the Nab Tower, Margaret Wells knew that they then depended for their lives on 'the gallant Porbeagle engine, with its limited fuel supply' – partially submerged though it was.

Having arranged to refuel before they left Deauville, they found the fuelling wharf unattended, leaving them with fuel for just four to six hours motoring, a factor that was thought to have fateful consequences. The skipper believed in having ample reserves of fuel at all times; 'a rule which will never again be relaxed.'

On Day 2 conditions deteriorated rapidly with a SW gale and squall after squall. Wisely, they abandoned making Shoreham, since the entrance is a nasty one in any weather. Soon it was evident that hopes of finding a lee under the Isle of Wight were groundless. Here, the seas were steeper and closer together and before they reached the forts the tide turned eastward, against them, and they were driven past the Nab towards the lee shore of Hayling. Below decks the stove jumped its gimbals, the saloon table lifted itself bodily; 'everything that was not screwed or bolted down became a potential menace'.

A few hundred yards off Hayling shore they let go both anchors, one a 2cwt CQR, the other a 2cwt fisherman. As the fisherman bit in, the chain vibrated so violently that the claw stopper jerked off and the whole chain went over the side, leaving the CQR to take the strain alone, until its chain , too, parted under water with 'a crack like a whiplash'.

When the engine bilge took a lot of water through the wheelhouse doors and a loose skin fitting, the bilge pump proved impossible to prime with the motion of the ship, so they had to bail with bucket and basin.

Almost invariably, matchsticks, shavings or labels from food cans found their way into the valves of those earlier bilge pumps, once the violent motion of the bilge water had swilled them from their hiding places.

27 *Girl Stella's* going

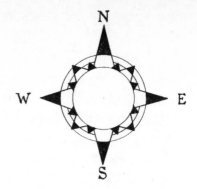

> **Yacht** *Girl Stella* (40ft gaff-rigged ketch)
> **Skipper** Frank Mulville
> **Crew** Richard Morris (mate), Celia Mulville, Patrick Mulville, Andrew Mulville
> **Bound from** Bermuda to England
> **Date of loss** 24 April, 1969
> **Position** Porto Piqueran, 1 mile N of Santa Cruz, Flores

On 1 August 1968, Girl Stella *left Heybridge Basin in Essex, on a voyage to Cuba. On board were Frank Mulville, his wife Celia, their two sons Andrew and Patrick and a friend, Dick Morris. The 24-ton* Girl Stella *was an ex-Cornish lugger, built in 1896, but completely rebuilt and fitted with a diesel engine by the Drake brothers at Tollesbury.*

On the way to Cuba, Girl Stella *stopped for a while in Spain, the Canaries and the West Indies, before spending Christmas in Kingston, Jamaica. They arrived in Santiago de Cuba on 28 December, and spent several weeks cruising along the south coast and around the western end of the island, including 24 hours aground on a reef in the approaches to Santa Lucia. For the last month of the ten-week stay,* Girl Stella *lay in the harbour of Havana, finally leaving Cuba on 15 March, 1969. After calling at the Bahamas and Bermuda, the Atlantic crossing began on 9 April.*

Being to the southward of our course had put the Azores almost in line between us and home. 'Of course we'll go in,' Patrick said, 'it will be nice to get a run ashore in a brand new island.' I was doubtful. 'Wouldn't it be better to go straight on home?' Celia and Adrian agreed. 'Let's go home,' Adrian said, 'we'll be late for school – and anyway I want to see the dog.'

Dick, if anything, seemed to be in favour of seeing the Azores. 'I must say I'd like to see the whaling boats,' he said. The argument kept us amused for days. 'Look here, Daddy,' Patrick said, 'you can't go right past these lovely islands and not go in.'

In the end I compromised. If we just went in to Flores, the most northerly of the islands, and stayed for a short time, two days at the outside, it wouldn't waste much time or take us far out of our way. We studied the pilot book. Flores had a harbour of sorts, although it didn't say much about it. It was a whaling island – the last place in the world, I believe, where whales are still hunted with pulling boats using hand harpoons. If the whaling boats used the island there was no reason why we should not, and the port of Santa Cruz was on the lee side and should be well sheltered. 'After all,' Patrick said, 'Sir Richard Grenville lay in Flores off the Azores, why shouldn't we?' 'All right – we'll go into Flores. But two days only,' I decided. 'We'll fill up with water,' Celia said, 'and get some fresh vegetables.'

It was a bad decision. I knew it was a bad decision because a little voice inside me told me so – a decision dictated not by considerations of careful seamanship and what the pilot book would call 'A proper regard for the safety of the vessel', but by nothing more tangible than a passing fancy – a set of frail desires. It was trusting to luck instead of careful planning. Once embarked on, it led inexorably on to other decisions, taken one by one and in themselves innocent enough, which built themselves up to produce a misfortune which, to our small world, was a disaster.

The wind worked its way round to the south-west as we got closer to Flores and the glass went down slightly – nothing to worry about, but if it was going to blow a gale from the south-west it would be just as well to be safely tucked away in the lee of a high island. There is no radio beacon on Flores and, unlike any other of our major landfalls of the voyage, I would have to rely completely on my sextant. Flores is not a big island, perhaps half as long as the Isle of Wight, and there was no other island within 130 miles of it, except Corvo – a very small island immediately to the north-east. I supplemented my sun observations with star sights in the morning and confidently pronounced an ETA. 'You'll see it at half past two this afternoon, lying on the port bow, and there's ten shillings for the first boy to sight land.' It was Tuesday, 22 April and we had covered 1700 miles in 13 days – an average speed of over five knots. At two o'clock Adrian sighted the island pushing its bulk out of low cloud fine on the port bow.

It took a long time to come up with the southern cape of Flores and it was evening by the time we rounded it and came along the east side of the island towards Santa Cruz – close under great cliffs and mountains that dropped sheer into the Atlantic. White houses high up on the mountainside blinked their lights at us – we could see the gulls wheeling in tight spirals against the sheer rock face, and ahead of us the small town of Santa Cruz could just be seen before the sun went behind the mountain and everything was suddenly submerged in darkness. 'What a pity. I thought we'd just get in before dark,' I said to Celia. 'We'll have to hang off till morning – how disappointing,' she said.

We took the sails down off Santa Cruz and just as we were making a neat stow of the mains'l, two bright red leading lights suddenly showed up, one behind the other, showing the way into the harbour. 'Well, what do you think of that?' I said to Dick. 'Do you think they switched on the lights specially for us?' 'Perhaps they did. Anyway it must be quite OK to go in at night otherwise the leading lights wouldn't be there.' I went below where Celia was. 'They've switched on two beautiful leading lights,' I said. 'I think we'll go in rather than flog about here all night.' 'I think we ought to wait till we can see where we're going,' she said. I consulted Dick again and we overruled her. 'Is everything squared up? – get the ropes and fenders up and we'll go in,' I said. I knew, deep inside myself, that it was a silly thing to do. The little voice told me so again. 'You're a bloody idiot, Mulville,' it said. 'Oh shut your blather – I'm tired – I want a night's sleep.'

When everything was ready to go alongside – the mooring ropes ready, fenders out, side lights lit, boathooks handy, anchor cleared away ready to let go if needed, I put the engine slow ahead and went straight for the leading lights and straight for the black cliff which was all we could see behind them. Soon we could hear the surf pounding against the rocks. 'I don't like it, Frank,' Celia said, 'I'm going below.' 'It's not too late to turn back,' the voice said. 'Don't be such a bloody fool.'

'Can you see anything, Dick?' I shouted to the foredeck. 'Yes – there's a gap right ahead – starboard a little.' 'Starboard she is.' 'Steady as you go.' 'Steady.' Suddenly we were between the rocks – close on either side. There was no turning now. A swell took us and swept us forward. 'Hard to starboard,' Dick shouted. I spun the wheel, my mouth dry as the bottom of a bird cage. 'There it is – right ahead – put her astern,' Dick shouted.

There was a small stone quay right beside us – a dozen men on it, all shouting at us in Portuguese. The swell was terrific. *GS* was rearing up and down alarmingly. Dick threw a rope, it was made fast and *GS* was pulled in towards the quay. 'We can't lie here,' I shouted to Dick, 'we'll have to get out again.' Just then *GS* grounded on a hard stone bottom. She only touched once, not hard, and I put the engine astern and brought her a few feet along the quay – but it was enough to be unpleasant. 'Anyone speak English?' I shouted. A big man came forward. 'I pilot,' he shouted. 'This harbour no good for you – tide go down – no enough water.' He and two of his friends jumped on board. 'Full astern,' he said. I put the engine astern and opened the throttle. The pilot took the wheel from me. 'Neutral – slow ahead,' he said. We seemed to be surrounded by rocks on all sides and the swell was playing round them, leaping into the air, and crashing down with a noise like a steam train pulling out of a station. The pilot manoeuvred us back and forth – turning *GS* round with great skill as if he had known her ways all his life. 'I don't know how you get in here,' he said, 'no one come in here at night.' 'Then what in Christ's name are the leading lights for?' I asked. 'Fishermen,' he said.

It was like the middle of Hampton Court Maze, but somehow the pilot got us out, backing and filling and turning until *GS* was clear in the open sea again. The saliva slowly came back to my mouth. 'Give me a drink of water,' I asked Celia whose white face was looking anxiously out of the hatch. "We take you Porto Piqueran. One mile up coast,' the pilot said. 'You OK there.' We motored for a quarter of an hour to the north and then the pilot put *GS*'s head straight for the rocks. 'Don't let him do it,' a voice said. 'Shut up for Christ's sake. I can't tell him his job.'

There were no leading lights here at all – only the black face of the rock. 'No worry,' the pilot said, sensing my apprehension, 'you OK here. Quite safe – no swell – I know way.' '*Ça va bien*,' one of the other men said, thinking for some reason that I was French and wishing to air his grasp of that language. '*Le Monsieur Pilot – il le connait bien ici.*' The pilot was as good as his reputation. He took us straight towards a tower of rock, looming sullenly in the weak light of the stars, then hard to port for a few yards, then to starboard and to port again until suddenly we were in a small cove – a cleft in the rocks no more than 60ft across but calm and still. 'Let go anchor. Now we tie you up.'

The pilot and his helpers climbed into our dinghy and ran out ropes to the rocks. They jumped nimbly ashore and fastened every long rope we had in the ship – three on each side. 'Best ropes forward,' the pilot said, 'bad ropes aft. Wind come from west,' he said pointing to the sky where the clouds were racing towards England. 'Always strong wind from west here.' I thought for a moment while they were working on the ropes. 'Pilot,' I said, 'suppose we have to go out quickly. Would it not be better to turn her round, so she's facing the sea?' 'No,' he said, 'strong wind from west – always face strong wind – best ropes forward.' The little person inside me said 'Make him turn her round, you weak idiot – this may be a trap.' 'Stop your bloody nagging.'

They tied us up thoroughly, made sure that everything was fast and strong and then they came down to the cabin and we gave them a drink. 'By God – you lucky get out Santa Cruz,' the pilot laughed. 'No ship ever come there at night before. You fine here – you sleep sound.' We put them ashore in the dinghy to a stone quay with a flight of steps hewn out of the rock face and they went off home. 'See you in the morning. You sleep OK.'

We did sleep soundly. *GS* lay as quiet as if she were in Bradwell Creek. The glass was dropping again and it was already blowing a gale from the south-west but Porto Piqueran was quite detached from the gale – the only evidence of wind was the racing clouds far up above and an occasional down draught which would sometimes break away from the body of the gale and find its way like some spent outrider round the mountain and down towards Porto Piqueran where it would hurl the last of its dissipated energy at the top of *GS*'s mast, stirring the burgee 40ft up, making a faint moaning sound and then dissolving into the night. Dick laughed, 'This is a hurricane hole all right – there isn't enough wind in here to lift a tart's skirt.'

'Don't laugh too soon,' the little voice said to me as I went to sleep.

Next day, Mulville met with some difficulty when customs officials accompanied him into Santa Cruz to the office of the International Police, who wanted to retain all the passports. After much argument Mulville managed successfully to plead with them.

'The wind might change in the night,' I said. 'We might want to go out at a moment's notice. We must have our passports.'

Before spending a second night in Porto Piqueran, they carefully checked all the warps before they went to bed and found nothing amiss.

'The two strongest warps we had were out over the bow, each made fast to a rock. On the starboard side there was a rope from aft to a ring bolt let into the rock by the steps and another to a stone bollard at the corner of the quay. On the port side the longest rope led from aft to a big rock on the south side of the cove and yet another from amidships. It was something of a work of art.

'If you got out your crochet needles you could make us a Balaclava out of this lot,' I had remarked to Celia. In addition to her ropes the anchor was down, although I doubted whether it was doing any good, as the bottom was hard and it had not been let go far enough out to be effective. Dick had been round in the day checking that the ropes were not chafing against the rocks and had served a couple of them with rope-yarns. 'I reckon she'll do,' I said to Dick and we went to bed.

A boat is always there – you never stop worrying about her whether you are aboard or ashore – she is always a presence in the mind and you're conscious of her at all times. She may be laid up in some safe berth for the winter or hauled out of the water in a yard, but wherever you may be – at home in your virtuous bed or roistering in some gay spot, a chorus girl on each knee and the air thick with flying champagne corks – a part of your consciousness is always reserved. When the wind moans round the eaves of the house it has a special significance, and you check off in your mind, one by one, the possible sources of danger. Men lie awake worrying about their bank balances, their waistlines, their wives, their mistresses actual or potential; but sailors worry about boats.

A boat is something more than an ingenious arrangement of wood and copper and iron – it has a soul, a personality, eccentricities of behaviour that are endearing. It becomes part of a person, colouring his whole life with a romance that is unknown to those who do not understand a way of life connected with boats. The older a boat becomes, the stronger the power. It gains in stature with each new experience – people look at boats with wonder and say 'She's been to the South Seas', or 'She's just back from the North Cape', and the boat takes on a reputation in excess of that of its owner. *Girl Stella* had become a very real part of our lives – we each of us loved her with a deep respect.

I slept badly, frequently waking and listening. At 2am it began to rain, softly at first and then more heavily so that I could hear the drips coursing off the furled mains'l and drumming on the cabin top. At 4am I heard a slight bump and wondered what it was – then I heard it again and I knew what it was. It was the dinghy bumping against the stern. I froze in a cold sweat. If the dinghy was bumping against the stern, the wind must have changed. I got up, put oilskins on over my pyjamas and went on deck. It was cold – the temperature had dropped three or four degrees – it was pelting with rain and a light breeze was blowing from east by north – straight into the cove of Porto Piqueran.

I undid the dinghy, took the painter round the side deck and fastened it off the bow where it streamed out clear. I went back to the cabin, got dressed and called Dick. I tapped the glass and it gave a small convulsion downwards. 'Dick – the wind's changed. We'll have to get out of here quick. The glass is dropping. We can't stay here in an easterly wind.' Dick got up and put his head out of the hatch. The rain was pouring down and it was as black as a cow's inside. I believe he thought I was over-nervous – exaggerating.

'We can't do much in this,' he said. 'If we did manage to get her untied and turned round, we'd never get her out through that channel in this blackness. All we can do is wait till morning and then have another look at it.' He went back to bed and was soon snoring peacefully.

The little voice said 'Get him up – start work – now.' 'Shut up – he's right – you can't see your hand in front of you – how the hell can we go to sea in this?' I walked round the deck. There was more swell now, and *GS* was beginning to buck up and down – snatching at her ropes so that sometimes the after ones came right out of the water. The forward ropes – the strong nylon warps – were quite slack.

I went down to the cabin, sat at the table and tried to read. I made myself a cup of coffee and sat with the mug warming my hands and the steam wreathing round my face.

Then I went on deck again. The wind was beginning to increase, a heavy swell was now running and small white waves were beginning to overlay it. The rain had increased and was now slanting with the wind and driving into the cove. *Girl Stella* was beginning to pitch and jerk at the two stern ropes with alarming force. Very slowly and reluctantly it was beginning to get light. I went below and shook Dick. 'Come on – not a minute to waste – it's beginning to get light.' I tapped the glass again and again it dropped.

It seemed an age before Dick was dressed in his oilskins and on deck. 'First we'll get the anchor up. It's doing no good there and it will only hamper us. Then we'll let go the head lines – leave them in the water, they'll drift to leeward and we'll come back for them later. Then we'll go astern on the engine and let her swing round on one of the stern lines.' We set to work. It was a relief to have ended the dreadful inactivity of the last two hours. As the anchor began to come up, Celia woke and put her head out through the hatch. 'What's happening?' 'We're going to get out of here – look at the weather – we're turning her round. Better get the boys up.' In minutes the boys were up on deck in their oilskins and Celia was dressed.

The anchor came home easily and I started the engine. We cast off the head lines and prepared another line which would take the strain after we had turned, passing it round the bow so that we could fasten it to the stern line to starboard, which would then become the head line to port. Now the wind was howling with real ferocity – increasing every minute. The swell had become dangerous and was slapping against *GS*'s blunt stern and sending little columns of spray into the mizzen shrouds. I moved the dinghy painter from the bow to the stern and the boat lay alongside, leaping up and down and banging against the top sides.

We were almost ready when there was a twang like someone plucking a violin string. I looked up and saw that the stern line on which we were relying had received one jerk too many. It had snapped in the middle and the inboard end was flying back towards the boat like a piece of elastic. *GS* immediately began to move towards the rocks on her port side. I jumped into the cockpit, slammed the engine into reverse, gave her full throttle, and put the rudder hard to starboard. She began to pick up. 'Let go the port stern line,' I yelled to Dick. He began to throw the rope off the cleat. 'Throw it well clear – she'll come.' The engine vibrated and thundered – the spray over the stern drove in our faces – the wind battered our senses but she was coming astern. 'Good old girl,' I muttered, 'we'll get you out.'

Then the engine stopped – suddenly and irrevocably – the bare end of the broken line wound a dozen times round the propeller. 'Now you're in trouble,' the little voice said.

GS began to drift inexorably towards the rocks – there was nothing to stop her – no ropes on the starboard side and no engine. 'Fenders, over here, quick,' I shouted to the boys and Celia. 'Fend her off as best you can. I'll go over with another rope,' I shouted to Dick. There was one more rope long enough to reach the shore, still in the fo'c's'le locker. The top of the locker was covered with toys and books belonging to the boys and with Patrick's accordion. I threw them off in a pile on the floor and brought the bare end up through the fo'c's'le hatch. 'Celia,' I shouted, 'pay it out to me as I go in the dinghy.' As I got over the side into the Starling I felt *GS* strike the rocks – surprisingly gently, I thought. Perhaps it was a smooth ledge and they would be able to cushion her with fenders until we got another rope out. I rowed desperately towards the shore, the end of the rope wound round the after thwart of the dinghy. The swell was washing violently against the stone steps. I could see the ring bolt but I couldn't reach it – as soon as the dinghy got in close it would surge up on a swell, strike the slippery surface of the steps and plunge back. I took my trousers and my shirt off, plunged into the sea with the end of the rope, upsetting the dinghy as I jumped out of it, and tried to clamber up the steps. But there was nothing to grasp and three times the weight of the rope pulled me back. With a last effort I managed to roll myself over onto the steps, reach up and keep my balance until I was able to grasp the ring. 'All fast!' I shouted to Celia. I swam back on board and clambered up over the bobstay. It was bitterly cold.

Dick and I took the rope to the winch and began to heave. The strain came on the rope and her head began to come round clear of the rocks, but she had moved ahead slightly and the rocks under her stern had shifted their position to right aft, under the turn of the bilge, and begun to do real damage. They were too far below the waterline for the fenders to be of any use. Then she stopped coming. The rope was tight but something was preventing her from moving forward. Dick went aft to look. 'She's all tied up aft,' he reported. 'Every bloody rope in the place is tied up round the propeller and they're all bar tight.' I looked over the stern. It was daylight now and I could see a tangle of ropes bunched up round the propeller. 'I'll cut them free.'

Dick gave me his razor-sharp knife and I jumped over the side again. I dived and saw that at least two ropes had somehow got themselves into the tangle – I managed to cut one and came up for breath. *GS*'s stern was just above me, the swells lifting it and allowing it to settle back on the rock with all the force of her great weight. I could hear the rock cutting into her skin – the unmistakable cracking sound of timbers shattering under blows of irresistible force. I knew then that she was done for.

I dived and cut the other rope, swam round to the bobstay with difficulty in the heavy swell and dragged myself on board. Dick and I wound furiously on the winch – she moved a little further, and then, as the swells came more on her beam, she lifted and crashed down with an awe-inspiring crunch. She would move no more. As I went aft Celia was working the hand pump and Patrick jumped into the engine room and switched on the electric pump. Adrian came up out of the saloon and I heard him say to Celia in a quiet voice, 'Mummy, I don't wish to alarm you but the cabin's full of water.'

'It's all over,' I said to Celia, 'everybody get into lifejackets. We'll have to swim for it.'

Celia and I went below. The water was knee-deep on the cabin floor and was rising as we watched. *Girl Stella* was still bumping, and every time she hit the rock we could hear the heavy frames splitting, the timbers crumbling. I looked at Celia. Her face was grey, her hair hanging in rat tails, and she had an expression of unimpeded sadness. We stood for a moment among the ruin. The ingredients of our lives were swilling backwards and forwards across the cabin floor, soon to be swallowed by the sea. Books given to us by the Cubans, their pages open and eager, as if they would convert the ocean to revolution, Adrian's recorder, clothes, an orange, the cribbage board, the kettle, a pair of chart rulers, rolls of film, my hat, Celia's glasses-case – objects which had somehow jumped out of their context to give mocking offence. The ordered symmetry of our lives was torn apart and scattered – haphazard and suddenly meaningless.

I could see in Celia's face that she had reached the end of a long journey. *Girl Stella* was a precious thing to her – something that was being thrown away in front of her eyes. The years of struggle with the sea were coming to an end – the pinnacles of achievement, the harrowing crises, the light-hearted joys and the endless discomforts had slowly spiralled upwards as we had progressed from adventure to adventure. Now they had reached an explosive zenith and for her there could be no going on. I knew in that moment she would never come sailing with me again. I had at last betrayed her trust – forfeited her confidence in me. Before, we had always come through – snatched victory out of disaster – but now she was facing a fundamental confrontation of truth. I put my hand in hers – pleading for a glance of sympathy.

Celia passed the lifejackets up the hatch to Dick, and then she gathered a plastic bag and put in it the log books – the ship's, the children's and her own – and a few oddments. I found myself unable to think – I was almost insensible with cold. I grabbed my wallet and a book of travellers' cheques, the last of our money, and stuffed them into the bag. I took one last look at the clock and the barometer shining on the bulkhead, the cabin stove, its doors swung open and the water ebbing and flowing through the grate, the lamp swinging unevenly with a stunted motion, and floating lazily across the floor, *GS*'s document box, *'Girl Stella* – Penzance' scrolled on the lid.

On deck the boys were calmly putting on their lifejackets. I bent down to help Patrick with the lacings. 'This is the end, Daddy,' he said quietly, 'the end of *Girl Stella* – poor, poor *GS*.'

Now she had settled deep in the water and her motion had suddenly become sickening. She had lost her liveliness and when she rolled to the swell it was with a slow, tired lurch. Her stability, the quick sense of recovery, the responsiveness that she always had, was gone. 'Quick. She may turn turtle – we must get off. I'll go first, then boys, then you, Celia and Dick last. Grab the rope and pull yourselves along it. I'll help you up the steps.'

I jumped into the sea, found the rope and shouted back, 'Come on, Pad, jump.' Patrick hesitated for a moment and then his body came flying through the air and he bobbed up, gasping with cold beside me – then Adrian, then Celia. We pulled ourselves hand over hand along the rope. Now the swell was much heavier and there were vicious seas breaking in the cove. It was much more difficult to get on to the steps. The ring bolt was high up out of the water and it was necessary to let go of the rope and swim the last few yards to the steps. My puny strength was of no consequence in the swell – like a piece of floating stick I was swept back and forth across the rock face, the small aperture of the steps flashing past as I was carried first one way and then the other. Then, more by some quirk of the swell than by my own efforts, I was dumped heavily on the bottom step and was able to scramble to my feet. I grabbed Patrick by one arm and heaved him up, then Adrian came surging past and I was able to grasp the back of his life-jacket and pull him on the bottom step. Celia was more difficult. She was all but paralysed by the cold – she was heavy and slippery and there seemed to be nothing of her that I could grip. Then she managed to get her body half on to the step, and with Patrick helping me we pulled and rolled and tugged until she finally got herself clear and struggled to her feet. 'Up you go – quick before the sea snatches you back again.'

Dick had not come. I looked up and saw that *GS* had moved ahead and was now lying athwart a towering rock pillar. I saw that he had been below and had brought up the two sextants and placed them on a narrow ledge of rock which he could reach. *GS* was now low in the water and sinking fast. 'Dick,' I shouted, 'come out of it – now.' If she sank before he came he would be denied the rope and I doubted whether he would be able to swim through the broken water without its help. He took a last and reluctant look round and then he jumped and we watched him working his way along the rope, hand over hand, until I was able to grasp his arm and he scrambled up the steps.

We stood in a dejected, shivering group on the little stone quay and watched *GS* work out this last moment of her span of life. A thing of grace and beauty – agile, sure-footed, tender in her responses to our demands – at the same time she was a block of solid assurance. We had always felt safe in her – we always knew that she would do whatever was asked of her. She was our home – she gave us a dignity which we would otherwise have been without.

She had come to her end not by any misdeed of hers – not through any wilfulness or delinquency – but by misuse – a sheer disregard of the elements of seamanship. I felt the dead weight of my responsibility settle heavily on my shoulders. It was a score against me that could never be wiped clean – nothing that I could ever do would relieve me of the knowledge that I had destroyed a thing of beauty.

From *In Granma's Wake* (1970), Seafarer Books

Lessons learned

Frank Mulville had a premonition that trouble would befall *GS* and never forgave himself for not heeding the 'little voice' that told him it was a bad decision, that night in 1969, to moor *Girl Stella* in Porto Piqueran, just north of Santa Cruz on the Island of Flores.

It was a bad decision 'dictated not by considerations of careful seamanship and what the pilot book would call "A proper regard for the safety of the vessel", but by nothing more tangible than a passing fancy – a set of frail desires. It was trusting to luck instead of careful planning.'

'We take you to Porto Piqueran. One mile up coast,' the pilot said. 'You OK there.'

'Don't let him do it,' the voice said. 'Shut up for Christ's sake, I can't tell him his job.'

Even when they had arrived in the 60ft-wide hurricane hole, Mulville remained uneasy. 'Pilot,' he said, 'suppose we have to get out quickly. Would it not be better to turn her round, so she'll face the sea?'

'No,' was the reply, 'strong wind from the west – always face strong wind – best ropes forward.'

The little voice within Mulville persisted: 'Make him turn her head round, you weak idiot – this may be a trap.'

'Stop your bloody nagging,' was the outer Mulville's reply.

After spending most of the next day in Santa Cruz, the crew of *GS* returned to find her 'lying peacefully at her moorings. But the voice said "Watch it."'

Mulville and his mate, Dick Morris, carefully checked all the mooring lines and went to bed, but as Mulville so rightly observes, 'A boat is always there – you never stop worrying about her whether you are aboard or ashore'. During the night the wind came in from the east and freshened until it became obvious that they must leave. They made swift but careful preparations and 'were almost ready when there was a twang like someone plucking a violin string. I looked up and saw that the stern line on which we were relying had received one jerk too many. It had snapped in the middle and the inboard end was flying back towards the boat like a piece of elastic. I jumped into the cockpit, slammed the engine into reverse, gave her full throttle ... then the engine stopped – suddenly and irrevocably – the bare end of the broken line wound a dozen times round the propeller. "Now you're in trouble," the little voice said.'

28 Bad luck in Boulogne

Yacht *Mary Williams* (Silhouette)
Skipper Clementina Gordon
Bound from Etaples (river Canche) to St Valery sur Somme, France
Date of loss 7 August, 1962
Position outer harbour, Boulogne

Many people began their cruising careers in Silhouettes, those small hard-chine bilge keel plywood boats designed by Robert Tucker; but not so many of them were women, and surely the Rev Clementina Gordon was the only ordained woman minister amongst them. In 1961, Clementina Gordon had won the Suzanne Trophy for her log of a remarkable cruise in appalling weather from the east coast of England to Zeebrugge in Belgium, and in 1962 she set out alone to cruise along the Normandy and Brittany coasts, but ran into trouble, as she relates in this simple but graphic account.

I was trying to cruise on the difficult north coast between Boulogne and Cherbourg, exercising great care, as the anchorages are dangerous with vile bars and ripping tides, also drying out 20ft and more. On Monday, 6 August, I left Le Canche river about 0345, negotiating the bar with a terrible ebb, and then the SW tide for St Valery sur Somme. At 0645 the forecast was a westerly gale coming from the Plymouth area, so as I hadn't a hope of making Dieppe, I ran back over a foul tide to Boulogne. (The Somme estuary is murder in onshore winds.) I came into Boulogne in pouring rain, and brought up just by the inner pier head, clear of traffic, and of course behind the big west breakwater. There I rested clear of the miseries of that inner basin and all ready to slip in when I had sorted myself out. I must have dozed off, thinking myself perfectly secure. When I came to, the wind had flown round, from offshore, to put me on the lee of the inner pier, about force 7. I thought it a risk to get under way, and placidly waited for a lull or a pluck in from a passing tug. My signals, even red rockets bursting 100ft, were unnoticed, so I had to hang on with very heavy ground tackle, two anchors and vast new warps and chain.

By midnight, the wind settled in the SW and increased, I guess to force 8, but another report said much more. I now had the far side of the harbour in my lee, down Cape Griz Nez direction, all rocks and old blockhouses, with heavy surf. She held till just before HW 3am, when the west break-water ceased to function, and a heavy swell came in almost unimpeded. I sent off the remainder of the big rockets (after I learnt that the inner pier-head, 80 yards away, was manned all night and the lifeboat station was 150 yards away!)

I then took the situation seriously and inflated my good rubber dinghy, as it was obvious that if the bitts were not torn out of her something would have to go. The surf and the rocks were so nasty that I had a drink of Madeira to steady my poor nerves, and stop my being sick all the time and therefore inefficient. Just after that there was a bigger heave than usual, and with a roar I found myself trapped under the cockpit with the boat on top of me. (Afterwards, examining the wreckage, I found that the new 2½ inch bow warp had parted about 15ft from the bitts, so I presume she was caught underneath by a steep wave and turned bow over stern.) Luckily, I held my breath, extracted my leg wedged under the boom, and got out, with the dinghy, which my safety belt was attached to. Then a gulp of air, before a monster of a wave crashed me down and down. Eventually I came up, and was rushed ahead for 250 yards or so, nearly torn away from the rubber dinghy. A pause, then crashed down again and pushed violently forward. This was repeated while I weakened physically.

Luckily, I missed the rocks sticking out, and after ¼ or ½ mile had slacker water, but a sheer cement wall with an overhang and railings right on top. It was just light, and a Frenchman fishing with a rod was there, so I yelled like an otter hunter, and he slithered down a drainpipe to help. I was too weak to keep hold of the rocks as the dinghy acted like a sea anchor and pulled me back by the safety line. He could not approach to pull me out, as he had a new pair of suede shoes, and leaped back for fear of wetting them. Even then I could see how funny it was! Eventually, I had the wits to pull the release of the belt, and was able to hang onto a rock.

I was hauled out. A baker's delivery man had now appeared to join in the fun, and then manhandled me into a pub where Madame had hysterics and tipped filthy French 'whisky' down me, such as the fishermen use. As I would insist on subsiding on to the floor in a pool of my own private sea, they sent for the ambulance and tucked me up in a nuns' hospital. There I stayed for a couple of days, as I had only a nightshirt lent by a nun, and it stopped short 1½ ft above my knees; so I was a prisoner of modesty.

The unfortunate boat broke up a quarter of a mile off shore. The local yacht club picked up the bits at low water and most of my gear was salvaged. Obviously the whole silly accident was quite unnecessary, I could easily have gone right inside before supper. But it is a sobering lesson on what a dangerous place a harbour is in a gale, and how useful an inflatable dinghy can be (no other dinghy would have had the buoyancy to bring me through that stuff), also on the improbability of one's distress signals being seen. Perhaps one ought to carry a minimum of a dozen rockets and a dozen flares, instead of three of each and some whites, as I had.

From *The Silhouette Owner*, September 1962

Lessons learned

It is sometimes difficult to realise that even in harbour a yacht can still be at great risk if conditions change rapidly. One might think, as Clementina Gordon did, that inside the outer breakwater of Boulogne there would be safety and a chance to rest; but as she relates: 'When I came to, the wind had flown round ... I now had the far side of the harbour in my lee, down Cap Gris Nez direction'. Her two anchors, one on a warp and the other on chain, held until just before 0300, 'when the west breakwater ceased to function and a heavy swell came in'. Soon after that, a bigger sea than the others came with a roar and turned the little Silhouette bow over stern. Fortunately the dinghy was inflated, and although she was unable to get aboard she managed to hang on to it and be swept ashore beneath the esplanade.

29 *Thelma* Parts her Cable

> **Yacht** *Thelma* (27ft gaff-rigged cutter)
> **Skipper** AW 'Bob' Roberts
> **Crew** AF 'Bully' Bull
> **Bound** round the world from England, westabout
> **Date of loss** 1 March 1935
> **Position** Chatham Bay, Cocos Island

Long before he won fame as a skipper of Thames spritsail barges, Bob Roberts and his mate 'Bully' had sailed the little gaff cutter, Thelma, *from England to Cocos Island in the Pacific, where she was lost when her anchor cable parted. The voyage is described in his entertaining book* Rough and Tumble. *Roberts had felt uneasy about the anchorage in Chatham Bay, but put his doubts behind him when Bully asked why he was worried. He takes up the story:*

It was an open anchorage and no place for rough weather, but being so calm it did not seem that there could be the slightest danger in lying there for a few days. It would not take us long to top up our water tanks and get away for the Galapagos. It was only those queer fancies of mine that made me dislike the place, and I even went so far as to reveal my thoughts to Bully as he stirred the porridge in the galley with a sweaty hand.

'I don't like this place much.'

'Want to move further out?'

'No, she's as safe here as anywhere with the hook in this patch of sand.'

'Well, what don't you like about the place?'

'Dunno. Just a hunch.'

In the meantime I altered my ideas about a kedge anchor. We were not so lavishly equipped as to have two anchor chains, and our custom was to lay out a kedge on a stout manilla warp. As our two-inch tripping line had already chafed through on the jagged bottom in only two hours, I felt it would be useless to use a kedge on a warp.

After solemn deliberations we decided that if the anchor chain did not hold her it was quite certain a chafing warp would not. Likewise, it was impossible for our main anchor to drag. It could not drag from that patch of sand because it was surrounded by mushroom coral. This mushroom coral grows some little way off the bottom and spreads out according to its name. Thus if the anchor dragged, the lower flukes would go under the coral and hold there so fast that it would be unlikely that we should ever get it up again.

So there did not seem to be much danger of *Thelma* dragging her anchor, especially as the weather was dead calm and there was no current to speak of in the bay itself.

Roberts and Bully spent three days watering ship by ferrying a cask to and fro between *Thelma* and the shore; and then, having met a man named Cooknell, they were persuaded to join in a search for the 'Cocos' treasure. The search was unsuccessful and throughout the five days Roberts remained uneasy and depressed. The return to Chatham Bay was in a ship's lifeboat.

I was glad to be on my way back. A cloud of depression seemed to be hanging over me all the time at Wafer Bay. While the others scampered in and out of the water and played golf on the beach with a round stone and a crooked branch, I could only sit around and mope. I must have been dull company.

I thought it was sheer tiredness after our efforts in the jungle, but as things turned out it was that vague mental warning to which the human mind is sometimes subjected when something dreadful is going to happen. At last, in the ship's lifeboat, we bore away to cross Chatham Bay; I felt no qualms at not sighting *Thelma*'s stumpy stick straight away. But as we grew closer I stood up in the prow and scanned the bay. *Thelma* was not there!

Wild thoughts ran through my head. Then, far away in a corner of the bay, I caught sight of her. She was but a few yards from the rocks. Even as I watched, a huge wave lifted her up and carried her in. We rowed like fiends, but the tide and current were against us. I stood there and saw her rise again and disappear. When the next breaker came she did not come up. She was down on her beam ends with the surf pounding over her.

There was very little wind but it was impossible to get the lifeboat alongside in the breakers. We anchored a little way off and veered down as near as possible. The sight before us almost broke my heart. There was the gallant little vessel, which I had loved and cared for all these years, which had brought us safely through fair weather and foul for nearly 7000 miles on this cruise alone, in her death throes on that lonely shore. All our worldly belongings danced and swirled among the rocks. A bunch of dollar notes disappeared in the foam. Pieces of timber floated everywhere. It was enough to chill the heart of the bravest soul. To complete the mournful scene, Jimmy the ship's cat, drenched and scared, meowed pitifully from the masthead.

I took one look at the way she lay and knew that the vessel was doomed. She hardly rose an inch to a breaking wave, and there was a sickening grinding and snapping of timbers with each cruel blow. Every wave broke clean over her and forced us to cling on for our lives.

We fought our way down into the tiny cabin. Each wave filled her up and we were imprisoned like rats until it subsided. We choked and gasped as we grabbed such things as were within reach and passed them out on deck. It was impossible to stay below for long at a time, and as I struggled in the cabin I could feel the rocks under my feet. The whole of her starboard side was ripped out. Something was sticking up through the cabin floor. There was nothing to be done except to try to save everything possible.

At low water *Thelma* was almost high and dry and I was able to discover the cause of the wreck. Trailing from her bow were many fathoms of anchor chain but no anchor. One of the links had been sawn clean through as if with a file. It was the work of the mushroom coral. So sharp was the edge of it that in five days it had cut through a heavy chain link as the vessel swung gently to her hawser. I should never have believed that coral could cut through solid iron so efficiently. Later we found pieces on the beach which would file through any iron or steel we possessed. But the knowledge came too late. The worst was done. Some time after the wreck we found that anchor still firmly embedded in the sand and it took four of us to weigh it from the lifeboat.

From *Rough and Tumble*, 1935, Sampson Low and Marston
Republished 1983 by Mallard Reprints

Lessons learned

Even 'heavy three-eighths-of-an-inch chain from a big Whitstable smack' could not prevent *Thelma* from blowing ashore when coral cut through the iron chain 'as if with a file.' Bob Roberts had felt uneasy about anchoring in Chatham Bay 'An open anchorage and no place for rough weather. It was one of those queer fancies of mine that made me dislike the place.'

Roberts considered laying out a kedge as well as the bower anchor, but decided that since 'our two-inch tripping line had already chafed through on the jagged bottom in the matter of two hours, it would be useless to use a kedge on a warp'. That was the danger signal he ignored. For if a warp could be chafed through in hours, even a chain might go the same way if left for days. In fact, they left *Thelma* for five days before returning to find her among the rocks. Anchoring in coral without careful checks can also run the risk of chain wrapping itself around a coral head, which can cause inextricable problems. Apart from the risk of being 'trapped', shortening the scope increases the shock loading, which can cause chain to snap, or put a fatal strain on deck gear.

Part five:

Collision

The huge tail fin of a blue whale which struck the fatal blow on Pionier.

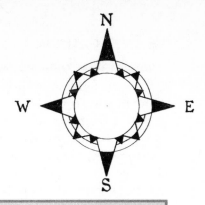

30 Run down, or rescued?

Yacht *Nuts* (Danish Bandholm 28)
Skipper Niels Blixenkrone-Moller
Crew Rikke and Rasmus Blixenkrone-Moller
Bound from Los Llanos, Tenerife, for Barbados
Date of loss 18 December 1999
Position 1,600 miles from Barbados

Danish schoolteacher Niels Blixenkrone-Moller, his wife Rikke and son Rasmus (11), were on a year's sabbatical and crossing the Atlantic to cruise the Caribbean when their rendezvous with a tanker went disastrously wrong.

O n 19 June I set sail from our home port of Nappedam on the east coast of Jutland, Denmark, with my wife, Rikke, a psychologist, and our 11-year-old son, Rasmus, aboard our 28ft yacht *Nuts*, a sturdy Danish Bandholm 28 design.

An uneventful North Sea crossing was followed by a rainy sail across Scotland, via the Caledonian Canal. From the island of Ghia we sailed to Ireland. Already we had made many wonderful sailing friends whilst enjoying Scottish and Irish hospitality. But by the beginning of August it was time to cast off from Kinsale for a five-day crossing to north-west Spain and down the Spanish and Portuguese coasts to the Algarve.

In the Canary islands we became part of the cruising community, planning to cross the Atlantic. The ARC (Atlantic Rally for Cruisers) sailors were busy preparing their yachts for the departure deadline. But we, and many others, believe that choosing your departure day should be done on the spot and not set a year in advance. Thus it was not until 7 December that we finally left Los Llanos, Tenerife, bound for Barbados.

By this time, Herb Hilgenberg's Atlantic weather SSB radio net (12359 Kilohertz), and others, suggested that we should sail SSW to at least 20° N to find the trade winds.

With a south-east wind we logged between 106-124nm each day, hoping always for a nice easterly. On the tenth day we discovered both that our batteries were too low to start the engine. We hoped our solar panel would feed one battery sufficiently to do the job. Otherwise we had enough dry-cell batteries to power our handheld GPS and torches.

We hadn't seen any ships since the first day. But at midday on the eleventh day we saw a large tanker approaching. We thought this was an opportunity to get assistance – either to get our battery charged, or to obtain a new battery.

We contacted the tanker by handheld VHF and although the radio contact was poor, they were prepared to help us. Our position was 18° N and 35° W. It was a sunny morning and we were sailing at 5 knots on a heading of 240°.

The tanker manoeuvred in a large circle and we thought they would stop on our port side to give us a lee from wind and waves. The sea was not rough, but the swell and waves were one to two metres.

But as the tanker approached, we were surprised to see steps lowered on its port side. We thought they had decided to send over a small boat. VHF communication was not working. But soon they were on our starboard, lee-ward, side, just a few metres away. Heaving lines landed like small bombs all around. Cries of 'Make fast!' and 'Get closer!' were in the air.

Although we were uneasy, we tied the heavy lines fore and aft, expecting to be able to stay off the ship's side by steering off.

Suddenly, we were sucked along the iron wall towards the huge tanker's rudder. To prevent disaster, we were pulled forward. Our mast banged against the giant.

In seconds the situation had changed. Our masthead lights and the mast's starboard spreader had gone. The teak cap rail was crushed and the pushpit bent.

With 1600 miles to go to Barbados our yacht was now disabled. In desperation we climbed the vertical steps to board the tanker. We were surprised to learn that we had been 'rescued' and 'saved'. The Arab and Pakistani crew seemed to feel that Allah had helped us.

We, however, felt that bad seamanship by the tanker's captain had severely damaged our yacht.

As the last of my family arrived on deck, I asked if *Nuts* could be craned aboard. The captain welcomed us aboard, but also informed me that our yacht would have to be abandoned as he refused to take her aboard as deck cargo. I asked if I could go back aboard *Nuts* with a volunteer sailor to salvage our personal effects. My wish was granted. But as we were on our way down the ladder, the second bridge officer came running and stopped us saying 'Is there really anything there worth risking lives for?'

All we had managed to bring with us were four carrier bags containing wallets, camera and films, but not much else. Now we were forced to abandon our lovely home, plus much valuable equipment aboard – including scuba diving gear, the liferaft, dinghy, outboard engine, plus three months' provisions and treasured possessions, like our diaries.

The captain asked if he could sink *Nuts* as a hazard to shipping. Instead, it was agreed that she would be left adrift and a sécurité message was broadcast. We informed Herb Hilgenberg's Atlantic radio net. Finally, we told friends over the SSB not to expect us in Barbados.

Soon we were shown to our new quarters – our home for the next 12 days – and we heard the ship's main engine start. The tanker was en route from America to Angola.

By now a strange double reality had developed. The tanker's logbook recorded 'Rescue operation'. But from our point of view we had been 'run down'. The captain insisted we had been 'lucky' to meet them.

Whatever our confused feelings, the friendliness and helpfulness of the tanker's crew were overwhelming. We were given shoes, clothes, toothbrushes and even Christmas presents for our son Rasmus.

On the evening of 28 December, 14 miles off the coast of Angola, we were told a helicopter would take us off the tanker on the morning of the 30th. The captain did not let us have our passports until I signed a paper saying that I was prepared to pay all expenses for our return to Denmark.

The helicopter arrived while the tanker was at anchor near a place called Soyo, an hour by plane from Luanda. We had been told by the captain that his company would pay for our journey home and then invoice us later.

However, once ashore we were told we had to pay on the spot for our tickets. Luckily, we were able to make arrangements with our bank in Denmark. Later that morning we flew from Soyo to Luanda, where we caught a flight to Paris, finally arriving in Copenhagen on 31 December. The cost of our return flights, including the help of an agent in Angola, totalled US $6,959.

A month later, on 2 February, the Danish Coastguard informed us that a Norwegian vessel had sighted *Nuts* at position 43° W and 19° N and had lifted her aboard. She was now on her way to San Cristobal, Panama.

There she was landed and a local agent inspected her and informed our insurers, Pantaenius, of the damage: *Nuts* had been dismasted and the starboard side of the hull had suffered a rupture one-and-a-half metres long by a metre. The pushpit and pulpit had been torn off. The yacht was insured for 300,000 Danish krona, but unfortunately, our onboard equipment was not covered separately.

From *Yachting Monthly* July, 2000

Lessons learned

With a young child aboard, and 12 days from Barbados, Niels still feels that he didn't make a wrong decision calling for assistance, although he admits 'we had enough dry-cell batteries to power our handheld GPS and torches'.

Sailing literature is full of horror stories involving small yachts having disastrous close encounters with big ships – either by design or accident. Invariably, the yachts are severely damaged.

Any experienced ocean sailor will tell you to give the widest possible berth to any ships that might approach too close, perhaps out of curiosity. Forces like drift, suction from prop wash, and wind eddies will guarantee you surrender all control over what happens next.

Sound preparation of yacht and confidence in your seamanship should mean that, even facing engine failure and flat batteries, you can complete an ocean passage safely under sail.

It was not until *Nuts'* batteries went flat that Niels discovered the crank handle to handstart the 17hp Volvo engine could not be turned, because movement was restricted by the construction of the galley.

As back-up against power failure next time, Niels could add a separate generator, bigger solar panels, or even a towing generator. Having full insurance for equipment and personal effects aboard is also a sound idea.

31 Fatal flotsam

Yacht *Gartmore Investment Managers*
Skipper Josh Hall
Bound from Charleston, South Carolina, to Cape Town
Date of loss 18 October, 1994
Position 500 miles off the coast of Brazil

While taking part in the first leg of the 1994–95 BOC Challenge Around Alone single-handed race, Josh Hall's 60ft racing yacht, Gartmore Investment Managers, *sank in cold, four-mile-deep South Atlantic water 500 miles off the Brazilian coast after colliding with a submerged object – probably a ship's container – at over 10 knots in rough seas.*

A s the BOC Around Alone fleet settled into the start of its fifth week at sea, Josh Hall, some 700 miles south of the Equator, had been in the south-east trades for about five days and was going great guns under full sail. The seas off this section of Brazil's coast had been unsettled, with bands of current kicking up some nasty, confused seas. Josh was hand-steering to stop the boat slamming over the backs of the waves.

Dusk was coming up with the wind blowing mostly over 22 knots true as *Gartmore* powered upwind at 10 knots. She came off the back of a wave, much like many others that threatened to loosen the fillings in the skipper's teeth. Josh nudged the wheel, expecting a soft landing, but was thrown up against it as the boat staggered to a standstill.

'It was the most horrendous landing you could imagine. The boat reared up and there was the most incredible rending sound as the bow came down. I realised something really bad had happened. It was almost as if we'd run aground,' he said.

As the yacht picked herself up again and started sailing, Josh rushed below, punching the Autohelm 7000 self-steering into action as he went.

BOC yachts have exceptional safety features, including a forward collision bulkhead designed to cope with just this sort of emergency. Already a huge amount of water had flooded the yacht through a 10ft-long gash. Water was halfway up the inspection and access hatch of the forward watertight bulkhead. Worse than that, the bulkhead itself had been fractured by the impact, allowing water to pour into the main part of the hull through a crack.

'My heart went to my stomach. It seemed as though it was happening to somebody else ... as if I was watching a bad movie. I had never felt so panicked or scared in all my time at sea. The fear came in waves. I didn't know what to do first. The real danger is a kind of paralysis from fear, not fear itself. In my mind I just knew I had to prioritise things. In a panic situation you try to quell the panic. I thought, "Is this it?"

'My adventure aboard this superb racing machine had turned into a nightmare. To get hold of myself, I was walking up and down very quickly in the cabin thinking "What do I do first? What do I do?" Suddenly there was so much to do that a full crew would be stretched to its limits.'

Josh's first priority was to get off a Mayday signal. He rushed to the chart table and hit the two red distress buttons on the Trimble Galaxy INMARSAT-C telex modem. He had to stop for a few seconds and read the instructions.

Within minutes UK Coastguard officials in Falmouth, Cornwall, alerted Charleston Race HQ that Josh was in trouble. It was 1950 GMT. At the same time Josh threw the switch on the INMARSAT-M satellite telephone, which would take about ten minutes to warm up. *Gartmore* was one of only three yachts in the race which was equipped to telephone direct to anywhere in the world.

Next, as water gushed in, he did his best to shore up the damaged area with floorboards and sailbags. Because she was holed in such a structurally strong area, Josh felt that *Gartmore* had struck the corner of something hard, like a shipping container. He switched on the big electric bilge pump forward of the watertight bulkhead and led another hose into the damaged area from a take-off on his water ballast pump. With all his pumps going he was shifting the best part of 5000 gallons (19,000 litres) of water an hour. Despite this, there were two or three feet of water throughout the yacht and it was rising.

He picked up the telephone to call Race HQ and let them know what was happening. Peter Dunning, an old friend, was on duty. As the co-ordinator of every BOC Challenge, Dunning has been through every crisis in the race and was typically calm and reassuring.

He agreed that Alan Nebauer on *Newcastle Australia*, 90 miles to the north-west, was Josh's nearest competitor. Charleston would try and raise Alan by radio or Standard-C to divert him to the rescue.

It was agreed that Josh would leave his SSB radio on the 4MHz frequency on which skippers chatted each night and he would wait for Alan to call. As a back-up rescue aid, Josh activated his 406MHz EPIRB (satellite distress beacon). Finally, he would talk to Race HQ on INMARSAT-M every hour to update the situation.

Outside, it was getting dark and Josh needed to get the mainsail down to stop *Gartmore* burying her bow under water. He also needed to turn around and start heading towards Alan, instead of away from him.

With half the staysail up, *Gartmore* was jogging along at some three knots with the whole foredeck awash. Josh hoped that slowing her down would stem the flood of water inside. The fact that the bows were down with the weight of water up forward helped to keep the batteries and engine dry at the back of the boat. Josh desperately needed them to maintain power to his bilge pumps and communications. He used pieces of floorboard to make a dam at the main bulkhead around the galley to stop water flooding the batteries.

'Once I got started, the effort and involvement removed the panic. What stood me in good stead was having dealt with other situations. I've been involved with dismastings, broken booms and personal injury. But my biggest asset, communications-wise, was the COMSAT satellite telephone.'

Some 20 minutes after Josh's Mayday, Charleston made contact with Alan Nebauer, who responded to their urgency message. At first Alan wondered if something had happened back home. Then, when he heard Josh was in trouble, he worked with communications co-ordinator Larry Brumbach to plot an intercept point for the two yachts. *Newcastle* proceeded on a southerly heading at seven knots, while *Gartmore* set a course to the west at four knots. This gave an average combined closing speed of 11 knots and put Alan some seven hours away.

By now Josh was coming to terms with the fact that *Gartmore* was fatally stricken. For a time he had thought he might be able to shore up the damage, stem the influx of water and limp somewhere. But the nearest land was more than 250 miles away. He accepted that his yacht was just going to be a floating island for him before rescue came. He would be lucky if she remained afloat. The creaking and groaning of the watertight bulkhead was frightening. If it burst open, the flow of water into the yacht would be doubled. *Gartmore*'s satellite phone was ringing every half-hour as Josh dealt with 15–20 calls over the next few hours before Alan's arrival.

Falmouth Coastguard, officially co-ordinating the rescue, called every hour and the Brazilian Coastguard on standby called four or five times. They were searching for ships nearby to divert to *Gartmore*'s aid, but were unable to locate any.

The Brazilian's English was undoubtedly better than Josh's Portuguese, but the language problems prompted some bizarre exchanges. As Josh failed in his polite attempts to explain that he didn't have time to answer bureau-cratic inquiries about the yacht's registration papers, he was forced to hang up on them saying: 'Sorry, I'm too busy!'

He also wanted to speak to Laura, his wife, back home in Ipswich. He didn't want to scare her, but was concerned that she might have been alarmed to receive a call from the authorities about his EPIRB distress signal. He wanted to reassure her. He also needed to hear her voice.

A few days earlier she had called him to say that she was expecting their second child. Now it was his turn to break the news that their yacht and life-savings were sinking under his feet.

Back home in Suffolk it was 10 o'clock in the evening when Laura picked up the phone. She had already spoken to Peter Dunning, who had spelled things out very well, so Josh didn't have to go through it all. But it was an emotional phone call.

'I broke down a bit at that point,' said Josh. 'We were a bit teary. I remember saying "I just want to be at home". Laura was very good. She's very solid and strong and I guess she'd had time to deal with the situation. Peter had assured her help was on its way to me. I phoned three times throughout the whole night's drama to let her know how it was going and also just to hear her voice. My parents drove over and spent the night with Laura. When my younger brother rang me a few minutes later for a chat I don't think he believed me when I told him the yacht was sinking and I was about to get into the liferaft.'

Time ceased to have much meaning for Josh as he pumped and prayed. He had first made radio contact with Alan some two hours after the fatal collision.

'I can remember the relief that he was on his way. He asked me if it was bad and I said "Yes, get here as soon as you can". But I didn't want to panic him because I knew he'd be sailing as fast as he could. At the same time, I wanted to impress on him the urgency of my situation. We agreed to speak on the radio every half-hour.'

In an attempt to defuse the tension in the midst of Josh's crisis, Alan Nebauer tried cracking a joke over the radio.

'What?' said Josh, failing to see the humour.

'Don't worry it's just my Aussie humour trying to cheer you up,' said Alan.

A few hours later, Alan had his own sense of humour failure when he 'lost contact' with Josh for more than an hour . . . Josh was busy trying to shore up the damaged hull and Alan's call was drowned out by the noise of the bilge pumps and engine running. Ninety minutes passed by before Josh remembered his radio schedule. Alan, meanwhile, had been 'freaking out', having called constantly and received no reply.

Down below on *Gartmore* it was a depressing scene with water still rising.

Josh, up to his hips in water, put on his survival suit. By now his concerns were concentrated on the integrity of his watertight bulkhead. If it gave way, or the pumps packed up, things would escalate rapidly. He decided to put his liferaft over the side, as an insurance.

'It was a six-man liferaft and I remember how heavy it was. I could only just pick it up ashore. But a frightened man has the strength of ten ... it went over easily and I tethered it alongside inflated so it was ready if I needed it. I was sponsored for all my safety equipment by a local company back home – Suffolk Sailing. When I left Shotley Marina to head to the start of the race, the boss, Graham Gardiner, came down to wish me well and I'll always remember him saying: "Unlike all your all other sponsors, I hope you never have to use what I've given you!" I was going to seriously disappoint him. There I was using everything he'd given me.'

Earlier, Josh had received a message from Peter Dunning asking him to hoist his SART (Search and Rescue Transponder) up the mast so that Alan could home in on it to find him.

In one of their radio calls Alan encouraged Josh: 'To try and save as much kit as you can.' In the drama and panic it was something that hadn't even occurred to Josh. Each hour from then on he spent about ten minutes between pumping, trying to grab bags which were already packed and throw them into the liferaft.

'I'd borrowed a couple of laptop computers and put them in the liferaft, but they got swamped. I grabbed family photos of Laura and Sam (his son aged two-and-a-half) which were stuck above the chart table. What do you take? My whole world was in that boat. You look at all the bits and pieces of gear that you accumulate over the years ... I felt we were one of the best equipped and prepared boats. I had to abandon all my navigation books and the sight reduction tables given to me by Robin Knox-Johnston. But I managed to grab my sextant. If I'd only managed to grab one thing it would have been the sextant.

'Alan was being updated on my position constantly by Race HQ, who were polling my GPS by the INMARSAT-C satellite. Ten miles away he also picked up the signal from my transponder on his radar. We agreed that to confirm my position I'd send up a red parachute flare, so I went on deck and fired one off. My masthead lights operated on a 24-volt system and were very powerful. He'd seen us!

'We were also fortunate that when Alan closed on my position there was almost a full moon at 0300 in the morning. Eventually Alan came up on the radio and said "Can you see me?"'

`I went up on deck and there he was in the moonlight, 200 yards away. He rolled up his headsail and we went over to talking on our waterproof handheld VHFs.'

As Alan Nebauer looked across to *Gartmore*, illuminated by her cabin and deck lights, he realised she was going down. She was a sad sight. 'If you love boats you just hate seeing them in those situations. I'd hoped maybe we could put a collision mat under the hole and sail to Brazil, but it was obviously not possible. *Gartmore* was very low in the water.' The Brazilian coast was also 500 miles away.

Conditions had improved as far as the sea state was concerned, but it was still too dangerous for Alan to come alongside. The pitching in the swell could have damaged *Newcastle's* hull. It was agreed that Josh would transfer to *Newcastle* in the liferaft. His final act before he abandoned *Gartmore* and his dreams was to turn off the bilge pumps and open up all her seacocks, thus ensuring that his prized yacht sank and did not pose a threat to any of the following yachts in the BOC fleet.

He found his longest line to hand, the mainsheet, tied it to the liferaft and jumped in. 'I thought it was important to stay attached to something at all times. But as it turned out it was a mistake.' The liferaft drifted 60–70 yards downwind and as *Gartmore* surged on the ten-foot waves the mainsheet snatched the liferaft, causing it to be swamped. Alan passed close by under reefed main and threw a line to Josh, but just as he went to grab it, the liferaft was violently jerked by its umbilical line to *Gartmore*. Letting go of Alan's line, Josh grabbed his knife and cut the line to *Gartmore*. Severing this last link to cut himself adrift seemed a final symbolic gesture.

'I was on my own for the next ten minutes as Alan did another circuit round the liferaft. It was the loneliest I've felt at sea. Sad and scared, even though he was close by, these were all fairly alien emotions to me. It felt strange to be bobbing around not tied to anything. *Gartmore* was such a tragic sight in the moonlight. The number of times I've pulled away from the yacht in the dinghy leaving it on a mooring . . . but from the liferaft it was awful to see her as she laboured hull-down.

'Alan's seamanship was superb as her rounded up on the raft for a second time. I tied on his line and he dragged the liferaft up to *Newcastle's* wide open transom. I scrambled on board, safe at last.'

'Welcome aboard mate,' said Alan.

'Thank you!' said Josh, in the understatement of the race.

'We were both very emotional,' said Josh. 'I stood for about an hour at the back of Alan's boat totally stunned by it all while he got organised to get under way.'

Josh's sudden sense of isolation set against the speed of modern day satellite communications was paradoxical enough to bewilder anyone, let alone a shipwrecked sailor.

As Alan stowed his bags down below, *Newcastle* jogged around under mainsail. It must have been over an hour before Josh got his survival suit off. They had to get rid of the liferaft and since it was impractical to bring it aboard they cut it up with a knife and let it sink.

'Neither of us wanted to stay around to see *Gartmore* sink. When we left, the light on the SART was still flashing just under the spreader. Despite the seas running the light wasn't rolling because the decks were awash.'

Twenty-two days later Alan and Josh crossed the Cape Town finish line.

The media were eager to quiz them about the mid-ocean rescue drama at a packed press conference. Josh was surprised at how emotional he was.

'I'd had three weeks to deal with it mentally and I thought I'd pretty much come to terms with it all. I started to give an account of what happened and just broke down in tears. I hadn't actually cried about the loss of the boat until then. It suddenly all came home to me.'

The Cape Town Harbour Master informed Josh Hall of the thought-provoking fact that in recent years over 40,000 containers had been officially reported as lost from the decks of Atlantic container ships.

'How many remain semi-submerged, suspended, waiting, is anyone's guess. I was lucky – I had superb communications on board, including a satellite phone. The skilled experience of the guys at BOC race HQ in Charleston coupled with the seamanship of Alan Nebauer meant I was plucked from the nose-diving *Gartmore* just eight hours after the collision.'

Extract from *The Loneliest Race*, by Paul Gelder,
published by Adlard Coles Nautical

Lessons learned

Josh used pieces of floorboard to make a dam at the main bulkhead around the galley to stop water flooding the batteries, which he desperately needed to maintain power to his bilge pumps and communications.

BOC yachts have a forward collision bulkhead designed to cope with just this sort of emergency, but still it didn't work. Josh did his best to shore up the damaged area with floorboards and sailbags. With all his pumps going he was shifting the best part of 5000 gallons (19,000 litres) of water an hour. But despite this, there were two or three feet of water throughout the yacht and it was rising. Because she was holed in such a structurally strong area, Josh felt that *Gartmore* had struck the corner of something hard, like a shipping container.

32 Anatomy of a sinking

Yacht *Sea Crest,* a Brewer 44
Skipper Joe Bass
Bound from the British Virgin Islands to Venezuela
Date of loss 16 June 1998
Position Two days south-west of US Virgin Islands

As a circumnavigator and highly experienced yachtsman, Joe Bass thought he was prepared for any emergency. Yet, he found himself in life-and-death circumstances, battling unexpected challenges which he had never have anticipated. What happened, the surprises he faced and vital lessons he learned, proved an eye-opener. 'If my experience can help one couple face a similar situation better prepared, this account will have been worth the effort,' he said.

Recently, I re-crossed the Atlantic once again in *Sea Crest*, my Brewer 44. After three years in the North Atlantic and the Mediterranean, I looked forward to the warmer seas and reliable trade winds of the Caribbean. I finished a re-fit in the British Virgin Islands and then it was time to sail to hurricane-free Venezuela, by way of Bonaire. Because my crew was called back to the USA, I decided to singlehand to Bonaire. *Sea Crest* was perfectly rigged for solo sailing. Between fully crewed voyages, I loved singlehanding as a way to 'stretch' my sea legs and become one with my boat on the open ocean.

Countdown to collision
14 June: At 0700 I upped the anchor and sailed out of St Thomas and set a rhumb-line course directly for Bonaire, some 400 miles distant. The winds were perfect, 20 knots out of the south-east, and the sailing was magnificent. *Sea Crest* was in her element on the open seas.

15 June: Once again *Sea Crest* sailed beautifully. Everything was right. It was one of those days which cruisers remember as sheer perfection.

16 June: The last day of her existence dawned with heavy clouds coming in from the south-east. The forecast was for a 'tropical wave' to move through the area, bringing squalls with heavy rain and gusts of up to 35 knots. Around 0900, squall after squall began passing through, bringing intense rain and high winds. Visibility grew more limited. By 1100, the frequency and strength of the squalls had increased. I furled the working jib and changed it to *Sea Crest*'s normal heavy-weather rig – double-reefed main and staysail. She sailed comfortably in 9ft seas, rising and falling gently as they swept past beneath her. We were 'snug and cosy' for the conditions and if it hadn't been for the limited visibility, it would have been an exciting sail.

At 1300, the squalls increased once more in frequency and wind speed. Heavy rain was driven horizontally towards us and there was very little visibility. I was down below monitoring the radar for any traffic.

Sea Crest charged ahead, riding well and comfortably, as I switched the radar from one range to another, watching for any signs of traffic. In one particularly strong squall, the wind speed indicator shot up to 38 knots, as she heeled sharply and moved ahead.

At that moment, *Sea Crest* rose up on what seemed to be a particularly large wave and came down into the trough. As she fell, heavily heeled over, I heard a loud bang. It was a rending, hard sound, unlike any I've ever heard from waves hitting a boat. She shuddered and veered off course, as though being bodily pushed or shoved aside. The autopilot quickly brought her back on course and as she continued sailing, the bilge alarm started its shrill warning signal.

I rushed up on deck to see what I had hit. Because of driving rain, the high seas and forward momentum of the boat, I could see nothing.

I hurriedly clipped on my safety harness and moved around the deck, looking over the sides from bow to stern for any sign of damage to the hull above the waterline. I could find none.

I dropped the staysail, made my way back to the cockpit and brought *Sea Crest* upwind, hove-to. I examined the leeward side of the hull, but I could see no sign of any damage above the waterline.

Rushing back down below, I opened the engine-room doors to inspect the bilge area. Every sailor's nightmare had come true. The bilge was rapidly filling and the water was already up to the engine block. I had to find the source of the inflow . . . and fast.

I moved through the cabin, pulling up the floor hatch covers to inspect the through-hull fittings. They seemed secure. But the bilge pump wasn't keeping up with water rushing in.

To my surprise, I quickly discovered that once the source of the water inflow was covered by rising water, it would be almost impossible to find, unless it was a big 'gusher'. My only hope was to find it by feel. I tried to trace the direction of the inflow and follow it back to its source. But with the boat both rolling and pitching, there was no 'direction' to follow – only turbulence.

I soon realised that 75 per cent of the possible area of damage, the underwater hull, was completely inaccessible from inside the boat due to the flooring, furniture, glassfibre liners or the four fuel and water tanks.

I left the futile search for the source of the water inflow to return to the engine room to get the portable high-capacity bilge pump I stowed there for just this kind of emergency. It had been used only once, in mid-Atlantic, when I answered the distress call of a 27ft wooden yawl which was sinking. This high-capacity pump saved the boat. Now, I desperately needed it to save *Sea Crest*.

I lowered the pump's intake into the bilge, ran its three-inch discharge hose out of the nearest opening port, secured it to a stanchion and directed the flow overboard. I hurriedly connected the electrical leads to the engine-starting battery with crocodile clips. The pump immediately started throwing water out at a high rate. It worked! The water level appeared to be dropping slightly. It had fallen two inches, from the top of the engine block. Clearly the breach in the hull was not large. With the pump working and buying me time, I started a systematic search for the damaged area. The pump was definitely reducing the water level, which meant the inflow was less than the pump's discharge. There was hope.

I grabbed my boat-saver 'umbrella' – a heavy canvas device which in its 'closed' mode is shoved through the hole in the hull and, once through, opened up like an umbrella and pulled tightly back against the outside of the hull, secured there by an adjusting clamp on the inside.

I had kept it ready to use, as well as underwater epoxy and a 'collision mat' – a heavy canvas with grommets, made for just this use.

I desperately searched every area of the hull I could reach, feeling and probing, hoping to discover any discernable rush of water or apparent direction of flow. But as *Sea Crest* rolled and pitched in the large seas, rising water was thrown about in every direction.

By the time I gave up this unsuccessful effort and got back to the pump, I was in for a terrible shock. The pump had been stopped most of this time – blocked at its intake. The water level was now covering the engine and spilling out into the cabin. The blockage was caused by oil absorbent pads stowed in the engine room. The pads had fallen into the deep bilge and were now clogging the pump's intake. I tried to pull them out, but they were very heavy in their soaked state and came apart, leaving a pulpy mass.

I cleared the intake and re-lowered it, only to see it clog moments later. Cardboard boxes with filters and engine parts disintegrated in the rising water, turned into pulp floating on the surface and clogging the intake. Every time I had to stop to unclog the intake, the water level rose.

As long as I could keep the pump's intake clear, I gained on the water level. 'I can save her!' I kept thinking to myself. But the pump repeatedly clogged and the water level rose. When I stopped to search for the source of the inflow, the water level rose still further. I was astonished at the incredible amount of debris and paper that was now floating on top of the rising water. The cabin sole hatch-board covers, which I had removed and replaced while checking the through hulls, floated up and off and became deadly hard-edged 'surfboards' and battering rams, being hurled from side to side on top of the water, as the boat rolled and pitched. One knocked the crocodile clips off the battery, stopping the pump. The clips seemed adequate at anchor but were all too easily dislodged when hit by floating debris. It became clear they needed to be much larger and stronger. I was losing the battle. I switched the battery leads to the separate and much higher 'house' battery bank, which was still above water. Repeatedly, the pump intake clogged.

I was losing the battle. I realised I was going to need outside help to save *Sea Crest*. I have always been reluctant to call for assistance, but I urgently needed a larger, petrol-powered pump – one that was not so vulnerable to clogging. I started a series of Mayday calls on VHF channel 16, hoping to reach a ship within range.

There were no replies. I turned the radar on to the 24-mile range, but there was nothing. I was out there alone. It was time for urgent action to get help. I grabbed the EPIRB 406 and taped it to the aft rail and activated it. Returning below, I made a distress call on the SSB emergency frequency. Getting no response and with water rising up my legs, I switched frequencies to WOM, the commercial high-seas marine operator in Miami, and they responded immediately. They relayed my position and situation to the Coast Guard and I went back to the pump. Then, I was confronted with another unexpected discovery – one which almost proved fatal.

As water rose above floor level, all ten cabin sole hatch-board covers had floated off, leaving ten large gaping holes hidden under the surging water. As I went forward to search again for the source of the leak, my right leg plunged deep into one of these gaping holes up to my knee.

My leg was jammed solidly under the water; wedged firmly between the top of the fuel tank and the bulkhead. I couldn't get it loose.

If I couldn't free myself, I would go down with my sinking boat. I realised I had to relax my foot and leg and slowly move it about, rather than pull it straight out by brute force. With great effort I managed to take a deep breath, relax and slowly move my foot and leg about. I lost some skin, but after ten of the longest minutes of my life, I was free.

An hour had passed. From now on I had to move about most carefully. There was no cabin sole left there were only holes . . . traps. The scene around me was one of chaos and destruction. I faced the shock of seeing my beautiful home transformed into a disaster area. The emotional distress was traumatic.

With every roll of the boat, hatch boards were thrown back and forth in the surging water. As the water rose, two heavy engine-room doors floated off their pintles and joined them. Just to remain standing in the rising water, as it surged from side to side with every roll of the boat, was difficult. To work in this situation was almost impossible. I had to use one arm to fend off the doors and hatch boards hurtling across the cabin with every roll. To do all this, and find and deal with the inflow and pump would have kept a full crew busy, much less a solo sailor or a cruising couple.

Though I had not yet thought of abandoning ship, it was now clear I had to face that reality. I launched the Avon liferaft and attached it to the aft rail. I was then faced with a cruel choice. If I took time to salvage my most important possessions it would keep me away from the pump intake, and almost certainly guarantee the loss of *Sea Crest*. I chose to put all my faith and effort into saving my boat. It was going to be all or nothing.

Two hours after the collision, I heard a great roar overhead and rushed up on deck with my handheld VHF radio – an essential piece of equipment in such a crisis. The rescue aircraft had arrived from Curacao. The pilot said he was going to fly off on a circular route to search for any vessels within range. I told him I needed a vessel with a large portable pump. When I returned below, the water was up to my waist. I had a battle to stay on my feet, avoid traps in the sole, fend off debris and keep the pump unclogged. The next 90 minutes were a blur.

The aircraft returned and the pilot told me that the nearest ship was about 60 miles away and would arrive in 2–3 hours. I told him I was going to keep trying to save the boat but would board the liferaft and cut loose only at the last moment before she went down. I have always said that my boat would have to leave me, by going under. I would not leave her. But, of course, I never really believed it would happen.

Several hours later, I heard the pilot calling on the VHF. A Norwegian ship, *Heros*, was arriving on the scene and he said I should immediately leave *Sea Crest*. I spoke to the captain. He didn't have a suitable pump on board. That news was the death knell for *Sea Crest*.

I went below one last time, grabbed my wallet, passport and ship's papers, put them into a plastic bag and secured it to my lifejacket. That's all I could take from what had been my home for several years. I had gambled that I could save it all. It had been so close. But it had not worked out that way.

I paused on the aft deck to bid farewell to *Sea Crest*. As the seas lapped over her decks, I stepped into the liferaft. I had poured my life, my work, and my worldly possessions into her. It was all going down with her. I didn't then, or now, regret that I gave her my best effort. She deserved at least that.

The captain explained the rescue procedure by VHF. I cast off from *Sea Crest* and the liferaft was driven by seas and winds towards the sides of the now stationary ship. As I watched the crew lowering the rope ladder, I heard them shout, 'Look out!' The same seas and winds driving the raft towards the ship were also pushing *Sea Crest* towards me. The ship and *Sea Crest* were going to collide – and I was caught between them.

The crew saw it before I did. I turned to see *Sea Crest* go down into the trough of a large wave. As she rose on the crest and was about to be thrown violently against the ship's side, I jumped from the liferaft back onto *Sea Crest*'s now awash deck – just in time. The liferaft was folded over and crushed by the violent impact of the two hulls. When *Sea Crest* drifted back away from the ship, the liferaft popped back to shape. As my yacht drifted away and sank beneath the waves, I grabbed the rope ladder and climbed to safety clutching the plastic rubbish bag containing my worldly possessions.

Aftermath and observations

The captain of *Heros* and I discussed what I may have hit. Some of the crew had seen semi-submerged logs in the area. We thought it was a partially-sunken container or logs. Both are often lost off ships in bad weather. I have seen several half-sunken containers as I've sailed around the world. Off Cape Trafalgar, near Gibraltar, I saw one directly ahead, with only its edge sticking up above water. I turned just in time, missing it by not more than 25ft. It's not an empty sea out there. During the same period that *Sea Crest* was lost, two other yachts sunk in the Atlantic after colliding with submerged objects. One shipping report states that more than 1000 containers are reported lost at sea each year. Many others are not reported. How many remain semi-submerged is anyone's guess.

From *Yachting Monthly*, February 2000

Lessons learned

Be prepared, it can happen to you – far out to sea or on a coastal passage. I was prepared for storms, gear failure, close encounters with ships or other mishaps. But the shock of hitting a submerged object caught me mentally unprepared. I thought collisions only happened with ships and I always kept watch for traffic and used radar fitted with a very loud alarm when sailing singlehanded.

You must have both a plan and equipment ready in the event of a sudden catastrophe. The handheld VHF was crucial in communicating with the aircraft and the rescue ship. The portable high-capacity bilge pump almost saved my boat. It could very well save yours. Built-in bilge pumps are often inadequate. An investment in a portable pump is not only extra insurance for your vessel, but could save any stricken sailboat you encounter.

Obviously, you must have an EPIRB 406. No one should go offshore without one. But it must be registered properly, with telephone contact numbers. I was very surprised to learn that the EPIRB did not give my position to rescue authorities on the first pass. They had to call the telephone numbers I gave on my registration. They reached my son who informed them I was sailing from the Virgin Islands to Venezuela. This helped them determine my location before the additional passes required for a fix – time you may not be able to afford. By this time, the rescue co-ordination centre had been informed of my SSB Mayday call with my exact position.

For the EPIRB system to work, you must register it and provide 24 hour telephone contacts if possible. And back it up with VHF or SSB calls if possible.

Surprises I faced

Though I have circumnavigated and sailed full-time for more than 10 years, I faced surprises I was not prepared for: I was amazed how difficult it was to trace the source of the inflow once the water level was above the source. Three-quarters of the possible area of damage was inaccessible from inside the boat due to the flooring, furniture, fibreglass liners, etc. I had only a few precious minutes before this happened. I should have made that search my first priority. It probably cost me my yacht. But my first instinctive reaction was to rush up on deck and see what I had hit. Then, I took time to carefully inspect the hull above the waterline.

By the time I got back below, the water level was already above the inflow source. That made it impossible to find the breach in the hull. Finding the source of the breach must be your first action. Everything else can wait.

You have only a short time to decide your actions. The first five minutes are the most crucial.

Set your priorities now . . . in advance. Be sure your mate or crew is as familiar with the procedure as they are with the man-overboard drill. Your earliest actions will be your most effective.

The cabin sole hatch-board covers became deadly hard-edged 'surf-boards' and battering rams as the boat rolled and pitched.

Another danger was that all ten cabin sole hatch-board covers floated off, leaving ten large gaping holes hidden under the surging water so that I almost lost my life by stepping into a hole. Secure yours in advance. This is vital in case of a capsize, of course, but few people think of it in the event of taking on water. Also put as many of those boxes and paper products as possible in waterproof plastic bags. I never expected to see so much pulpy paper floating and submerged . . . and it proved devastating to the pump's operation.

I have always sailed with a small brass plaque next to the navigation station. It reads: 'Hope for the best. Organize for the worst'.

So, expect trouble. Do your planning and preparation now.

33 That sinking feeling

Yacht *Bits* (36ft Kim Holman-designed Twister)
Skipper Noel Dilly
Bound from the Azores and Madeira
Date of loss
Position off the coast of Casablanca

Noel Dilly is an eye surgeon in London and has been sailing for 45 years. He keeps his Kim Holman-designed Twister, Bits, on the River Medway. His previous boats were a Stella and a Westerly Centaur. In this account he describes the sudden holing and sinking of a 36ft yacht off the coast of Casablanca:

It was a beautiful starlit night with virtually no wind and just a gentle Atlantic swell running. We were a few miles off Casablanca, on a return voyage from the Azores and the Madeira Islands. We had just begun to round the headland with the lights of Casablanca harbour in sight when there was a bang as the hull hit something under water.

We brought the yacht on to a reciprocal course, but after about 10 minutes there was a second thump, much gentler than the first because she was travelling much more slowly. However, the usual precaution of pumping immediately after hitting something revealed that we had taken on water in the bilges. They had been dry after the first strike. A shout from forward revealed that water was welling up through the floorboards. The next shock was that it was not possible to remove the floorboards to try to locate the source of the leak.

Amazingly, they had been screwed down at the last refit. Worse still, the

222

weight of inrushing water was buckling the floorboards and bending the screws so that they could not be turned with a screwdriver. It was imperative that we remove the floorboards if we were to stand any chance if saving the yacht. First we used a winch handle and then a large hammer to try to smash through the boards, but they were of quality teak and the hammer hardly dented the surface!

The biggest screwdriver we forced into the gap between the boards bent when it was used as a lever. By now the board was under water and efforts from inside the yacht became futile. We decided we would have to tackle the leak from the outside.

The bilge pumps were doing their best, but the boat was filling visibly. What had not been taken into account was the action that had been going on above decks while the battle was being fought below. The engine was still running, and as it was obvious to the rest of the crew that we were in danger of sinking, they had steered the yacht towards the apparent safety of the shore.

The swell was breaking on the beach and we were pitching about in the beginnings of the small but frequent waves. Our attempts to get underneath the wildly gyrating bow proved hazardous and only a half-hearted attempt was made to find the leak. While this was going on, the water level had reached something vital, stopping the engine. Then the boat started settling quite rapidly. We tried draping a sail under the bow, but this did nothing except sink the bow, and the extra weight up forward caused an increased rush of water. The entire crew then moved their combined weight to the stern, but still the hole remained below the waterline. With no wind, no engine, and sinking with no chance to stop the leak, it seemed a good idea to consider abandoning ship.

The idea had hardly been mentioned when one of the crew, who was obviously under considerable stress, threw the liferaft overboard. It was not much more than 200m to the shore, and it would have been much easier to have pumped up the inflatable dinghy. However, as the liferaft was inflated and ready we decided to use it.

The crew went gingerly below to collect their valuables and put on extra clothes. Surprisingly, everyone reappeared in smart 'going ashore' gear. The valuables were hastily thrown in the rucksack normally used for shopping, which was put in the raft; then everyone climbed in.

With the canopy doors open, the paddles were used to head the liferaft towards the shore. However, as the liferaft entered the breakers it capsized and we were washed overboard. Then we realised that the vital rucksack had been lost. Bedraggled, we swam the liferaft up the beach, and stood up dripping to face a car full of Moroccan policeman.

Fortunately, they had seen the yacht slipping beneath the waves. But bureaucrats are bureaucrats the world over and the full entry formalities still had to be fulfilled. The senior policeman then asked what we would like to do.

The skipper announced: 'Take us to the best hotel in Casablanca!'

Just after midnight, five dripping yachtsmen were deposited in the hotel's foyer. A haughty and obviously horrified manager surveyed us and saw that we had no baggage. Drawing himself to his full height he demanded: 'And how do you intend to pay?'

The skipper then fished a sodden handkerchief from his top pocket and ceremoniously unwrapped an American Express credit card.

'That will do nicely, sir!'

It was at that point that everyone fell about laughing.

Next morning, intent on salvage, we went down to the beach where the yacht had been washed ashore. The hole in the bow was not much bigger than a fist. If only there had been a wrecking bar aboard to smash our way through the floorboards.

From *Yachting Monthly*, May 1995

Lessons learned

The single most startling, but I suspect almost universal, fault that this incident revealed, was that no emergency plan had been agreed before or during the cruise. The distress, although dire, had not been communicated to anyone. No one had been delegated to send a Mayday, nor to inflate the dinghy. Certain sensible things should be agreed from the outset.

The skipper with a few words can decide who launches the liferaft and who sends the Mayday, should the need arise. On my own yacht we have the whole format for the Mayday message written on a notice alongside our radio so that even the most inexperienced crew member knows what to do.

Immediately after striking anything below the waterline, or falling off a large wave, it is a good idea to pump the bilge. This way you have a dry bilge as a starting point from which to assess if you are making water when you try to pump later. Or, of course, you may not be able to pump the bilges dry, which will signal that you are taking a significant amount of water aboard.

If you start taking in water, close all the seacocks. It was an amazing sight to see water pouring through the marine toilet once the basin lip was below sea level. Water rushing into the cockpit via the cockpit drains was probably the last straw that provoked the panic launch of the liferaft.

Never, ever screw down the floorboards. It is prudent to think about how you would get to the below-the-waterline hull of your boat. Most people who consider this problem end up buying a lump (club) hammer and a wrecking bar to add to their tool kit. The item frequently forgotten is a substantial pair of bolt croppers to free a mast that has fallen overboard. Research reveals that this is the most common cause of being holed below the waterline.

How big a hole would sink your yacht? There is a whole science of fluid dynamics, but a reasonable estimate is that if the hole letting in the water is bigger than the smallest part of the bilge pump pipework, then, unless you can make the hole smaller, you will surely sink.

A good engine-driven bilge pump will shift about 40 gallons per minute under ideal conditions. The average hand-operated one is about half that amount. Bilge pump ratings in the manufacturers' claims are usually for 60 pumps per minute against no resistance, and with no need to lift the water (to a particular height above sea level) before discharging it. A head of 7ft will halve the output. Any length of piping will rapidly reduce the efficiency of the pump, as length of pipe plays an important role in generating the resistance against which the pump is working.

Just to depress you further, you cannot pump faster than the time it takes for the pump to fill and empty. Otherwise the pump loses efficiency. Next time you pump your bilges just time a complete cycle. The classic 'frightened man with a two-gallon bucket' will shift about 20 gallons a minute. That involves lifting and throwing 20lbs of water every six seconds. One way of working-out to keep fit!

It is a reasonable assumption that the flow of sea water through a hole is directly proportional to the fourth power of the radius of the hole. A two-inch hole will let in four times as much water as a one-inch hole would in the same time. Do not make the hole bigger by exploring it, if you can avoid doing so. Any means of decreasing the size of the hole will be richly rewarded by a big decrease in inflow. Do not despair if you seem to be getting nowhere pumping the boat out after you have plugged the hole. There is an awful lot more water about than is visible, and a great deal has to be shifted before there is any visible fall in the waterline.

Do not, repeat do not, make for the shore. The breakers are dangerous and in our case had the boat remained in calm water, she might have been saved. Breakers are no place for small liferafts. Even the inflatable dinghy would have had problems.

A surprising problem arose after the liferaft capsized. Two crew members had been wearing automatically inflating lifejackets; once they were thrown in the water the jackets inflated. As designed, the jackets turned them face up. It proved extremely difficult for them to overcome this righting tendency so they could swim to the shore.

34 The loss of a 'friend'

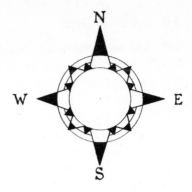

Yacht *Yondi* (T24)
Skipper Peter Jackson
Bound from Plymouth for a daysail
Position Five miles south of the western end of Plymouth Breakwater

Peter Jackson began sailing in the Solent as a Sea Scout aged 12. Years later, a spur of the moment decision to go for a sail ended in disaster when his yacht Yondi *struck a submerged object off Plymouth and began to sink.*

I was standing on the outer pontoon of the Clovelly Bay Marina with the sound of the Plymouth Lifeboat's powerful engines receding in the distance. I must have looked both ridiculous and pathetic. I was wearing a garment that looked like a giant Babygro, about four sizes too big, and a pair of size 11 boots on my size 7 feet. In my arms was a lifejacket and a small bundle of wet clothes. Tears were just beginning to run down my face. Our yacht *Yondi*, which had been so much of our life over the past four years, was gone for ever.

We first met *Yondi* in an open barn on a farm in the middle of Gloucester, where her owner had been replacing much of the wooden cockpit and fitting a new diesel engine. She was a T24, built in 1965 by D C Perfect of Chichester, and was the deep fin, tall mast version.

As soon as we saw her we knew she was right for us, and we quickly agreed to buy her. Over the next four years we used her as often as we could. We learned to sail in all conditions and were soon competent navigators.

We explored nearly all the deep-water harbours and anchorages from Dartmouth to the Isles of Scilly and across to the Channel Islands. She became a home away from the stress of work for both my wife and myself.

It was near the end of September, and I should have been sailing west with my son on what would probably have been the last trip of the season. But the forecast had predicted gales, so the trip was postponed and I decided, instead, to change the filters on the engine. When I'd finished, I should have gone home. Instead, I decided to give the engine a test and *Yondi* and I were soon heading out into Plymouth Sound.

There was a fresh breeze blowing from the north-west which meant that although the wind was about force 5, the sea remained fairly calm. Since I was already late home I decided to throw caution to the wind and have a short sail. Soon we had cleared the breakwater and were heading for the open sea. *Yondi* was going perfectly and we were both thoroughly enjoying ourselves. She was a heavy boat with a deep keel and needed a good wind to go well. Conditions were ideal and she was flying along at near 7 knots. Soon we were well on the way to the Eddystone Lighthouse. What time did I say I'd be home?

I'd just left the tiller to prepare the sails to go about and return home, when there was a tremendous crash and *Yondi* seemed to stop dead. I was thrown forward on to the cabin bulkhead. I thought we must have collided with another vessel, but nothing was in sight. I was very confused. I knew that there were no rocks in the vicinity, and then I saw it: a huge log – no, a tree – just under the surface of the water. It was about 30ft long, and around 5ft in diameter, covered in weed and goose barnacles.

I went below to look for damage and was surprised when I found no big holes in the hull. In fact, I could find no damage at all, except for a slight seepage of water into the bilge pump. I wasn't concerned as the electric pump could easily deal with it. I felt it prudent to return to harbour as soon as possible, so rather than make a long beat back against the wind, I dropped sail and started the engine. As I had not replaced the cover on the bilge sump I could see the water level from the cockpit, and soon noticed that the level was slowly rising. I wasn't worried as I had a large capacity Whale bilge pump I could use if the electric pump couldn't cope. Although the sea was reasonably calm, there was a swell running and without sails *Yondi* was rolling.

After about 10 minutes the water level had reached the top of the sump, so I started using the bilge pump, quickly reducing the water level. I examined the sump again but still couldn't see any holes or cracks. I deduced that the water must be seeping up around the keel bolts, which had perhaps been loosened by the impact of the tree on the keel. I realised that, if this was the case, the movement of the boat was likely to exacerbate the leak and I could see no way of stopping it. The water level was now rising steadily and I was using the bilge pump continuously. Unfortunately, I was no longer able to keep the level within the bilge and water was beginning to slop around the floor of the cabin. I still felt that I would be able to reach Plymouth safely, as I knew *Yondi* would have to be nearly full of water before she would sink. Then matters took a turn for the worse.

The water reached the lower lockers where all of our tinned food was stored and the labels were being washed off and sucked into the pump strainer, slowing its efficiency.

Although I cleared the strainer several times, it blocked almost immediately and the water level was climbing quickly. I decided that I needed help. A quick look around showed no other vessel in sight. I went to the VHF radio and, microphone in hand, went through the lessons that I'd received when training for my radio licence. Should I put out a PAN PAN call, meaning that I need assistance, or a Mayday, used when life is endangered? At this point *Yondi* rolled and the water covered one of the berths and me up to my waist. The engine stopped. I made the call: 'Mayday, Mayday, Mayday, this is yacht *Yondi*, yacht *Yondi*, I am five miles south of the western end of Plymouth Breakwater. I have hit a submerged tree and am taking water on board. I am on my own and am in danger of sinking.'

The Coastguard responded immediately and calmly. Help was on its way. I put my lifejacket on and went to inflate my dinghy which was on the foredeck. I'd just started inflating it when the lifeboat called to obtain a radio fix on my position. I'd started inflating again when another yacht called to ask me to fire a flare so he could do the same. This I did, burning my hand in the process.

Once again, I turned to the dinghy, but now the Coastguard called again for an update. The water seemed to have levelled out but I realised this was only because it was filling the full volume of the hull. The cabin was now a dangerous place. Every time *Yondi* rolled, all kinds of floating debris was being thrown around the cabin, and the force of the water was so strong that I was unable to unblock the pump strainer again. Fortunately, I had installed the radio so that it could be operated from the cockpit and, surprisingly, it was still working, although the batteries had long been under water.

The first help to arrive was a fast rigid inflatable boat (RIB) from Fort Bovisand Diving Centre with three fit young men on board. They were soon bailing with buckets. When another RIB from the same centre arrived it was decided to pass lines under *Yondi*, attached to these boats, to try and keep her afloat. The bailing seemed to be making no difference to the water level.

There were now several boats standing by and the lifeboat arrived. They launched their dinghy to bring a large petrol pump over to *Yondi*. I felt a big sense of relief as I was still very uncertain about being held up by those RIBs. *Yondi* was a very heavy boat. This relief didn't last for long, however, as the lifeboatmen couldn't start the pump. It was decided to bring the lifeboat alongside and use its internal pump, even though this meant casting off from the RIBs.

We were alongside the lifeboat and I was just taking the hose from a crew member when the coxswain ordered us all to leave *Yondi*. No one moved. This time we were given the same order in much stronger and louder language. This convinced us. As I went to do so, my lifejacket became entangled with one of the rear mast stays and for what seemed a lifetime I was firmly attached to the boat. Eventually, I freed myself and jumped into the sea. I turned immediately and was just in time to see the top of the mast and the new, expensive furling foresail disappearing under the water. I remember thinking that I'd hardly used that sail. *Yondi* sank like a stone, leaving just a few pieces of debris floating on the surface. Even the partially inflated dinghy which had been untied did not appear. There was nothing to show that my beautiful boat had ever existed.

I was soon on board the lifeboat, dressed in rather large but warm clothes and being given a hot drink. The crew were embarrassed about not being able to start the pump but perhaps they were just as unfortunate as I was when I hit the tree. We all know that any mechanical item will always fail at a critical time and for no apparent reason.

Perhaps only those who have owned a boat, and used it as intensively as I did, can begin to understand my tears as I stood on the pontoon. Certainly some of the tears were due to release of the tension of the past hours, but there was also a feeling of having lost a close friend, a friend with whom I had shared so much. Experiences such as meeting dolphins for the first time, watching them swim alongside, so close that we could touch them, and watching them swim under the boat and jump out of the water. We will never forget sailing in warm weather through hundreds of jellyfish and watching sunfish, basking sharks and pilot whales, or arriving in harbour and meeting many wonderful and interesting people and discovering new and fascinating places.

I feel that sailing is a physical, intellectual and emotional experience and for me *Yondi* was part of these emotions. At times, sailing can be very challenging. On a long trip in poor weather with a pitching boat, the physical effort of operating the sails efficiently, or even just keeping on course, can be extremely demanding. For me, navigating is an intellectual challenge and it was always very satisfying to arrive at an intended destination. But, ultimately, it's the feelings that are the most important. I find it impossible to describe the emotions we felt when we first met the dolphins, or the joy of sitting on the boat in a quiet anchorage, or of just being at sea using the wind to take us wherever we wanted to go. My wife says that the moment that I sat in the dinghy to row out to *Yondi* on her moorings I relaxed and changed. For me *Yondi* was freedom.

No only had we lost *Yondi* but also many of our possessions. Because we spent so much time on her, she was always fully equipped for us to live on. We lost clothes, cameras, binoculars, books and artist's materials, besides all the normal items found on a well-equipped yacht. Months later we were still remembering lost items, but the saddest loss was our log book, describing all the adventures we had shared.

I suppose now I am a little wiser and I have certainly learned from this experience. I would never have considered the possibility of colliding with a submerged tree or of a lifeboat's pump failing to start. I was pleased with the way I coped with the situation, and my only doubt is whether I delayed too long before calling for help. I have not been put off sailing, but unfortunately it will not now be on my own boat. The biggest error I committed during this sad affair was to calculate how much money owning *Yondi* had cost us. The figures made it clear that we had never been able to afford her and that she could not be replaced.

A chance meeting with a tree in a most unexpected location had deprived me of my 'friend' and one of the most fulfilling activities I have ever enjoyed.

From *Yachting Monthly*, June 1998

Lessons learned

Although Peter Jackson cleared the bilge pump strainer several times, it blocked almost immediately and the water level was climbing quickly. When the water reached the lower lockers, where all the tinned food was stored, the labels were being washed off and sucked into the pump strainer, slowing its efficiency.

Fortunately, Jackson had installed a VHF radio so that it could be operated from the cockpit and, surprisingly, it was still working, although the batteries had long been under water, when he sent his Mayday.

35 Hard chance in a nutshell

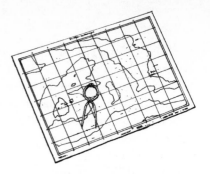

Yacht *Dorothea* (Harrison Butler-designed 32ft Bermudian cutter)
Skipper Peter Tangvald
Bound from Cayenne, French Guyana to Fort Lauderdale, Florida, USA.
Date of loss 12 March, 1967
Position approximately 40 miles S of Barbados

When I told the ocean-wanderer Peter Tangvald that I was preparing this book, he replied, from Las Palmas, that he had himself once thought of compiling a list of 'yacht disasters', with the intention of making a book out of it. However, he had abandoned the idea – 'after having submitted a few of the examples for the approval of the various skippers concerned, who are all very offended by my conclusions, which generally put the blame on them; as they themselves, in every case, considered the fault to lie with everybody else but themselves!'

Nevertheless, Peter did kindly give me permission to use his own account of the sinking of the Dorothea *in the Atlantic. I have used the title he originally intended for the story.*

Dorothea, a Harrison Butler-designed cutter, was built in Whitstable in 1935. Peter Tangvald bought her in 1959 and during the next five years sailed her round the world before writing his book Sea Gypsy. *After marrying his faithful crew Simone, and while in South America, they decided to build a larger boat and to sell* Dorothea *in America, where she could be expected to fetch a higher price. Tangvald left Cayenne on 7 March, sailing single-handed, with the intention of making a stop on the way at Charlotte Amalie in the Virgin Islands, where he hoped to meet old friends.*

My wife stayed behind in our newly leased house to watch over the huge pile of lumber and all the machine tools already purchased for the new ship. She told me later it had been a beautiful sight to see the ship tack down river towards the sea. Had she seen me when I crossed the bar, however, she would not have said the same thing, as one huge breaker swept the ship from end to end, soaking me to the skin in the process, while I wondered how strange it was that man is able to shoot rockets to the moon, yet be incapable of making oilskin which is truly watertight. Being wet and cold I decided to anchor for the night in the lee of the Iles du Salut about 30 miles from Cayenne.

Next morning, without having gone ashore, I set sail again, this time in much improved weather, well rested and cheerful. The wind was right on the beam and very fresh and gave *Dorothea* her maximum speed. In fact from us leaving these islands till the moment of the accident, she made the greatest average speed of her life, covering 170 miles a day from noon to noon; but I must add that about 40 of these miles were probably due to the strong South Equatorial Current helping us along.

Then on the night of 12 March it happened. The weather had covered up with black clouds and rain squalls. The night promised to be dark as there was no moon. Although the ship steered herself with her self-steering gear, I sat by the tiller, breathing in the last rays of daylight. The evening meal was on the stove down below and would soon be ready. Then when the new night was complete and I had just decided to go down below for dinner, the ship struck.

She struck so hard that she shuddered. But then she kept on going as before. I knew that I was many miles from the closest land and had about 1000 fathoms of water below me, and thus could not have bounced on a reef. For an instant I thought that I had collided with a native fishing boat, as they often don't bother to use any lights, but dismissed the thought immediately, as I knew that I would have heard not a little swearing. Indeed, shining my electric torch all around the horizon revealed nothing but water. Thus I can only presume that what I had hit was possibly a large tree trunk or some wreckage which had been floating at, or just below, the surface of the sea.

Down in the saloon I was horrified to see the water already washing above the floorboards. The collision had sprung a very serious leak in the ship which until then had never leaked more than a bucket of water a year. I immediately realised that at the rate the water was coming in, the ship would soon sink unless I was able to localise the damage and make temporary repairs, but this proved an impossibility due to the inside ceiling which hid the planking with its damage. Thus water was leaking in between the outer and inner skin of the boat with no possibility of access for me to the damaged spot. To look for it from the outside would no doubt have been possible in a calm sea and in daylight, and I might then have been able to nail over it a piece of canvas; but as it was, with a rolling ship, in heavy seas and pitch darkness it was an impossibility, and perhaps even suicide as the copper sheeting had no doubt been torn and its sharp edges would soon have cut me to death.

To realise suddenly that one is on a sinking ship, far from land, outside of any shipping lane and with no lifesaving equipment on board is most depressing, and perhaps even more so on a pitch dark night, windy and with frequent rain squalls. But however unhappy I was, I never stopped trying to figure out how to save my own life.

The dinghy was just 7ft long and of flimsy plywood construction, while the seas were heavy and frequently breaking; but with luck even the smallest boat can survive quite rough conditions. Down in the chart room, with water swirling around my legs, I saw that the closest land was Barbados, about 40 miles away but dead to windward of me and thus out of the question for me to reach; but to leeward was the long chain of the Grenadine Islands about 55 miles away. Presuming that the dinghy would not be swamped before then, these should be easy to reach with a following wind, and the only navigational difficulty and danger would be to avoid letting the wind and current sweep me between two islands and into the Caribbean Sea where we would have no more land to our lee until the American mainland.

Thus with the greatest possible care I launched the dinghy and was greatly relieved when I had been able to do so without damaging it or letting it be filled with water. To get a dinghy in the water singlehanded is not the easiest job in the world even in a calm harbour, but in a heavy sea and a rolling ship it is very awkward indeed. I let her drift off to leeward on a long painter so that she would not get damaged against the side of *Dorothea*, and then went below to assemble all the gear I considered desirable for increasing my chances of making land alive.

First of all I took the two plastic bottles, each containing 2½ gallons of fresh water which I always kept as emergency rations should *Dorothea's* single tank have sprung a leak; then I half-filled a sailbag with food; then another sailbag with some clothes, then the chart and the compass; then an awning, a short gaff and some rope with the idea of a makeshift rig to cover the many miles to land; then the dinghy's folding anchor with a very long line, with the idea of having a last defence against being swept into the Caribbean Sea, should I miss the islands, hoping, of course, that I would get close enough to shallow water for it to be of any use. Then my two flashlights with spare batteries; then my lifejacket; and finally my papers and the cash I had in the boat, which I put in a watertight bag together with the spare batteries. I assembled all the gear by the cockpit, and as I walked up the companionway my eyes fell on the dinner-pot still on the stove. I had just been ready to eat when we struck, so not wanting to waste the work of cooking, took the pot along. When all was ready on deck, I pulled the dinghy alongside, quickly threw in all the gear, jumped in and pushed off.

I soon realised that I had grossly overloaded the little boat, as almost every wave shipped water into her, so I lost no time in throwing overboard part of the gear, as obviously even the most desirable piece of equipment would lose all its importance should the dinghy founder. The anchor with its line went over the side, then one of the two water bottles, then the life-jacket, as, come what may, I was not going to swim 55 miles. Then, thinking that I would either make land within a couple of days or not at all, I half-emptied the other water bottle.

This lightening made a tremendous difference, and if I now sat in the bottom of the boat instead of on the thwart, in order to lower her centre of gravity, the dinghy was both very stable and buoyant, lifting over every wave and hardly letting in any water at all. I let go the painter but held on the yacht's mainsheet for a while, looking at her with my torch, somehow reluctant to abandon her and to be on my own in that black night; but then a very strong squall came whistling down and I was unable to hold on any longer for fear of capsizing, even though *Dorothea* was hove-to. So I let go the sheet and drifted off to leeward. About 50 minutes had elapsed since the collision and *Dorothea* was lying very deep in the water. I saw her lights for a while and then suddenly they disappeared.

I felt utterly lonesome, wet, cold and rather worried about the future. I was, however, soon relieved to see how well that little dinghy managed in the heavy seas. She really floated like a cork and even when the top of a crest was breaking and overtaking us in a white foam, making me at first think that 'that one will swamp us', even then the little boat lifted bravely and the foam disappeared harmlessly below us.

I soon gained enough confidence to make the jury rig which I knew would be necessary if I did not want to spend days at sea before reaching the land. I then discovered that I had forgotten to bring the knife. I was extremely annoyed at myself for that, as I really had tried to do my best not to overlook anything. Fortunately I was able to tear the awning to the right size anyway by using my teeth to get the rip started. But I was entirely unable to cut the rope without a knife so I had to make the whole rig with one continuous length of rope, lashing one side of the 'squaresail' to the gaff which was to serve as square yard, then lashing the middle of that gaff to the end of one of the oars which was to serve as mast. From that same intersection I got out two lines to act as shrouds and then two more lines to the lower part of the sail as sheets.

When I had everything ready, I hoisted the 'mast'. The sail filled immediately but before losing control I was able to tighten the shrouds by taking up the turns around the thwart. I let the mast lean forward, thus not needing any forward stay which would have been very difficult to rig. Then by adjusting the sheets and steering with the remaining oar, the little boat scooted right along at a fair speed. Before I was able to rejoice much, however, I was suddenly dismayed by seeing the water rise in the bottom of the dinghy at a frightening rate. I then understood that it was the pressure of the sail which depressed the bow enough to let the water wash above it. The sail, hiding the bow from where I sat, had prevented me from seeing the danger. By moving quickly right aft and leaning over the stern thwart, then bailing out the dinghy, everything seemed under control.

At about 0130 I was startled and overjoyed to see a steamship coming toward me. This was almost unbelievable luck as these were little-frequented waters and this ship was, in fact, the first ship I had seen on the voyage since leaving Cayenne, not counting a few fishing boats along the coast of French Guyana. I flashed continuously the international distress signal, SOS, with my powerful long-range torch which I trained straight at her.

The ship came slowly closer and in my thoughts I prepared how I should board her. I presumed that the steamer would come alongside me at very slow speed and then throw me a rope for getting on board. I decided that I would make no attempt to save either the dinghy or anything in her except my papers and money. I would as quickly as possible tie the rope around my chest right under the armpits and make fast with a bowline. This knot never slips.

The ship was now very close and I could see her moving through the seas. I expected to see her slow down and set the course straight for me; but to my dismay the minutes passed without the ship altering course at all, then her bright red port light faded, as did her two masthead lights only to be replaced immediately by a single white light; her stern light. She had not seen me after all!

As the steamer's lights disappeared below the horizon, I stopped thinking about her and told myself that, after all, if the dinghy had managed these many hours, there was no reason why she should not continue doing so until I reached land. My thoughts wandered over to the new dreamship I was going to build and I decided that I would incorporate two strong, watertight bulkheads so that I would not again be put too easily in such an awkward situation. I also secretly thought that next time I would have a bigger dinghy and a real sailing dinghy at that, but I did not dare linger too long on any criticism of my present dinghy for fear it would bring me bad luck. After all, she was doing her best to save my life.

The night was long, sleep was impossible and I was shivering with cold, all my clothes being soaking wet. At last daylight came. And best of all, about an hour after daybreak, I saw land in the distance. It was a most comforting sight, but I soon realised that my makeshift sailing dinghy, which seemed only able to sail with the wind aft, could not point high enough to reach it.

An hour later two more spots of land appeared, so with three peaks from which to take cross-bearings with my compass I soon found on the chart the only three places it matched and could thus determine my own position. Then to my great joy I realised that the land I was seeing was not at all the closest land to me but that a lower land still below the horizon was much nearer and easier to reach as it was almost straight downwind. All I needed to do was to alter the course by a few degrees.

I became very cheerful, despite my tiredness from the lack of sleep, the cold, the uncomfortable position in the bottom of the dinghy, the strain of steering and having to counteract every wave, and now the glare and the heat of the tropical sun, not to speak of the emotional strain. After a few hours land did indeed appear dead ahead of us as expected and I could then steer straight for it, using the compass for checking crosscurrents which soon proved to be so strong that, had I not had the compass, I might not have realised their force until too late and then missed the island.

When I got close to the island and felt safe, I became careless and sat up on the middle thwart in order to get a better view to choose the best place to land. Immediately the bow plunged under the sea and the dinghy began to fill up. In a desperate move, I grabbed the 'mast,' uprooting it and let it fall over the side. The dinghy was at once relieved but already so full of water as to have lost all stability and threatened to capsize or fill up completely. I was close to land but still much too far to swim for it. As quickly, but also as carefully as possible, I undid all the ropes holding the rig to the boat, then threw over the side the remaining bottle of water to give me more room for bailing and then bailed for dear life while all the time I kept shifting my weight to counteract the effect of the surging water. I breathed a sigh of relief when the dinghy was dry and had regained her stability. Without the rig I felt it was safe enough to sit up on the thwart and at long last stretch out my legs.

The island I had come to was called Canouan and was a small island in the Grenadines group. Its northern part was steep cliffs and impossible to land on, but its southern part seemed to be low sandy beaches. Unfortunately that part of the coast was bordered by a long reef on to which the whole Atlantic broke heavily. I was well aware of the danger of trying to land through such breakers and the sensible thing to do would, of course, have been to land on the island's lee side; but I was just too tired to even consider sculling all that way and I was also worried about the current perhaps being stronger than I and making me miss the lee side altogether. Thus I preferred to take the chance on shooting the reef.

As I came closer, an islander high on the cliff signalled to me not to come any closer but to go round the island; however as I disregarded his advice and he realised that I really intended to go through the surf, he directed me to the best place where the rollers were not too big. I tried to time it so that I would get over the critical spot between two rollers but my dinghy was not fast enough and a huge breaker came foaming against me. I expected to be capsized but hoped to have enough strength to swim the rest of the way.

Much to my surprise the brave little dinghy just popped up on top of the broiling mass of water and shot forward at great speed. When the wave died down I found myself in smooth water. In the meantime, the islander on the cliff had jumped into a rowboat and was now coming toward me. He then towed me into the bottom of a quiet bay and helped me up the beach to lie down as my legs were so weak as to hardly be able to carry me. I was so tired I felt sick, but I knew that once more the words of the fortune-teller who had told me at the age of fifteen that I was like the cat, born with nine lives, were still right. In fact, I should have two or three more to go!'

From *Yachting World*, September 1967

Lessons learned

It must be a terrifying conundrum for a singlehanded sailor aboard a badly-leaking monohull to choose between pumping, stopping to search for the cause of the leak, or abandoning ship while there is still time to launch the liferaft or dinghy and collect essentials.

When Peter Tangvald's *Dorothea* collided with something at night SW of Barbados, he knew that the leak was serious because water was above the floorboards almost immediately. His heavily ballasted boat would soon sink unless he could quickly locate the damage and make temporary repairs; but 'this proved to be impossible because of the inside ceiling which hid the planking'. In such circumstances, some yachtsmen have been known to use a 'wrecking bar' (similar to a crowbar) to get past the obstruction.

Tangvald's story is proof that a small wooden dinghy can, under favourable circumstances, serve as a lifesaving craft, giving the shipwrecked sailor a more active role in self-preservation. Tangvald's 55-mile voyage to safety in his 7ft plywood dinghy was occasioned because *Dorothea* carried no liferaft. Fortunately, he had time to grab many essentials to construct his makeshift rig for the dinghy, but he forgot his knife. Once again, the importance of having a pre-prepared 'grab bag' of essentials for emergencies is demonstrated.

36 Whalestrike

Yacht *Guia III* (44ft ocean-racer)
Skipper Jerome Poncet
Crew George Marshall (navigator) Giorgio di Mola, Claudio Cuoghi, Giovanni
 Verbinni, Francesco Longanesi
Bound from Rio de Janeiro, Brazil, to Portsmouth, England
Date of loss 9 March, 1976
Position approximately 500 miles SW of Cape Verde Islands

The Italian-owned Guia III *had sailed for Australia in their 1973 Admiral's Cup team under the name Ginkgo, but under her new ownership she had subsequently taken part in two of the three legs of the 1975–76 Atlantic Triangle races, the last one of which was between Rio de Janeiro and Portsmouth. The third leg started on 22 February, 1976, and until 9 March the race continued without incident. Thereafter, George Marshall, navigator and sole Englishman on board, tells the story:*

We started from Rio de Janeiro with a very good chance of winning the Atlantic Triangle; everything required to make the boat a winner had been checked and replaced where necessary. One item that needed doing was the liferaft; its certificate was out of date and only the eagle-eyed scrutineers spotted this. Like most long-distance sailors we had only made sure that we had one. The raft arrived back only hours before the start and was placed in its customary position in the centre cockpit.

The race soon became the usual long-distance ocean racing routine. Up to the equator we averaged 150 miles a day, hit the doldrums on 6 March, but during the night 8/9 March the wind increased to 35 knots, moderating as the sun came up.

At 2000 the watch changed and I, with the other two on watch, went below for what was normally the best sleeping time. After a very quick breakfast of hot chocolate, cookies and cheese, I wrapped a sheet around myself and was into the land of nod.

From the middle of a deep sleep I was awoken by a sudden crack and lurch upwards, and all the watch below sat up on their bunks. From the deck came the cry of 'Orca! Orca!' – even my limited Italian was enough to translate this as whales. The head of a crewman appeared in the hatch and pointing forward he shouted 'water in the boat'.

I put my feet onto the cabin sole and found that, indeed, there was water in the boat, over the tops of my ankles.

Looking forward through the tunnel joining the forepeak to the main cabin I saw water rushing back. Diving forward into the forepeak I saw that the water was coming from the port side through the sail bins. I went back to the main cabin, got the knife that was always available on the galley, and went back to join Jerome our skipper and Giorgio from the deck watch. We cut the sail bins free and found what to us looked like an enormous hole. It was about 2ft below the waterline and just abaft the fore bulkhead. It was an egg-shaped hole 3ft long and 2ft deep. The planks had been forced from the bottom to the top and it was very obvious that whatever had done the damage had hit the boat with great force.

The water gushed in, and for a second or two we just gaped at the damage in disbelief. Jerome and I then tried to force the wood back into the hole but the strength of the remaining fibres of wood were too much for our combined weight. As we were doing this the remainder of the crew were handing the sails to take way off the yacht, the initial inrush of water making it impossible to tack or heave-to. As it became obvious that we were not going to get the damaged portion of the hull back over the hole, Jerome told Giorgio and me to go on deck and try to get a headsail over the hole. He continued to try and plug the hole from the inside with spinnakers and anything else to hand. The water was waist deep at this time and as fast as he pushed a sail in the gap it was forced back.

Giorgio and I went up on deck and freed the No. 2 genoa from the lifelines. I took the head of the sail and stepped over the lifelines with the idea of jumping down past the hole and carrying the sail with me under the hull so that the water pressure would suck the sail into the hole.

Looking down into the very clear water I could see the jagged hole with long cracks, fore and aft. Also lying alongside the yacht about 2 to 3ft down I could see a very big fish which was at least half the length of the yacht and appeared about 6ft wide. Giorgio also saw it and very emphatically told me to stay on deck. In truth, I had already changed my mind as I didn't fancy making a snack for whatever it was.

We then tried to take the sail around the bows, but by now the deck was awash and this proved impossible. Jerome appeared in the main hatch and said it was time to abandon ship. The rest of the crew had already started to get stores up from the cabin and I went down below to start my part of the abandon ship drill. As I waited for the hatch to clear I looked around *Guia* and saw on the port side a pod of killer whales circling around about 50ft from the beam. They are unmistakable with their white patches and tall fins, and for the first time I realised what had happened. On the starboard side a school of dolphins, fairly large and with a mottled green and black skin, were sounding.

Down below I found that the water was thigh deep and the boat rocking, swishing the water from beam to beam. The radio had been switched on and I soon had the first Mayday out on 2182 kHz. I knew that there was very little chance of it being picked up as we were by this time too far from land for the set to reach. A quick switch to the race control frequency of 4136.3 kHz and again a Mayday. The output meter on the set showed that the power was rapidly going as the sea water came over the tops of the battery. The water all this time was rising rapidly and soon Jerome and I were chest high. I continued sending Maydays on alternate frequencies until it was obvious that the set was only working on a bare minimum of power. As I was sending the signals I was helping Jerome by passing anything that floated past. All our kit that we kept for emergencies had already been passed up on deck and we knew that the liferaft had inflated and was being loaded.

Jerome then gave a very Gallic shrug and said to me that we must say *au revoir* to *Guia*, and told me to go on deck and get in the liferaft. I pushed the emergency signal button on the radio and noticed that it was transmitting, but at a very reduced output from normal. As we waded back to the hatch through the now neck-high water we managed to save a few more items – cans of fruit – a bag of mine that contained my camera and personal washing kit and a notebook and some cans of condensed milk.

A shout from outside said that *Guia* was going. This made us move up on deck just in time to see the bows dip and in about 10 seconds from a boat awash there was only the stern and the top of the mast out of the water.

I slid into the water and swam the short distance to the liferaft. As I clung to the side of the liferaft *Guia* gave a very loud prolonged sigh as air trapped in the stern escaped and she disappeared entirely. I then attempted to board the dinghy and found to my alarm that something was holding me down in the water. Jerome tried to pull me in with help but couldn't. We soon found that the sea anchor had wrapped itself around me and that this was keeping me in the water. It then became a simple matter of hauling it and me into the raft.

On entering the raft I saw that it was just a heap of bodies, kit, food containers and clothing. Everyone just sat for the first few minutes and I am sure that they felt as I did. To see a fine yacht like *Guia* disappear so suddenly was a shock to us all. Also the realisation that we were many miles away from both land and frequented shipping lanes made us all a little unhappy about our chances of survival. Looking around there was no sign of anything; no boat wreckage, no whales; just the sea and sky. It was a very lonely feeling.

We started to organise the inside of the raft and take an inventory of what we had, and after we had inspected everything, decided that we were not too badly off. There was plenty of food, enough to last a month with care, a box of flares, Helly Hansen suits and waterproofs for us all. Three blankets, 800 cigarettes, matches, lighters, torches, lifejackets and three kit-bags with personal kit, including mine, with all my spare pullovers and some sailing trousers were on the raft.

All the food was in polythene casks and we were glad that we had decided that this system was used on *Guia*. We thought that if the liferaft was badly damaged then we might be able to make a float with the food containers.

Our only shortcoming was water. We only had 15 litres and we knew that we would be in trouble if we didn't get some rain or make some from a still. However, we were pretty sure that we could last until a rain cloud came along as the area we were in always produced some rain.

After sorting out the raft and the stores we all changed into the thermal underwear and on the advice of Giorgio rested and talked about our chances. After a long discussion we agreed that we were going to survive come what may, and that we had three chances of being picked up. It was clear that the only place that we could go was towards South America, with the odds of ending up somewhere in Venezuela. On the way we thought that within three days we should be somewhere near the mid-Atlantic route between the North American ports and Cape Town, then two weeks later on the shipping route between Panama and Cape Town and finally the inshore routes along the coast of South America.

After two hours, the sea anchor was hauled in and we set off from the scene at about 2 to 2½ knots. The sea anchor had made us decide to leave, as its violent snubbing was liable to damage the raft and we would sooner take our chance with a possible long trip than end up with a sinking liferaft.

A food container and two lifebelts on the end of a 20ft line kept the back of the liferaft to the wind and sea. It also broke up the worst of the waves so that only very occasionally did water come onto the canopy.

The motion of the raft was fairly comfortable, the floating anchor keeping us from dropping too fast down the front of the waves. The only discomfort was from the damp on the bottom of the raft and from the conglomeration of legs in the centre. The oilskins and blankets made the floor comfortable but the only answer for the legs was to grin and bear it. Giorgio was told that he might be getting some practice in amputation if we had to spend too much time in the dinghy.

As night fell the watches were set for everyone to do one and a half hours in rotation. During the day only whoever was near the door had kept lookout as we knew that the best chance of seeing a boat was during the dark.

The lookout was stationed at the entrance with the torches, pumps and flares to hand. Each lookout was allowed two cigarettes and a cookie to keep him going during his watch.

As my turn was not until midnight I settled down to get what sleep I could. This proved easier than I thought but not until all the legs had been arranged to our mutual comfort.

At midnight Claudio Cuoghi, the youngest member of our crew, woke me and told me it was my turn for *guardia*. After a long complicated manoeuvre I extracted myself from the pile of bodies and sat at the entrance of the raft. A shared cigarette with Claudio and a chat about the sinking, then he wormed his way into the pile of bodies and I was left alone with the sea. The wind was still about 25 knots and the sea about 9 to 12ft high, but the raft was behaving perfectly well. Without moving I soon realised that I could cover 360° of the horizon every two to three minutes as the raft swung at the end of the floats.

I can't say that I thought any great thoughts during the time I was on watch except that I probably felt very much at rest. The sea is so huge that it is difficult to feel anger or sorrow at anything that it or its inhabitants may do to you. Like the jungle the sea is neutral, and all that man can hope to do is live with it and accept all its moods.

After sitting for two hours, I gave one of the crew a shake and he took over the watch from me. It was more difficult to get a comfortable space on the floor and it took me a while to get into that half dozy state that precedes sleep. Just as I had got warm and comfortable someone leaned across me and shook Jerome. 'I think that I can see a light,' he said, 'but it could just be a star rising.'

I was at the entrance before he finished speaking, as I knew that there were clouds all around the horizon and it was almost certain that he had seen a ship. The three of us sat in the entrance staring out over our limited horizon. After what seemed an age we spotted a light dipping to windward. I wanted to put up a flare straight away (I had been delegated the job of igniting them as I had more practice than the others).

However, Jerome suggested we wait until we could see what it was and what course it was on. This seemed to me an even longer wait, but soon the second masthead light of a steamer showed itself. It became apparent that it would pass us about three miles downwind, and I put up the first parachute red flare. It went straight up and burst into a very satisfying red glow. After about 30 seconds it went out and we all stared at the lights of the ship willing it to alter course. We waited 10 minutes and then discharged two more para flares one after the other, aiming to send them across the bows of the ship. They both worked and as they drifted down, we saw the ship flash an Aldis lamp at us and the angle of her lights alter. Moments later all her deck lights came on and within minutes she went past us at a distance of 200 yards and stopped about a mile away. All our torches were lit, the buoy lights set flashing and I set to igniting the handheld flares.

The next two hours were probably the most trying of my life. The ship made four passes at us but seemed to have great difficulty in seeing us. We only had ten handheld flares, and some of those proved useless. My chief memory of those two hours is of violent curses against the people who sell such unseamanlike objects and gratitude to the sane ones who made the ones that worked.

Eventually the ship stopped downwind of us and we tried to paddle the lifeboat to it, but as the ship was drifting faster than us we gave up and waited to see what they would do. From round the stern a ship's lifeboat appeared. It was only when we saw it that we realised what size sea was running. Most of the time it was out of sight and at first went away from our position. The last hand flare brought it back towards us, and soon we transferred to the lifeboat, taking all our kit from the liferaft with us.

The raft was secured alongside, and soon we found ourselves alongside the *Hellenic Ideal*. We still had to manage the ladder but the deck officer in charge made us all tie a lifeline around ourselves before allowing us to climb to the deck from the lifeboat; a very sensible precaution as it turned out. Not one of us after the climb was able to stand, and each of us collapsed against a bulkhead; I think it was more from relief than weakness. After a cigarette and a tot of something very strong we were led down below to the passengers' dining room. The captain then came down from the bridge, made sure that we were complete, and said that the ship was at our disposal until New York.

It is difficult to express your thanks to someone who saves your life, but to the seaman who spotted our flare, and the Captain, Dimitros Dimitri, and the crew of the *Hellenic Ideal*, thank you. Your skill, seamanship and hospitality will never be forgotten.

From *RNSA Journal*, Spring 1976

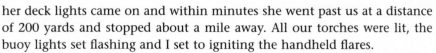

Lessons learned

Both *Guia III* and *Pionier* (see There She Blows page 248) were lost after colliding with whales while racing. In 1972 and 1973 there were also high profile losses of the yachts *Lucette* and *Auralyn* which sank after striking whales not far from the Galapagos islands. Their stories are told, respectively, in Dougal Robertson's book, *Survive the Savage Seas*, and Maurice and Marilyn Bailey's *119 Days Adrift*. In the two latter cases, the survivors had a long time during which to reflect on their wisdom in deciding to take both a liferaft and an inflatable dinghy with them on their world voyaging.

After striking a whale, the skipper and crew of *Guia III* did not abandon ship until they were compelled to do so. George Marshall recounts how they made desperate efforts to staunch the flow of water. 'The water gushed in, and for a second or two we just gaped at the damage in disbelief. Jerome and I tried to force the wood back into the hole but the strength of the remaining fibres of wood was too much for our combined weight ... Jerome told Giorgio and me to go on deck and try to get a headsail over the hole. He continued to try and plug the hole from the inside with spinnakers and anything else to hand. The water was waist deep at this time, and as fast as he pushed a sail in the gap it was forced back.' The attempt to cover the hole from the outside also failed, because the bow of the yacht was awash by this time.

One or two accounts in this book describe sending distress calls using the MF band. *Guia III* operated an MF radio on the 2182 kHz International Distress Frequency, but as George Marshall recalls, 'Down below I found that water was thigh deep and the boat rocking, swishing water from beam to beam. The radio had been switched on and I soon had the first Mayday out ... The output meter on the set showed that the power was rapidly going as the seawater came over the tops of the battery.'

Guia's skipper and crew were experienced ocean-racing types, and it was expected they would be well organised so that even while some of them made last-minute attempts to keep *Guia III* afloat, others 'had already started to get stores up from the cabin. So by the time their skipper made the decision to abandon, 'All our kit that was kept for emergencies had already been passed on deck, and we knew that the liferaft had inflated and was being loaded.'

There was enough food, with care, to last a month; a box of flares (which were to prove their saviour); Helly Hansen suits and waterproofs for all; three blankets, torches, lifejackets and three kitbags with personal gear ... All the food was in polythene casks, 'and we were glad that we had decided to use this system in *Guia*.' The only shortcoming was water. As it happened, they were rescued by a ship within 24 hours. But they were lucky.

Just as there are differences of opinion on the influence a sea anchor will have on the behaviour of a yacht in heavy weather, so there are uncertainties about the value of a sea anchor or drogue when attached to a liferaft. When it had been decided to try and reach land by drifting with the wind, *Guia III*'s sea anchor on the liferaft was hauled in, since it would slow progress. But George Marshall also pointed out: 'The sea anchor's violent snubbing was liable to damage the raft and we would sooner take our chance with a possible long trip than end up with a sinking liferaft.'

In recent years the design of liferaft sea anchors has improved, following tests which revealed that the snatch loads generated between a liferaft and its sea anchor in 20 knots of wind, with seas of 3 to 5ft, can increase to 10 times the normal steady loading. The once commonly used 'handkerchief' type of drogue offered too much resistance and has since been replaced by a conical-shaped sea anchor made from porous material so as to reduce loading to a more tolerable level.

Five of the six-man crew of *Guia III* were trying to sleep during the first night in the liferaft, when the lookout said that he thought he could see a light. George Marshall wanted to put up a flare straight away, but the skipper insisted on waiting until they were certain. 'It was soon apparent that the vessel would pass about three miles downwind, and I put up the first para-chute red flare . . . After about 30 seconds it went out and we all stared at the lights of the ship, willing it to change course. We waited ten minutes and then discharged two more para flares, one after the other. They both worked, and as they drifted down we saw the ship flash an Aldis lamp and the angle of her lights alter.'

Getting aboard a rescue craft from a dinghy or liferaft is never easy in a rough sea if the rescue ship is a large freighter or tanker with decks high above the water. In such cases it may be safer to carry out the rescue in two stages, as the captain of the *Hellenic Ideal* decided to do when he stopped his ship downwind of the liferaft. George Marshall says: 'From round the stern a ship's lifeboat appeared; it was only when we saw it that we realised what size sea was running,' but they safely transferred to the lifeboat, taking all their kit with them, and soon they were alongside the *Hellenic Ideal* where 'we still had to manage the ladder, but the deck officer in charge made us all tie a lifeline around ourselves before allowing us to climb to the deck from the lifeboat. A very sensible precaution as it turned out. Not one of us after the climb was able to stand, and each of us collapsed against the bulkhead.'

37 There she blows

Yacht *Pionier* (32ft sloop)
Skipper Gordon Webb
Crew Jennifer Webb, Tony Keeney, Peter Flockemann, Willi Schutten
Bound (racing) from Cape Town, South Africa to Rio de Janeiro, Brazil
Date of loss 23 January 1971
Position approximately 1600 miles W of Cape Town

A few years before the loss of Guia III *(see Whalestrike), the South African yacht,* Pionier, *had also sunk after striking a whale while racing across the South Atlantic, and although there is much similarity between the two incidents some of the experiences of the crew of* Pionier *are of particular interest. The following extracts are from an account written by Anthony Hocking after interviews with the survivors from* Pionier. *The 1971 Cape to Rio race had started on 11 January and the 'strike' occurred when* Pionier *was eleven days out from Cape Town.*

Tony Keeney was on watch, sitting among the cushions in the cockpit behind the wheel as midnight approached. It was a dark night, with only a sliver of moon and a few brave stars appearing through the cloudy haze. Tony had been there since 2200, alone while the other four rested below, reading, sleeping, plotting. Since the second day *Pionier*'s crew had been watching alone, two hours at a time through the day and night. Gordon Webb, *Pionier*'s skipper, was due to relieve Tony at midnight.

Gordon took control, standing with one hand on the wheel looking out into the blackness ahead while Tony eased himself from the cushioned seat beside him, en route for his bunk. He had been at the wheel most of the day. There was not much to say. Both Gordon and Tony knew the implication of the position report. *Pionier* was placed to win, the wind was right, they were heading in straight for Rio. Almost, though neither of them would have dreamt of suggesting it out loud, the race was in the bag.

Suddenly there was a shuddering crash. *Pionier*'s bow shot high, arching out of the water in the darkness ahead, pointing to the stars as she crashed into some terrible obstruction. As she plunged down again, a fraction of a second later, there was a second bang, a sickening smash, this time from under the hull, as *Pionier* was hurled bodily to starboard.

The men struggled to keep their balance; there was not much light around. The binnacle light was on, there was light filtering from the cabin, a token glimmer from the sky, the stern light. Gordon looked aft, as *Pionier* fought gamely to recover from the cruel shock. In the glow of the stern light he saw the huge tail fin of a blue whale, 2.5 metres across and forked, strong, majestic and now disappearing into the deep.

Tony had seen it too, just. Halfway into the cockpit, he had turned at the two crashes, and though he was low in the boat, he could see the end of the tail over the dodger and the life-rings, as it dipped slowly out of sight.

The boat lurched crazily as dazed wits gathered. Gordon still held the wheel, Tony was standing in the hatchway. Down below, Willi in the fo'c's'le had taken the full force of the first blow; Jennifer, the wife of the skipper, the second. Willi had thought the boat had hit rough weather and wondered where it came from. Jennifer had felt the impact of the second blow under her head. She was thrown up and half out of her bunk, and she let her feet fall to the deck to steady herself.

It was then she felt the water. Creeping up through the cabin planks, from down somewhere by the keel, she could feel it lapping her ankles as the boat heeled over under full sail. She screamed her discovery up to Gordon on deck. Gordon and Jennifer eased up the planks to see if they could find the hole admitting the water. But it was coming in too fast. Gordon told Peter Flockemann to get on to the radio.

Peter tuned the transmitter to 2182 kHz, the distress frequency. It was supposed to be left free for emergencies like this one, and all ships were supposed to keep a watch on it. But there was the usual cacophony of messages broadcast in abuse of the international agreement. Peter could hear a conversation going on, by the sound of it not far away. He switched on the transmitter and began broadcasting the Mayday. *Pionier* was sinking, he called. He gave the position they had calculated most recently, 24°30'S, 07°06'W. Again he repeated it, appealing for rescue. But when he switched on the receiver to see if anyone was responding, he drew a blank.

Gordon had abandoned any plans to save the ship from the inside, though Willi had begun to bale with a bucket. The water was swirling knee deep in the saloon by this time, the ship was sinking to the gunnels. Gordon had read somewhere of a way of saving a holed ship with sails, by draping them over the side and allowing suction to pull them into the hole and seal it off. He outlined the plan to Tony and Willi, and they set about the job. There were two spinnakers in the cockpit, and they took one from its bag and draped it over the port side. The boat had lost way by now, and they draped the second spinnaker in its place.

But still the water poured in. Now it was waist deep in the cabin. Gordon was out in the cockpit, taking the liferaft from its cover. He pulled the inflation trigger, it opened with a loud hiss, and he put the raft over the side. He shouted down to Jennifer to cut free the plastic jerry cans of water lashed to the legs of the saloon table below, the extra water *Pionier* was obliged to carry in addition to the water in her tanks, to comply with the race rules. She tossed four of the jerry cans to Willi up in the cockpit. They weighed 22.5kg apiece, but she hardly noticed.

Jennifer's next thought was of food. She scrambled to collect all she could find in the provision lockers and pass it to Willi on deck, who by this time had hold of the liferaft alongside. Anything she could find, most of it floating around her, tins, cereals, eggs in their boxes, vegetables, jars, anything within reach. As she passed the provisions up to Willi, Gordon remembered they would need the tin-opener. He reminded her, and Jenny turned to open the door where it was kept. But it was jammed. Peter left the radio to wrench it open for her, then went up on deck to help Tony with the spinnakers. Jennifer took over the radio, and had time to shout out two more Mayday signals before the radio went silent as the flooded batteries died.

Willi had remembered to grab flares before going up on deck. He took a full box of them, ordinary night flares, unfortunately, rather than the parachute flares he had been looking for. And he grabbed an heirloom from the days when he had sailed his first yacht, *Falcon*, years before. His one and only smoke flare. It had sailed with him on *Falcon* and his second yacht *Sprinter*, without a moment's anxiety, and now it was with him on *Pionier*. He threw it into the raft.

Tony's thought was of clothing. He had read an article on liferaft survival before the race. It had pointed out that though water was a high priority in survival at sea, almost as high was – not food or flares – but shelter. It had advocated clothing as protection both from heat and cold, and it was this thought that drove Tony to the nearest clothes locker, his and Willi's. He grabbed armfuls of whatever came to hand. Sodden jerseys and trousers, anything, he passed them to Willi in the cockpit. Peter, equally practical, found a sleeping bag and a bottle of whisky.

Gordon ordered everyone on deck. The boat was sinking fast. Willi was in the liferaft, holding it to the gunnel of the yacht in the heavy swell, still wearing nothing but his underpants. Gordon told Jennifer to climb in with him, after her Tony, after him Peter. He looked down the yacht. The bows were under but the stern was still above water. He wondered if there was a bubble of air keeping her afloat and if there was a chance of saving her after all. He began bailing, but only for a moment. He knew there was no hope, and he thought of something else. Their passports. He knew they were in a wallet down below. He went down, the cabin almost full of water, and dived down to the locker where they were kept. He found them, surfaced, and found, too, his precious sextant and navigation books floating by. He took them in his arms and climbed into the liferaft – able to step straight from the gunnel into the shelter, so low was the yacht.

The liferaft stood off some way, for the yacht was rolling over. Slowly she dipped at the bows, further under water as the pulpit disappeared, and as she heeled over, as if in final, tragic salute, a short somewhere on the electric panel produced the last cruel joke. All *Pionier*'s lights flashed on, her masthead lights, the navigation lights, the lights on her spreader, and over she rolled, her bared poles sinking under the waves as like a whale herself she showed her underside, deep fin keel with rudder still intact on the skeg – and the long, jagged rip in her hull which told *Pionier*'s crew what they needed to know: that they could never have saved their ship. The yacht disappeared, and they were alone.

There they sat, in the dark. They had a torch, but to conserve its batteries they used it only sparingly. They had brought one packet of cigarettes, and a box of matches. But the matches were soaked in sea water and would have to be dried out. Some tried to sleep, ignoring the cramp of legs intertwined uncomfortably with four other pairs. And every so often came an unnerving hiss of escaping air from the raft beneath them, the only sound besides their close breathing and the lap of the water. There was nothing to say.

At dawn with light to see what they were doing, they began to organise their raft. It might be their home for weeks. The sail they had brought as a sea anchor was already trailing overboard. Gordon decided the three white plastic jerry cans should be trailed as well, once he had made sure their plastic caps would not let in sea water. Fresh water being lighter than salt, they would float. So the jerry cans were tied together with a rope, and gently let into the water.

While they were securing the jerry cans overboard, conversation turned to food, and the five investigated the contents of the sailbag. Tins galore, boxes of dehydrated vegetables, broken eggs in their boxes, muesli breakfast cereal, the sodden packets spilling their contents; even a hunk of Christmas cake wrapped in tinfoil and a jar of honey. Jennifer set about preparing something. Her eye fell on Gordon's sextant box and she commandeered it. The sextant was ejected, and the box became a serviceable pot. She mixed the muesli cereal and some broken eggs into a tasty paste, with Christmas cake to follow. Nobody noticed the tang of salt water.

Breakfast over, they opened the emergency survival pack they had found in the raft. Nobody had any idea what might be in it, so it was like opening a Christmas parcel. First, they found a hand pump for the raft, with instructions which, among other things, explained the disturbing hisses of air they had heard in the night. These had come as air was let out of the raft to counteract its heavy load. There were sponges, to help in drying out the raft, which was itself ankle deep in water from the night before. There were six 3-pint tins of water, and a can-opener, with a measuring cup. Instructions with the water advised regular rationing. No random drinking, but instead a cupful early in the morning, one at noon, and a third at night. Though they had plenty of water in the jerry cans, Gordon decided they would follow the directions. Glucose sweets, an emergency medical kit and a funnel to catch rainwater completed the provisions.

There was not much conversation. Gordon had told them at the outset they were in quite a spot. They were way off the normal shipping lanes, and it would be a miracle if their Mayday signal had been picked up. The rest of the fleet would not miss them as a number of yachts had not been heard of in days, in most cases because of the failure of their generator plants. So it might be weeks before anyone thought of mounting a search for them. On the other hand, they had plenty of water, the means of catching more, and clothing and covering enough to shelter them. They knew that even without food they could survive for weeks on the water alone.

What was suggested openly was that it would not be long before a few legs were amputated and thrown overboard. All were in agonies of cramp, unable to move their legs without dislodging the whole arrangement of the raft. But nobody complained.

Noon arrived, and it was getting hot. Somebody had tossed a sodden sheet into the raft, Jennifer's tropical sleeping bag – an ordinary sheet sewn double along three-quarters of its length. They had a couple of large sombrero hats with them too. It was found one way of keeping the watch-keeper cool during his 20-minute agony was to soak the sheet in sea water and drape it over his back and neck, while he wore one of the hats. Noon was the time for more water rations, and each received his measure from the cup. Nobody wanted food.

So the watches went on through the afternoon, 20 minutes turn and turn about, the raft bobbing to the top of the swell and giving a view for three miles around, and then dropping back into a hollow. The watchkeeper wearing his sheet and his hat, the other four cowering in the shelter, without speaking. On the raft's canopy, all the clothing there was room for, drying in the sunshine. And the precious matches, being dried for the pleasure of the packet of cigarettes still to be smoked.

Tony was sitting outside again, passing in to the others the clothes that had been drying in the sun. Then someone asked for the matches. Tony did not smoke, but he looked for the matches and found they had disappeared. It looked as if they had gone over the side as they had been threatening to all along. With disgust the others resigned themselves to survival without cigarettes, and the apparently useless packet was thrown overboard. Two minutes later the matches turned up – among the dried clothes in the liferaft.

Scanning the horizon for a sail, the shapes of clouds had played cruel tricks with the hopes of the watchkeepers, so much so that they had taken to looking many times before daring to believe their eyes. And each time it had turned out there was nothing there. But when Tony noticed a movement on the horizon, as the liferaft rose to the top of a swell, he felt a curious burst of excitement. It was a new shape, to the north-west. But it was far distant, and he knew he could be wrong. He looked to the south, to the east, looking for a sail, anywhere but to the north-west. But he had to look again. This time he was sure there was something there. What looked to him like goalposts, the derricks of a big bulk carrier, or tanker, perhaps. But he wanted to be sure.

He carried on watching as the liferaft rode the swells, watching as the ship came closer. He could see his 'goalposts' clearer now, and he was sure it was a ship. But still he said nothing. He watched as the ship emerged clearer from the mist on the horizon, and looked again at the approaching rain squall, getting dangerously close. He could see the ship's bows and her bridge. His heart was beating fit to burst, but he stayed quiet, until he was confident there was hope of rescue, and his eyes were not betraying him. He called Gordon.

'I think there might be something over there,' he said, leaning towards the opening in the canopy.

'What, a ship?'

'I don't know. It might be.'

The atmosphere was electric as Gordon slowly crawled across the craft, its bottom heaving, and knelt in the opening to see what Tony had spotted. He was not over-optimistic. Clearly there was a ship, but he estimated she would pass three miles away.

Tony had been watching it for some minutes now. He told Gordon he felt she had changed course. Gordon did not allow his hopes to ride too high.

The three left inside the shelter were hanging on to every muttered word that passed between the two men. The ship was five miles away.

Gordon thought quickly. How could he attract the ship's attention to the tiny ball of orange adrift between swells? He was revising his ideas of how far away the ship would pass. As she came closer, he thought it might be something like two miles. But she was still far away.

There was suddenly pandemonium on board. The box of flares Willi had saved was useless in daylight, and this was a blow. The white flares in the box would not be spotted if they were fired now. The only hope rested with the orange smoke flare, but it was years old. Gordon read and re-read the instructions on its side, to make sure he made no mistake in firing it. And while the five waited in a tension of fright for the approach of the ship, the flare was passed from hand to hand as each strove to find a new significance in the simply listed instructions.

There could be no doubt now that the ship would be passing close by, even if she had not seen life on the raft. But she was still miles away, and it would be too late to fire the flare when she came abeam. As Gordon knew well, in a lonely ocean like this there might be no one on the bridge. So Gordon read the instructions on the flare for the last time, and all wills were with it as Gordon pulled its triggering mechanism and flung it through the air. It landed nine metres away and worked, scattering bright orange smoke over a wide area of ocean. But hearts on the liferaft sank to their lowest ebb. The wind scattering the smoke kept it only half a metre or so above the sea's surface, and for all but a fraction of the time it was as invisible to the ship as the raft itself. If they could not see the ship, how could it see the liferaft?

But the ship kept coming, and Gordon was beginning to agree it might come close after all. Peter and Tony grabbed two bright orange jackets which had been salvaged with the clothes, Jenny's and Willi's, part of the crew's uniform. They stuck them on the two short paddles that had come as part of the liferaft kit, and began waving them furiously through the opening of the shelter, waving till their arms refused to work more and dropped in exhaustion. And it was then the ship responded with three long blasts of her whistle.

There was pandemonium on that liferaft. Jennifer Webb burst into tears and flung herself at the necks of each man in turn, her husband first and then Willi, Peter and Tony, and on each face there was a smile as big as it could take. They were cheering, everyone was talking at once. Everyone realised they had been rescued without going through any ordeal at all, only 16 hours in the water when they had feared they might be there for ever.

Up came the ship, more than 13,000 tons of her, rusted and wave-worn. A ship they would not have spared a second glance if they had seen her in harbour. But now she was the most beautiful ship the five had ever seen. A bulk grain carrier, and on her bow they could read her name: *Potomac*. She manoeuvred to within 100 metres of them, as they wriggled eagerly in what seemed eternity, waiting for their deliverance. On deck they could see the crew making ready. A pilot's ladder was lowered over the side, and deck-hands were standing ready with a rope. Others were swinging a lifeboat overboard, still on its davits. On the bridge stood several officers, one of them with a loud-hailer. He tried to shout down instructions to them, but his words were carried away on the wind. The crew members not involved with the preparations were standing at the rail, many of them with cameras.

The *Potomac* came up close. A line was thrown across, but missed the raft. As it was thrown, a rain squall, which had been threatening all afternoon, arrived. Driving rain forced them back under the canopy, even finding its way through the air vents. The sky grew dark, the sea green and the swells white-capped. The *Potomac* lost way and had to start her engines. Their wash swept the tiny liferaft astern to her, and away into the gloom. The

Potomac disappeared, ahead, over the swells half a mile away.

'They'll lose us,' cried Jennifer. The smiles disappeared as new anxious thoughts crowded in. The squall was dangerous. It was as if the sea had reacted in fury as it saw its victims all but snatched from its clutches, and was taking its revenge on them. But they could see the *Potomac* circling round, and she came up from behind, this time further away. They watched as the lifeboat on its davits was lowered into the water, with its crew of seven aboard. And they watched as it crossed the swells separating them from the ship. On the ship, the crew were rigging a scrambling net forward.

The sea was rough and it was a dangerous manoeuvre as the lifeboat chugged in to relieve the excited survivors. But soon it was alongside and brawny arms helped first Jennifer, then each of the men into the lifeboat. Peter carried the bottle of whisky with him, still all but full as they had consumed only a part of it on the raft. The other things were left on the raft, which was towed to the ship behind the lifeboat. And the survivors met their rescuers.

They were Americans. The *Potomac* was from Portland, Oregon, on America's west coast, and was on her way to Cape Town. In command of the lifeboat was the man they had to thank for their deliverance, Third Officer Roy Newkirk. He had been on watch on the bridge, soon to be relieved, when he saw the tiny orange dot in the distance, three miles off the port bow. He thought it might be a buoy drifting. But he did not want to take chances, and told the *Potomac*'s master about it. Vernon Hansen, from America's deep South, had been asleep in his cabin, but climbed to the bridge immediately. Through binoculars it was obvious the orange dot was a liferaft, and Hansen ordered a change of course. But there was no sign of life aboard. Just then Hansen spotted the trail of orange smoke from Gordon's flare. It drifted over a wide expanse of water. 'There's life all right,' he told Newkirk.

He ordered a lifeboat to be prepared and Newkirk himself asked to be put in charge of it. He wanted to find out what people were doing out in the middle of nowhere where nobody ought to be, he explained.

The lifeboat pulled alongside the ship, heaving in the swell, and the crew helped the survivors grab the scramble net and clamber up the deck, a vertical climb of 24 metres. Jennifer and Gordon went first, Jennifer a little worried about the bikini bottom she was wearing as its elastic had broken. She had tied a piece of string to it taken round her neck as a kind of suspender. Willi went next, hampered by his injured leg and clambering up with the strength of his arms. Peter and Tony brought up the rear, and the lifeboat was winched back on deck.

From *Yachting in Southern Africa*, 1972
Purnell & Sons (SA) (Pty) Ltd

Lessons learned

The international distress frequency 2182 kHz is supposed to be left free for emergencies and for all ships to keep a watch, but as the crew of *Pionier* discovered there is often a cacophony of messages broadcast in abuse of the rules.

Gordon had read of the method of saving a holed ship with sails, by draping them over the side and allowing suction to pull them into the hole and seal it off. They took one spinnaker and draped it over the port side. The boat had lost way by now, and they draped a second spinnaker in its place. But still the water poured in. Theory is all very well, but you need almost perfect conditions to put it into practice.

When the liferaft was launched Jennifer cut free the plastic jerry cans of water lashed to the legs of the saloon table. *Pionier* was obliged to carry extra water in addition to the water in her tanks, to comply with the race rules. But this is a good idea in all circumstances, in case the tanks become contaminated, or spring a leak.

The next problem was that the parachute flares could not be located. Willi managed to grab a full box of ordinary flares. But, ironically, it was 'an heirloom from the days when he had sailed his first yacht, *Falcon*, years before' that proved to be the crew's salvation . . . His one and only smoke flare.

Tony's thought was of clothing. He had read an article on liferaft survival which pointed out that though fresh water was a high priority in survival at sea, almost as high was – not food or flares – but shelter. It had advocated clothing as protection both from heat and cold. Tony grabbed armfuls of sodden jerseys and trousers, anything. Something that Willi, wearing nothing but his underpants, would be grateful for later.

When a ship was sighted in daylight, all hopes rested with the orange smoke flare. It was the trail of orange smoke that prompted the rescue ship's skipper to remark: 'There's life all right.'

Part six:

Fire or explosion

The 55ft Nicholson yawl, Lord Trenchard *was destroyed by a gas explosion at Poole Town quay.*

38 LPG – a disaster waiting to happen

Yacht *Lord Trenchard* (55ft Nicholson yawl)
Skipper Colin Rouse
Date of Loss 30 June 1999
Position Poole Harbour

On 30 June,1999, the 55ft Nicholson yawl, Lord Trenchard, *owned by the Armed Forces and used for adventure training for servicemen and women, was destroyed by a gas explosion whilst alongside Poole town quay. Two people were injured, one very seriously. This first-hand account of the accident, by Gavin McLaren who was Mate aboard at the time, makes sobering reading for anyone with a gas system aboard their yacht.*

The sound of people moving around the cabin and quiet conversation wakes me. It is broad daylight and I glance at my watch. Five to seven – I can doze in the quarter berth for a few more minutes. I pull the bunk curtain aside just in time to see two of the crew disappear up the companionway with their shower gear. The skipper, Colin Rouse, is up and about. 'What's the weather like?' I ask.

'Fine,' he answers. 'Looks good for Cherbourg. The kettle is on.'

I lie back and think about the plan for the day. Seven new crew members will be joining us after breakfast and in my mind I run through the briefing that they will need before we can sail. I hear the generator, fitted below the cockpit, turn over as Colin tries to start it from the control panel by the saloon steps. It doesn't start the first time and then I hear it turn over again.

Chaos. I am conscious of the most excruciating pain. The whole of my right leg feels as though it is being electrocuted. The agony goes on and on and on. I can't see, I'm covered in something white and translucent. There is no noise, and then I hear screaming. Deep male cries of agony; it takes a finite time for me to realise that the screaming is coming from me. Illogically, I think that something must have happened to the generator and live cables have dropped across my leg. After what seems like an age the pain starts to ease. Faintly I hear a voice. 'He's lost his leg'. I turn my head to the right and see a severed leg lying beside my bunk where the chart table seat should be. For one dreadful, heart-stopping moment I think that it's mine. Then I realise that the leg is deeply tanned and wearing a shoe and sock – it can't be me.

I think I lose consciousness at this point and the next thing I am aware of is someone dragging me from the remnants of the quarter berth. They are pulling shattered sheets of glassfibre off me. I am lying on the bare hull, the bunk has disappeared from under me. My rescuers drag me through the gaping whole where the coachroof had been. There is a stink of glassfibre, as though I was in a moulding shop. My face and eyes are covered in blood and something seems to have happened to my right foot – it's bleeding and won't take my weight. I look back into the wreckage of what had been the saloon. Colin is lying there with people working on him. The stump of his leg is pointing straight toward me. The cabin is devastated – I cannot conceive what has happened. There is blood everywhere.

I recall nothing else until I step onto the jetty from TS *Royalist*, alongside which *Lord Trenchard* had been berthed. There are police cars and ambulances all over the quay and more are arriving. I only hear their sirens faintly. There is a lot of broken glass and a crowd is beginning to form, held back by the police. A sergeant is talking to me, but I can't really absorb what he is saying. He shakes my shoulders. 'How many people were on board. How many?' I try to pull myself together. 'Four!' I answer.

I look back at *Lord Trenchard*. The whole of the cockpit and after deck has disappeared, leaving a gaping hole some 20ft long. The mizzen mast has fallen forward and the aft end of the coachroof has been torn off. I can see a deep split running down the hull from the coaming to the waterline. The whole deck has been lifted and all the windows blown out. Only at this moment does my mind register what has happened – explosion. I want to go back to the boat to help Colin but, sensibly, I'm not allowed to. 'He's all right – he's being looked after,' I am told. Still dripping blood I am put into an ambulance and driven away.

That is the reality of a gas explosion. The violence of the event is beyond belief. The blast was heard over four miles away and windows blown out on the quay, despite being shielded by the bulk of *Royalist* inboard of *Lord Trenchard*. The other two crew members on board, who had, like me, been lying in their bunks, were miraculously uninjured, but very shocked. The two crewmen who had just stepped onto the jetty probably saved Colin's life. They recall looking round to see parts of the boat – including the complete wheel and binnacle – flying high in the air. They came back on board and administered first aid, helped by officers from *Royalist*, until medical help arrived.

The emergency services deserve every praise. Poole lifeboat came alongside and together with *Royalist* supported *Lord Trenchard* to keep her afloat; she was making a lot of water from the splits in the hull and damaged seawater systems. After Colin had been taken ashore she was towed to the other side of the harbour to be lifted out. I spent some time in casualty, together with members of *Royalist*'s crew, who had suffered cuts and bruises. I had the gashes in my foot stitched up – the cuts to my face were only superficial – and discovered that both my eardrums had been burst. The initial pain in my leg, which had been only a few inches from the seat of the blast, was explained to me; the shock of the explosion had stimulated all the nerves in it at once, a common blast effect.

Whilst being treated I heard that Colin's left leg had been amputated above the knee. His other leg was badly damaged but had mercifully been saved. He also had injuries to his hand and neck and, although critically ill, was out of immediate danger.

Later that day I went back down to *Lord Trenchard* to try to retrieve some of my personal kit. She was still being kept afloat, but was half full of water and diesel fuel. The interior was almost unrecognisable with virtually nothing left intact. The explosion had obviously happened under the cockpit and the blast had torn forward through the boat, ripping out the joinery, bulkheads and cabin sole. The forehatch, which had been secured with a massive wooden strongback, had been torn off. The chart table had been blown forward through the saloon, together with the radar and all the instruments. It seemed impossible that four people could have survived. Mixed in with the shattered fragments of glassfibre and plywood were the pathetic remains of personal possessions – shredded clothing and sleeping bags, books, toilet gear, Colin's battered flute. It was a very shocking sight, made worse by the evidence of Colin's injuries – splashes of blood and blood-soaked clothing.

How could such an accident happen? The Joint Services Adventurous Sail Training centre in Gosport has been running a fleet of 24 boats, including nine Nicholson 55s, for nearly 30 years. The boats are deployed world-wide – three of them were racing across the Indian Ocean when this accident happened. They have a regular programme of refits and maintenance and, because many of the service personnel who sail in them are novices, safety procedures and routines are paramount. The Marine Accident Investigation Board carried out a very thorough enquiry into the explosion on behalf of the Health and Safety Executive.

Like the other service Nicholson 55s, *Lord Trenchard*'s gas system consisted of two 3.9kg propane cylinders, mounted in a gas locker sunk into the deck abreast the cockpit. Both cylinders were connected by flexible hoses to the regulator via a wall block and from there a single continuous gas pipe ran to an isolating valve by the cooker. A retaining plate secured the cylinders in the locker with just their shut off valves exposed. One cylinder was turned on whilst the other, shut off, was a standby, available when the in-use cylinder ran out. Whenever the cooker was not in use the isolating valve beside it was kept shut. A gas alarm was fitted, with two sensors, one beneath the cooker and one below the cockpit.

The evening before the accident the in-use gas bottle ran out whilst supper was being cooked. It was turned off, the standby cylinder was turned on and a note made to change the empty cylinder next day.

The accident report identified three failures that caused the explosion. First, the standby cylinder, which had been turned on the previous evening, had not been properly connected to its flexible pipe. The cylinder was recovered after the event and the connection was loose. It had been attached during a previous cruise made by *Lord Trenchard* a fortnight earlier and had been the 'standby' cylinder since then. Thus, when, twelve hours before the explosion, this cylinder was turned on, high-pressure gas leaked undetected directly from the bottle into the gas locker.

This gas should have drained overboard. However, examination of the gas locker, which was also recovered, revealed that it was not completely gas tight. So an unknown proportion of the escaping gas leaked into the watertight compartment below the cockpit.

The final cause of the disaster was that the gas alarm failed to operate. The reason for this could not be determined – the alarm system was so badly damaged in the explosion that testing it was impossible. The report concluded that the generator starter motor supplied the spark that ignited the gas.

Written specially for *Total Loss*

Lessons learned

So three failures, one human and two material, caused this catastrophe. The most obvious lesson is that gas cylinders should always be turned off AT THE BOTTLE when gas is not being used. But in many boats this is inconvenient – the gas locker is outside in the cold and wet and it is often difficult to get at. It is worth noting that a solenoid shut off valve, often fitted to overcome this inconvenience, would not have prevented this accident, as it would have been 'downstream' of the loose connection.

But there are other lessons too. Gas on boats is inherently dangerous and to keep it safe we have to actively do things. We must turn the gas on and off at the bottle every time the cooker is used and test our gas alarms by injecting butane into the sensors at regular intervals. We must periodically check that our gas lockers are indeed gas tight and that the drains from them are not blocked. We must check pipework and replace flexible hoses, test flame failure devices. Human nature is such that not all of these things will unfailingly get done.

We should all consider whether we really do need gas on our boats. Nowadays there are more alternatives available than the old-fashioned traditional Primus stoves. There are user friendly diesel cookers on the market, now with ovens. Larger yachts with modern, quiet inboard generators might use electricity for their cooking.

On a happier note, Colin made the most remarkable recovery, due largely to his amazing cheerfulness and fortitude together with the unstinting support of his partner Janis. Within a week he was terrorising the nurses in hospital and within a fortnight he was home. Although the adjustment has not been easy he gets around well on a marvellous artificial leg. He no longer works as a Nicholson skipper but has not given up sailing.

Accidents happen but ones involving gas are more horrible than most. We were fortunate that no one was killed on *Lord Trenchard*. Had the explosion happened the previous day, with the yacht at sea and everyone on board in the cockpit, or had we all been sitting round the saloon table, undoubtedly lives would have been lost, quite possibly the whole crew. To prevent such a disaster happening to you, if you must have gas on your yacht, always, always turn it off at the bottle.

39 A blazing yacht in the Ionian

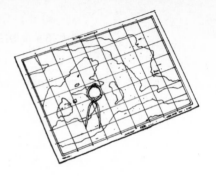

Yacht Charter yacht
Skipper unknown
Bound from Mourtos in the Northern Ionian to Parga
Date of loss 1997
Position Sivota Islands, Ionian Sea, Greece

Derek and Carol Asquith's charter holiday got off to a hair-raising start when they were called to rescue the crew of a burning yacht.

It was the second day of our flotilla sailing holiday in the Northern Ionian. The winds were light, the sea was flat and the sun was shining as we left Mourtos for Parga. The fleet was a mix of 9.7m (32ft) Jeanneau and 11m (36ft) Beneteau yachts and my wife Carol and I, who sail a 7.3m (24ft) Snapdragon at home in North Wales, had looked forward to the comfort of a larger boat for the holiday.

We sailed between the Sivota Islands and the mainland, cruising slowly down the coat. After a couple of hours the wind died completely so we started the engine. The sea was calm as we motored at a comfortable 4 knots towards the next headland in the distance. We noticed the lead boat close inshore three or four miles ahead of us, with only one or two boats of the flotilla in sight.

Suddenly the radio came to life with one of our group calling the lead boat in a fairly calm way saying they had a fire. We turned the volume up and scanned the horizon but could see no signs of smoke anywhere. Our lead boat responded on the VHF channel that the flotilla was using, asking if they had found the source of the fire and made any effort to extinguish it. They replied that the fire was in the engine compartment and one extinguisher had made no difference.

The lead skipper then asked their position and from their reply we realised they were perhaps half-a-mile ahead of us with no one else around. The flotilla lead skipper then told them not, on any account, to open up the engine compartment, but to try to use the second extinguisher through the hole in the companionway steps panel. After some tense moments they came back to say that their efforts with the second extinguisher had proved unsuccessful.

At this stage, I called the lead skipper to tell him we were closing with the boat. We increased speed towards the, now visible, smoking yacht and saw four men waving frantically and more smoke pouring from the cabin. When we were within about 25m (80 ft) we could hear them shouting.

'Hurry up, it's going to blow!'

Carol turned to me and quietly asked if I thought it would really explode. I crossed my fingers and replied confidently: 'Diesel won't explode, it will only burn.'

Pulling alongside the stricken yacht, we found three crew amidships and one standing in the pulpit, as far from the smoke and burning as possible. Carol held a fender over the side to prevent the stanchions and guardrails becoming entangled as we came alongside in the swell. We did not want to be trapped against a burning yacht, even for a few seconds.

The three men amidships scrambled aboard, calling for the fourth in the pulpit. In his panic, the fourth man jumped overboard into the sea. We veered slowly away and Carol threw a fender to the man in the water who could not swim as fast as the boat. She then took a mooring warp from the cockpit locker and we reversed very slowly until she could throw him the line. With the engine in neutral we pulled him towards the bathing platform and after a successful recovery motored clear to take stock of the situation.

The crew of the blazing vessel were all wearing T-shirts and shorts and had only two lifejackets between them as the others were stowed below in cabin lockers which were impossible to reach because of the fire. Carol made them hot coffee, gave the wet crew member a towel and a large sweater, and called the lead boat to inform them that we had transferred the crew.

The lead boat arrived a short while later, but by now the fire had really got hold and no one could have safely gone back aboard. As we watched, the shrouds gave way and the mast collapsed and fell into the sea. Soon the gas bottles exploded in the cockpit and that was the beginning of the end. The lead boat later tried to tow the hull but, when it became obvious she was sinking, they took her back to deep water where she soon went down.

As we returned the four crew to Mourtos, they told us that, as with all the flotilla boats, they had a liferaft and inflatable dinghy; but since no one had been given instructions in launching the liferaft, they had failed to inflate it. They had tried to pump up the dinghy, but felt it was taking too long and had given up. No doubt the proximity of our boat had led them to feel they had more chance of escape with us. Luckily, all survived unharmed.

From *Yachting Monthly*, September 1997

Lessons learned

We instantly moved our lifejackets from the cabin into the cockpit lockers and made sure we knew everything we needed to about out how to launch the liferaft.

It was our first real man-overboard and, although the stern bathing platform is considered the wrong place from which to recover a person, on an almost flat calm day the platform with a ladder made it easy.

Should you be unfortunate enough to have an engine fire aboard, throw the gas bottles and any spare fuel cans overboard to prevent them exploding.

A longer lead on the VHF microphone and a hand-held set in the cockpit would have helped. Apparently, the cabin of the blazing yacht filled with black smoke so quickly that it was soon impossible to go below.

I intend to fit bigger extinguishers on our Snapdragon, including one in a cockpit locker. And make sure than anyone who comes aboard has a thorough safety briefing and knows where everything is stowed and how it is operated.

40 *Strumpet* was Gone!

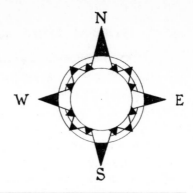

Yacht *Strumpet* (28ft GRP replica of a Morecambe Bay prawner)
Skipper Henry Irving
Crew Barry Speakman, Jondo Irving, Joe Irving
Bound from Wainfleet Haven, Lincolnshire, to Wells, Norfolk
Date of loss 3 August, 1980
Position 1 mile S of Gibraltar Point, approximately 6 miles S of Skegness

Henry Irving, author of the pilot guide Tidal Havens of the Wash and Humber, *has sailed those waters, summer and winter, for many years, usually in his own boat* Venture, *but this time in a friend's yacht,* Strumpet. *They had set sail from Wainfleet Creek at the northern corner of the Wash and were bound for Wells, some 30 miles away on the north Norfolk coast.* Strumpet *was a reinforced glassfibre replica of a Morecambe Bay prawner – a strong and sea-kindly vessel. Besides Barry, an old friend and experienced cruising companion, Irving had his two young sons, Jondo and Joe, on board. In company as they left the creek was another friend, Peter Tomlinson, in his steel yacht* Temptress, *with a crew of four. The mood was merry, Skegness had been good, the day promised to be good and Wells promised to be even better. Fifteen minutes later, all eight of them were aboard* Temptress *and* Strumpet *was a blazing inferno. Henry Irving takes up the story.*

Tide time arrived that morning in the middle of ablutions, so it was necessary to postpone breakfast, start the engine and cast off lines. Wainfleet permits little dallying on the ebb. As I steered *Strumpet* down the tortuous creek between the withies, Barry prepared breakfast and served it up to Jondo and Joe. Since we were nearing the haven mouth, I suggested that he kept our breakfasts warm in the oven whilst raising sail. A leisurely breakfast under sail appealed to me much more than something crammed down astern of a noisy diesel engine. Jondo, fearing that he was missing something of interest, bolted his breakfast and rushed on to the foredeck to assist. Joe, unwilling to abandon his carefully prepared bread soldiers, stayed below to savour his food. Something, however, was spoiling his childish pleasure:

'Dad, there's an awful smell of fumes.'

'Oh, shut up. It's only the diesel. Eat your breakfast. I'll switch it off in a minute.'

The sails went up, I bore off, and switched off the engine.

'I can't stand these fumes. I'm going to eat my breakfast out there.'

By this time, I could smell something, so I summoned Jondo to the helm and scrambled below. A quick glance at the galley showed me that Barry had left no pans on the gas, and a peep into the oven revealed a reassuring pile of bacon, mushrooms and tomatoes, warmly awaiting the arrival of the as yet uncooked eggs. I looked at the engine temperature gauge. All fine. To check, I lifted the engine cover and smelled fumes, but the engine did not feel excessively warm. Thinking it must have been an oily rag on the exhaust, I climbed into the cockpit to check this, unhurried because the engine was now quiet and presumably cooling. Nothing amiss in that department so I looked at the sails and sea scene once more, assuming that the smell would soon go.

Joe finished his breakfast so I asked him to go below and start cooking the eggs for Barry and myself. He disappeared, only to re-emerge immediately to say that black smoke was now pouring into the cabin from the fo'c's'le. I seized the large CO_2 extinguisher from the cockpit locker and scrambled below, but the dense black smoke prevented me from getting anywhere near the fo'c's'le. I held what breath I had and directed the extinguisher into the smoke for a few futile seconds then rushed out on deck. The hatch boards were stowed in the aft locker so I could not quickly fit them. When I got my breath I realised that Peter, a friend in another yacht *Temptress*, had come close alongside and had hurled his extinguisher at Barry. We went on to the foredeck and I opened the hatch so that Barry could direct the extinguisher on to the source of the smoke. Immediately, a roar of black smoke and flame shot out of the hatch, igniting the staysail and causing us both to stagger back with black faces and singed eyebrows.

My thoughts then turned to saving life rather than fighting fire. *Temptress* was still at hand so I called Peter to come alongside and take off crew. The sea was quite choppy, but the manoeuvre was well executed and the boys and Barry got safely on to *Temptress*. I attempted to unfasten the inflated dinghy from the cabin roof, but as I did so the forward section burst into flame so I abandoned the attempt. I called for a tow rope and managed to make it fast to the forestay, thinking that a sandbank was a better place to sink than a swatchway. By this time, the heat was becoming so intense that *Temptress*'s sails and rigging were endangered, and the boys were clearly in distress, so I jumped aboard. We towed *Strumpet* on a long line, which finally burned through while we were atop the Outer Dog's Head. The maelstrom that ensued was awesome to behold: sails burst into flame, the mast tumbled, the Calor cylinder exploded in the aft locker making an insignificant contribution to the overall scene and finally the hull slowly melted away till she sank. *Strumpet* was gone.

Written for this book by Henry Irving

Lessons learned

Naturally the insurance company required a full explanation. As the nightmare subsided, to be replaced by a dull, numb feeling of loss, I spent hours trying to sift through the events in order to provide one. I could only think of one possibility. There was no natural light in the fo'c's'le of *Strumpet*, so the boys, who were sleeping there, used a Camping Gaz lamp which the owner had left hanging on a hook for this purpose. That morning, they had used it to dress and had put it out before emerging to accompany me to the toilet. As I have previously said, our ablutions that morning were hasty, so it was only a matter of minutes before we had cast off and were motoring down the creek. At the haven mouth there was a chop in the water which caused the boat to dance about. I can only think that this motion caused the lamp to jump off the hook and fall with a still hot glass on to one of the sleeping bags, causing it to burn. The sleeping bag must have ignited the Dunlopillo mattress (which I subsequently simulated with horrifying results) and the mattress in turn generated sufficient heat for the GRP and plywood of the fo'c's'le to catch fire. The speed of these events was of an order that I would never have imagined possible. From Joe's olfactory misgivings until the evacuation of the boat was no more than 15 minutes.

It is certainly possible, and perhaps useful, to make the usual set of recriminations – the checklist of guilt and the vows for the future. Camping Gaz lamps on hooks are out; the Dunlopillo mattresses were suspect (though they continue to be temptingly comfortable, and I still sail with one on *Venture*, albeit with a robust cover on it); GRP boats have never been my favourite kind of craft and I would now hesitate to undertake a serious cruise in one. So much for materials; what of human action and inaction? I will always remember to seal up a boat on fire rather than to mess about with silly extinguishers. I have always preferred to cruise in company for social reasons; this incident revealed practical ones. But at the end of the day the basic lesson to be learned is that disaster can strike a small cruising yacht very quickly and cause loss of life. If you can't cope with this, then don't go to sea. But don't get into a car either, and don't cross the road to get your morning paper.'

Footnote

Irving found he couldn't get through the cabin to the source of the fire in the fo'c's'le. He knew that he should close the companion hatch to reduce the air flow into the boat, but the washboards were stowed in the aft locker so he couldn't fit them quickly enough. A valuable lesson learned. Instead, he went forward on deck and opened the forehatch 'so that Barry could direct the extinguisher onto the source of the fire. Immediately, a roar of black smoke and flame shot out of the hatch'. Another lesson. Finally, when he attempted to unfasten the inflated dinghy from the coachroof, the forward section burst into flames, so he had to abandon the attempt. If *Temptress* had not been on hand to take them off, the crew of *Strumpet* would have been forced to jump into the sea.

41 A chance in a lifetime

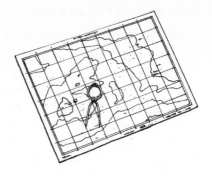

Yacht *Freedom To* (34ft motor-sailer)
Skipper C Binnings
Crew J Warrington
Bound from Hamble, Hampshire to Newport, South Wales
Date of loss 20 May 1981
Position 5 miles S of Eddystone Lighthouse

Freedom To, a Westerly Vulcan, was brand-new and on her way from the Solent to Newport, South Wales, which was to be her home port when she was struck by lightning.

We left Hamble at 1100 on Tuesday, motored down to the Solent and took our departure from the Needles. As we came on to 260°, the wind came up dead astern and with the roller headsail full out and the revs down to 2200 we made 6½ knots – pleasant sailing.

A week previously I had sent form CG66 to Swansea Coastguard and accordingly informed Solent Coastguard of our departure, as well as Portland and Brixham as we passed. We had planned for Dartmouth, but changed our plans when the afternoon brought a blue sky and the evening a good moon. We decided to make for Penzance.

At 0100 we saw flashes of lightning way to the south. By 0400 it was raining and the flashes were getting nearer. Visibility was by now down to about two to three miles. We continued to run under full headsail and 2200 revs.

Jim had the 0200–0600 watch and at 0530 he joined me below in the main cabin, saying that he would steer from the inside position for a while. He had done more than his fair share of helming on the previous day.

Feeling sufficiently awake, I said I would take over and settled myself into the helmsman's seat with a glance at the compass.

I would liken it to a television tube exploding. Our first thoughts were 'the engine', but it appeared to be running normally enough. We raced to the cockpit to look for visible damage and as I looked I noticed the aerial had gone. Jim switched off the engine and gas bottle in the nearby locker. A thick, tanny brown smoke was rolling up the companionway to be straightened and carried away by the wind. It's still raining, I thought, I'm going to get wet out here without oilskins. I quite believed that it was only a matter of waiting for the smoke to clear. I had other thoughts. If the situation deteriorated further, sending a Mayday was impossible now with the aerial gone. Top priority was the dinghy, flares and lifejackets.

I took a deep breath and leapt down the companionway. Visibility nil. The lifejackets were in the hanging wardrobe and the flares under the settee berths, but access was still a stranger and familiarity not yet an ally. The attempt was aborted, but I did manage to grab a fire extinguisher which was clipped under the saloon table.

By now Jim was in the cockpit with a full bucket of water, but with smoke issuing from every quarter it was difficult to know where to start the attack. We lifted the cockpit locker to get at the dinghy – more dense smoke. This is a big 7ft deep locker with the dinghy at the bottom under a mound of carefully stowed warps and fenders, the outboard motor and five gallons of spare diesel. I came out gasping for air. The dinghy was firmly lodged. We climbed to the weather side to avoid the toxic fumes, while *Freedom To* continued to turn. As we came up on to the starboard side we saw the first lick of flame from the main hatch. It was impossible to believe, the possible avenues of retreat were rapidly being whittled away: we had no VHF, flares or lifejackets. A stuck dinghy and two horseshoe buoys were all that was left.

With Jim making a last ditch effort to free the inflatable, I grabbed at the horseshoes, freeing one. Still no flames in the cockpit locker as the dinghy finally freed. We yanked it clear, the rubber warm and sticky. By now the flames were at Jim's seaboots as we hauled the dinghy down the weather side outside the lifelines. By now the cabin roof was melting, with flames breaking through to leeward. We stood in the pulpit together, desperately trying to inflate the dinghy by mouth. The heat on our backs was appalling, as all deck features folded in before taking on a mantle of flame.

Flame and heat accelerated our departure from the deck and with the dinghy only perhaps 20 per cent inflated we followed it into the water. 'That's it, we can stand it no longer.'

With the partially inflated dinghy folded like a clam we searched with our mouths for the inflation holes which were some way under water. The dinghy by now was alongside the starboard beam, although I have no idea why. We continued to inflate – it was taking shape, holding air. Then down came the mast immediately above us. Six or seven feet from the hull and it would have hit us, but we were close enough to the side for safety as it lay at right angles into the sea. Seconds later the boom came tumbling into the water alongside the dinghy. It was still, however, attached to the gooseneck and lolled, burning, inches from the rubber. The mainsail which had been left wrapped on to the boom had burned and the metal was molten with heat.

Jim was still busy blowing air. I thumped him for his attention and four hands sent water flying to douse this, our latest hazard. This was followed by our next concern, the danger of explosion from the 40 gallons of diesel on board and the two gas cylinders. Using our hands as paddles we made some distance from the wreck. Ten, fifteen, twenty feet and I looked astern.

She lay in the water, her superstructure gone, a floating cauldron with her spars dangling. We could still make out her lines. We paddled further and as I lifted my head on the next crest I saw the coaster, maybe 700 yards off. You're not safe yet, I thought, she's probably on autopilot. As she neared we could see figures on deck and heard the sounds of reversing engines. Through salt drenched eyes I could read the name on her bows. Will I ever forget that name *Moray Firth*? Never.

As we were helped up the side and up on to the bridge, the first of two explosions wracked *Freedom To*. She was last reported burnt to the water-line. We informed the Coastguard of our safety.

From *Yachting Monthly*, September 1981

Lessons learned

Flares must be kept dry and to hand – not under the settee berths, as they were on *Freedom To* when she was stuck by lightning. Manufacturers go a long way towards ensuring that their flares do keep dry, by packaging them in waterproof plastic containers, but it will always be down to the skipper to decide where they are stowed. Any container used for storing distress flares must not only be instantly accessible but must also be easily opened on the roughest, blackest night, so that the correct flare or rocket can be found without fumbling or delay. Flares are marked with an expiry date, so don't count on them to work successfully after that time.

When a boat is on fire and the fire is out of control, there is no time to be wasted. But if the inflatable dinghy has been stowed in a locker and is inaccessible the situation can be frightening as the crew of *Freedom To* discovered.

The 'big 7ft-deep locker' had the dinghy at the bottom under a mound of carefully stowed warps and fenders, the outboard motor and five gallons of spare diesel! The skipper came out gasping for air. 'The dinghy was firmly lodged . . . we had no VHF, flares or lifejackets. A stuck dinghy and two horse-shoe buoys were all that was left.' When they did eventually manage to yank the dinghy clear it was warm and sticky, so it must have been a very close thing. Then they had to inflate it without a pump, using their mouths instead. When they could stand the heat no longer they tossed the partially inflated dinghy into the water and followed it. Having no oars, they had to paddle with their hands to get clear of the yacht, which, with its tanks of diesel fuel and gas bottles, was likely to blow up at any moment. Somehow they managed to get more air into the dinghy to keep her afloat until they were rescued by a passing coaster. They were extraordinarily lucky and their experience should warn against stowing a dinghy in a locker while underway.

42 One touch of the button

Yacht *Ladybee* (30ft gaff-rigged double-ender)
Skipper James Houston
Crew Margaret Houston
Bound from Puilladobhrain, Argyll to Tobermory, Isle of Mull, Scotland
Date of loss: 10 June 1972
Position two miles south of Duart Point, Sound of Mull

Ladybee was a double-ender of the Colin Archer type, heavily built by Weatherhead of Cockenzie in 1929. She was originally called Lady Bridgella of Rhu *and was well known on the Clyde.* Ladybee *had served well as a slow but comfortable family cruiser for James and Margaret Houston and their children. The engine was a petrol/paraffin Kelvin, and in the spring of 1972 it was giving a lot of trouble.*

O ur cruise this year began with the Lamlash Race when we took up our customary position of being last. Sunday was an absolutely perfect day for soaking up the sun, not to mention Jimmy Gillespie's cocktails before lunch. It came as quite a disappointment, however, to find that the absence of wind was soon to be joined by the absence of engine. It seemed that nothing short of oars would get us past the old wreck on Holy Isle until we secured a welcome hitch from one of these common white yachts.

Despite regular attention by notable engineers our engine had given trouble all spring, and we were more than a little despondent to find that things were still not right and that the palliatives like stripping and cleaning the carburettors, renewing the plugs, etc, made little or no difference.

We thought it better to have the engine examined properly even at the expense of losing another precious day of our fortnight. We found that a manufacturer's engineer was coming down to Fairlie the following day, and so we were able to secure his services at short notice. We finally got away on Tuesday morning, and had a fine sail all the way to Ardrishaig. The engine started reassuringly as we approached the breakwater. But it packed up again as we circled around to await the opening of the sea lock gates. We ended up having to rush at the lock from some distance with plenty of impetus to carry us in. Help!

The next day a very competent and helpful young man from the garage fitted a shining new starter switch, starter button and solenoid. He tested and re-aligned the starter motor and it was reassuring to see that everything at long last appeared to be functioning perfectly. One touch of the button – marvellous.

It was with confidence and perhaps a touch of bravado that we demonstrated our skill in gliding our 10ft beam serenely through what looked like a 9ft half-gate. At the sixth lock we found a small fishing boat having engine trouble and as the skipper was quick to notice our great power and manoeuvrability, he actually requested a tow! I really couldn't help laughing. Later on I felt quite superior by being able to diagnose the fault of his engine, and instantly produced a proper-sized jet-spanner to remedy it. I could see he was quite impressed by my knowledge of the engine and I secretly hoped that Margaret wouldn't spoil my act by revealing to him that his engine was exactly the same as ours.

The previous year, the first two weeks of June were sublime and we had fond memories of cloudless skies, sparkling water and warm southerly winds keeping the eternal swell crashing into the depths of Fingal's Cave. We drifted round the Mull in swimming costumes to arrive home the colour of Indians and stating knowledgeably that everyone should take their holidays in June, when the weather is always at its best.

This year the cold northerly wind blew through the buttonholes of our oilskins as we pounded our way with the tide up the Sound of Luing. Tacking back from the Mull shore found us near enough to Puilladobhrain to have us thinking of the warm pub over the hill at Clachan Bridge, so we fairly tore into that well-known sheltered lagoon. The cold wind dropped in the evening so that we could sit comfortably in the fading light and admire the nice new woodwork and homely interior of our saloon. But it rose again with us in the morning so the ham and egg breakfast was not to be enjoyed in the exposed cockpit.

We set off for Tobermory, choosing our time for wind and tide to be in the same direction, making for a flatter sea, but unfortunately these elements were coming almost exactly from the direction of our destination. Before leaving the shelter of Kerrera on our third tack, we brought the grey inflatable dinghy on board as it had been snatching at the painter while out in the Firth. Although it does spoil the view we always like to keep it inflated, not so much for its immediate availability for use as a liferaft, but more because it is such a tiresome task having to blow the thing up again! Anyway, the air valves had been leaking a bit in the spring, and although it had been serviced by the agents in Glasgow we noticed that sudden deflation was less frequent when the full pressure was maintained. Several thoroughly secure lashings kept the dinghy a good three inches clear of the boom, and I managed to film some good shots as we left Bach Island rapidly to port, but it didn't look as though we had a hope in hell of leaving Duart Point to port. The best we made was a couple of miles south of that, and we felt rather tempted at the time to motorsail up the coast to save another tedious tack into the Firth.

But there was no particular hurry, so we went about as usual and turned our backs to the fresh wind and hauled the sheets in tight. Soon, however, a combination of good ideas like having coffee now, and perhaps reaching the Mishnish before closing time, prompted a reconsideration of the motor-sail idea. The coffee was therefore extracted from the cupboard on the uphill side of the boat and I reached forward from the cockpit for one touch of the button. The boat blew up.

Margaret was shouting something about her leg and I couldn't understand where she had disappeared to, or why I could now see the whole engine which had hitherto been concealed by the heavy plywood covers: or where all the flames suddenly appeared from; or where the companionway was that used to be bolted over the engine covers.

Ladybee must then have been given her head for I remember using both hands from a crouching position to tear, I think ineffectively, at a red jersey levering itself up into the cockpit. We were absolutely stunned. I remembered a fire extinguisher decorating a bulkhead at each end of our boat so here was the chance to try one out as I always wanted to. It wasn't necessary to open the forehatch because it had already disappeared and fragments of plastic could be seen clinging to the wet deck around the windlass, against which the hatch had undoubtedly smashed. The extinguisher had fallen from its bracket to the floor and in searching quickly for it I noticed the bulkhead was slightly deformed and the doorway which used to open into the saloon was now opening slightly into the fo'c's'le.

Anyway the extinguisher was a bit of a disappointment. The wind carried some of the white stuff into the sea and the remainder was soon to be exhausted. The jet seemed to choke a bit when directed towards the flames surrounding the engine and I wished that I had another extinguisher to try out because it looked like the petrol in the tanks would soon be on the boil. We forgot about coffee.

Meanwhile, we decided that it was now an appropriate time to secure a line of retreat. The lashings on the dinghy suddenly became fused to the rails and the fingers began to fumble frantically until we saw that the bow of the Avon had a great hole in it. The shock of this observation must have caused us to take stock, because we began to tackle the lashings in a more orderly manner; and perhaps we realised that despite the decompression of one half of the dinghy, the other half was miraculously staying fully inflated. We wasted no time in launching the dinghy which was tethered by Margaret while I collected oars and the pump. By this time we had agreed that it might be prudent to actually use the line of retreat before the petrol tanks blew up. As with fire extinguishers, we had also wondered about flares. A hasty return to the fo'c's'le confirmed that the flares along with the lifejackets were unobtainable in the saloon, but in any case there was as much smoke trailing across the Firth of Lorne as any flare would have made. I caught a glimpse of the fenders which we had been using to go through the canal and it occurred to me that they would have made quite good emergency floats when tied together.

I also hesitated to consider the new outboard motor but decided against that. We were getting a bit fed up with engine trouble anyway and surely nothing much could go wrong with a pair of oars. So we cast off at 1310 and *Ladybee* pulled rapidly away. Margaret gathered the deflated loose part of the dinghy around her waist to keep the water out as we began to row towards the Mull shore and we suddenly felt very sad indeed.

A second explosion perhaps ten minutes later confirmed that we were now in the safer vessel. While it had seemed that we were alone on the Firth of Lorne we suddenly noticed a steamer abeam of Lady Rock lighthouse, presumably on her way from Craignure to Oban, and we saw her alter course. Perched on each successive wave crest we could see *Ladybee* sailing now on a more southerly course back towards Puilladobhrain and away from the steamer. A flash of white light, followed a second or two later by a loud report, must have been the gas cylinders blowing up, and we wondered what the skipper of the steamer would be thinking. It looked as though he was getting quite close to *Ladybee* – if only we could let him know there was nobody on board. We did worry in case someone would get hurt trying to find out, but we were now miles away and a half-sized grey rubber dinghy is not the most conspicuous object on a dark grey sea.

We discovered later on that a report was issued at Southend (Argyll CRHQ) at 1331 hours from Oban radio to the effect that the car ferry *Columbia* was going alongside a yacht with a blue jib and white mainsail about one mile south-west of Kerrera Island. No one could be seen on board. It seems that Mr Devine, the Coastguard in charge at Oban, was immediately informed and within a few minutes he had put to sea in the

Callum Cille and was making for the position.

We had, however, been spotted by someone on Mull, and it seems that Captain Leslie, the Coastguard Reporting Member at Grasspoint on Mull, was soon able to inform the *Columbia* that we were safely ashore. We didn't know this at the time, of course, but we did notice the arrival of other vessels in the area and saw with some relief that *Columbia* was able to depart.

I had been told as a child that if I ever fell out of a balloon (which I could never understand) I would be sure to land on a feather bed. It was only to be expected, therefore, that the rocky shore we suddenly gaped at as we made our diagonal journey should give way to the most beautiful sheltered sandy bay, precisely at the point where it seemed we would fetch up. Margaret dissolved in tears as we walked up the beach. She had left her make-up case behind!

Looking around the hillside revealed no immediate signs of life until two figures appeared standing in the bracken some distance away. I approached them to be informed (believe it or not) that 'some boat was in trouble out there'. As I followed the sweep of the gentleman's arm I screwed up my eyes incredulously. Perhaps people had a habit of coming ashore there with blackened faces and singed eyebrows.

From *Yachting World*, September 1972

Lessons learned

The two major causes of boat loss by fire or explosion – about equally responsible – are petrol and bottled gas. Petrol engines are something of a rarity in yachts these days now that small lightweight diesel units are available. *Ladybee*'s dual petrol/paraffin engine was designed to start on petrol and then to run on paraffin, which was cheaper than petrol. They tended to be troublesome, as James Houston found. His own explanation of the explosion that cost him his boat is given in a letter – 'After motoring out of Puillodobhrain and hoisting sail, we had a beat for a couple of hours towards Mull, during which time petrol from the carb, or somewhere, must have leaked into the bilge below the engine. The engine was enclosed in a watertight box in which the right mixture must have accumulated to be ignited by a spark from the new starter motor when we decided to restart it.'

What happened immediately after *Ladybee* caught fire is instructive. With the engine surrounded by flames and the companion steps blown away, Houston's first concern was to help his hurt wife out of the cabin and into the cockpit. He then remembered 'a fire extinguisher decorating a bulkhead at each end of our boat'. He discovered that the forehatch had been blown clean off and the forward extinguisher had fallen to the floor, whence he retrieved it, only to find that in use 'it was a bit of a disappointment, because the wind carried some of the white stuff into the sea and the remainder was soon exhausted; the jet seemed to choke a bit when directed towards the flames'.

It would seem that Houston was using a foam-type extinguisher, and because he had no choice but to work from the deck its effectiveness was negligible. Extinguishers smother the fire by denying it oxygen and the blanketing substance, whether powder, foam or gas, must reach the root of the fire. But quite often, when fire breaks out in a small yacht, it quickly becomes impossible to stay below, and the chances of aiming an extinguisher at the source of the fire are greatly reduced. The best compromise would seem to be to install at least two extinguishers; one of them just inside the main hatch and easily reachable from the cockpit, and the other accessible through the forehatch.

The flares, along with the lifejackets were unobtainable in the saloon, but 'there was as much smoke trailing across the Firth of Lorne as any flare would have made'.

An inflatable dinghy, whether lashed on deck or stowed in a locker, becomes very vulnerable when a yacht catches fire. *Ladybee*'s dinghy, already inflated, was on deck, but 'the lashings suddenly became fused to the rails ... and we saw that the bow of the Avon had a great hole in it'. Fortunately the stern half of the dinghy remained fully inflated, so Houston and his wife were able to get ashore safely in half a dinghy. Even when only half inflated, a rubber dinghy can serve as a small liferaft – provided there is no rough water to contend with. A liferaft, packed in a glassfibre canister, would not catch fire as quickly as an unprotected dinghy and there would, of course, be no delay involved while inflating it.

Part seven:

Being towed

Jester, *Mike Richey's famous junk-rigged folkboat, lost under tow on her 14th transatlantic passage.*

43 Typhoon Brenda and the tow

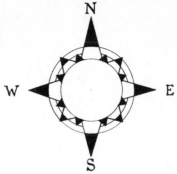

Yacht *East Wind of the Orient* (Contessa 38)
Skipper Major Philip Banbury
Bound for Hong Kong from the Philippines
Date of loss May 1989
Position less than 100 miles SSW of Hong Kong

Major Philip Banbury describes the dramatic sinking of a Contessa 38, which was being towed away from the path of a typhoon in the South China Sea.

For a number of years, HM Forces stationed in Hong Kong ran an adventure training exercise in the Philippines, sailing their Contessa 38 *East Wind of the Orient*. It usually took place between January and May, enabling eight crews of eight servicemen and servicewomen to spend a fortnight sailing in one of the most attractive cruising areas of the world. Lest the taxpayer should question the value of such 'exotic' training, I should point out that during those months the prevailing wind is the northeasterly monsoon and often provides fast, exhilarating sailing which be can more testing than adventurous.

The last leg of the exercise was from 5–20 May, 1989. A week would be spent cruising the local waters of the Philippines and the last week sailing *East Wind* back to Hong Kong. The skipper, who had assembled and briefed the crew and done the initial passage planning, had to drop out at the last minute, so I flew to Manila and joined the yacht two days after the other seven crew members.

After a few days' local sailing, enjoying sun and swimming, we sailed 300 miles north to San Fernando, the little port which provides the jumping off point for the shortest distance from the Philippines to Hong Kong, 480nm.

On Tuesday morning, 16 May, we had been in San Fernando 36 hours. I returned to the yacht having cleared with immigration and customs. Major Bruce Denton, our doctor, heard that a tropical depression was forming to the south of us. A motor-yacht in the harbour with a weatherfax promised to give us an update at 1700. Meanwhile, I telephoned our exercise control in Hong Kong to see if they had any weather information. As a result of information provided, I decided to set sail as soon as I got the weatherfax from the motor-yacht.

I cannot now remember the precise location of the depression. The dominating feature was a high pressure area over mainland China, which I thought might provide us with north-east winds. We set off immediately for Hong Kong under engine, as there was very little wind.

Throughout Tuesday night and most of Wednesday we motored, because I wanted to keep ahead of the depression and make best speed for Hong Kong. During Wednesday the wind started to pick up and because it was blowing from dead ahead we continued under engine. We listened to the weather report on Rowdy's net (an amateur radio net) at 0800 and also got a weather update at 0900. Both confirmed the depression was moving north and gave predictions for 24, 48 and 72 hours ahead, which I plotted on the chart.

At this stage, there was no knowing the precise path the depression would take, though it was clearly going to enter the South China Sea. It had been given the name Brenda and was classed as a tropical storm.

By Wednesday evening the wind was blowing 25 knots from NNE and the sea was getting up. Thinking that the wind would get stronger during the night, and because it was still on the nose, we set storm jib and trysail, as much to steady the yacht as to make headway under sail. By Thursday morning the wind had increased and veered a bit. We were able to sail on a course of about 315°. At some stage that day we switched off the engine to save fuel. I wanted to conserve enough to meet a real emergency and to charge batteries, so we could maintain radio communications. Throughout Thursday, 18 satnav fixes confirmed we were making a lot of leeway because of both wind and waves. By nightfall the wind was force 7 gusting 8. I decided that of the four men on watch only two should be on deck at a time to avoid crew getting unnecessarily cold and wet and to conserve as much energy as possible.

On Friday morning we were about 100 miles SSW of Hong Kong. The wind was blowing a constant 35–40 knots and gusts would occasionally take it off the windspeed indicator at 50 knots. During our morning radio schedule with Hong Kong we were told the storm had now been classed as typhoon. Its path could still not be predicted, so we continued to sail as close to the wind as the sailplan allowed in the direction of Hong Kong.

During the morning we tried to start our engine to charge the batteries, but despite the fuel tank being between a half and a third full, the engine would not start; for some reason the fuel was not getting through to the engine. Our engineer tried to bleed the system without success. We think the fuel tank was probably a bad design and the positioning of the outlet pipe meant that all the fuel could not be utilised.

We got a satnav fix at 0810 on Friday. The course continued to be plotted by DR/EP on the chart. I estimated that we were making good a course of 310°.

At around midday, our contact in Hong Kong, having received the latest information on Typhoon Brenda, said he would be asking if HMS *Plover*, one of the Royal Navy's patrol craft, could be sent down to 'stand by' us.

We established communications with *Plover* on our HF set and she arrived in our general area at about 1700. The first flares fired were not seen and it was clear that our estimated position was not sufficiently accurate to avoid her having to search for us. It was now getting dark. At 1818 one of the crew on deck reported sighting a merchant vessel several miles astern. This information was passed to *Plover*, which saw the vessel on their radar and were then able to establish our location. A few minutes later we also got a satnav fix and passed it to *Plover*. By the time they sighted us just after 1930 the wind was force 9 or 10 and the waves 8–9m high.

Because we were directly in the path of the typhoon, *Plover* informed us that they proposed to take *East Wind* under tow and were preparing a line to be passed to us. I agreed to accept this and they gradually manoeuvred to come abreast of us. After requesting we lower the trysail, they fired a heaving line. This was unsuccessful, as was the second attempt. Eventually, we picked up a line floated astern of HMS *Plover* and the tow was secured just after 2200.

Having been taken under tow, HMS *Plover* started to pull us clear of the predicted track of the typhoon. Up to now, I had spent most of my time at the VHF radio in contact with *Plover*, and the chart table, whilst yelling instructions through the companionway hatch to the crew on deck.

Because the remainder of the crew had been on deck while the tow was being secured, I now took the helm and Major Jonathon Swann kept me company in the cockpit. Under tow the yacht behaved well but had to be steered. She would surf down the front of the waves, which were following us at great speed, seeming at times to be in great danger of catching up with the stern of *Plover*. When this happened, the tow rope obviously went slack.

At midnight, I handed over to Captain Simon Pashley and Major Bruce Dunlop, the first two crew of the other watch. Jonathon and I went down below to rest. The next thing I knew, someone on deck was shouting that the tow must be stopped. I radioed *Plover*. Down below we were taking in water fast. The area by the companionway was immediately affected. I roused the crew and told them to get on deck. It was clear from the speed that water was coming in that we would have to abandon ship.

Everyone, except two of us (including me), was wearing a lifejacket. The liferaft was launched. There had been some difficulty getting it out of the storage locker. Once it was in the water, we saw that the canopy entry door was facing away from the yacht, so we jumped on to the canopy itself, which collapsed, leaving us exposed to the elements. But before anyone even jumped on to it there was an explosion and one of the inflated rings burst. Simon was also having difficulty untying the painter from the yacht. No one had a knife and he patiently untied the knot while someone held in the slack.

We tried to move the liferaft to the bows of *East Wind*, believing that the original orange line, by which we had collected the towing warp, was still attached to both *East Wind* and *Plover*. This would have enabled us to pull the liferaft towards *Plover*. It wasn't, and we concentrated, instead, on try-ing to push ourselves from the rapidly sinking *East Wind*. We were just a few yards from her when she went down at the bows, up at the stern, and disappeared under the sea, a mass of air bubbles marking the spot.

It was just four minutes since I had radioed *Plover* to stop the tow.

To watch our yacht plunge to the bottom, like some scene from the sink-ing of the *Titanic*, is something I would not wish to experience again.

We shouted towards HMS *Plover*, which had spotted our plight. For me, cold and without a lifejacket, this was the only moment that I ever felt frightened. I wondered what would happen if our partially inflated liferaft capsized or sank. *Plover* was turning around and, beam-on to sea, coming back to pick us up. Scrambling nets were lowered over the side and, after some nasty moments, during which we seemed to be inspecting the under-side of her hull, we all clambered up and were hauled over the ship's rail by the waiting crew.

Down below in the wardroom, Simon explained what had happened while he was at the wheel. He had been experiencing the same problems with *East Wind* surfing towards the stern of *Plover*. One moment all was well, the next the stern of *East Wind* was pulled around and yacht was being dragged backwards through the water. There was no response from the helm.

The only explanation seems to be that the slack in the towing warp had got caught around the rudder and skeg and the tremendous force exerted had ripped them off, creating a large hole in the aft section of the hull which so rapidly filled with water.

From *Yachting Monthly*, December 1990

Lessons learned

If you are towing, or being towed, you need a tow rope that covers at least the distance between two waves in the sea conditions prevailing.

A good tip for the yacht being towed is to shackle the end of the tow rope to the shank of the anchor and then deploy the anchor and a considerable amount of anchor chain. This avoids the problems of chafe and the weight of the chain also acts as a shock absorber, hopefully, avoiding the problem of over-running the tow rope and getting a bight of rope caught around the keel or rudder and skeg, as seems to have happened with *East Wind*.

An alternative, but less bulletproof, method is to lash weights, like anchors or water-filled fuel cans to the middle of the tow rope. There must be enough weight on the rope to prevent all of it from coming out of the water at once and snatching.

The vessel being towed should also trail a drogue or warps which will help to prevent over-running the tow rope as she surfs down a wave.

Using bridles connected to the primary winches makes any adjustments easier.

May is a typhoon month in the Philippines and South China Sea, but the frequency of typhoons in May in the area is very low. Throughout the time we were sailing back to Hong Kong the weather bulletins we received were based on the best information available, provided by the Royal Observatory, Hong Kong, supplemented by the US base at Guam in the Pacific. Opinions between the two differed on the course that Typhoon Brenda might take and I have accepted that having set sail and passed the point of no return, *Brenda* followed a course at a speed which resulted in our being right in its path.

Perhaps the first lesson when passage-planning during the period when typhoons are even remotely possible, is that every depression should be treated as a potential typhoon and one should remain within a few hours of a good bolt hole to see how things will develop before making a lengthy passage.

I mentioned that the engine would not start, despite the fuel tank being one third or half full, and attributed this to a poorly designed tank. It has since occurred to me that, by going about, we may have freed any blockage and allowed the fuel better access to the delivery system. On the other hand, in rough seas it is common for sediment in the bottom of the tank to be shaken up and cause a blockage.

In any situation which is potentially dangerous, the whole crew should be ordered to wear lifejackets and safety harnesses (which they were wearing). Off watch and under tow we should also have slept in our lifejackets.

Another crew member and I were without lifejackets. I had left mine below while making sure the crew were getting up on deck. I tried to seize one of the two horseshoe lifebuoys mounted on the pushpit, but each was securely tied to a stanchion and I didn't have my knife on me, nor did anyone else. A knife is always an essential item for any yachtsman to have at hand at all times. This could have cost me my life in less favourable circumstances without HMS *Plover* close at hand.

Our liferaft had been serviced and tested a few months earlier, but still a part of it exploded and deflated. I don't know why, or whether it could have been prevented, but I can imagine that if kept too close against the side of a vessel it only needs a barnacle to cause a puncture.

44 The loss of *Jester*

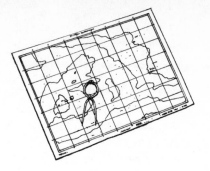

Yacht *Jester*
Skipper Michael Richey
Bound from Plymouth to Newport, Rhode Island
Date of loss 15 July, 1988
Position 470 miles south-east of Halifax, Nova Scotia

Both Michael Richey and Jester *had crossed the Atlantic many times and the 1988 Carlsberg Singlehanded Transatlantic Race, from Plymouth to Newport, Rhode Island, was to be their last. But when he left Plymouth on 5 June, Richey could not have anticipated what lay ahead. On 15 July 1988, in position 39°08'N, 58°43'W, some 470 miles south-east of Halifax, Nova Scotia,* Jester *was abandoned and her skipper taken off by the MV* Nilam, *a 60,000-ton bulk carrier bound for New York. It was* Jester's *eighth OSTAR and her 14th transatlantic passage. The incident, a knockdown, occurred some 40 days out.*

Beyond the fact that *Jester* had participated in every Singlehanded Transatlantic Race since the event's inception in 1960 and that her entry would thus be widely welcomed, there was, I suppose, little point in doing the race. *Jester* was unlikely to distinguish herself. However, it would almost certainly be my last opportunity to participate and so I entered with the prime intention of enjoying the sail, probably along a route that would neither be too demanding nor stretch the nominal distance too far.

Jester had attempted most of the accepted routes over the years, from the far northern passage with Blondie Hasler in 1960 and 1964 to the trade wind route in 1968, with varying degrees of success. The path one follows in practice is largely determined by what the wind does in the first few days of the race. Nevertheless, for the small vessels, so vulnerable to the effects of current and whose windward ability may well be limited, some overall strategy seems to be called for. On this occasion my intention had been to head south-west to a position sufficiently west of the Azores to avoid the calms associated with the archipelago, cross the ocean south of the core of the Gulf Stream in about 37°N, and then come up to cross the Stream at a broad angle in about 65°W. The route approximates in its early part to the low-powered steamer route shown on the US pilot charts, but the difficulty under sail is the tendency for the wind to head when west of about 50°W, forcing the boat into the Stream prematurely.

When *Jester* emerged from Mayflower Marina on the morning of the race, there was some excitement among the spectator fleet and we were applauded by many of those on board the ferries. Four years earlier, she had been similarly received by the competitors as she sailed into Millbay Dock. The start itself was unmemorable, but for a while *Jester*, *Suhaili* and *Galway Blazer* kept company – a distinguished fleet indeed.

The early part of the passage was uneventful, the first few days inevitably a period of settling down, for I had not sailed the boat that year, fighting lethargy and a tendency to hibernate. By the end of the first week we had covered over 700 miles in a direction 250°T – a highly satisfactory state of affairs.

Jester effectively sailed herself and, although one could reef or put on more sail from time to time, and occasionally adjust the self-steering gear, there was no deckwork and life on board became a matter of eating, sleeping, cooking, navigating and, much of the time, reading. There were, of course, long periods when one was simply looking at the sea.

Navigation, as always, was by sextant and chronometer, the latter being one of the handsome quartz clocks once manufactured for Brookes & Gatehouse. Nowadays, of course, quartz crystal wristwatches, even quite cheap ones, are so accurate and reliable that the problem of time at sea has virtually disappeared. On ocean voyages I found it convenient to keep the digital display, which was less liable to reading error, set to GMT for sights and the analogue display to the zone time. All calculations in *Jester* had for some years been made by hand-held computer, not so much for speed or accuracy but rather for convenience. However, I have found, particularly with astronavigation, that it becomes even more necessary than with tables and plotting to know what you are doing because mistakes will not be so readily apparent.

One of the great pleasures of navigation for me has always been using the tools of the trade and in *Jester* I have been able to ensure that they were of the finest. Many of them, too, have particular associations. The sextant, for example, a lovely Plath dated 1939, its mirrors as clear as the day they were made, was acquired from a U-boat towards the end of the war; with its maker's name there was a swastika emblazoned on the index arm. Its box was bolted to the shelf on the starboard side just below the sidehatch and in cloudy weather I would keep it open to avoid delay if the sun showed itself for a fleeting second. *Jester* was the ideal boat for taking sights since, supported firmly in the control hatch, both hands can be used without fear of falling overboard. I used to rejoice in the art and, when my eyes were somewhat sharper, would often take morning and evening star sights in mid-ocean when the results would have little navigational significance.

The dividers were made of solid silver with stainless steel points and a nylon bush in the joint to prevent slippage. They were the most beautiful pair I have ever used, the gift, suitably inscribed, of the talented silversmith who made them. The Walker's Excelsior log which has trailed behind for so many thousands of miles was presented to the boat by the author of that remarkable work *The Principles of Navigation*. The Brookes & Gatehouse sounder, which has seen the boat over the Nantucket and many another shoal, came out of Richard Gatehouse's own yacht *Electron*. And so on. Alas, it was destined to be the last time I would use any of them.

By 15 June the generally northerly airstream gave way to a period of unsettled weather with intermittent calms and fog. The Azores Current was setting us fast to the south-east and I began to wonder whether we should weather Corvo. At times the current could be seen on the surface of the water, creating steep wavelets in a wind of no more than force 2. North-west of the Azores there was very little wind and several days of complete calm on 26 and 27 June we only logged 2½ miles in 36 hours and set some 20 miles north-east.

Apart from the periods of flat calm, the weather during this time, west of the Azores, was unbelievably pleasant and I spent long hours looking at the waters, admiring in particular a pair of dolphins that stayed with the boat for days, with their extraordinary turn of speed. On one occasion, thousands of sardines broke surface, fluttering like butterflies; occasionally great schools of dolphin would pass by, usually in the evening, as though some migration was under way. One evening later in the voyage I saw two large fins about 20 yards ahead of the boat and had, at the last moment, to seize the whipstaff and put the helm over, the self-steering still engaged, to avoid collision with two whales on the surface, apparently oblivious of our presence. I scraped past them a few feet away; one of them started to follow the boat and then gave it up. It shook me slightly, even though they probably live on shrimp.

The sixth of July was my birthday, a dry day as it happened because I had finished the wine, but celebrated nevertheless by a remarkable run (over 25 hours, for the clocks had been retarded) of 161 miles, 35 of which could be attributed to a lift from a Gulf Stream eddy.

The following day the wind backed south-westerly and by 9 July we were being pushed up towards the 40th parallel into the foul current.

It is always difficult to know how far one is justified in taking the losing tack in order to avoid a foul tide or current, especially perhaps in a boat of limited windward ability. Staying on the master tack in this case meant pointing roughly in the right direction but making less and less progress; going south meant pointing in the wrong direction to get into an area where one might expect, if not a favourable eddy, at least no foul current. At noon on the 9 July I took the losing tack south and by noon the next day we were some 48 miles further away from Newport. The wind piped up to about force 6 or 7 for a few hours during the afternoon and backed westerly. 'After an infernal afternoon,' I wrote in the log, 'virtually hove-to under a single panel of sail in appallingly confused seas bursting all over the place in quite alarming peaks. The gale quite suddenly ceased and we proceeded northward under two and later three panels of sail.'

Whether the confused seas we were to meet from now on were entirely due to the Gulf Stream, or were due to some other factor, I am not certain. The Stream was certainly running much faster than the mean speed given on the pilot charts (0.7 knots) and when the MV *Nilam* was standing by with her engines stopped she recorded 3 knots made good over the ground. On the other hand, there was an occluded front to the westward and I later remembered a letter I received in May 1968 from C J Verploegh of the Royal Netherlands Meteorological Office on the general subject of weather in the North Atlantic.

'There is,' he wrote 'one situation you should be warned of because it is seldom detected on weather charts. Sometimes a wavelike disturbance will develop on an occlusion which is moving slowly eastward between two well developed cells of high pressure. Gale force winds may occur, southerly on the eastern side and northerly on the western side, over an area no more than about 40 miles on both sides of the front. Within this small area, waves may be as high as five metres and west of the front a heavy southerly swell will be running against northerly gale force winds. I have had reports from routed vessels (Verploegh was in charge of weather routeing) and it seems that as the ship approaches the front the wind suddenly increases to gale force with correspondingly steep seas.'

The extent to which my own situation corresponded to that described is perhaps irrelevant, but certainly whatever local conditions prevailed, super-imposed on a strong-flowing Gulf Stream, created conditions that not only made progress on either tack difficult but were at times alarming. In addition, I was concerned about a slight movement at the heel of the mast much aggravated by pitching in confused seas. I had used metal shims several times at the adjacent floors and twice taken up the soft-wood wedges at the partners but had been unable to stop the movement, which on occasions sounded as though it was tearing the boat to bits.

In these somewhat disturbed conditions, where much of the boat's movement must be accounted for by a current of unknown velocity, there was generally some ambiguity in the observed position based on a run between sights.

On the morning of 13 July, a merchant vessel, bound northwestward, crossed two or three miles ahead of us. I swallowed my pride and asked him for a position. He gave it, in a Scandinavian voice, as 39°32'N, 58°41'W, which surprised me a little. He then said he could not see me but presumed that the vessel I had in sight was one he could detect on his radar some 12 miles to the south. I found this a bit perplexing but decided to bear all the possibilities in mind until I got some kind of noonday sight (which indeed confirmed that I was well south of my estimate).

We had a sharp blow, up to about force 7, around noon, although I was able to get the information I wanted from a series of shaky sights. I went down to bare pole for a while because I thought we would make little progress and it would save breaking the boat up. By 1600 we were under way again with two panels up, heading for Labrador.

'Extreme discomfort aboard,' I noted in the log. 'For the past three days every stitch of clothing has been soaked, every towel is dripping, the matches won't strike and so on.'

It is extraordinary how, even in a boat with full enclosure like *Jester*, living so close to the surface in hard weather the water seems to permeate everything, like an atmosphere. 'If only,' I wrote, 'we could have a fine day to dry everything out.'

Morale seems to have been sagging. By the evening, the wind had got up again and by midnight it was blowing a full gale from the south-west. I went down to a single panel and hove the boat to under the self-steering gear. In the early hours I went down to bare pole. The centre of the system must have gone through my position, for at about 0500 the wind dropped completely and a downpour of tropical dimensions went on for about an hour and a half; it ceased as suddenly as it had started, as though a tap had been turned off.

At about 0800 the wind came in again, rising quickly to gale force and getting up a steep and confused sea. 'Some of the breakers quite frighten me,' I wrote in the log. 'They come at you hissing, generally just across the wave train, and carrying you along for a while, generally on your beam ends.' By 1000, it was blowing perhaps force 9 with visibility affected, but the seas flecked rather than covered with spume. There was not much I could do but wait hopefully for the storm to pass. At about 1030, surveying the scene from the control hatch with as much equanimity as I could muster, I saw a plunging breaker coming at us from the port side and said out loud, 'Oh hell, here's a knockdown,' as indeed it proved to be.

The boat was smashed down to starboard and carried along with her mast below the horizontal until the wave had passed and the weight of the ballast keel brought her upright again. She was full of water, with floorboards, cushions, books, charts, sleeping bags and food all floating free. More important, the starboard sidehatch had been stove in, totally demolished with only its bronze hinges hanging loose. The boat was now open to the sea.

The first thing was to get the water out and I started bailing with the plastic bucket but it seemed a losing game as more water poured in through the open hatch. Eventually, I suppose, the gale subsided and my efforts had more effect, I was able to reduce the water to a level where the bilge pump would be able to deal with it. But whilst in the throes of the storm, and obsessed with the idea that the boat was open to the seas, I became convinced that I should need assistance to sail on. I activated the EPIRB. A few hours later I thought I must have gone mad.

It is difficult to recall precisely one's motives in a moment of crisis. I was later to regret not having waited until the gale had blown itself out before activating the EPIRB, or indeed in retrospect having activated it at all. But in the throes of the gale I thought the boat, open to the seas could well founder, and that in any case with a 121.5/243MHz 'line of sight' system a considerable delay could be expected. Once switched on, of course, the EPIRB should not be switched off until rescue.

By nightfall I had pumped the boat more or less dry, but I was too exhausted to attempt any kind of clear-up. Earlier, when I had thought the boat might founder, I had launched the liferaft and thrown into it a few stores such as a barricoe of water, some flares and a panic bag of sorts. I now transferred them all back. I spent the night on the bunk aft, a wet sleeping bag draped over my knees and my head on some protrusion, wondering between snatches of sleep what action I should take when help came. Having summoned it, I should be prepared to take it. But I earnestly wished the course now lay open to me to reconsider the whole situation.

In the morning, I was able to get one burner going on the cooker to make a cup of tea. Clearing up seemed too large a task and I concentrated on getting the boat operational, seeing how much of the navigational gear was still functional, what, if any, charts survived, what state the instruments were in and so on.

It was a pleasant enough day, the storm now through. I had little idea where we were and took the sextant from its box. The telescope had misted up from the inside but I took a series of shots without it. The reduction tables, like the charts, were effectively pulped and the hand-held computer, predictably, had packed up. *Macmillan's Nautical Almanac*, however, had been on a higher shelf and was virtually untouched. Unfortunately, after many attempts I failed to extract a sensible quantity for hour angle and declination, for the good reason I was to discover later that I had somehow contrived to drop a day from the date.

Shortly after 1000, an aircraft flew low over the boat with her lights on and I switched on the hand-held VHF on channel 16. The pilot identified the plane by number from the US Coast Guard Rescue Services and enquired, with great politeness, addressing me as 'Sir' all the while, as to the nature of the emergency.

I reported the damage and wondered whether any ship in the vicinity would be able to render assistance, perhaps a tow or hoisting the boat inboard. I should in any case require water if I were to sail on, for two of the barricoes had managed to empty themselves as a result of the upset. The pilot undertook to find out what shipping was in the area and meanwhile instructed me to switch off the EPIRB. He attempted to drop me an SSB (with, for some reason, some apple juice), but unfortunately I was unable to pick up the drop, hindered in my manoeuvring ability by towing the life-raft. The pilot then announced that the MV *Nilam*, a bulk carrier, some 20 miles away, was prepared to help and was closing. He had to refuel but a new aircraft was on its way.

When the new aircraft arrived, we went through the extent of the damage again and I emphasised that, whilst it was of little consequence in good weather, the boat could well founder in a gale. I suggested that the ship, when she arrived, should provide me with some water, if possible some tins of food and some stout canvas with which to effect a temporary repair. This information was passed to the MV *Nilam* and in due course, when she came up with us, she dropped over the stern three barricoes of water, some tins in a large plastic bag and the canvas. I told the pilot there was no chance of picking up the drop without getting rid of the liferaft and then cast it off, manoeuvring astern of the ship to recover the stores.

At this stage the possibility of abandoning *Jester* had neither been raised nor contemplated. I asked the aircraft for a position which he gave as 39°08′N, 58°43′W. My nearest landfall, he volunteered would be Halifax, Nova Scotia, some 470 miles north-west. How long, he asked, would that take me? I thought about a week and he then undertook to get me a weather forecast for each of the seven days. Meanwhile, the ship stood by with her engines stopped and the plane circled overhead.

After about half an hour the pilot came back and said he now had the forecast. Before reading it, however, he had to make clear that in view of the deteriorating weather situation both the Canadian Coast Guard in Halifax and the US Coast Guard Co-Ordination Centre in New York strongly urged me to terminate the voyage now. He then read me the forecasts. Without a chart before me I found it difficult to envisage any kind of weather pattern. I picked up one wind forecast of 34 knots and asked what that was on the Beaufort scale (I still think in sea states); I was told force 7–8.

The advice to abandon the yacht came as a blow. I asked for a few minutes to consider the matter but I found it very difficult to think. With a plane circling overhead and a 60,000-ton ship standing by, and after 40 days on one's own at sea, a balanced judgement was almost impossible.

Would that I had a friend with whom to discuss the issue. The response I felt must be quick, positive and decisive. I agreed to accept the Coast Guard's advice.

It would be impossible for me to approach the ship's accommodation ladder on the lee side without being blanketed (*Jester* has no engine), so we agreed that I should sail *Jester* two or three hundred yards ahead of the ship's lee bow and she would then steam gently ahead and drift down on me. I got the boat under way, one reef down, the boat sailing as prettily as she can and then suddenly felt I could not go through with it.

I contacted the aircraft again and, now emotionally fraught, said, 'Do you think the captain would be very annoyed if I decided to go on?'

The question must have sounded as silly as it was rhetorical and I don't remember the reply. I then asked if I could talk to the pilot man to man, irrespective of what the authorities had said.

What, I wondered, would he do in my circumstances?

'I don't know,' he said, 'I have never sailed the Atlantic singlehanded. It must be your decision, but I think you ought to accept the Coast Guard's advice.'

He could scarcely, I imagine have said anything else.

The transfer was effected, the master manoeuvring his ship with great skill with so little way. I had furled the sail and lashed it neatly, put up the canvas dodger, disengaged the windvane, handed the log and (lest it be damaged going alongside!) brought the recorder inboard. As soon as I was on board the ship, I was called to the bridge where the pilot of the aircraft wanted to sign off. I thanked him profusely and before we had finished the master asked me to tell him he would attempt a tow, although he had little hope of success.

It was a quixotic gesture, for at that speed a boat of *Jester*'s size could but be towed under.

In due course I was given a cabin facing aft and some dry clothes. After a shower I watched *Jester* through the scuttle at the end of her long tow. I suddenly realised she was getting smaller. I had taken a quick turn on the king post with a hawser far too large whilst getting aboard, and I suppose it had jumped. 'That's that,' I said out aloud, without emotion, for there could be no going back. But as I watched her recede into the distance, looking as trim and pretty as ever, I realised how much I had loved her. Men personalise their boats as no other artefact. I felt I had failed her, that I should have stayed with the boat.

It was one of the unhappiest moments of my life and a passage occurred to me from the sad soliloquy at the end of Joyce's story *The Dead*: 'Better pass boldly into that other world in the full glory of some passion than fade and wither dismally with age.'

Jester had been if anything a passion.

From Yachting Monthly, November 1998

Lessons learned

Whether there are useful lessons to be drawn from the episode is hard to say, writes Richey. The side hatches were not strong enough. After the boat's capsize on the way back from Nova Scotia in 1986, I had them remade and I suppose they could have done with an extra lamination or two. It is not always easy to envisage the forces that can be unleased in an ocean storm. For safety, as Blondie Hasler would maintain, 'a boat's upper-works and hatches should be as strong as her bottom'.

Jester had now been knocked down or capsized three times in three successive years and one cannot help wondering whether there is any significance in that fact. For various reasons I had the WEST epoxy process applied to her whaleback coachroof in Nova Scotia and when she was repeatedly knocked down and finally rolled on the way back, I did wonder whether the extra weight might have affected her stability. It seems improbable and, in any case, so violent were the seas in that appalling storm that any such consideration seems irrelevant.

In 1987, the boat was knocked down and her windvane and boom smashed by a rogue wave just on the shelf break off Cape Finisterre whilst running under bare pole. She then had a new mast of Douglas fir some 25lb heavier than the original spruce although slightly shorter. This year, I had fitted a radar reflector at the masthead which gave me more weight in that position than I would have liked, but my anxiety was more for the unstayed mast than anything to do with capsizing moment.

One must conclude, I think, that due to some curious circumstances *Jester* happens to have met, in three successive years, waves of just the right size, frequency and shape to knock her down. On each occasion she had, it so happens, been under bare pole; but looking back on each I would not handled her differently.

Somewhere, many years ago, that great cruising seaman Eric Hiscock wrote that in the (to him improbable) event that he were asked to organise a race across the oceans, his first rule would be that there should be no radio transmissions. 'We do not', he went on, referring to yachtsmen, 'have to go to sea and we have no right to call on anyone for help.'

It sounds a bleak attitude, but there is much to be said for it. Emergency beacons such the EPIRB are made compulsory in such races as the Singlehanded Transatlantic, as much to protect the organisers as the competitors, for there is a real possibility nowadays of an organising club being sued in the event of a disaster. For the competitors they are perhaps a mixed blessing.

In 1986, with no mast, no forehatch cover and an injured back, I was glad enough of help. The boat was saved. (She was lifted aboard a Geest banana boat.) In 1988 help was again summoned and the boat was lost. Paradoxically, one cannot help wondering if she would have been saved had help not come. It is an idle speculation but there is a sense in which an umbilical cord compromises the responsibility of the skipper for his own vessel.

Some days after the rescue, I reflected bitterly that, after all, the Coast Guard's advice could scarcely have been otherwise; and that had I sought it at the beginning of the voyage the temper would have been the same. Whether the predicted weather arrived, and whether the boat would have survived it without a side hatch, is now to some extent irrelevant. The safest course is not necessarily the right one to take. But a grain of comfort came in a letter from Bridget Hasler. She felt that after the boat's achievements it was a fitting end; and that the only thing Blondie would have minded was if all the fun we had both had out of the boat had ended in my being lost.

There was, of course, a faint hope that *Jester* would still be afloat, drifting in the North Atlantic like the *Marie Celeste*. For initiating steps to locate her I am particularly grateful to Rear Admiral Sir David Haslam of the International Hydrographic Bureau and to Vice Admiral Sir John Webster, C-in-C Plymouth and a member of the Royal Cruising Club. I must also thank Senator Clayborne C Pell of Rhode Island for his efforts to get something going in the States.

My principal thanks are of course due to the United States Coast Guard Rescue Co-Ordination Centre in New York and in particular the pilots of the HU 25A Falcon Jet from Cape Cod and the HC 130 from Elizabeth City which took part in the rescue. To Captain Pecunia of the MV *Nilam* of the Ultramar Company, I am grateful for delivering me to New York in such a friendly way, and in such comfort. I am grateful, too, to Racal Limited for the loan of the EPIRB which so effectively summoned help, but which I was unable to return.

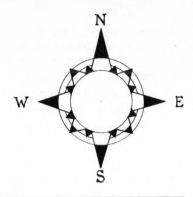

45 *Mischief's* Last Voyage

Yacht *Mischief* (45ft Bristol Channel pilot-cutter)
Skipper Major HW Tilman
Crew Charles Marriott, Simon Beckett, Kenneth Winterschladen, Ian Duckworth
Bound from Jan Mayen Island to Norway (under tow)
Date of loss 4 August, 1968
Position off east coast of Jan Mayen Island

Between 1954 and 1968, when he lost her off Jan Mayen Island, Bill Tilman sailed Mischief *some 110,000 miles. Sea Breeze, her successor, also a Bristol Channel pilot-cutter and even older than* Mischief, *was lost in 1972 on the south coast of Greenland. Tilman sailed mostly to places where there was snow, ice, mountains and very few people. In 1968 he chose Iceland and Jan Mayen Island as his goals and* Mischief *left Lymington on 31 May, after the crew had subscribed for the hire of a liferaft. Having called at Thorshavn in the Faeroes, they were in Akuryri on the north coast of Iceland by 26 June, where they stayed for a few days, leaving on 7 July, bound for Jan Mayen, some 300 miles to the north. The long axis of Jan Mayen Island runs from south-west to north-east, the middle of the island being barely two miles wide. Almost the whole of the north-eastern half is filled by Beerenberg's massive bulk. This 7000ft peak was of course Tilman's climbing goal. Because the chart agent had mistakenly told him that there was no Admiralty chart of Jan Mayen, Tilman was using a chart on which the 30-mile-long island occupied little more than one inch.*

Variable winds and too much fog marked our passage to Jan Mayen. On the 17 July we luckily got sights which put us some 10 miles from the island, so we steered, once more in fog, to clear South Cape by five miles. In fact, that afternoon some very impressive rocks suddenly loomed up only two cables away. These we identified as Sjuskjæram: a group of seven rocks a mile off the cape. Next day we anchored off the old Norwegian weather station at Mary Musbukta on the west coast.

What few anchorages there are on either the east or west coast of Jan Mayen are wide open, but the west coast is preferable as it is free from dangers. Nor was there any ice in the vicinity of Mary Musbukta, though three miles to the north we could see pack-ice extending westwards. However, I thought we ought to let the Norwegians know that we were there, with designs on Beerenberg, so after anchoring I went in search of their new base. On the east coast, south of Eggoya, where the beach is very wide, and thick with driftwood, originating probably in Siberia, I found a party at work. We had no common language and, except that I had no beard, they must have thought I had been left behind, possibly under a stone, by some earlier expedition. I got a lift in a truck five miles to the present Norwegian station where we were just in time for supper. It is a large installation comprising some 50 men, mostly technicians. The Commandant was surprised to see me, for a Norwegian naval vessel, approaching by the east coast, had been turned back by ice. He showed me a small bay close by which they used for landing stores and suggested that we lie there. We were, so to speak, uninvited guests, so I thought it best to comply, though the bay was more than half covered with ice floes. From this mistake all our troubles stemmed.

We started round on Saturday, 20 July, a brilliant morning on which we enjoyed the only view we ever had of the ice slopes of Beerenberg, the mountain we hoped to climb. The brilliance soon faded, and once more we rounded South Cape in thick fog, having to tack twice to weather it. The wind died at night, and having steered east for two miles to get an offing, we handed sails and let her drift, waiting for the fog to clear. The coast runs SW–NE so that by steering east we had not gained that much offing, and although the ship had no way on, it was a mistake to think she was not moving. I had the midnight to 0200 watch and on the false assumption that we were not moving I sat below, taking a look round on deck every 15 minutes. It was, of course, fully light, but miserably cold and damp, visibility less than a quarter mile. Accordingly, I told my relief Ian that he need not remain on deck all the time, provided he went up at frequent intervals. He interpreted this liberally and must have remained below most of his watch.

At about 0350 a terrible crash roused me. We were almost alongside a lone rock pinnacle lying about half a mile off the coast – I could have touched it with a boathook – the slight swell bumping us heavily on its plinth. This result of his neglect seemed to have unnerved Ian, who had already pulled the cord of the liferaft without troubling to launch it, so that a huge yellow balloon now filled most of the starboard deck. To make doubly sure of getting off he had also cut the dinghy lashings. Once the engine had started she slid off easily, but not before having struck hard at least six times. She proved to be leaking a lot but the Whale pump and deck pump together kept it under control. To hit this rock we must have drifted in the course of the night some three miles to the north at a rate of nearly half a knot.

Owing to fog and a lot of ice close inshore, we had trouble in finding the bay. About 0700 we anchored off it while I went ashore to tell the Norwegians what had happened. They said, and I agreed, that the only thing to do was to beach her to get at the leaks. So we brought her in through the floes until she grounded on a beach of black sand. We started taking out the ballast (some 5 tons of pig iron), drained the water tanks, to float her further up, and put ashore the anchor and cable. The rise and fall of the tide was only 3ft (*Mischief* draws 7ft) and the beach shelved quickly towards her stern, so that we could not get at the garboard strake or the planks above it, except at the forefoot. On heaving her down with a bulldozer and examining what we could of the port side at low water, we saw no sprung or started planks; in places the caulking had spewed out, and aft about 10ft of the false keel had broken away.

With the help of the Norwegians, who generously supplied anything needed, we covered the likeliest leak sources with tar, felt, and copper. Then we turned her round and hove down to get at the starboard side where, too, there were no obvious signs of damage. The leaks had been reduced though not cured, but I thought that we could easily sail her back to Iceland or even home. Ian thought otherwise and had already arranged a passage to Norway in *Brandal*, a sealing vessel chartered to bring stores. Charles, I knew, would stay with *Mischief*, while the two younger crew, though apprehensive, were willing to try.

Meantime the ice, which the day after our arrival had moved in almost to fill the bay (thus helping us by damping any swell) began to move out. Before refloating her we put back the ballast, all but a ton – no doubt, another mistake. By Saturday, 27 July, there remained only an unbroken line of massive floes close to the beach, most of them probably aground. The Norwegian who had been helping me realised better than I did that *Mischief* was now in peril. By means of a wire led from the stern to a block slung on an adjacent rock and thence to a bulldozer we tried to haul her off. She moved a foot or two, but anyway there was no forcing a passage between the floes and no means of hauling them away.

Next day, Sunday, 28 July, the Commandant came down and managed to break up with dynamite a floe threateningly close to our rudder. A floe lying only a yard or so from our port side was too big and a series of underwater explosions close aboard might have damaged the ship. That morning it began blowing hard from the south, causing the ice to surge forward, bumping *Mischief* heavily on the beach, and edging her higher up. I rallied the crew for a last effort to get her off by means of a warp to the anchor winch and the engine. She would not budge. With a couple of bulldozers we might have succeeded, but when I ran to the base for help there was no one about. By the time I got back the ice had battered a hole in her hull below the engine water intake and started several planks. That evening, in despair, I wrote her off.

She was one-third full of water so we took ashore the gear below deck. Charles, who had not been well, now collapsed and retired to a bed in the base sick-room. On first beaching *Mischief* we had all lived in a small hut close to the beach.

Next day a powerful red-bearded Norwegian, whom I called the Viking, had taken to heart *Mischief*'s plight and was as anxious as myself to save her. He suggested that she should be hauled right out so that in the winter he could repair her. I doubted the feasibility because it meant hauling her at least 50 yards over very soft sand sloping up at about 15°. Clutching at straws, I agreed. Once more we took out the ballast and that evening the Viking and a bulldozer moved her about two yards. She still lay among the breakers, the wind continued blowing, and the swell rolling in lifted and dropped her heavily on the sand. A big float with an outboard engine used for bringing ashore stores, on which we had deposited the ballast, lay hard by on the beach; and the next night *Mischief*, driven ever higher by the seas, had her bowsprit broken on the float in spite of our having reefed it.

The idea of hauling her right out seemed to be tacitly abandoned. Instead, on 30 July, we put a big patch over the hole, having arranged with *Brandal*, then about to leave Norway, to tow us to Bodo. She was also to bring out a small motor pump to cope with the leaks, which by now were well beyond our two hand pumps. With another gale on 1 August the breakers tore off *Mischief*'s rudder, but *Brandal*, with whom the base spoke by radio telephone, reckoned they could still tow. *Brandal* arrived on 2 August, fetching up north of the island, in spite of radio beacons, radar and Loran, and that morning the big patch we had put on was torn off by the seas.

Upon this the Viking and I reverted to the idea of leaving her there hauled out for the winter, but the Commandant thought little of it and said she must be towed. So on 3 August the Viking and I again put on a patch, a wet job since waves were sweeping the stage we had slung overside to work from. That evening I went on board *Brandal*. They agreed to lend us a small electric pump to reinforce the petrol pump they had brought, which we had already installed in the cockpit. I had to sign a guarantee against the loss of this pump. The Commandant also arranged for a walkie-talkie set and a field telephone to keep *Brandal* and *Mischief* in touch.

Overnight we rove a 3-inch wire through a big block slung on the nearby rocks and passed a length of 6-inch nylon rope twice round *Mischief*'s hull. At 0700 on Sunday, 4 August, a fortnight to the day since we first limped in, the Norwegians rallied in force to get us off. Although the ballast was out it took some doing. Either the sand had piled up or she had dug herself in, so the biggest bulldozer, a real monster, dropped its scoop into the sand and using the sand as a cushion advanced on *Mischief* and pushed her bodily sideways. The two bulldozers in tandem then coupled on to the wire, a big dory with an engine pulled from seawards, and *Mischief* slid slowly into deep water. Simon and I were on board with the pump going. It needed to be, for she leaked like a basket.

Having secured astern of *Brandal*, lying half a mile out, we remained there, tossed about in a rough sea until late afternoon. Meantime, the float made two or three trips out to *Brandal*, the last with seven men from the base and the remaining three of our crew. Charles was to travel in her while the other two helped in *Mischief*. Since we were to be closely attended, Ian had consented to come. Our only contact with *Brandal* was by the float, and in the evening it came alongside with three of her crew to arrange the tow line, the electric pump, field telephone, walkie-talkie set, and a liferaft. Our own had no gas cylinder, that having been expended when Ian prematurely pulled the string a fortnight before. He and Ken now joined us, and were promptly seasick.

For the tow they used a nylon warp shackled to 10 fathoms of our anchor chain on which they hung three big tyres to act as a spring. The remaining 35 fathoms of our chain with the 1cwt anchor attached, we led to *Mischief*'s stern to drop over when the tow started. This served in place of a rudder and kept her from yawing. The heavy electric cable to supply current from *Brandal* to the pump they merely dropped loose into the sea. Its own weight imposed a heavy strain, no current ever passed, and immediately the tow began *Brandal* told us it had broken. Had it been hitched to the tow line or to another line *Mischief* might have survived. This meant that the little petrol pump must function for three days without fail. I did not think it would. Since early morning Simon and I had been running it for five minutes in every 10 to keep the water at bay.

At about 2000 in a rough sea the tow began. At 2100 Simon and I lay down, leaving Ken and Ian to carry on until 0100. With the water sloshing about inside, sleep was hardly possible and for food we made do with hard tack and a cup of tea. Just before midnight I learnt that the pump had given up; the engine ran but was not pumping. Three of us were ready enough to quit and I confess that the skipper and owner, who had so much more at stake, had no longer the will to persevere, a fortnight of trouble, toil, and anxiety having worn me down.

Brandal had already been told. She lay to about a cable away and told us to bring off only personal gear. So we collected our gear, launched the life-raft, and abandoned *Mischief*. She had then about three feet of water inside her. Paddling over to *Brandal*, we climbed on board while three of her crew returned in the raft to salvage the two pumps and the telephone. The electric pump, which weighed a lot, we had already hoisted on deck through the skylight. The pumps met with scant ceremony, being thrown overboard on the end of a line to be hauled through the sea to *Brandal*. While *Brandal* got under way I remained on deck watching *Mischief*, still floating defiantly, until she was out of sight. We were then 30 miles east of Jan Mayen.

As I have said, ice conditions in 1968 were unusually bad; in a normal year Jan Mayen is clear of ice by the end of May. And, apart from human failings, ice was the principal cause of the loss of *Mischief*. For me it meant the loss of more than a yacht. I felt like one who had betrayed and then deserted a stricken friend, a friend with whom for the last 14 years I had probably spent more time at sea than on land, and who, when not at sea, had seldom been out of my thoughts. Moreover, I could not help feeling that by my mistakes and by the failure of one of those who were there to safeguard her, we had broken faith; that the disaster or sequence of disasters need not have happened; and that more might have been done to save her. I shall never forget her.

From *Roving Commissions 9* (1969)
published by the Royal Cruising Club

Lessons learned

Not many. *Mischief*'s problems began with the unusually bad ice conditions of that year. Perhaps Tilman regretted his too kind considerations towards his relief watch in the 'miserably cold and damp' conditions that fateful night. Visibility was less than a quarter mile and having told Ian that he need not remain on deck all the time, it seems he 'interpreted this liberally and remained below most of his watch'. Less than two hours later 'a terrible crash' roused Tilman. Despite valiant efforts to save the vessel over the following days, even the redoubtable Tilman confessed he was worn down by toil and anxiety. The eloquence and depth of his regrets will strike a chord with any skipper.

Index of boats and yachtsmen

Aikenhead, Phil 3
Ana (Modi Khola) 25–31
Asquith, Derek and
  Carol 264–6
Autissier, Isabelle 68–77

Baggeley, Jason 25–31
Banba IV 160–3
Banbury, Major Philip
  283–8
Bandholm 28 203–6
barge, ketch-rigged
  148–53
Bass, Joe 214–21
Beckett, Simon 299–304
Beilby, Malcom 167–72
Bennett, Alex 3
Bermudian cutter 232–9
  ketch 84–92
  sloop 60–7
Berret, Jean 68–77
Binnings, C 271–4
Bits 222–26
Blixenkrone-Moller
  Neils 203–6
boier, 45ft yawl-rigged
  175–81
Brewer 44 214–21
Bristol Channel Pilot
  Cutter 45ft 299–304
Brodie, Beth 141–7
Bull, 'Bully' 197–200

Catalac catamaran
  78–83
catamarans 3–9, 78–83,
  93–8
Catherineau, Alain 32–7
Chartreuse 134–8
Clark, Ed 141–7
Colin Archer 30ft
  275–80

45ft gaff-cutter
  122–25
Contessa 38 283–8
Conway, Peter 32–7
Cownie, Hugh and Sue
  108–14
Crowther, Peter 15–20
Cuoghi, Claudio 240–7
Curtis, W L 60–7
cutter (60ft) 68–77
  gaff-rigged 160–3,
  197–200

David, Brian 112
di Mola, Giorgio 240–7
Dorothea 232–9
Duckworth, Ian
  299–304

East Wind of the Orient
  283–8
Ecureuil Poitou Charentes
  2 68–77

Flockemann, Peter
  248–56
Freedom To 271–4

gaff-cutter 122–25,
  160–3, 197–200
gaff-rigged cutter 160–3,
  197–200
gaff-rigged double-ender
  30ft 275–80
gaff-rigged ketch
  182–93
Galway Blazer 21–4
*Gartmore Investment
  Managers* 207–13
Gelder, Paul 68–73
Geoff, Graham 3
Girl Stella 182–93

Gordon, Clementina
  194–6
Goss, Pete 3–9
Graham, Neil 32–7
Griffin 32–7
Griffin, Ann 122–25
Griffin, Lt Cdr James
  122–25
Guia III 240–7
Gulf Streamer 38–50

Hall, Josh 207–13
Harmonic class sloop
  51–9
Harrod-Eagles, George
  115–21
Harvey, Bob 84–92
Heavenly Twins catama-
  ran 93–8
Hindley, Andy 3
Hodge, Eloise 49
Hornby, John 77
Houston, James and
  Margaret 275–80

Irving, Henry, Joe, and
  Jondo 267–70
Island Princess 84–92
Islander 29ft trimaran
  167–72

Jackson, Peter 227–31
Jester 289–97
Joner, Jimmy 141–7

Keelson II 108–14
Keeney, Tony 248–56
ketch 84–92, 101–7
  gaff-rigged 182–93
Kim Holman 222–26
King, Bill, Cmdr 24

Ladybee (Lady Bridgella)
  275–80
Larsen, Paul 3
Lazy Daisy 78–83
Lealand, Anthony 51–9
Linsay, Jay 141–7
Livery Dole 154–9
Longanesi, Francesco
  240–7
Lord Trenchard 259–63
Lottie Warren 93–8

Maalust 175–81
Macek, Steve 112
Maid of Malham 160–3
Mariah 141–7
Marriott, Charles
  299–304
Marshall, George 240–7
Martinet 148–53
Mary Williams 194–6
May Bee 15–20
McLaren, Gavin 259–63
Merlan 60–7
Millar, Michael 126–33
Miller, Lionel 78–83
Mischief 299–304
Morecombe Bay
  Prawner 28ft 267–70
Morris, Richard 182–93
Morrison, Phil 25
Mulville, Patrick,
  Andrew, Celia and
  Frank 182–93
Munroe, Michael 84–92

Nainjaune 101–7
Newell, Paul 134–8
Nicholls, John 167–72
Nicholson 55ft 259–63
Noel Dilly 222–26
Northern Light 122–25
Nuts 203–6

ocean-racer 44ft 240–7
Offshore One-Design 34
  32–7

Passmore, John 93–8
Paulsen, Bruce 141–7
Payne, Bob 84–92
Penn, Richard 125–33
Philips, Frank, Freda,
  Nichola and Peter
  175–81
Pionier 248–56
Poncet, Jerome 240–7
Porter, Nigel 10–14
Primrose, Angus 24

Quarrie, Stuart 32–7
Quiver 126–33

Rankin, Bruce 78–83
Richey, Michael 289–97
Riot 10–14
Roberts, A W (Bob)
  148–53, 197–200
Robson, Malcom and
  Merrill 160–3, 164–6
Rouse, Colin 259–63
Rowe, Nigel 73
Rushcutter 51–9
Rustler 31 15–20

Sadler Barracuda 45
  10–14
schooner, 86ft staysail
  141–7
Schutten, Willi 248–56
Sea Crest 214–21
Shaw, Brian 60–7
Sky Catcher 73
sloop ,26ft twin-keeled
  115–21
  32ft 248–56
  31ft half-ton 134–8
Song 115–21
Speakman, Barry
  267–70
St Clair, Matthew 'Doc'
  84–92
Stanley, Gordon 15–20
Stephens, Bill 39–50
Storm, Elizabeth 141–7

Strumpet 267–70
Super Sovereign 35ft
  ketch 101–7

T24 227–31
Tangvald, Peter 232–9
Team Philips 3–9
Temptress 267–70
Thelma 197–200
Thomason, Jerry
  148–53
Thompson, Adrian 3–4
Thunder, Barry 15–20
Tilman, Major H W
  299–304
Tomlinson, Peter
  267–70
trimaran 38–50, 154–9,
  167–72
Triventure 167–72
Tudor, Richard 3
Tulloch, Bill and
  Charlie 78–83
Twister 36 222–26

Vancouver 32 108–14
Verbinni, Giovanni
  240–7

Walker, Eric 60–7
Warmsley, Jenny
  15–20
Warrington, J 271–4
Webb, Gordon and
  Jennifer 248–56
Weld, Phil 38–50
Wells, John P, Margaret,
  Peter 175–181
Westerly Vulcan 271–4
Wilde, Annette 51–9
Williams, Chip 141–7
Winterschladen,
  Kenneth 299–304

Yondi 227–31
Young, Keith Douglas
  60–7